Lecture Notes in Computer Science 7768

Commenced Publication in 1973
Founding and Former Series Editors:
Gerhard Goos, Juris Hartmanis, and Jan van Leeuwen

Services Science

Subline of Lectures Notes in Computer Science

Emmanuel Bertin   Noel Crespi
Thomas Magedanz (Eds.)

Evolution of Telecommunication Services

The Convergence of Telecom and Internet:
Technologies and Ecosystems

 Springer

Volume Editors

Emmanuel Bertin
Orange Labs Caen
42 rue des Coutures
BP 6243
14066 Caen Cedex 4, France
E-mail: emmanuel.bertin@orange.com

Noel Crespi
Mines-Telecom
9 rue Charles Fourier
91011 Evry, France
E-mail: noel.crespi@mines-telecom.fr

Thomas Magedanz
Fraunhofer Institute FOKUS
Kaiserin-Augusta-Allee 31
10589 Berlin, Germany
E-mail: thomas.magedanz@fokus.fraunhofer.de

ISSN 0302-9743   e-ISSN 1611-3349
ISBN 978-3-642-41568-5   e-ISBN 978-3-642-41569-2
DOI 10.1007/978-3-642-41569-2
Springer Heidelberg New York Dordrecht London

Library of Congress Control Number: 2013950390

CR Subject Classification (1998): C.2, H.4, D.2, H.3, I.2, H.5

LNCS Sublibrary: SL 3 – Information Systems and Applications, incl. Internet/Web
and HCI

Typesetting: Camera-ready by author, data conversion by Scientific Publishing Services, Chennai, India

Printed on acid-free paper

Springer is part of Springer Science+Business Media (www.springer.com)

Foreword

Of late, we have witnessed a new and encouraging phenomenon that telecommunications are not confined to being a commodity, but are increasingly becoming an enabler for an open-ended spectrum of customizable service offers in ever-new application domains of our daily life. The convergence of technologies and ecosystems in telecommunications, entertainment, and Internet industries started 10 years ago with the introduction of next-generation networks (NGN). We have since seen new players arriving on the market, pushing innovative ideas and rolling out new products faster than ever. Needless to say, this convergence, coupled with allied ecosystems enabled by telecommunications, unlocks unparalleled growth potential for business as well as society, be it healthcare, disaster management, environment sustainability, or city management, to name a few. However, this convergence also comes with its own set of challenges, both for network operators in terms of business sustainability, as well as for society in general, be it identity and security issues, infrastructure sabotage, financial fraud, etc. Technology awareness, research, innovation, and market orientation will be key for a successful evolution towards a new telecom ecosystem.

In principle, we see four developments shaping our industry: (a) shift to all-IP, (b) cloudification, (c) webification, (d) software-enabled productivity increase. It is obvious that technology and society evolve together with transition to all-IP. While the initial advances in telecommunications were primarily hardware-driven (imagine human-operated telephone switching centers), software soon became the key factor in Internet transmission technology, as exemplified by Internet traffic forwarding elements like switches and routers. This has led to a separation of infrastructure from the services, giving birth to the over-the-top (OTT) domain, where anybody with a smart idea can offer services over the underlying Internet infrastructure, without the need to own or control the infrastructure. The popularity of Google Chromebook and its cousins, along with the transition of most big businesses to cloud applications, speaks for itself about the benefits of cloudification. An increasing number of complex applications can now be run over a Web browser. A case in point is WebRTC, which provides high-quality voice over the Web, enabling Web developers to easily create communication applications. What once required millions of euro in communication equipment investment, is now possible with a couple of backend servers and some smart software code – welcome to webification! Lastly, software-enabled productivity is increasing manifold through use of open source, software libraries and APIs. Consider this – to produce 100 K lines of software code, the employee cost has reduced by a factor of 8 to 10 in the last 10 years, accompanied by improved bug fixing and shorter software cycles.

This book offers insights into this complex but exciting world of telecommunications characterized by constant evolution, and approaches it from technology as well as business perspectives. The book is appropriately structured in three parts: (a) an overview of the state of the art in fixed/mobile NGN and standardization activities; (b) an analysis of the competitive landscape between operators, device manufactures and OTT providers, emphasizing why network operators are challenged on their home turf; and (c) opportunities for business modelling and innovative telecom service offers.

I feel sure that students, researchers and industry executives alike will find it a good investment of their time and energy to absorb the contents of this book. All the best!

Dr. Heinrich Arnold,
Senior Vice President, Research & Innovation,
Global Head of Telekom Innovation Laboratories,
Deutsche Telekom

Preface

In the telecom world, services have usually been conceived with a specific mindset. This mindset has defined the traditional characteristics of these services; services distinguished by their linkage with the access network, tight control over service use (e.g., authentication, billing), lack of deep personalization capabilities (mass services only), and reliance on standardization to achieve end-to-end interoperability between all the actors of the value chain (e.g., operators, platform manufacturers, device manufactures). In addition, telecom operators – which we will also refer to as "Telcos" in the following – have been used to holding a brokering position because of their control of communication networks.

Many aspects of the telecom business model are being challenged by Web actors – often referred to as Over-The-Top (OTT) players – who also offer communication services, but services that are:

- Network-independent (relying on the universal internet network and on the web technology)
- Loosely controlled (e.g., light authentication, credit card payment, and no monthly billing)
- Largely customizable (e.g., based on each user's profile, request history, context-awareness)
- Non-standardized, and often without interoperability between actors
- Where consumers may also become producers (e.g., Web 2.0 wave, Apple 'app' model)

These IT actors rely on sharp software competencies that enable them to quickly develop, test and deploy services. The Web development methods provide flexibility and faster time-to-market (TTM) and thus easier integration and validation for new service deployments along with lower costs thanks to the use of massively deployed open-source information technology (IT). Moreover, these Web players benefit from a strong brokering position based on their key assets: e.g., a search engine for Google, a social network for Facebook, mobile devices and a closely linked and easy-to-use App Store for Apple.

In response to the emergence of these new players, telcos are trying to reinvent their organizational networks and business models in line with this emerging service paradigm. This book surveys the major shifts in the telecom services ecosystem, from both technical and business viewpoints, and introduces possible responses by telcos within three timeframes: *now* (the IP Multimedia Subsystem – IMS age), *tomorrow* (the post-IMS age), and *afterwards* (the Future Internet age). Each of the chapters' authors are recognized experts, working for key players in the telecom market: operators (Deutsche Telekom, Orange, Telecom Italia, and Telefonica), standards organizations (ETSI), regulators (ARCEP), manufacturers (Alcatel-Lucent Bell Labs, Ericsson, and Tekelec), IT vendors (HP,

SAP) and academia (Fraunhofer FOKUS, Mines-Telecom, Politecnica Madrid, TU Berlin, and Zurich University).

The first part of the book reviews the main telco assets in terms of services and their current disruptions, in order to better understand where the industry is coming from and how it stands now. Chapter 1 focuses on the network and control layer evolution. It first introduces broadband network evolution as a highway for services, with the Fiber-To-The-Home (FTTH) optical access network and the Long-Term Evolution (LTE) wireless access network. It then depicts the convergent core network evolution of fixed and mobile all-IP networks. It also deals with the evolution of the controlling and enabling layer. Chapter 2 surveys how the application layer is evolving towards a convergence of telecom and Web services. Applications have been the main driver for the incredible growth of OTTs. Telcos are now preparing to open up their assets to third-party service providers to enrich their application offerings. In addition, service composition has become a key value-added capability that enables end-users to adapt services for their own needs. The requirements for service delivery (e.g., identity management, service brokering, service enablers) are presented first, followed by a survey of the various service delivery solutions, with their strengths and weaknesses. Chapter 3 is a showcase focusing on Value-added services (VAS). It contains an in-depth anthology of the evolution of the techniques supporting the creation of Value-added services. This includes a break-down of the fundamental building blocks and how these building blocks are used to build VAS for the evolving/future multi-access multimedia communication networks. Chapter 4 presents the current trends in the standardization landscape, from the perspective of a standard development organization (SDO). It describes the recent key technical achievements, as well as the standardization process and the collaboration between different SDOs.

The second part highlights the new issues raised by the rise of the OTTs and the possible medium-term strategies beyond the IMS/NGN paradigm. The importance of an ecosystem model is emphasized, as well as the key regulation principles of the telecom market and their evolution. Chapter 5 recalls the history of the VoIP standards that paved the way to many OTT multimedia communication offers. Chapter 6 comes back to the main assumptions that have driven the construction of telecom architectures during the last ten years (with the NGN paradigm), investigates how these assumptions were or were not realized, and offers perspectives for the future. Chapter 7 presents an IT viewpoint on standardization. It especially questions when, why, and how the absence of standards might be a strength. Beyond standardization, it introduces the "common platform" model and its importance for the IT mindset. It emphasizes the main options for building such platforms (e.g., open-source or ecosystems). Chapter 8 investigates the shifts in the roles of players and business models. It details the respective strengths and weaknesses of telcos and OTT players, and investigates whether an ecosystem model is suitable for telcos. Chapter 9 deals with the shifts in public regulation. The telecom operator business is indeed highly driven by regulation. This chapter details the current regulatory trends, for both telcos and Web players. It also addresses net neutrality issues.

The last part is dedicated to the long-term service evolution driven by future Internet research, especially virtualization, the Internet of Things, and service engineering. Chapter 10 surveys the rise of the service marketplace and application stores, as well both native and Web apps. It details how telcos may compete in this area with a three-screen strategy (i.e., PC, mobile, TV). Chapter 11 explains the rise of cloud computing and how telcos might operate cloud services in a de-perimeterized way, i.e., independently of access networks or regional markets. Chapter 12 focuses on the corresponding network function virtualization and software-defined network trends. It introduces the new network architecture models and technologies (e.g., Open Flow), and shows how telcos may exploit it for more economic service provision. Chapter 13 presents the stakes and challenges of the emerging Web of Things by applying the lessons learned from current machine-to-machine (M2M) services. It also introduces possible business opportunities for telcos in the Web of Things. Chapter 14 covers the shifts in service consumption. It introduces the paradigm shift from products to services, as well as the key concepts from service science and engineering. This chapter provides a prospective view on services customized according to individual needs, along with a detailed survey of the research on that topic.

We would like to thank all of the authors for their diligent efforts and outstanding contributions to making this book a reality. We hope readers will enjoy reading the book and come to some fresh insights on this challenging field.

Emmanuel Bertin
Noel Crespi
Thomas Magedanz

Table of Contents

Network and Control Platforms

Marius Corici[2], Julius Müller[1], Dragos Vingarzan[2], and Thomas Magedanz[1]

[1] Technische Universität Berlin, Straße des 17. Juni 135, 10623 Berlin, Germany
julius.mueller@tu-berlin.de
[2] Fraunhofer Institute FOKUS, Kaiserin-Augusta-Allee 31, 10589 Berlin, Germany
{marius-iulian.corici,dragos.vingarzan}@fokus.fraunhofer.de

Abstract. The Internet as the largest global recognized communication system is in constant change and evolves in dimensions of technology, capacity, availability and size continuously since its beginnings in the late 1960's. The openness and its continuous change became characteristics of the Internet nowadays, but were no available in its origins. This chapter presents an overview about the telecommunication network and control platform evolution from classic fixed Circuit-Switched (CS) on to current fixed and mobile Next-Generation-Networks (NGN) towards future networks trends. Furthermore the Fixed-Mobile-Covergence (FMC) is presented and technology specific details are presented exemplarily.

1 Introduction

The Internet is the largest global recognized communication system, which evolved in dimensions of technology, capacity, availability and size continuously since its beginnings in the late 1960's. Information is transported via packets without differentiating between individual application characteristics over manifold access and core network technologies. The openness and its continuous change became characteristics of the Internet nowadays.

This chapter presents a chronological overview on the evolution of telecommunication networks and control platforms in the last decades, transition from closed to open networks, the fixed and mobile convergence and finally outlines trends of future networks. This chapter focuses on connectivity and builds the fundament for the following chapters especially for the Application Layer Evolution chapter, which outlines the application layer evolution, which is aligned on network layer evolution. Both presented trends influence each other.

The structure of this chapter is as follow. An introduction, which positions the presented work and provides the historical background, is followed by section 2, which introduces the concept of Intelligent Networks (IN) as a classical closed telecommunication system initially designed for fixed networks with a limited set of functionalities. Intelligent Networks or its mobile variant Customized Applications for Mobile Enhanced Logic (CAMEL) are introduced as classic telecommunication systems circuit-switched networks. Section 3 presents the concept, architecture and key functionalities of the IP Multimedia Subsystem (IMS) standardized by 3GPP. IMS is presented as network layer abstraction for 3GPP GPRS and UMTS or non-3GPP, cable,

E. Bertin et al. (Eds.): Telecommunication Services Evolution, LNCS 7768, pp. 1–24, 2013.

digital-subscriber-line (DSL) networks with the goal of providing unified interfaces for SIP based services. Section 4 presents the architecture, main protocols and key functionalities of the 3GPP All-IP Evolved Packet Core (EPC). The need for standardizing the Evolved Packet Core System (EPS) consisting of the radio part LTE and the core network part EPC is motivated and outlined. Section 5 discusses the role of Over-The-Top (OTT) applications and their growing impact on the application diversification, which directly influences the classic telecommunication value chain. Section 6 presents the trend of Machine-Type-Communication (MTC) in form of standardization activities. Section 7 outlines the trend of Open Networks by motivating the concept of network virtualization and presenting ongoing research and development activities. Section 8 summarizes and concludes the chapter. A list of acronyms and references are attached to the end of this chapter.

2   Intelligent Networks

The term Intelligent Network (IN) describes a framework, which provides an open platform support for uniform creation, introduction, control and management of services in an abstract way. The concept of Intelligent Networks separates control and switching logic what in turn introduces flexibility in static telecommunication networks. Logic is pulled out of the network switches (SSP) into dedicated network nodes (SCP), what accelerates the overall performance to real-time signaling and eases the deployment of new service features for the whole network. One main benefit is the reusability of basic services to shorten the time-to-market duration of introducing novel and complex services on top of existing standardized simple services (enabler), without changing the deployed switches. The other benefit is the achieved network and service independence.

Global System for Mobile Communications (GSM) networks were deployed in parallel to fixed line IN. The concept of IN was applied on GSM networks with regards to mobility of the subscriber over network provider boarders. The ETSI standard for IN in mobile networks is called Customized Applications for Mobile Enhanced Logic (CAMEL). The CAMEL architecture supports Operator specific services (OSS) to mobile subscribers even when roaming in another network (international roaming).

IN for fixed CS networks did never support service interoperability, but in mobile networks we are confronted with roaming users and have strong heterogeneity of service platforms, which require seamless and transparent interoperability.

CAMEL evolved within four phases, in which basic call control functions for GSM calls, charging of services in visited network domains, enhanced mobility management and interworking with IMS were introduced step by step.

2.1   Network Elements

Service Switching Points (SSP) connects subscribers' telephones and terminal equipment with the network. SSPs contain large switching matrices in order to switch the high volumes of traffic from the interconnected subscribers. A finite state machine, namely the Basic Call State Machine (BCSM), represents an abstract two-party-call containing all stages. Trigger hook between two adjacent states and invokes further services after reaching this state.

Service Control Functions (SCF) request SSF/CCF to perform certain call and connection processing functions (routing, charging, etc.) and requests Service Data Functions (SDF) to receive/update service data information.

Service Switching Functions (SSF) determine when IN service logic should be invoked. The SSP represents the point of subscription for the service user, which is responsible for detecting special conditions during call processing that cause a query for instructions to be issued to the SCP.

Signaling Transfer Points (STP) act as SS7 routers and give alternate paths to destinations when one possible route to a destination fails.

Signaling Control Points (SCP) provide database and data processing functions within the network, such as billing, maintenance, subscriber control and number translation. The SCP validates and authenticates information from the service user (such as PIN information), processes requests from the SSP and issuing responses.

The Intelligent Peripheral (IP) or Specialized Resource Function (SRF) provides additional interaction functions, which provides additional voice resources to the SSP for playing back standard announcements. Therefore DTMF tones are detected when gathering information from the user.

Service Management System / Operations System (SMS) deploy, manage and configure services. Monitoring data is collected to charge service usage and to provide statistics to the service operator.

Service Creation Environment (SCE) provides to service designer capabilities to construct chains realizing services (service features).

CAMEL and IN have share the same concept, therefore the components of them are quite similar and displayed in the same Fig. 1.

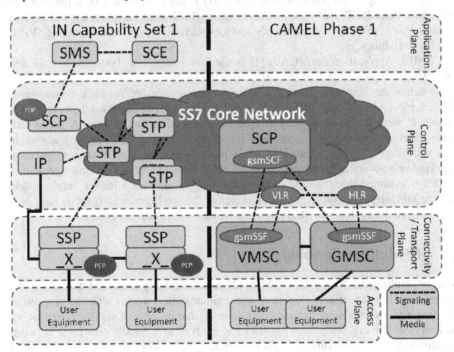

Fig. 1. Intelligent Network and CAMEL Architecture Overview

The Home Subscriber Register (HLR) stores the information relevant to the current CAMEL subscription (CSI). Its counterpart in the visiting domain, the Visitor Location Register (VLR) stores the O-CSI and T-CSI as a part of the subscriber data for subscribers roaming in the VLR area.

The Gateway or Visitor MSC (GMSC/VMSC) receive an O/T-CSI from the HLR, indicating the GMSC to request instructions from the gsmSSF, in case the processing of a subscribe call requires CAMEL support. The MSCs monitor on request the call states (events) and inform the gsmSSF of these states during processing, enabling the gsmSSF to control the execution of the call in the specific MSC.

The gsmSCF functional entity contains the CAMEL service logic to implement OSS. It interfaces with the gsmSSF and the HLR.

The gsmSSF functional entity interfaces the MSC/GMSC to the gsmSCF. The concept of the gsmSSF is derived from the IN SSF, but uses different triggering mechanisms because of the nature of the mobile network.

2.2　IN Key Protocols

Common Channel Signaling System No. 7 (i.e., SS7 or C7) is a global standard for telecommunications defined by the International Telecommunication Union (ITU) Telecommunication Standardization Sector (ITU-T) used in IN. The SS7 network and protocol are used for basic call setup, management, and tear down. Signaling links are logically organized by link type ("A" through "F") according to their use in the SS7 signaling network, depending on the connected network components.

INAP (Intelligent Network Application Part) is used between a wire line Service Switching Point (SSP), network media resources (Intelligent Peripherals), and Service Control Points (SCPs). It supports IN services such as enhanced call routing, VPN, number portability, etc.

CAMEL Application Part (CAP) [1] is used for interactions between the SSF and SCF. Mobile Application Part (MAP) queries the HLR.

Switches are complex, powerful, efficient and expensive network components. Once deployed in the telco network, it is difficult to apply changes on them. Switches of the IN were designed to work simple without having much logic. A Basic Call State Machine instance is instantiated for every incoming call reaching a switch. Trigger Points (TP) are located between these individual Call States, to perform blocking or non-blocking actions to control call establishment and call management.

It was assumed that the idea of the Basic Call Model has a longer duration than service logic deployed on each switch, therefore the intelligence in form of logic was moved from the switch into SCP (high availability server cluster) nodes.

3　IP Multimedia Subsystem

The IP Multimedia Subsystem (IMS) [2] was originally designed to merge the Internet and the carrier grade operator telecommunication worlds with the purpose of creating a platform able to enhance and diversify the process of service provisioning and service delivery. Subsequently, IMS has evolved as a middleware layer between the different access networks and their afferent core network functionality including 3GPP architecture for GPRS and UMTS as well as WiFi and WiMAX from the mobile telecommunication and NGN fixed networks interoperating with legacy PSTN fixed and mobile communication. With the fast deployment and gradual adoption of the LTE access network which offers only packet based communication, IMS is foreseen as the feasible support for voice and other telecommunication services support in the future mobile broadband communications.

IMS represents a generic service provisioning platform widely adopted in the design of Next Generation Networks (NGN) as operator mediation of the service control between the various fixed and mobile devices and the specific application servers enabling the support of the services through the various NGN transport architectures including the 3GPP architecture for 2G and 3G access networks and later for LTE as well as the integration with third party and operator controlled WLAN accesses, the 3GPP2 architecture for the CDMA technologies and ETSI/TISPAN NGN architecture for fixed communication.

Over these multiple accesses, IMS is able to provide a unified QoS and charging mechanisms. Independent of the various access networks, IMS is able to provide service personalization and localization as well as flexible charging schemes based on content and an integrated authentication and authorization.

This brings, as shown in Fig. 2, a large number of benefits including:

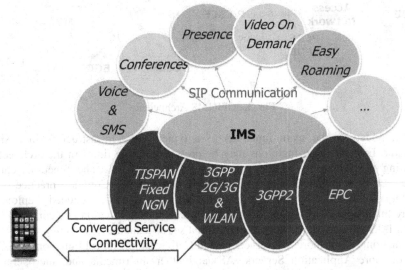

Fig. 2. 3GPP IP Multimedia Subsystem: The Multimedia Service Convergence

- Rapid service creation and system integration – part of the functionality usually required for a specific service is maintained by the service provisioning platform, therefore it does not have to be developed for the specific services such as presence, conferencing, push-to-talk, content sharing etc.
- High degree of interoperability is achieved through the usage of standard interfaces. Same functions are shared among several applications and a more complex service logic can be achieved. This enables service providers to build and customize their own multimedia services.

- The system was design to be highly scalable with build in redundancy mechanism, enabling the easy support of the carrier-grade multimedia communication needs of the fixed and mobile operators.

3.1   IMS Architecture

IMS follows an approach called functional decomposition, which is superior to the traditional vertical integration models in which common functions are replicated for each application. By contrast, IMS offers a layered architecture consisting of an access network, a transport layer, a control and an application/services layer.

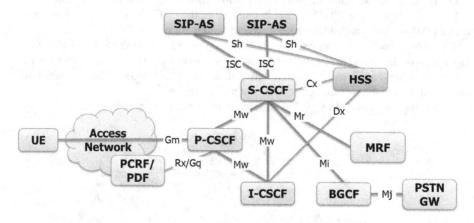

Fig. 3. 3GPP IMS Architecture

Fig. 3 depicts the main functions of a typical IMS infrastructure in a single operator. Each of these functions may be present multiple times in the architecture, ensuring the scalability of the operations of the system. The functions can be collocated or split between multiple physical components. Common practice of the vendors shows that co-location can be used in specific reduced deployment environments; however the most vendors implement each function as a component.

An IMS infrastructure is composed from a set of databases containing user related information, one or more SIP servers named Call Session Control Functions (CSCFs), one or more Application Servers (AS) and other multimedia and interoperability functions.

As main database, IMS includes the Home Subscriber Server (HSS) which contains the subscription profile of the user enabling the handling of the multimedia services as well as IMS platform information such as location, security, authentication and authorization, permissions and current network entities handling the device. If more than one HSS is used in a specific deployment, then a static Service Location Function (SLF) database enables the redirection of the subscription information exchange to the appropriate HSS.

The Call Session Control Functions (CSCFs) are SIP servers which are handling the subscriber signaling in the IMS. There are three types of CSCFs depending on the functionality they provide:

- P-CSCF (Proxy-CSCF) – the P-CSCF terminates the IMS domain towards the user endpoint acting as an inbound/outbound SIP proxy. The P-CSCF includes authentication and authorization functionality related to the usage of IMS services for the mobile device. Additionally, it enables the encryption and the compression of the communication of the mobile device. In relationship with the access networks, it makes resource reservation and charging requests towards the specific transport networks.
- I-CSCF (Interrogating-CSCF) – the I-CSCF is a static SIP proxy located at the border of an administrative domain. Its main function is to determine the service SIP proxy for a specific subscriber. For this it communicates with the HSS to determine the current node serving the subscriber.
- S-CSCF(Serving-CSCF) – the S-CSCF is the central node in the user signaling acting as a SIP registrar, maintaining the binding between the current contact address of the device and its public identity. Additionally, the S-CSCF routes the SIP messages to the appropriate Application Servers, PSTN interoperation nodes, other S-CSCF or the P-CSCF representing the User Endpoint.

A SIP Application Server (AS) hosts and executes a service such as presence, location, conferencing etc. Depending on the type of service, the AS can have multiple SIP functions. As the SIP AS may require information related to the subscription profile, an interface to the HSS is included.

An IMS infrastructure may include additional functions such as a Media Resource Function (MRF) providing the media content addressed to the user endpoint. For interconnection to the PSTN network, a supplementary Border Gateway Control Function (BGCF) and a gateway to the PSTN domain may be deployed enabling the location of the device in the PSTN network and the translation of the communication signaling and data information.

In order to be able to reserve resources and to transmit charging differentiation information towards the specific access networks, the IMS architecture is communicating with the policy decision entities for the specific transport network architectures such as Policy and Charging Rules Function (PCRF) for the Evolved Packet Core, the Policy Decision Function (PDF) for the UMTS and for the fixed network transport infrastructure. Through this interface data path resource requirements are transmitted enabling the appropriate QoS reservations and notifications related to the connectivity of the devices are received.

3.2   IMS Key Protocols

The Session Initiation Protocol (SIP) [3] is used for the signaling and the control of the communication between the User Endpoints or between a User Endpoint and the IMS CSCFs or one or more Application Servers. SIP enables the provisioning of information in the correspondent parties required for establishment and termination of specific services. Specifically for multimedia services such as voice or video calls SIP is transporting in the body of the messages the information in the form of the Session Description Protocol (SDP). SDP is a text based protocol which contains information on the multimedia end points, codec information and optionally indicates the communication data rates.

In case of SIP based sessions, the IMS infrastructure plays an intermediary role enabling the reachability of the correspondent parties, the transport of the resource negotiation and charging information as well as the communication of the different messages through the application servers which are involved in the specific service establishment. The basic SIP protocol was extended for enabling carrier grade communication as well as for supporting the required scalability features of the multimedia signaling.

The actual multimedia data is carried through protocols such as the Real-Time Transport Protocol (RTP) [4] which provides end-to-end real-time transmission. The data encoded with a specific codec is encapsulated into RTP data packets which include additional timestamp and order information enabling the receiver to decode and to render the information at the appropriate time interval from the previous message.

For specific services such as Instant Messaging and Presence, the SIP protocol was extended to transport other type of information such as plain text messages, subscriptions and notifications for specific events and XML formatted information related to the subscribed devices. The extension of the SIP protocol enables the IMS infrastructure to support additional services apart from the classic multimedia.

For the communication with the transport networks the IETF DIAMETER protocol [5] is used, extended for the specific purpose of resource reservations and event notifications. Diameter is additionally used as signaling protocol between the different control entities of the transport layer and it is further described in the next subsections.

3.3   The Role of IMS in the Future Internet Networks

Driven by the deployment of LTE access network, the current carrier grade network providers are also deploying all-IP based infrastructures in the mobile networks, similar to the evolution towards NGN in the fixed communication. In this context IMS plays a major role as the only standardized and highly flexible network architecture.

In order to be able to provide basic Voice Sevices in the all-IP infrastructure, the Next Generation Mobile Alliance (NGMA) adopted and further developed a set of IMS specification under the umberella of VoLTE which enable the basic call setup using IMS, roaming and voice call continuity to Circuit Switched communication through this simplifying the IMS standard to a level where inter-operability can be received with minimal costs.

Additionally, carrier grade operators are planning the deployment of rich communication suite services addressed to smartphone communication and extending the current telecommunication services towards high data exchanges and other user and community services. These services are currently standardized by the NGMA requiring an IMS infrastructure.

IMS can be deployed also independent of the various access networks acting as an Over-The-Top multimedia platform. From this perspective, the carrier grade operator networks are able to offer the services not only to their own subscribers, but also to other subscribers which are bale to communicate via IP. In this case an IMS infrastructure is not limited only to the specific operator, enabling it to act on a larger market targeted to specific users and not bound to a specific geographic region. This use case is addressing especially other industries than the telecommunications such as automated communication with consumer devices, sensors and actuators of automotive industry etc.

4   Evolved Packet Core

With the progress towards high data rate wireless access technologies, a complimentary evolution was required from the side of the core network architecture. As observed from the evolution of the fixed communication, the services that the user requires over broadband access are not any more limited to voice and reduced data exchange such as email over 3G networks. Instead, they are using all of the resources available which transforms the mass broadband wireless environment into an IP data dominant one. In order to face this challenge, the novel architecture is considered to rely on IP communication only and to use a similar forwarding mechanism as the Internet, adapted to the wireless environment and more efficient due to the increased deployment and operational costs compared to the fixed infrastructures.

Following the indications of the NGMN Alliance[11], the 3rd Generation Partnership Project (3GPP) initiated the standardization procedures for the Evolved Packet Core (EPC)[6][7], an all-IP core network architecture specifically designed for the communication requirements of the LTE access and offering IP convergence for the heterogeneous access networks in a transparent manner to the applications as depicted in Fig. 4.

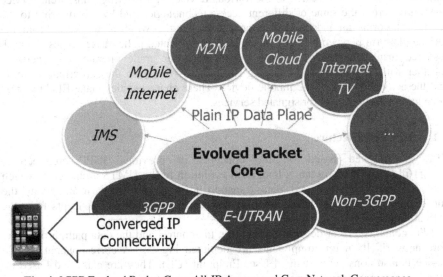

Fig. 4. 3GPP Evolved Packet Core: All-IP Access and Core Network Convergence

As the EPC is the only core network architecture supporting the LTE access technology and as the LTE is gradually deployed with a time horizon of more than ten years until complete deployment, the EPC architecture represents a technology landmark for the core network development. Furthermore, the further scientific development of the EPC core network will most probably be integrated in the next generations of the core network architecture as it was until now done throughout the evolution of the mobile core networks.

Other architectures are available from other standardization organizations such as the NGN architecture from ITU [16]. These architectures exhibit the same functional features as they offer the same type of connectivity support to the devices. However, either their standardization status is still in very early stages or the specific access technologies for which they are developed are not having a global momentum similar to LTE. Therefore, they will not be further presented here.

As LTE is still in its first releases in standardization, it is foreseen that the architecture is not yet completed. Major requirements are expected to be further received from the first deployments as well as with the increase in scale of the number of connected subscribers and of the number of applications especially tailored for the mobile environment[12]. Because of this a large space for novel concepts and innovation is envisaged.

Additionally, the EPC sustains also in an integrated manner the other heterogeneous accesses such as 3GPP e.g. UMTS, EDGE, GPRS and non-3GPP e.g. WiMAX, CDMA etc., being able to interconnect with any available or future wireless technologies including fixed communication [3],[4]. EPC provides for the mobile devices connected to these accesses full convergence at IP connectivity level including the support for identity, authentication and authorization, policy and charging control and mobility management.

Through the convergence at network level, the EPC is enabling efficient connection of the mobile devices to the network and their communication with the different service platforms such as the IP Multimedia Subsystem (IMS) [8] or the Internet, being able to control the resources allocated to the various devices and offering transparent service continuity across the same or different access technologies and by this offering to the service platforms an independent connection over the wireless accesses. From the service platform perspective, EPC manages event oriented policy based access control, resource management and mobility in single carrier grade operator core network together with accounting and charging functionality based on the subscription profile and the active services of the mobile device. These characteristics make EPC the next generation transport level for signaled services.

4.1   EPC Architecture

EPC is designed based on the concepts of previous 3GPP architectures ([12][16][8][9]). It represents a long term evolution of the UMTS architecture which was designed for voice and data transport [10]. Additionally, it maintains the subscriber differentiation based resource reservation and mobility concepts from the IMS architecture.

EPC contains a clear delineation between the control and the data path through the core network. Its main components are depicted Fig. 5. A correspondent mobile device is also considered, named User Endpoint (UE). They are classified based on their functionality as follows:

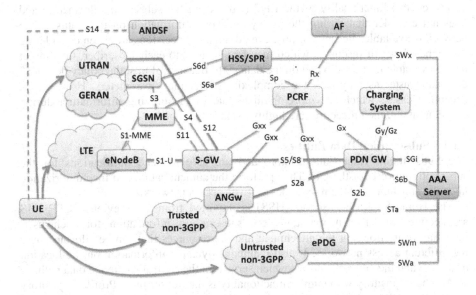

Fig. 5. 3GPP Evolved Packet Core Architecture

- Subscription Data Entities (e.g. HSS, AAA Server etc.) - These entities store, update and are able to transmit notifications on the subscription profile of the users and to perform authentication and authorization procedures. Additionally, they contain dynamic user information such as current allocated IP addresses.
- Control Entities (e.g. PCRF, MME, ANDSF) - These entities make policy based decisions regarding the connectivity, the access control and the resources required by a UE. Based on various subscriber related triggers, they make the decisions which are afterwards installed on the UE and on the various data path components.
- Gateways (e.g. Serving GW, PDN GW etc.) - These data path entities are forwarding the data traffic of the UE and ensure the access control, QoS and mobility support according to the decisions made by the control entities. They are also able to transmit subscriber related events to the control entities in order to adapt the policy decisions accordingly.

Together these entities enable that the IP Connectivity is provisioned and the resources are allocated according to the profile of the user and based on the requirements of each application. The applications are considered external to the EPC architecture and they are generically named Application Functions (AFs). The role of the AF can be taken by an IMS architecture, by a service broker, by an intermediary node of the operator on the application path or directly by infrastructures of third party service providers. Additionally, the operator may deploy traffic detection tools which can also transmit events which generate policy decisions modifying the IP Connectivity.

Furthermore, EPC contains accounting functions enabling the charging services for the IP connectivity. The charging is based on the data path sessions and can be executed synchronous or asynchronous to the data sessions.

The control functionality of the EPC is based on the subscriber information and does not consider that during the policy decisions information on the status of the network is available. Because of this, even though the decisions are taken considering the highest level of resources which may be allocated to each subscriber, they might not be available in the radio and on the data path. Because of this, the policy decisions are taken faster as they lack the complexity of the input parameters. However, in exception cases, which are more frequent due to the missing information during decision taking, the procedures are highly extended.

4.1.1   Subscription Data Entities

The Subscription Data Entities store and are able to send notifications for the subscription profile of the UE. They perform the authentication and the authorization upon the attachment of the mobile device to an access network.

The Home Subscriber Server (HSS) is imported from the previous 3GPP IMS architecture. In EPC, it maintains the subscription information for each user, including restrictions for the attachment and the resources that can be allocated over the different access networks. It also maintains dynamic information on the location of the UE and the network entities which serve it in the control and in the data path.

Another repository with similar functionality is the Subscription Profile Repository (SPR). It is a logical function which maintains the subscription related information necessary for the policy based decisions for access control and resource reservation. As the current standards do not specify the internal data structure of this repository and following the standardization direction in 3GPP to unify the different subscription data entities, the SPR is associated in this paper with the HSS, because of their similarities.

The AAA Server was initially defined for the inter-working between the 3GPP and WiFi and it was extended in the EPC for supporting authentication and authorization in non-3GPP accesses ([22][23]). It retrieves and updates the subscriber profile information from the HSS allowing also report generation for charging based on the authentication requests received from the non-3GPP trusted network or from the ePDG. In the roaming case, an AAA Proxy is located in the visited domain for forwarding the requests related to the user to the home domain.

4.1.2   Control Entities

The control functions of EPC manage the access control, the mobility and the resource reservations. The control mechanisms of EPC are triggered by events. When the user profile from the repositories, the attachment of the UE or its resources required change or the access network context is modified then policy based decisions are made which are further enforced in the gateways.

The Mobility Management Entity (MME) is the central management entity for the LTE accesses [21]. It is responsible for the connection of the UE by selecting the gateway through which messages are to be exchanged and a level of resources for the UE in cases of attachment and handover. It provides also authentication and authorization and location tracking using the HSS and intra-3GPP mobility (e.g. between 2G/3G and LTE).

The Policy and Charging Rules Function (PCRF) is the control entity making policy based decisions for service data flow detection, admission control, QoS and flow based charging [25][26][27][28]. It maintains a complete subscription state for each UE with decisions made on a per-user base. PCRF cannot be associated with a management entity as it does not maintain information on the resources available in the different access networks. Instead for each decision an enforcement procedure is to be executed in order to determine whether the requirements can be fulfilled by the gateways.

The Access Network Discovery and Selection Function (ANDSF) makes subscription based decisions and transmits to the UE information on the preferences of the operator for the discovery of accesses in specific locations and handover decisions of the UE [29]. The ANDSF uses the location of the UE, a Coverage Map and the subscription information, to make these decisions. As inside 3GPP accesses the preference of the operator is controlled by the MME, the ANDSF addresses only handovers with non-3GPP accesses.

4.1.3 Gateways

In EPC, the gateways ensure the forwarding of the data packets between the UE and the network core within the parameters enforced by the control entities. They also support the execution of different mobility protocols and transmit notifications for data related events for each subscriber to the control entities.

The Packet Data Network Gateway (PDN GW) is the entrance and the exit point for data traffic in the EPC. It provides connectivity from the user devices to the external packet data networks. Additionally, it acts as central mobility anchor. The PDN GW performs policy enforcement and packet filtering for each data flow of each subscriber. For this, it maintains the context for each connection of the mobile device, the traffic flow templates for the active services, the QoS profile and the charging characteristics.

The EPC is able to offer a unified enforcing of the policies for the different access networks. For each class of access networks, a different gateway is defined. For the 3GPP accesses a Serving GW (S-GW) is used. Additionally, a Serving GPRS Support Node (SGSN) is used for the 2G/3G access technologies. The non-3GPP technologies are separated based on the security the operator is able to provide over the access network in trusted and un-trusted non-3GPP accesses. In the untrusted non-3GPP accesses additional security levels are to be established. As gateways, for the untrusted non-3GPP accesses an evolved Packet Data Gateway (ePDG) is used while for the trusted non-3GPP a generic Access Network Gateway (ANGw) is deployed, differing in the specific requirements and parameters of the different accesses.

All the gateways, they include the Bearer Binding and Event Rules Function (BBERF) which provides policy based enforcement and event notifications from the wireless link to the PCRF and gating functionality for the data traffic. They also include the attachment and mobility related functionality for both the control and the data path.

4.2   EPC Key Protocols

EPC bases on IP protocols, as standardized by IETF and OMA, enhanced by the 3GPP specifications. It is able to communicate over IPv4 or over IPv6 or over a mixture of the both. Three main categories of protocols are considered, depending on their goal in the EPC: active management protocols, mobility protocols and mobile device management from the network.

Diameter is used as a singular management protocol[5]. The basic IETF standard was enhanced by 3GPP for supporting not only authentication and authorization, but also policy based decisions and event notifications related to the connectivity and the different data flows of the subscribers. Diameter is deployed on the interfaces between the subscription repositories, the control entities and the data path entities supporting the operations required for access control, QoS and events.

As mobility protocols, multiple options are available like GPRS Tunneling Protocol (GTP), Mobile IPv4 (MIPv4)[31], Dual Stack Mobile IP (DSMIP) [32] and/or Proxy Mobile IP (PMIP) [33][34]. Each of these protocols has different capabilities and is in a different development stage. Although they may function independent of the architecture itself directly on the data path, as specified by IETF, in EPC, the entities defined in these protocols are interconnected with the Diameter control interfaces which supply parameters and through which different events and operations are to be triggered. All these mobility protocols have some similar characteristics. First, they are transparent to the correspondent nodes, enabling the communication to any IP based service which may or may not pertain to the carrier grade operator which deploys the EPC. Secondly, the mobility protocols rely on a centralized anchor node which enable the mobility of the all the devices in all the accesses and in all the locations of the EPC.

In EPC, the access network discovery and selection functionality was included as part of the operator con-trolled management of the mobile device. Thus OMA Device Management (DM) protocol was chosen as transport protocol because it is already integrated in the existing mobile network architectures [35]. A novel Management Object was defined specifically for the access network discovery and selection for conveying the in-formation from the network to the mobile devices [21].

4.3   EPC Functional Features

EPC is designed to provide a number of key capabilities over the IP basis required for the support of the seamless and efficient service delivery. The main functionality includes network access control functions, resource control and mobility support.

4.3.1 Network Access Control Functions

The network access control functions enable the UE to connect to the EPC and then over the EPC to the different service providers. They include the authentication and authorization, admission control, selection of the entities which will serve the UE (e.g. the PCRF, the PDN GW etc.) and the establishment of a minimal context which enables the UE to be reachable in the IP domain and its basic communication with the service platforms.

The authentication and authorization procedures are dependent on the access network selected by the UE for attachment. In the case of LTE, the MME retrieves the profile of the subscriber directly from the HSS during the attachment, while in the case of non-3GPP accesses, the ANGw or the ePDG request the information through the AAA Server from the HSS after the UE attached to the wireless environment when it requests an attachment to the EPC [36]. In case of the other 3GPP accesses, the standard procedure is executed, considering that the role of the GGSN is taken by the Serving GW.

Then, the IP reachability context is created for the UE. In case of GTP or PMIPv6, upon an address request from the UE, a data tunnel is established between the gateway of the specific access and the PDN GW. In case of MIP or DSMIP, an address is allocated locally and the tunnel is established directly between the UE and the PDN GW.

During the tunnel establishment procedures, the PDN GW initiates the procedures for the basic resources which allow the UE to communicate with the service platforms. In this procedure, the PCRF makes a policy based decision whether the UE is allowed to communicate over the access network and which default level of resources is to be allocated for the basic communication.

After this decision is enforced and the mobile device receives the IP address over which it is able to communicate, the attachment procedure is completed and it may exchange data over the access network and the EPC - it has a Packed Data Network (PDN) connection.

The network access control functions allow the EPC to coherently apply policies during the attachment and detachment of the mobile devices according to the subscription profile of the user in the SPR/HSS.

4.3.2 Resource Control

The EPC has a central notion for resource reservations the IP Bearer, an aggregation of IP data flows that receive a common QoS treatment (forwarding, scheduling, queuing, shaping etc.) established between the UE and the PDN GW.

In EPC there is a clear distinction between the access network and the core network resource reservation. The access resource reservation is technology specific and does not influence directly the EPC operations. On the other hand, EPC was designed as support architecture for LTE, thus the MME is managing the resources inside this access technology.

For all the access technologies, the core network resource reservation can be triggered by the UE or by the service platform. The UE trigger is received by the gateway of the specific access which forwards the request to the PCRF. The service platform trigger is transmitted directly to the PCRF. By this centralization into the PCRF, the consistency of the QoS rules enforced for an UE is maintained. Then the PCRF makes the subscription based policy decision whether the UE is allowed to reserve the required resources. The decision is enforced to the PDN GW and to the gateways of the specific access networks and from here using specific mechanisms to the wireless access network.

As PCRF does not manage the resources available on the different wireless accesses and gateways, this enforcement may fail. From this perspective, PCRF is not a resource control entity as it is not able to consider the context in the different accesses, but as a user control entity because it sustains its decisions on input regarding the UE and its applications. This allows the concentration of the functionality on the UE itself and not as much on the momentary context of the accesses, enabling a scalable flat decision mechanism.

In order to reduce the complexity, EPC considers that the default bearer established at the attachment to the EPC and the subsequent bearers, requested by the UE or the service platform, are reserved using the same procedures. This allows, from the perspective of the EPC to regard the network access control functions as resource management functions.

4.3.3 Mobility Support

EPC integrates multiple access technologies. In order to be able to support mobility between the different access networks a set of mechanisms was defined which include the access network discovery and selection and the correlated attachment to the target access and detachment from the source access relying on the existing mobility protocols like GTP, Proxy MIP and Classic MIP.

LTE was designed to be a direct extension of the other 3GPP accesses, as UMTS was an extension for the GPRS architecture. The Intra-3GPP mobility management bases on the MME to select the next attachment cell and to initiate a preparation procedure. When it is completed, the MME transmits a handover command to the mobile device.

In case of non-3GPP technologies, 3GPP cannot influence directly the handover procedures, due to the various standardization groups involved for access networks specifications. Thus a complete network controlled handover cannot be realized. In order to limit the effect of the UE independent selection of the target access which leads to congestion of some accesses while others are capable to sustain seamlessly the communication, the ANDSF was introduced in the architecture. Based on the location information, it transmits to the UE the preferences of the operator for target accesses in case a handover becomes necessary. The functionality of the ANDSF restrains to this general indication. The UE has to consider the policies received and decide independently when a handover is to be executed.

The effective handover procedures are separated logically in the attachment to the target access network and the detachment from the source access network. In the handover with optimization case, like in the intra-3GPP handovers, a preparation phase is executed which creates the user context on the target access network. However this is not possible in handovers from and to non-3GPP accesses, as the decision on the handover is taken by the UE. In this case, the mobility relies on the mobility protocol deployed, e.g. GTP, PMIP, classic MIP. It presumes that at the moment when the UE attaches to the target access network, the data traffic is forwarded to the new access even though the source access network connection is still available. From this perspective EPC is able to execute soft intra-3GPP handovers and hard handovers with the non-3GPP accesses.

As all the mobility protocols deployed in the EPC rely on a centralized anchor node and as the handover procedures are triggered by the changes of the location of the device in the network, currently the EPC does not provide any mechanism in which the data path can be adapted for each subscriber depending on the current network status and according to the applications delay requirements.

4.3.4 Interconnection with Application Platforms

EPC provides a transparent convergent network layer for the IP applications. From the perspective of a service provider without a modification of the application, it enables a degree of satisfaction similar to the fixed IP applications, by transparently supporting features like access control, QoS insurance, seamless mobility between the different access networks, prioritization and security. Based on this it is foreseen that the mobile application environment will adapt and integrate the ones previously deployed on the fixed Internet.

Also due to the resource reservation mechanisms, the services have a guarantee of the quality of the communication which is an addition to the typical IP communication and a high added value for broadband communication on mobile devices with reduced processing power.

EPC Support for Applications	EPC Independent Applications	EPC Aware Applications	Applications using extensively EPC Enablers
Access Control	•	•	•
QoS Insurance	•	•	•
Seamless Mobility	•	•	•
Prioritization	•	•	•
Security	•	•	•
QoS adaptation		•	•
Access Network Information		•	•
Location Information			•
Ambient Information			•
Identity Insurance			•

Fig. 6. Application support in EPC

EPC provides also a control interface between the service platform and the network core [26]. Through this inter-face, the EPC aware applications can transmit indications on the resources that have to be reserved for the specific users. They can also receive upon request information on events happening at the link and network layers e.g. the UE lost connectivity or a handover to another access net-work occurred. By these mechanisms, the applications can be adapted to the momentary context of the mobile device and to offer services customized not only based on the service level user profile, but also to the mobile device in use and to the surrounding network context. In this class of applications may enter the services offered by the operator or by third parties having an agreement with the operator, like IMS services, mobile cloud computing etc.

Although not yet standardized, EPC is able to export a set of enablers to the applications which offer even more flexibility in the service delivered to the mobile user. For example, services may use the location of the UE or even ambient information on the vicinity of the UE and the subscriber identity of the mobile device, in order to further more adapt to the environment conditions and to ensure a more secure communication. In this category fall the future mobile applications adapted to the subscriber and to his surrounding environment.

With the development of the mass broadband environment offering data dominant broadband communication, a novel evolution of the applications that the mobile users will be using is foreseen. This is due to the complete personalization of the mobile device as communication instrument which allows the specific user to exchange data anytime and anywhere. In order to face this challenge the novel architecture is limiting its goal in offering added value at the level of network connectivity and of different enablers for the service platforms which enhance the communication (e.g. resource reservation enabler). This increases the acceptance of the overall system and of the novel mobile applications and thus the acceptance of the mass broadband wireless environment.

5   Over-The-Top

Over-The-Top (OTT) applications gain huge interest due to its competitive service offers towards the telecommunication provider and operator. Network (cloud) storage, news, social networks as well as classic telco provider services as voice, video and messaging are offered alternatively and partially for free.

The huge success of OTT can be measured in number downloads of apps, active users and generated data traffic. All of these numbers positively influences the acceptance and grows of the mobile domain, but challenges the telecommunication business in the domain voice, video and messages and finally reduces the operator business to a pure IP connectivity provider. The number of Short-Message-Services (SMS) and voice minutes is decreasing continuously since years.

The deployment of all-IP network infrastructures such as the 3GPP Evolved Packet Core enables the network operators to reserve resources and to differentiate the data traffic for charging reasons based on the requirements received from the service platforms.

At this point in time, OTT services mainly rely on best-effort data transport and do not consider resource reservation for specific applications or traffic classes. Current state-of-the-art research is presented in the 'Network Layer Evolution' chapter under Cross-Layer-Composition.

OTT services mainly rely on proprietary solutions, without taking interoperability into consideration. Usually the communication offered to subscriber of a OTT services (Skype, Facebook, Google, WhatsApp, etc.) is limited to other subscriber of the same system, but not includes subscribers of other OTT services.

GSMA as an alliance over 900 companies (including over 700 operators) facing the challenge of interoperability, by standardizing a generic interface specification (Rich-Communication-Suite/RCS) for a basic set of services (RCS-enhanced/RCS-e) such as voice, video, messaging, presence and enhanced phonebook. The main idea of RCS(-e) is to provide services over network operator domain boarders, being device independent and providing native interfaces in the device operating system in order to provide high quality communication.

6   Machine-Type-Communication

The term Internet-Of-Things (IOT) is a hot topic for academia and industry and is also referred as one view on the Future Internet. Machine-2-Machine (M2M) – as one single aspect of IOT - is a paradigm in which the end-to-end communication is executed without human intervention. In general, M2M is not a direct subscriber service.

IOT in general and M2M in particular gain importance through the global forecasted numbers in term of connected devices and expected data traffic. Network operators are facing a huge increase in data traffic in orders of magnitudes caused only by M2M [38][39].

The range of bandwidth varies huge given the different M2M scenarios. A humidity sensor in a museum may signal only 4bytes from time to time, whereas a surveillance system may stream multiple MB/s High Definition (HD) multimedia content continuously. Efficient concepts, mechanisms and technologies are required to transport M2M data traffic with large variations in capacity. Standardization activities address these challenges. The work of ETSI is briefly described in the following.

M2M ecosystem mainly consists of standardization bodys (IETF WG Constraint RESTful Environments (CORE), ETSI TS M2M, 3GPP Machine Type Communication[40], ISO, ITU-T, ZigBee, etc.) together with vendors, network operator and service provider.

The standardization within ETSI on MTC is ongoing. A current state is presented in the following. ETSI identifies three main components: device, gateway and server as depicted in Fig. 7. ETSI defines a set of standardized Service Capabilities (SC) [40] in M2M Core and M2M Device/Gateway, to provide functions that are to be shared by different M2M Applications

Currently ETSI defined 11 M2M Service Capabilities to

- Provide recommendations of logical grouping of functions
- Expose functionalities through a set of open interfaces
- Use Core Network functionalities
- Simplified, optimized application development and deployment through hiding of network specificities from applications

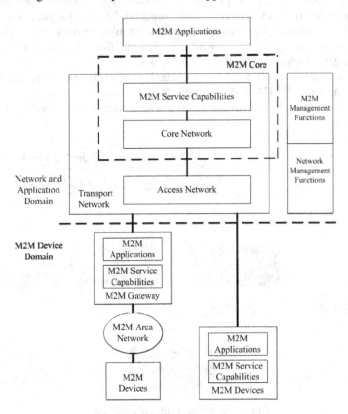

Fig. 7. ETSI General M2M Architecture

The ETSI M2M Release 1 fully specifies the 3 interfaces: mIa, mId, and dIa, which are specified to ensure interoperability towards operator domain boarders.

7   Open Networks

Resource sharing enables more efficient resource utilization and might result in cost savings. Virtualizing a network enables the operation of multiple protocols in parallel and independent of each other, providing a smaller closed partition of a larger network, or enables security by providing access control by separating network entities.

Network virtualization exists in manifold variations and can be applied on different layer in the network and on various technologies. Network virtualization mainly refers to network resources such as switches or routers from a hard- and software perspective.

Virtual local area networks or VLAN is the concept of grouping different hosts to a virtual topology, which is independent of the underlying hardware. The VLAN membership is software defined and not realized over physical links. Traffic related to one specific VLAN is marked with the same VLAN-tag or 802.1Q header within the header of an Ethernet frame.

The OpenFlow technology [41] is a famous representative for virtualizing networks, in order to run independent experiments on the same hardware environment by separating switching from control. OpenFlow enables networks to support traffic isolation, creates an open environment and flexible flow definition by individual flows, aggregated flows or post-IP protocol support.

OpenFlow defines itself as 'open standard to deploy innovative protocols in production networks' [42] and is Open Source available. Commercial internet switches, routers and wireless access points are supported what eases the setup of test infrastructures.

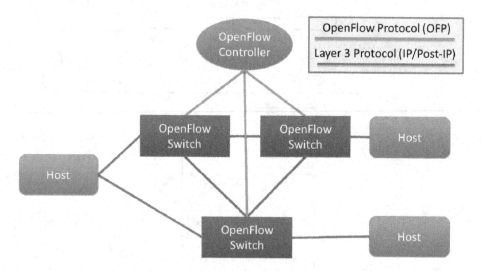

Fig. 8. Basic OpenFlow Architecture

Network packet routing consists first of routing decision followed by packet forwarding, what is done in the same entity (switch/router) in classic networks. OpenFlow separates routing and packet forwarding by extracting the routing decision in a separate box namely OpenFlow Controller (e.g. NOX [43]) from the switch, which functionalities are limited to packet forwarding as depicted in Fig. 6. The SSL secured OpenFlow Protocol (OFP) is used for communication between controller and switch to request and signal routing decisions.

8   Summary

The Internet is the largest global recognized communication system, which evolved in dimensions of technology, capacity, availability and size continuously since its beginnings in the 1960's. Information is transported via packets without differentiating between individual application characteristics over manifold access and core network technologies. The openness and its continuous change became characteristics of the Internet nowadays. Classical telecommunication networks transport voice over circuit-switched network initially, before adapting packet transport to the underlying network in order to increase the overall network performance.

This chapter presents a chronological overview on the evolution of telecommunication networks and control platforms in the last decades, transition from closed to open networks, the fixed and mobile convergence and finally outlines trends of future networks. The introduction chapter focuses on connectivity and builds the fundament for the following chapters especially for the Application Layer Evolution chapter, which outlines the application layer evolution, which is aligned on network layer evolution. Both presented trends influence each other.

The structure of this chapter is as followed. An introduction, which positions the presented work and provides the historical background, is followed by section 2, which introduces the concept of Intelligent Networks (IN) as a classical closed telecommunication system initially designed for fixed networks with a limited set of functionalities. Classic telecommunication systems as Intelligent Networks or its mobile variant Customized Applications for Mobile Enhanced Logic (CAMEL) rely on circuit-switched networks. Section 3 presents the concept, architecture and key functionalities of the IP Multimedia Subsystem (IMS) standardized by 3GPP. IMS is presented as network layer abstraction for 3GPP GPRS and UMTS or non-3GPP, cable, digital-subscriber-line (DSL) networks with the goal of providing unified interfaces for SIP based services. Section 4 presents the architecture, main protocols and key functionalities of the 3GPP All-IP Evolved Packet Core (EPC). The need for standardizing the Evolved Packet Core System (EPS) consisting of the radio part LTE and the core network part EPC is motivated and outlined. Section 5 discusses the role of Over-The-Top (OTT) applications and their growing impact on the application diversification, which directly influences the classic telecommunication value chain. Section 6 presents the trend of Machine-Type-Communication (MTC) in form of standardization activities. Section 7 outlines the trend of Open Networks by motivating the concept of network virtualization and presenting ongoing research and development activities. Section 8 summarizes and concludes the chapter. A list of acronyms and references is attached to the end of this chapter.

9   Acronyms

3GPP	3rd Generation Partnership Project
ANDSF	Access Network Discovery Selection Function
API	Application Programming Interface
AS	Application Server
EPC	Evolved Packet Core
EPS	Evolved Packet System
ETSI	European Telecommunications Standards Institute
HSS	Home Subscriber Server
IMS	IP Multimedia Subsystem
IN	Intelligent Network
INA	Information Networking Architecture
INAP	IN Application Protocol
IoS	Internet of Services
IoT	Internet of Things
IP	Internet Protocol
IPTV	Internet Protocol Television
ISC	IMS Service Control
ISUP	ISDN User Protocol
IT	Information Technology
ITU-T	International Telecommunication Union-Telecommunication
JAIN	Java APIs for Integrated Networks
JCP	Java Community Process
M2M	Machine 2 Machine
MTC	Machine Type Comminucation
NIST	National Institute of Standards and Technology
NGN	Next Generation Networks
NGSI	Next Generation Service Interface
OCCI	Open Cloud Computing Interface
ONA	Open Network Access
OND	Open Network Doctrine
ONP	Open Network Provision
OSA	Open Service Access
OTT	Over The Top
PBX	Private Branch Exchanges
PES	PSTN Emulation System
PGW	Packet Data Gateway
POTS	Plain Old Telephony Service
PS	Packet Switched
PSTN	Public Switched Telephone Network
QoS	Quality of Service
SaaS	Software as a Service
SCIM	Service Capability Interaction Manager
SCP	Service Control Points
S-CSCF	Serving Call Session Control Function
SDP	Service Delivery Platform
SGW	Serving Gateway
SIP	Session Initiation Protocol
SLEE	Service Logic Execution Environment
SMS	Short Message Service
SOA	Service Oriented Architectures
TMN	Telecommunication Management Network

TINA	Telecommunications Information Networking Architecture
TINA-C	Telecommunications Information Networking Architecture Consortium
TISPAN	Telecoms & Internet converged Services & Protocols for Advanced Networks
VAS	Value Added Services
VPN	Virtual Private Network
VoIP	Voice over IP
WWW	World Wide Web

References

1. 3GPP TS 29.078, CAMEL Application Part (CAP) specification
2. 3GPP TS 23.228. IP Multimedia Subsystem (IMS); Stage 2
3. Schulzrinne, H.: RFC3261, SIP: Session Initiation Protocol
4. Schulzrinne, H.: Real-Time Transport Protocol (RTP), RFC 3550 (2003), http://de.wikipedia.org/wiki/Real-Time_Transport_Protocol
5. RFC3588, Diameter Base Protocol
6. 3GPP TS 23.401, General Packet Radio Service (GPRS) enhancements for Evolved Universal Terrestrial Radio Access Network (E-UTRAN) access
7. 3GPP TS 23.402, Architecture enhancements for non-3GPP accesses
8. 3GPP TS 23.203 V10.0.0 (2010-06), Policy and charging control architecture (Release 10)
9. 3GPP TS 22.278 V10.1.0 (2010-03), Service requirements for the Evolved Packet System (EPS) (Release 10)
10. 3GPP TS 36.300, Evolved Universal Terrestrial Radio Access (E-UTRA) and Evolved Universal Terrestrial Radio Access Network (E-UTRAN)
11. NGMN Alliance, Next Generation Mobile Networks Beyond HSPA & EVDO, v3.0 (December 2006), http://www.ngmn.org/nc/downloads.html
12. 3GPP TR 23.882, 3GPP system architecture evolution (SAE): Report on technical options and conclusions, v8.0.0 (September 2008), http://www.3gpp.org
13. NGMA, Analysys Mason Limited, The momentum behind LTE worldwide (2011)
14. ITU-T Y.2018, Mobility management and control framework and architecture within the NGN transport stratum, ITU-T(September 2009), http://www.itu.int
15. 3GPP, Overview of 3GPP Release 12 (January 2012), http://www.3gpp.org
16. 3GPP TS 23.228, IP Multimedia Subsystem (IMS), v11.3.0(December 2011), http://www.3gpp.org
17. 3GPP TS 23.203, Policy and Charging Control Architecture, v11.4.0 (December 2011), http://www.3gpp.org
18. 3GPP TS 24.301, Non-Access-Stratum (NAS) protocol for Evolved Packet System (EPS), v11.1.0 (December 2011), http://www.3gpp.org
19. 3GPP TS 24.302, Access to the 3GPP Evolved Packet Core (EPC) via non-3GPP access networks, v11.1.0 (December 2011), http://www.3gpp.org
20. 3GPP TS 23.060, General Packet Radio Service (GPRS); Service description, v11.0.0 (December 2011), http://www.3gpp.org
21. 3GPP TS 29.272, Evolved Packet System (EPS); Mobility Management Entity (MME) and Serving GPRS Support Node (SGSN) related interfaces based on Diameter protocol, v11.0.0 (December 2011), http://www.3gpp.org
22. 3GPP TS 29.273, Evolved Packet System (EPS); 3GPP EPS AAA interfaces, v11.0.0 (December 2011), http://www.3gpp.org

23. 3GPP TS 29.274, 3GPP Evolved Packet System (EPS); Evolved General Packet Radio Service (GPRS) Tunnelling Protocol for Control plane (GTPv2-C), v11.1.0 (December 2011), http://www.3gpp.org

24. 3GPP TS 23.234, 3GPP system to Wireless Local Area Network (WLAN) interworking; System description, v10.0.0 (March 2011), http://www.3gpp.org

25. 3GPP TS 29.212, Policy and Charging Control (PCC) over Gx/Sd reference point, v11.3.0 (December 2011), http://www.3gpp.org

26. 3GPP TS 29.213, Policy and charging control signalling flows and Quality of Service (QoS) parameter mapping, v11.1.0 (December 2011), http://www.3gpp.org

27. 3GPP TS 29.214, Policy and charging control over Rx reference point, v11.3.0 (December 2011), http://www.3gpp.org

28. 3GPP TS 29.215, Policy and Charging Control (PCC) over S9 reference point, v11.3.0 (December 2011), http://www.3gpp.org

29. 3GPP 24.312, Access Network Discovery and Selection Function (ANDSF) Management Object (MO), v11.1.0 (December 2011), http://www.3gpp.org

30. Calhoun, P., Loughney, J., Guttman, E., Zorn, G., Arkko, J.: RFC 3588. Diameter Base Protocol. Internet Engineering Task Force (September 2003), http://www.ietf.org

31. Perkins, C.: RFC 2002. IP Mobility Support. Internet Engineering Task Force (October 1996), http://www.ietf.org

32. Soliman, H., Tsirtsis, G.: Dual Stack Mobile IPv6. Internet Engineering Task Force. Work in progress, ietf-draft-soliman-v4v6-mipv4 (July 2005)

33. Gundavelli, S., Leung, K., Devarapalli, V., Chowdhury, K., Patil, B.: RFC 5213. Proxy Mobile IPv6. Internet Engineering Task Force (August 2008)

34. 3GPP TS 29.275. Proxy Mobile IPv6 (PMIPv6) based Mobility and Tunnelling protocols, v11.1.0 (December2011), http://www.3gpp.org

35. Open Mobile Alliance (OMA). OMA Device Management Protocol, v1.3 (December 2009), http://www.openmobilealliance.org

36. 3GPP TS 33.401, 3GPP System Architecture Evolution (SAE); Security architecture, v11.2.0 (December 2011), http://www.3gpp.org

37. 3GPP TS 33.402, 3GPP System Architecture Evolution (SAE); Security aspects of non-3GPP accesses, v11.2.0 (December 2011), http://www.3gpp.org

38. Cisco Visual Networking Index: Forecast and Methodology, 2010-2015, White Paper (June 1, 2011), http://www.cisco.com/en/US/solutions/collateral/ns341/ns525/ns537/ns705/ns827/white_paper_c11-481360.pdf

39. Cisco, Whitepaper, Cisco Visual Networking Index: Global Mobile Data Traffic Forecast Update, 2011–2016 (February 14, 2012)

40. 3GPP TR 23.888. System improvements for Machine Type Communications (MTC), http://www.3gpp.org/ftp/Specs/html-info/23888.htm

41. McKeown, N., et al.: Stanford University, OpenFlow Switch Specification, Version 1.0.0 (December 31, 2009), http://www.openflow.org/documents/openflow-spec-v1.0.0.pdf

42. McKeown, N., Andershnan, T., Parulkar, G., Peterson, L., Rexford, J., Shenker, S., Turneron, J., Balakris, H.: OpenFlow: Enabling Innovation in Campus Networks. ACM Computer Communication Review 38(2), 69–74 (2008)

43. Gude, N., Koponen, T., Pettit, J., Pfaff, B., Casado, M., McKeown, N., Shenker, S.: NOX: Towards an Operating System for Networks. SIGCOMM CCR 38, 105–110 (2008), http://nicira.com/docs/nox-nodis.pdf

Telecom Applications, APIs and Service Platforms

Niklas Blum[1], Julius Müller[2], Florian Schreiner[1], and Thomas Magedanz[2]

[1] Fraunhofer Institute FOKUS, Kaiserin-Augsta-Allee 31, 10589 Berlin, Germany
{niklas.blum,florian.schreiner}@fokus.fraunhofer.de
[2] Technische Universität Berlin, Straße des 17. Juni 135, 10623 Berlin, Germany
julius.mueller@tu-berlin.de

Abstract. In the late 1980s, the open telecommunication services market was proclaimed in many vision statements and research papers, and regulative actions were taken to establish it. Today, due to the convergence of telecommunications, information technologies, Internet, World Wide Web and finally entertainment together with global markets and competition, we are living in an open multimedia services market and the information society is reality. As the competition between operators and service providers in the communications sector increases through, the actual value of networks and communications is decreasing. The remaining assets for future growth of the companies rely on the value of services, content and end systems that are increasing substantially within the new world of convergence and the much more complex multimedia services value chain that has emerged. The split of networks, service platforms, services and content requires on the one hand clear positioning of market players to face these challenges and on the other hand to establish a technological foundation for open business models. In this chapter, we want to trace the evolution of service and service platform concepts in telecommunications and outline technologies for converging networks and services and their latest developments.

1 Introduction

We are living in a global communications society and mobile multimedia communications have become a commodity in the daily life of many of us around the globe. In addition, the integration of communications, information services and entertainment under the umbrella of the multimedia Internet and the Next Generation Networks (NGNs) is going to change our life and the related industries completely. In this regard, the (tele-)communications market has in the last two decades been both driven and challenged by the convergence of network / information technologies and the Internet and additionally the related steady innovation and increased competition. This means that after 20 years of discussions, research and development we are finally seeing an open market for multimedia services provided on top of different fixed and mobile networks by different service providers in competition with each other. The spectrum ranges from over the top providers, like Apple, Google and Amazon, up to classic network operators, such as Deutsche Telekom or Vodafone. Most important, the Internet with its open nature has put the telecommunications

E. Bertin et al. (Eds.): Telecommunication Services Evolution, LNCS 7768, pp. 25–46, 2013.
© Springer-Verlag Berlin Heidelberg 2013

industry under strong pressure as the role of network-centric service intelligence has decreased in benefit of increasing intelligence in end systems and cloud-based service infrastructures outside the network core. The separation of the provisioning of services and content from service platforms enabling service delivery on top of multiple underlying networks is marking a drastic change in the value chain. The need to provide, i.e. to design, create, deploy, provision, execute and manage efficiently new multimedia services in accordance with market demands, customized to the individual end user needs on top of a common but extensible service platform requires the abstracting from the network details and a highly efficient and scalable service architecture.

In the early 1990s research was started as part of the evolution of the Intelligent Network (IN) to implement value-added services in fixed and mobile networks, particularly integrating IN with emerging telecom management standards, such as the Telecommunications Management Network (TMN). This research joined up with the Telecommunications Information Networking Architecture (TINA) initiative in the mid 1990s investigating integrated multimedia service control and management and looking also at middleware issues implementing the underlying distributed processing environment. This was succeeded at the end of the 1990s by promoting Parlay and 3GPP Open Service Access (OSA) Application Programming Interfaces (APIs).

With the broader role of the Internet and the emerging notion of Voice over IP (VoIP), the Session Initiation Protocol (SIP) was invented and more radical multimedia communication service implementation concepts inspired by Information Technologies (IT) and web programming, such as SIP servlets, were developed at the beginning of the new century. With the increasing significance of Next Generation Networks (NGNs) and the planned evolution of fixed and mobile networks towards a single, Internet Protocol (IP) based core network, namely the 3GPP IP Multimedia Subsystem (IMS) emerged in the middle of this decade as a practical combination of SIP and VoIP protocols. IMS is still very much aligned with and based on IN concepts. It is mainly promoted by the telecommunications industry as the a de facto standard for integrated triple play and quad play service architectures.

In face of the emerging web as a global service platform, many network operators are currently searching for possibilities and options for a so-called Telco 2.0 environment. This environment is ideally based on a Service-Oriented Architecture (SOA) for network-centric service enablers providing their specific capabilities to 3rd parties and application stores.

In this chapter, we want to trace the evolution of open service concepts and technologies for converging networks and outline technologies for converging networks and services and their latest developments regarding virtualized infrastructures and cross-layer network/service approaches.

The following section introduces the drivers for value-added services, open network interfaces and Service Delivery Platforms (SDP). The third section introduces TINA and looks at the Intelligent Network as the first SDP framework in the telecoms domain. Section four goes beyond TINA and paves the way for section five introducing Open Network APIs, such as Parlay, 3GPP OSA and JAIN. The sixth section is devoted to the impacts of IT and Internet technology on the telecommunication service domain. Section seven looks at the integration of core networks and service delivery platforms under the banner of SOA and Web 2.0

leading to a new Telco 2.0 environment. The eighth section describes current trends towards cloud-based telecommunication service environments, where virtualization and cloud brokering mechanisms are exploited for optimizing SDP utilization and operation. Section nine introduces the concept of Cross-Layer Composition describing a SOA-based approach to networking. A brief outlook into future R&D concludes this chapter.

2   The Open Service Market Vision Driving the Need for Open Service Interfaces and Service Delivery Platforms

Since the beginning of the 19th century, telecommunications was basically driven by the concept of the Plain Old Telephony Service (POTS), which used to be a closed-loop communication service. Serving the basic needs of people all around the world for more than a century, namely to communicate with each other over distance, we have observed a big change in telecommunications over the last three decades. New user needs and technical progress have led to the introduction of so-called supplementary or Value-Added Services (VAS) extending the functional capabilities of basic telephony services in regard to routing, charging, and user interaction patterns. Providing extra value for users, VAS have been correspondingly charged extra to a basic call. In addition, we have witnessed the broadening of the spectrum of telecommunication services, for example the rise of mobile telephony and data services, different types of messaging, multimedia streaming and conferencing services, and most recently search, social networking and group communication features, which today form our communication service space.

Conceptually, creating a telecommunications service meant that a corresponding architecture was developed describing how different functional components interact with each other by means of a protocol structuring and the exchange of control and content information to deliver services to the end users. In this regard, we can state that the telecommunications environments have always been service-driven or service-oriented, but not necessarily from a technology point of view.

The International Telecommunications Union (ITU-T) defined a three stage modeling approach for protocol definition [1], which starts with a description of a service and its capabilities from a high level end user perspective and is followed by the definition of a functional architecture (namely the required functional components and their information exchanges) in the subsequent stage. The 3rd stage leads to the definition of physical elements and the corresponding protocols to be used between them.

Due to the complexity of telecommunication systems, corresponding development times and applied technologies, the early systems were very service specific. Even in the context of supplementary and value added services, this approach was continued, leading to the implementation and installation of many service specific nodes within the network operator's infrastructures. This approach is often referred to as the stove-pipe architecture of an operator's service architecture as illustrated in Fig. 1 since each service requires its own infrastructure and functional systems which are more or less independent of other services. In face of limited services this approach worked very well and business cases could be calculated easily.

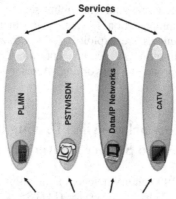

Fig. 1. Classic Telephony Stove-pipe Service Architecture

The notion of an open and potentially global service market is one of the driving forces of the information society. Different service providers offering network capabilities and services in competition were expected by politicians and regulatory frameworks have been established allowing a liberalized telecommunications market resulting in cost-based access to network and service infrastructures. Open Network Access (ONA) was the name for this initiative in the United States, Open Network Doctrine (OND) in Japan, and Open Network Provision (ONP) in Europe. These initiatives mainly demanded the clear definition of functional capabilities and prices for open network interfaces to be provided by incumbent network operators to open the market for new entrants and create benefits for the customers due to increased competition.

In face of the increasing competition requiring faster delivery times for new services, a new thinking in the Telecom industry emerged. The industry started to recognize the potential of Information Technologies within the telecommunications world in the early 1980s, and people started to think about a plug'n'play system for telecommunication services in which the network should be as easily programmable as a computer. An SDP providing programmability and abstracting from the network details should hide similar to operating system the hardware specifics from the applications.

3   TINA: Intelligent Network Evolution in Face of Object-Oriented Middleware

The IN evolution expressed by the capability set approach was targeted towards a so-called IN Long-Term Architecture. In the mid 1990s, programming languages like C++ and Java and especially middleware concepts, namely the Object Management Group's (OMG) *CORBA* (Common Object Request Broker Architecture) and the Java Remote Method Invocation (RMI) allowed implementing scalable and distributed service delivery platforms and provided abstraction from the details of underlying network signaling and transport protocols [4]. In face of this IT evolution and the considered impact on telecommunications, many operators and vendors started to investigate an object-oriented IN. This architecture was targeted for future multimedia mobile broadband environments (providing video conferencing and video on demand type), taking into account the newest network types and IT.

Inspired by Bellcore´s Information Networking Architecture (INA) developed for this purpose in the early 1990s, the international Telecommunications Information Networking Architecture Consortium (TINA-C) was established succeeding a set of international workshops on that topic. The TINA consortium defined a unified service control and management architecture, which should make use of distributed object middleware on top of emerging broadband networks and supporting existing and particularly new business models (see Fig. 2).

The result was a set of architectures, namely the Business Architecture, the Service Architecture and a Network Resource Control Architecture enabling Quality of Service (QoS) based service provision. This architecture allowed a decoupling of networks from the service architecture and the flexible distribution of service platform components across different physical. Most interesting was at that time the notion of a Service Retailer / Broker providing single sign-on capabilities for aggregated services by a set of service providers in a walled garden approach.

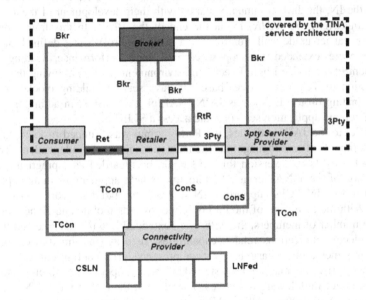

Fig. 2. TINA-C Service Architecture

However, TINA failed as the consortium specified architectures mainly in a walled garden approach and lacked a clear migration path from existing IN architectures. Furthermore, the proposed middleware technologies did not meet the operational requirements of operators at that time.

4   Beyond TINA – Open Application Programming Interfaces

Even as TINA finally failed, it has to be considered as one of the biggest collective "brain storming" activities that has ever been undertaken by the Telecom industry in face of a major IT paradigm shift. Based on the major TINA findings and thanks to the progress of IT in terms of performance and applicability, subsequent developments were more successful. In the loss of momentum of TINA, which led to its official termination in 2000, a more pragmatic activity was started in 1998: the definition of *Application Programming Interfaces (APIs)* for telecommunications. These APIs allow the flexible implementation of services in application servers accessing the network functions via dedicated interface operations defined by the API, independent of the underlying network signaling protocols and thereby ideally supporting network and vendor independence. Service independence is provided by the extensibility of the API. The major target of an API approach, however, is when publishing the API specifications openly to allow the creation of services by a 3rd party community and thereby gaining more service innovation.

Inspired by the Computer Telephony Integration (CTI) environment, Private Branch Exchanges (PBXs) were programmed for implementing sophisticated enterprise telephony applications. These were quite similar to IN Virtual Private Network (VPN) services, but implemented at the edge of the network and much more flexible and innovative. Expanding the idea of programming now for the public network and thus replacing the IN, the Java community started with their development of the *Java APIs for integrated Networks (JAIN)* [5] at the end of the 1990s. In this framework Java classes for carrier-grade call control (Java Call Control) were defined and Java containers were extended to support carrier grade performance, leading to the development of a Service Logic Execution Environment (SLEE) allowing the creation and execution of Telecom services based on Java service building blocks on top of various signaling protocols, such as JAIN INAP or JAIN ISUP. In addition, by using Java RMI, remote application servers could access a SLEE.

In parallel to the JAIN activities, the Parlay group was founded in 1998, targeting the development of a language independent and network independent Telecom services API. In its first version this API could be regarded as a pragmatically cut down version of the TINA Service Architecture, where applications in an application server on top of IN SCPs supporting INAP CS-1 for fixed networks provided the services. With the extension of the Parlay scope towards mobile and IP networks and a growing number of members, the APIs were extended in a market-oriented way and featured telecommunications related capabilities, such as (multimedia) call control, conferencing, messaging, charging, location, presence, group definitions, etc.

In order to prove openness, Parlay started an early cooperation with other standards bodies and major middleware initiatives. Therefore at the end of the 1990s, the 3GPP Open Service Architecture (OSA) APIs were aligned and merged with the Parlay APIs, and a bit later the JAIN initiative also joined the specifications with its Service Provider Access API.

In principle, all these APIs make telecom service implementation much easier and faster compared to the traditional IN approach by providing abstract service interfaces and leave the application developers the choice of using state of the art service development tools. As mentioned before, the basic idea of the API approach is that Application Servers (ASs) host the application logic, accessing via a secure network connection these APIs being provided by a dedicated network operator service gateway. This gateway maps the service interfaces to available resource interfaces that are not exposed to the applications as depicted in the following Fig. 3:

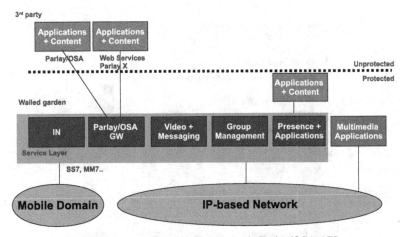

Fig. 3. Service & Network Exposure via Parlay/OSA APIs

The ASs could be operated by the network operator itself or even by 3rd parties depending on the business model. The idea was that network capabilities could be exposed to 3rd parties to take advantage of their creativity and create win-win business models for both operators and application providers. Corresponding interoperability specifications for the Parlay APIs were developed by ETSI TISPAN (Telecoms & Internet converged Services & Protocols for Advanced Networks) and should ensure the interoperation of different application servers and gateways.

Whereas the Parlay APIs are based on CORBA, the Parlay group started in 2003 the definition of Web Services based APIs labeled as Parlay X [6]. Parlay X is not considered as a successor of Parlay but rather an alternative, allowing the initiation of Telecom functionality via high-level functionality. On the one hand, this approach does not provide the developer with the functionality of creating sophisticated communications services with deep control of features. On the other hand, Parlay X hides most of the complexity of the Parlay APIs and can be considered as an offering for non-Telecom service developers that want to make use of Telecom features for their services.

Although this API technology was very promising, particularly as it provides some kind of enterprise application integration (EAI) within a network operator infrastructure, market acceptance has taken a very long time as most network operators at that time were still not ready to open up their networks believing that network and service ownership are most important. Additionally, the APIs themselves were still quite complex for non-telecommunications experts and telecommunications engineers were not used to utilizing such advanced information technologies, too. However, today in face of changing network technologies, i.e. the migration from circuit switched to all-IP networks, the value of OSA/Parlay APIs is fully recognized as they allow services to be provided on top of both networking domains in parallel.

Parlay/OSA as a standardization body was terminated in 2009 and further API definition was handed-over to the Open Mobile Alliance (OMA) as part of Next Generation Service Interfaces (NGSI) initiative to define a set of new service APIs in order to stimulate the usage of various service enablers fostering the development of new services and applications. NGSI as depicted in the following Fig. 4 defines extensions beyond today's Parlay X APIs and define several new APIs:

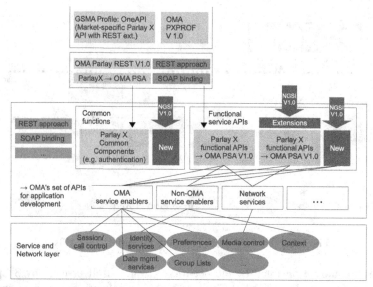

Fig. 4. OMA NGSI release 1 architecture

In order to allow for advanced service creation based on multiple services/enablers, interface functionalities for identity federation and related obligations as well as configuration for the composition of services are included.

5   Service Principles in IMS

As illustrated in the previous chapter, 3GPP started as part of its emerging core and access network evolution towards an all-IP network the specification of the IP Multimedia Subsystem (IMS). IMS was designed originally as an overlay on top of the GPRS domain within the 3GPP Release 5 specifications, published in 2003, for the provision of real time multimedia services, but has evolved since then as a general NGN control overlay network on top of any mobile, fixed and even cable network. The major target of IMS is to provide a standardized and structured "over the top" architecture in contrast to the Internet for better security, QoS, flexible charging within a single sign on framework. IMS allows the integration of service platforms for efficiently implementing various multimedia communication applications, including VoIP, video calls and conferencing, instant messaging, presence, group lists, Push to Talk, and also interactive IPTV (Internet Protocol based Television). In addition, new convergent service concepts, such as PSTN Emulation Services (PES), Fixed Mobile Convergence (FMC), Triple Play (3Play) and Quadruple Play (4Play) are targeted by an IMS infrastructure.

3GPP has defined a function within the SIP application layer of IMS managing interactions between application servers. This function can be considered as a service broker for SIP services and has been labeled Service Capability Interaction Manager (SCIM) and defined in [7] as depicted in Fig. 5:

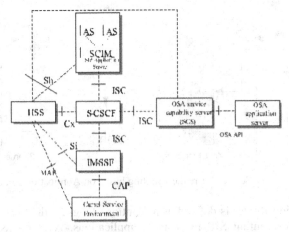

Fig. 5. 3GPP Service Capability Interaction Manager

However, the service interaction management functionalities of SCIM are not specified. Research in this field has been in progress over the last years [8]. As part of release 8, 3GPP investigates [9] impacts on defined control architectures through service brokering. A service broker is defined in this context as a logical function that manages service interactions among services hosted on single or multiple Application Servers. The main focus of the investigation is related to feature interaction between applications that are executed in a chain to form a complex service. Beyond the scope of [9] are service integration between SIP and non-SIP applications available via the IMS service architecture and the support of service integration across multiple service providers. It is considered as a functional part of the IMS Service Control (ISC) reference point interfacing IMS Serving Call Session Control Functions (S-CSCF) and Application Server functions. These considerations by 3GPP extend the static invocation mechanism as part of the S-CSCF through initial Filter Criteria (iFC).

3GPP differentiates between centralized and distributed service broker functions as depicted in the following Fig. 6:

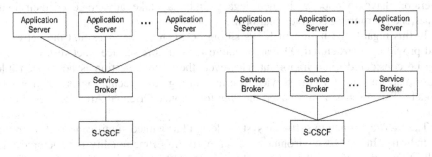

Fig. 6. 3GPP centralized and distributed broker functions

The Java Community Process (JCP) adopts the idea of a 3GPP SCIM as a so-called Application Router (AR) as part of its SIP Servlet 1.1 specification JSR 289 [10] as shown in Fig. 7:

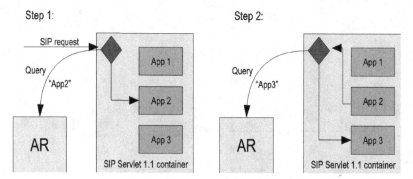

Fig. 7. SIP Servlet 1.1 request routing based on Application Router

The Application Router is defined as a function alongside the Servlet container. It is responsible for routing SIP requests to applications. As soon as the container receives a new request, it calls the Application Router; the AR determines which application should be selected and returns the name of that application to the container. The container then passes the request to the selected application. The AR is aware of what applications are deployed on the container, and it knows the request and the request context. Nevertheless, the AR is only limited to broker applications within a JSR 289 compliant container. The application is able to proxy the SIP request back out to the container, where it will again be passed to the AR to find the next application in a chain.

6   SOA and Web Impacts on Telecommunications

The telecommunications value chain is becoming increasingly complex and the role of traditional operators and vendors has to be redefined in face of this new structure of the service space and market. The provision of networks and services has to be clearly distinguished. In contrast to green field service providers, which may aim for service-specific over the top (OTT) architectures having content as a major asset, classical operators have to cope with their legacy and may take advantage of their long experience in running complex platforms.

In this regard, the notion of SDPs sitting between the services and the networks and providing a structured OTT architecture for multiple service / network offerings can be considered quite important. However, the major question is how extensible these platforms are for new service offerings in regard to technologies and business models. This discussion has paved the way for Service Oriented Architectures (SOA) [11].

The SOA approach to software system design has gained significant traction in the IT industry. In a SOA environment, an IT portfolio's functionality is structured into collections of services that are highly interoperable and loosely coupled (often communicating with each other through a service bus middleware). SOA promotes re-use, rapid application development, and simplification of inter-service communications. The development of a highly scalable SOA infrastructure enables strategic agility and cost efficiencies in an environment of mergers, acquisitions, and business model transformations. From a SOA perspective, the telecommunications estate can be encapsulated as services through the definition of dedicated service enablers and the abstraction of specific networking technology. But the most recognizable SOA today is the World Wide Web (WWW). Surveying the Web environment, one can recognize that there is no single common standard but a set of best practice technologies used in innovative multimedia applications, which have all gained in an interestingly short time an amazing user acceptance and momentum. Common to all is the notion of social networks and user-generated content, which in the end have extended the well known user-to-user communication and broadcasting into interest group specific communications and content production and consumption.

The WWW is by nature community driven, not only with regard to content but also from a technical point of view. Simple protocols such as HTTP, description languages such as HTML and architecture paradigms (e.g., Representational State Transfer - REST) made the Web successful and simplicity is the decisive factor for the developer community's acceptance of extensions to the Web technology stack. The evolution of the Web is less a question of novel technologies but rather a question of how existing technologies are applied to create services tailored to user needs and requirements.

In this respect, client-side active scripting and the inherent capability of HTML to integrate content from different sources plays a major role. Active scripts are shipped along with the web content to control content presentation and interactivity. The object-based programming language ECMAScript [12], better known as JavaScript, is today's most used scripting language for Web pages and mobile applications based on HTML5. In addition to operations on the associated document, all noteworthy Web browsers allow active scripts to self-reliantly utilize the HTTP client interface in a pared-down configuration. This feature of active scripts to access their origin server for the exchange of messages is referred to as Asynchronous Java Script (Ajax) [13]. The varieties of client-server interaction given to active scripts through Ajax, include Remote Procedure Call (RPC) and Publish-Subscribe.

The above technologies comprise a powerful client-side foundation for a novel approach to creating web applications, called *mash-ups*. A mash-up is a composition of 3rd party service building blocks resulting in a new, customized web application. While the outgoing web server of a mash-up provides the description of the composition and thus the actual services, adding value to the building blocks, the rendering and execution of the mash-up happens on the client-side. Consequently, mash-ups potentially decrease the need for intelligent ASs and avoid bottlenecks since mash-up clients access 3rd party service building blocks directly. Furthermore, mash-ups enable the rapid creation of powerful applications, even with limited engineering skills.

Through the ongoing process of the convergence of access networks and the entry of new players into the telecommunications market, traditional operators and carriers are desperately seeking for new business models in order to increase their revenue. Looking at the Internet and the WWW in this respect, the business models are completely different from the classical Telecom environment as either venture capital and/or advertising is financing free service offers. In addition, content is possibly charged for as well as premium memberships as part of premium service offerings. Thus, telecommunications operators have to position themselves within this converged services market. Considering a long tail approach, in which probably a huge diversity of niche services has to be provided with short service development times to end user communities, the import of service capabilities from big Internet players and more importantly the export of service capabilities via APIs towards Internet service providers becomes crucial. These APIs are integrated into a SOA, which takes advantage of an open SDP and possibly, but not necessarily an underlying IMS platform. Besides call control, messaging, location and presence interfaces, most importantly charging, identity management, QoS and connectivity capabilities are considered as most essential to gain a strategic position in the value chain. In addition, it is relevant that a decoupling of these capabilities from the underlying network(s) is also becoming increasingly significant as it could be expected that in the near future even more non-telecommunications network features will become fundamental, such as user profiling, advertising and e-commerce/shopping interfaces. Communications will most probably become a free enabler for much more complex higher layer services.

7   Converging Internet and Telecommunications Services

The emerging digital service marketplace presents an important opportunity for telecommunications operators to sell their own capabilities as services as illustrated above. Many Telecom operators have launched their open development portals (e.g., Deutsche Telekom developer garden [14] or Orange Partner Programme [15]) and started with communication related enablers like SMS, voice call, IP location and conferencing. The target of these portals is to expose simple Application Programming Interfaces (APIs) for developers, who use these services as enablers to create new integrated services. Via the portals, 3rd party service developers get access to core network functionalities using Web Services or REST-based interfaces. Some of these portals and activities have failed, e.g., BT with Ribbit [16], as the planned Return Of Investment (ROI) did not take place.

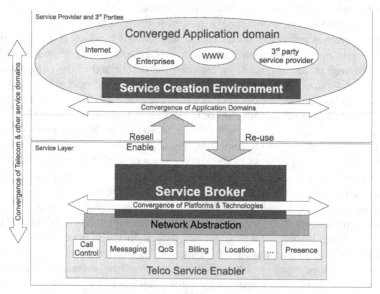

Fig. 8. Role of Service Broker for converged Telco services

Allowing the combination of features in a converged Telecom/Internet service space, well-defined and formalized programming paradigms in IT need to be applied to the telecommunications service domain and combined with fast evolving non-standardized, sometimes poorly described service principles in the Internet and WWW. To cooperate with the highly agile service domain of the Internet, a certain degree of flexibility needs to be incorporated into a Telecom application to adapt to changing requirements and business models.

A service broker function provides in an open telecommunications service environment vertical convergence between the business-driven service provider domain and the communications sector and horizontal convergence for platforms and technologies within a Telecom SDP. The following Fig. 8 illustrates the role of a service broker function for the telecommunications service layer and its interaction with service providers and application domains.

Such a service broker allows the definition of relationships between service developers, users and service providers to operator-owned telecommunication service enablers based on policy evaluation and enforcement. The service broker selects the appropriate service provider for a request, based on business and/or operations policies to optimally route service requests. Through policies, adaptation and personalization of services according to specific preferences does not require specific adaptations in the core system or a service, thus enabling policy-based composition of services implicitly during service execution time. Such an approach efficiently maximizes the value derived from the underlying IT resources through the application of service discovery and service execution-based rules. The underlying principle of rule-based service access and execution are defined as Policy Evaluation, Enforcement and Management (PEEM) by the OMA in [17].

An instantiation of such a service broker platform delivers the promises of SOAs by enabling a dynamic and robust integration infrastructure that is applicable to both middleware of next-generation telecommunications services as well as legacy services.

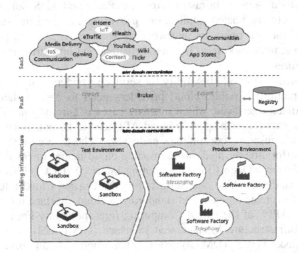

Fig. 9. Inter-domain Service & Platform Enablement with Service Broker

To accelerate service deployment and to provide a platform for open innovation, a service broker may be extended for service developers by providing a development staging environment and development sand boxes as illustrated in the following Fig. 9:

The service broker provides by its mechanism for defining and enforcing interaction patterns a generic composition platform for service development and deployment. This is referred to as a Platform as a Service (PaaS) environment. It is tightly connected to an enabling infrastructure providing communication-centric services and a development environment and has access to services from multiple domains provided as SaaS (Software as a Service).

8   Providing Elasticity and Virtualization of Services

Cloud hosting and computing mechanisms have gained broad attention in recent years attracting steadily increasing numbers of service providers by providing means to optimize storage and compute resource consumption to allow for outsourcing of infrastructure and service management costs.

For efficiently and economically operating telecommunication service platforms, cloud computing mechanisms are continuously becoming more and more relevant for telecommunication service providers, by offering the possibility to dynamically scale resource utilization, including "hybrid" cloud models [18] which allow for on-demand outsourcing of required computing capacities. Generally speaking, and following the National Institute of Standards and Technology (NIST) cloud definition [19] three cloud service models can be distinguished: Infrastructure as a Service (IaaS), utilizing a suite of virtual hardware through specific cloud management APIs, PaaS, providing application developers with application software, middleware, databases, and development tools and SaaS clouds offering complete cloud-based applications ranging from customer relationship management, communication, collaboration, business processes-oriented applications.

Of specific interest to telecommunication service providers seeking to consolidate and streamline their service infrastructures are PaaS and IaaS solutions that are agnostic to the actually hosted application, providing mechanisms such as elastic resource scaling and are open for interworking with external cloud platforms in a hybrid fashion, i.e. interworking of internal, private cloud infrastructure with external cloud infrastructures.

However in order to provide flexibility for service providers to dynamically choose external cloud platforms, public cloud providers need to expose their IaaS cloud through standardized interfaces, which in many cases is currently not the case. As a workaround, adaptors for each specific cloud API need to be implemented which can be a time and resource-consuming endeavor. There are currently several standardization efforts being made to harmonize cloud management APIs, of which the Open Grid Forum's Open Cloud Computing Interface (OCCI) [20] is currently a very promising candidate. Also other efforts like the Unified Cloud Interface Project [21], "an attempt to create an open and standardized cloud interface for the unification of various cloud APIs" of the Cloud Computing Interoperability Forum (CCIF) [22] and the Cloud Infrastructure Management Interface (CIMI) [23] of the Distributed Management Task Force (DMTF) show that there is an urgent need for standardization and unification of interfaces.

Elastic cloud computing, defined as the capability of cloud platforms to dynamically up- and down-scale resources, flexibly responding to variable load situations, is one of the most important mechanisms of an IaaS. By exploiting virtualization mechanisms, it allows for efficient resource utilization, enabling pay-per-use cost models strongly related also to Green-IT and autonomic computing mechanisms.

As described above, by utilizing converged, all-IP, access-network-independent service and session control platforms such as the IMS, Telecom service providers are currently consolidating their service infrastructures towards converged SDPs. Although these SDPs are sought to greatly reduce new telecommunication service time-to-market, significant upfront investments into IT service infrastructures and SDPs are still required. Thus, in many cases service roll-outs are still risky enterprises with an uncertain ROI. With cloud computing mechanisms applied to IMS/NGN-based service infrastructures, service providers are charged on a pay-per-use basis, significantly lowering the risk of unsuccessful investments. By efficiently combining service and cloud brokering mechanisms NGN service providers are empowered to efficiently provide different service qualities to different user segments allowing for additional cost saving strategies.

Currently available elastic cloud computing mechanisms provide cloud provider specific elastic computing mechanisms, thus they are not empowering service providers to flexibly deploy and release resources across multiple cloud provider platforms. These solutions do not support dynamic and seamless migration of services between multiple cloud provider infrastructures and platforms, fostering cloud provider lock-ins, rather than empowering service providers to exploit the increasing competition in the cloud provider market. Furthermore, they are not sensitive to and not aware of network performance metrics (between core network and cloud service platforms), which, to a lesser degree affects typical web applications, but to a significant degree affects real-time communication service quality (voice/video, conferencing, messaging). Therefore, cloud brokering mechanisms are currently investigated, which operate in the premises of a service providing network operator, passing back full control of utilized internal as well as external cloud resources to service providers.

IMS-/NGN-based telecommunication service platforms can indeed be deployed on multiple cloud platforms. Even the cloud-based deployment and hosting of an IMS itself, including the idea of offering a cloud-based IMS as a service is currently investigated and no more a far-out vision. By combining cloud brokering mechanisms with standardized NGN service brokering mechanisms, telecommunication service providers are empowered to flexibly provide a broad range of services that can be shaped to specific customer segments. This stems from the fact that state-of-the-art NGN service brokering mechanisms as described in chapter 7, already provide means for policy-based, user-centric access to multiple service endpoints; endpoints which surely can surely be cloud-based. These service brokering solutions provide means for exposure of telecommunication services hosted on multiple cloud platforms. Based on finely granular cost models for different user segments, service brokering is capable of providing a broad range of service qualities (from best-effort to highly reliable service qualities). Combining service brokering mechanisms with cloud brokering mechanisms, optimized resource utilization without the need for previously required over-provisioned service infrastructure, low-risk service roll-outs exploiting pay-per-use costs models and differentiated service provisioning can readily be enabled.

A Cloud Broker for NGN-based services, as shown in Fig. 10, is capable of simultaneously interworking with multiple cloud platforms and capable of dynamically, i.e. elastically up- and down-scale cloud resources to migrate cloud resources across multiple cloud platforms on-demand.

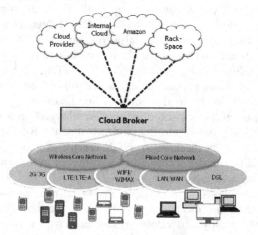

Fig. 10. A Cloud Broker for distributed cloud-based service platforms

The benefit of integrating service brokering mechanisms with cloud brokering mechanisms is obvious. Users of Web-based telecommunication services as well as 3rd party developers are provided with a single point for accessing telecommunication service. The invocation of backend services and service enablers is being conducted entirely transparent to the users, based on a specific user profile, service brokering mechanisms allow for exposure and invocation of one and the same service, hosted on multiple, e.g., differently expensive cloud-based platforms providing different service qualities.

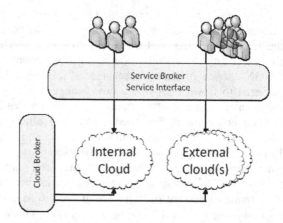

Fig. 11. Cloud and Service Broker Integration

By doing so, telecommunication service providers are empowered to flexibly allocate different cloud-based service resources to different user segments, where best-effort cloud resources can be exposed to budget users and highly reliable cloud resources can be exposed to premium customers as shown above in Fig. 11. By doing so additional cost savings are enabled, and furthermore the same scenario allows for risk-free deployment of new services / service trials, which can initially be hosted on external cloud infrastructures and seamlessly migrated to internal cloud platforms if service-uptake is successful and improved service quality is desired.

9   Cross-Layer Composition

The layered ISO/OSI model divides communication systems such as the Internet into horizontal and independent layers - each communicating only to its adjacent layers. The separation-of-concerns concept aggregates functionalities of the same type and assigns them to a specific layer. For this reason, IP applications assume pure best-effort IP connectivity, without implementing specific routing, session or mobility functionalities or adjusting access network specific parameters for the underlying connection.

On the one side the layered architecture eases the creation of new applications and the integration of new IP networks, which is one of the success factors of today's Internet. On the other side the existing and well-established Internet Protocol creates a high burden for introducing new network layer protocols (e.g., IPv6) addressing the weaknesses of IPv4 as address shortage, mobility support and insufficient security. Furthermore, additional transport protocols such as Stream Control Transmission Protocol (SCTP) [24], [25] or Multipath-TCP [26] could not be integrated into the network layer easily.

Cross-Layer Composition (CLC) is the concept of bridging the gap between application- and network-layer through creating awareness of each other by applying service-oriented concepts to networking for enabling direct control message exchange. The G-Lab DEEP project [27] introduced an intermediation layer in between the application and network layer, for enabling such communication and ensuring backwards compatibility to legacy networks at the same time. The main benefit of introducing CLC is the realization of network-awareness for applications to adjust data traffic control based on service layer requirements and application-awareness for networks to adjust active application-layer sessions based on network types or current traffic situations. To achieve this, CLC needs to support bottom-up as well as top-down layered signalling. Thereby client or service side applications are enabled to signal application layer demands over (ideally) standardized interfaces towards the underlying fixed and mobile access and core network and vice versa. Fig. 12 depicts the three layers: application, mediation and network:

The application layer represents an abstraction of any IP or post-IP service such as a single service, complex IMS and/or SDP. Network-aware applications support direct influencing/control of the underlying network or demanding network resources at the mediation layer, which enforces network specific parameters. Such applications may receive a notification event in case of network changes or guaranteed bit rate violation. The main purpose of the mediation layer is optimizing IP connectivity. Therefore generalized application layer network resource requests are transformed

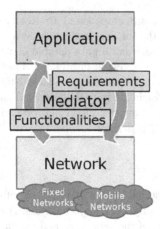

Fixed
Networks   Mobile
                Networks

- Abstract generalized mediation concept
- Application layer
  - Abstraction of any IP or post-IP service
  - Requirement statement towards network
- Mediation layer (loop)
  - Optimizing between application layer requirements and network layer functionalities
- Network layer
  - Any IP or post-IP transport layer
  - Fixed and mobile access and core networks

Fig. 12. Cross-Layer Composition Concept

into specific access – or core network resource requests. Incoming application requirements are transformed into network specific requests. A negotiation logic computes the optimized parameters which are enforced within the network. The optimization process may includes loops or rounds in which a solution is computed, fulfilling the initial application requirements (QoS, security, prioritization) to align with the available network capabilities (utilization, bandwidth, delay, jitter). This requires a trusted relationship between the network operator and service provider.

This mediation layer needs to work transparent for today's applications, which are not network aware. It is directly addressed by network-aware applications in order to perform network control and management tasks. The correct mapping of requested and available resources is a challenge, in which meta requirement descriptions are transformed into specific network resource parameters, while keeping the same level of information.

The network layer may encompass 3GPP and non-3GPP fixed and mobile access and core networks. Such a network may be a Next-Generation-Network (IMS or Evolved Packet Core) or Future Internet (virtual or functional composition) [28]. The network has to enable a northbound interface for exchanging control messages with the upper layers, namely the mediation layer.

The project G-Lab DEEP prototyped such Cross-Layer Composition architecture with special focus on security and to analyse novel functionalities of combining IMS with SIP-based application servers to support multimedia services with a functional CLC framework.

10   Summary and Outlook

This chapter traces the evolution of open service delivery platform concepts and technologies for converging networks and outlines the latest developments in a chronological order. An introduction outlines the evolution from closed to open telecommunication networks motivated by an economical and technological point of view. Section two motivates the open service market vision as a driver for VAS, open network interfaces and SDPs are presented and discussed. Section three introduces the Telecommunications Information Networking Architecture (TINA) and paves the way for section four introducing Open Network APIs, such as Parlay/OSA, JAIN and OMA NGSI. The fifth section is devoted to the impacts of IT and Internet technology on the telecommunication service domain enabled through the IP Multimedia Subsystem (IMS) and services using Session Initiation Protocol (SIP). Section six looks at the integration of core networks and service delivery platforms under the banner of Service Oriented Architectures (SOA) and Web 2.0 leading to a new Telco 2.0 environment. The seventh section introduces the service broker concept for converged telecommunication services. The eighth section extends the open service concept to the infrastructure layer by illustrating how virtualization and cloud computing, providing elasticity hybrid platform approaches may realize a completely flexible service layer that adapts to business and operational requirements. Section nine introduces the concept of Cross-Layer Composition, illustrating the application of service-oriented concepts to the network layer.

The described evolution and state-of-the-art concepts of realizing flexibility on programmability on all layers become of further importance realizing the Internet of Things (IoT) and providing connectivity and information platforms for smart cities. A smart city may be defined as one that makes optimal use of all the interconnected information available today to better understand and control its operations and optimize the use of limited resources [29]. To provide such a large scale platform connecting all relevant things in a city for providing information into (possibly) cloud-based platforms running business intelligence algorithms, flexibility on many layers and fine-granulated control of network access and transport is required. On-going research in this field and the Future Internet leads the way to a generic service platform providing connectivity to many service verticals as currently performed by the EU in the context of the Future Internet initiative [30].

11   Acronyms

3GPP	3rd Generation Partnership Project
3Play	Triple-Play
4Play	Quadruple-Play
Ajax	Asynchronous Java Script
API	Application Programming Interface
AR	Application Router
AS	Application Server
CORBA	Common Object Request Broker Architecture
CTI	Computer Telephony Integration
ECMA	European Computer Manufacturers Association
ETSI	European Telecommunications Standards Institute
EU	European Union
IaaS	Infrastructure as a Service
IMS	IP Multimedia Subsystem
IN	Intelligent Network
INA	Information Networking Architecture
INAP	IN Application Protocol
IoS	Internet of Services

IoT	Internet of Things
IP	Internet Protocol
IPTV	Internet Protocol Television
ISC	IMS Service Control
ISUP	ISDN User Protocol
IT	Information Technology
ITU-T	International Telecommunication Union-Telecommunication
JAIN	Java APIs for Integrated Networks
JCP	Java Community Process
NIST	National Institute of Standards and Technology
NGN	Next Generation Networks
NGSI	Next Generation Service Interface
OCCI	Open Cloud Computing Interface
ONA	Open Network Access
OND	Open Network Doctrine
ONP	Open Network Provision
OSA	Open Service Access
OTT	Over The Top
PaaS	Platform as a Service
PBX	Private Branch Exchanges
PES	PSTN Emulation System
POTS	Plain Old Telephony Service
PS	Packet Switched
PSTN	Public Switched Telephone Network
QoS	Quality of Service
RMI	Remote Method Invocation
ROI	Return of Investment
RPC	Remote Procedure Call
SaaS	Software as a Service
SCIM	Service Capability Interaction Manager
SCP	Service Control Points
S-CSCF	Serving Call Session Control Function
SDP	Service Delivery Platform
SIP	Session Initiation Protocol
SLEE	Service Logic Execution Environment
SMS	Short Message Service
SOA	Service Oriented Architectures
TMN	Telecommunication Management Network
TINA	Telecommunications Information Networking Architecture
TINA-C	Telecommunications Information Networking Architecture Consortium
TISPAN	Telecoms & Internet converged Services & Protocols for Advanced Networks
VAS	Value Added Services
VPN	Virtual Private Network
VoIP	Voice over IP
WWW	World Wide Web

References

1. ITU-T. Recommendation I.130: Method for the Characterization of Telecommunication Services Supported by an ISDN and Network Capabilities of an ISDN. published in Fascicle III.7 of the Blue Book, Melbourne (1988)
2. Ronayne, J.P.: The Digital Network. In: Introduction to Digital Communications Switching, 1st edn. Howard W. Sams & Co., Inc., Indianapolis (1986) ISBN 0-672-22498-4
3. 3GPP. 3GPP TS 23.078. Customized Applications for Mobile network Enhanced Logic (CAMEL) Phase X; Stage 2 (1999)
4. Herzog, U., Magedanz, T.: Intelligent Networks and TINA - Migration and Interworking Issues. In: The Intelligent Network: Current Technologies, Applications, and Operations, pp. 109–122. International Engineering Consortium (IEC), Chicago (1998) ISBN: 0-933217-43-9
5. Java Community Process. JSR21 JAIN JCC Specification (2002)
6. 3GPP. 3GPP TS 29.199-XX V8.0.0, Open Service Access (OSA); Parlay X Web Services (September 2009)
7. 3GPP. 3GPP TS 23.002 V5.12.0, 3rd Generation Partnership Project; Technical Specification Group Services and Systems Aspects; Network architecture (Release 5) (September 2003)
8. Gouya, A., Crespi, N.: Service Broker for Managing Feature Interactions in IP Multimedia Subsystem. In: Sixth International Conference on Networking (ICN 2007), April 22-28, pp. 54–54 (2007)
9. 3GPP. 3GPP TR23.810 V8.0.0. 3rd Generation Partnership Project; Technical Specification Group Services and System Aspects; Study on Architecture Impacts of Service Brokering (Release 8) (September 2008)
10. Java Community Process. JSR289: SIP Servlet v1.1 (2008)
11. Magedanz, T., Blum, N., Dutkowski, S.: Evolution of SOA Concepts in Telecommunications - A Déjà vu? Special Issue on Service Oriented Architectures. IEEE Computer (November 2007) ISSN 0018-9162
12. ECMAScript Language Specification, 3rd edn. (1999), http://www.ecma-international.org/publications/standards/Ecma-262.htm
13. Garrett, J.J.: Ajax: A new Approach to Web Applications (2005)
14. Deutsche Telekom, http://www.developergarden.com
15. Orange Partner, http://www.orangepartner.com/
16. Ribbit, http://www.ribbit.com/
17. Open Mobile Alliance (OMA). Architecture Document OMA Service Environment. Approved Version 1.0.4 (Feburary 1, 2007)
18. Bojanova, I., Samba, A.: Analysis of Cloud Computing Delivery Architecture Models. In: 2011 IEEE Workshops of International Conference on Advanced Information Networking and Applications (WAINA), March 22-25, pp. 453–458 (2011), doi:10.1109/WAINA.2011.74
19. Mell, P., Grance, T.: The NIST Definition of Cloud Computing. v. 15, National Institute of Standards and Technology Special Publication 800-145 (September 2011), http://csrc.nist.gov/groups/SNS/cloud-computing
20. OCCI-WG. GFD-P-R.183 Open Cloud Computing Interface – Core (2011) http://occi-wg.org
21. Unified Cloud Interface Project, http://code.google.com/p/unifiedcloud
22. Cloud Computing Interoperability Forum, http://www.cloudforum.org

23. Distributed Management Task Force (DTMF). Cloud Infrastructure Management Interface (CIMI) Model and REST Interface over HTTP. Version: 0.0.35 (2011),
    `http://dmtf.org/sites/default/files/standards/documents/DSP0263_1.0.0a.pdf`

24. Stewart, R. (ed.): IETF. Network Working Group. RFC 4960: Stream Control Transmission Protocol (2007), `http://tools.ietf.org/html/rfc4960`

25. Ong, L., Yoakum, J.: IETF. Network Working Group. 3286: An Introduction to the Stream Control Transmission Protocol (SCTP) (2002),
    `http://tools.ietf.org/html/rfc3286`

26. Scharf, M., Ford, A.: Multipath TCP. MPTCP Application Interface Considerations draft-ietf-mptcp-api-04. Version 4 (Feburary 16, 2012),
    `http://tools.ietf.org/wg/mptcp/`

27. German Lab DEEP Project Website, `http://www-g-lab-deep.de`

28. Mueller, J., Magedanz, T., Corici, M., Vingarzan, D.: UE & Network Initiated QoS Reservation in NGN and Beyond. In: 2011 International Conference on the Future Internet, Network of the Future (NOF), November 28-30, pp. 62–67 (2011) ISBN: 978-1-4577-1605-8, doi: 10.1109/NOF. 2011.6126684

29. IBM. Smarter Cities Series: A Foundation for Understanding IBM Smarter Cities. IBM Redbooks (2011), `https://www.redbooks.ibm.com/Redbooks.nsf/RedbookAbstracts/redp4735.html`

30. EU FP7 Future Internet Core Platform Project FI-WARE,
    `http://www.fi-ware.eu/`

Value Added Services
in the Evolving Multimedia Communication Network

Rogier Noldus

Business unit Support Solutions, Ericsson Telecommunicatie b.v.
P.O. Box 8, 5120 AA Rijen, The Netherlands
rogier.noldus@ericsson.com

Abstract. With the introduction of IMS based multimedia communication services, the need rises for a framework similar to Intelligent network (IN). The IN standard is used for augmenting Circuit switched (CS) networks like PSTN and PLMN (GSM, 3G). The IN standard is grafted on CS network paradigms and principles and is, in its native form, not suitable for IP communication networks like IMS. Within IMS, communication services are realized through Application servers (AS). AS's are connected to IMS core network in a manner that resembles, to some extent, Value added services (VAS) for CS networks. The combination of IMS core network and IMS Application servers provides network architecture for 'basic multimedia communication', including, but not limited to, telephony, video calling and messaging. In order to go beyond this set of basic communication services, the concept of VAS is equally needed in IMS. But in a different way! At the same time, network operators want to safeguard their investment in VAS in the CS network. In addition, operators require 'service parity' when introducing IMS. Hence, the introduction of VAS in the IMS network shall comprise a level of backwards compatibility. The introduction, and further development of, VAS in IMS gives rise to interesting network architecture, allowing for seamless integration of CS network and IMS network, augmenting the communication services, such as telephony, as is appropriate for the class of network used by the served subscriber. Protocols and procedures will be different, but fundamental service principles remain the same!

1 Introduction

The present chapter describes the development in Value added services (VAS) for the evolving multimedia communication network. The advent of advanced access network and core network technologies like LTE, EPC, Multimedia telephony (MMTel), VoLTE, Session continuity etc. require a re-definition of the way in which operators can enhance (enrich) and personalize their communication service offering to the end-users. This chapter will contain an in-depth anthology of the evolution of techniques for VAS. This includes a break-down of the fundamental building blocks for VAS and how these building blocks are used to build VAS for the evolved multi-access multimedia communication network.

E. Bertin et al. (Eds.): Telecommunication Services Evolution, LNCS 7768, pp. 47–76, 2013.
© Springer-Verlag Berlin Heidelberg 2013

This chapter will also describe the implication on service development and service deployment for heterogeneous networks, considering a mix of techniques like (not exhaustive) IMS centralized service (ICS), Circuit switched fallback (CSFB), Voice over LTE (VoLTE) and Single radio voice call continuity (SR-VCC). Since access network, core network and service network are being developed at different speeds, such heterogeneous networks will be a reality and will require careful network design. We may expect heterogeneous networks, with varying degree of technology evolution (and a mix of 'old' and 'new') for the coming 10 - 12 years.

2   Introduction into Value Added Services – Back to Basics

Value added services (VAS) is a concept that's been around for close to 25 years[1] and various books have been published on this topic, such as [1], [2] and [3]. So one may wonder whether it still requires introduction. The answer is a resounding 'yes'. In order to appreciate the role of VAS in the different networks, including the current 4G mobile network, it is essential to understand the fundamentals on which VAS has been built. In the present section, we will provide a network-independent view on VAS. Such view allows us to understand how VAS should be applied in evolved network architecture, such as IMS and Multimedia telephony (MMTel). Fig. 1 provides the rudimentary, basic picture of VAS as we know it from 'the old days'.

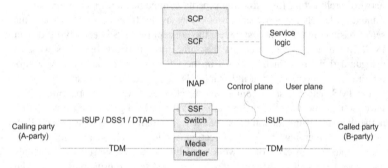

Fig. 1. Basic view on value added services

Legend for Fig. 1			
DSS1	Digital Subscriber Signaling System #1	SCP	Service Control Point
DATP	Direct Transfer Application Part	SSF	Service Switching Function
ISUP	ISDN User Part	TDM	Time Division Multiplex
SCF	Service Control Function		
Refer to 3GPP TS 23.002 for further information and background on these network components and for further references to technical specifications (standards).			

---

[1] See e.g. ITU-T recommendations Q.1200 series.

Fig. 1 depicts a 'switch' (digital switch), for which we may typically think of a switch in the PSTN (such as the ISDN), or a switch in the PLMN (such as the GSM network or the UMTS network). An example of the former is a Local Exchange or Transgate Exchange. An example of the latter is a Mobile service switching centre (MSC). The picture shows control plane and user plane. The control plane is the *signaling plane* in the telecommunications network that carries signaling messages needed for call establishment, call release and, where applicable, supplementary service control. The user plane is the media plane; this plane is formed by the entities that transfer media, i.e. digitized speech or digitized video, between parties involved in a call. Common practice is, especially in mobile networks since 2000, to deploy control plane part and user plane part of a switch as separate nodes. The user plane, for example, is built up from Media gateways (MGw). One reason for said separation of control plane and user plane is it allows for dimensioning control plane and user plane separately, which may, in turn, lead to more optimized network resource usage and allows for easier network expansion. VAS interacts strictly with the control plane.

Generally, VAS entails that the process of *basic call handling* in a digital switch is augmented with functionality that goes beyond the standardized set of basic telephony. Hereto, we distinguish the following layers in communications. See Fig. 2.

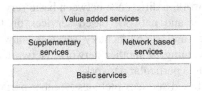

Fig. 2. Layered view on telephony services

Basic Services. Basic service represents the service of being able to establish a phone call (or video call) between two persons. The persons may be subscribers of different networks and may reside in different countries. When one or both of the involved subscribers is a 'mobile subscriber', she may reside outside the country of the network where she is a subscriber of, i.e. may be 'roaming'. Basic services includes call establishment, dialed number analysis, call routing (sending a call establishment message towards the telephony exchange through which the destination party can currently be reached), call progress announcements, call clearing, call charging etc.

Basic services is typically a *subscribed service*. This implies that a user of the telecommunications network must *subscribe* to this basic service(s), i.e. must have a subscription setting in a designated subscriber database. Within the GSM/3G network, this designated subscriber database is the HLR. Besides voice calls and video calls, basic services comprises (not exhaustive) data calls, fax calls (!) and Short message service (SMS).

Supplementary Services. To enhance the user experience, the basic services may be enhanced with supplementary services. Supplementary services were introduced in the PSTN and PLMN at a later stage, i.e. when the basic services were already introduced. Examples include Call forwarding (e.g. to voicemail), Call barring (e.g.

international calls), Call hold & retrieve and Call waiting. These services are also subscribed services, i.e. the user of a telecommunications network needs to have explicit subscription to these services.

Basic services and supplementary services are realized through functionality inside the exchanges in a telecommunications network and through signaling between exchanges in the network. ISUP, being the control plane protocol for ISDN, comprises specific control plane signaling for the supplementary services. In addition, basic services and supplementary services require specific capability in the end-user's terminal and may require functionality on the media plane, such a speech recognition, text-to-speech conversion and DTMF detection.

The ensemble of basic services and supplementary services is known as *basic telephony*.

Network Based Services. This category of services also enhances basic services. This category of services is realized through functionality (capability) in the core network. A difference between supplementary services and network based services is that network based services don't require subscription. They may be offered to all users in the telecommunications network. For a mobile network like GSM, this includes, where applicable, both *home subscribers* and *inbound roamers*. When considering a mobile network, a difference between basic services and supplementary services on the one hand and network based services on the other hand, is the following. Basic services and supplementary services may be used by a mobile subscriber, even when roaming in another network. Network based services, on the other hand, are confined to a particular network.

Examples of network based services includes Number portability, Optimal routing and Dialed number correction.

Value Added Services. Value added service (VAS) constitutes the concept, methods and protocols, for further enhancing basic telephony. Whereas basic telephony is accomplished through signaling and methods within the telecommunications core network (i.e. the switches / exchanges), VAS is achieved through designated infrastructure, the *service layer*. VAS enables operators to create service offering that goes beyond basic telephony. This enables operators to distinguish themselves from other operators. VAS is generally a method for achieving shorter time-to-market for new services, compared to standardized basic or supplementary services.[2]

Examples of VAS includes Prepaid, Virtual private network, Short number dialing, Location based service (e.g. Home Zone / Office Zone), Number correction and Incoming / Outgoing call screening.

VAS may be deployed as *subscribed* service, as *network based* service or as *endpoint service* (see below). Subscribed VAS entails that the subscriber of a network has an individual subscription to that particular VAS. An example of this category is Home Zone service. Network based VAS entails that the network uses VAS for a particular service that may be offered to all subscribers or to a group of subscribers,

---

[2] This is especially true for VAS that does not have extensive integration with the operator's business support system (BSS).

without the need for subscribing to this service. An example of this VAS category is Free divert to voicemail (toll-free forwarding to voicemail when roaming abroad).

A further category of VAS is Freephone and Premium rate (0800/1800, 0900/1900). These services are operated by a network operator and are typically offered to all subscribers within the country (or region) of the operator. This category of services is referred to as 'End-point services'.

Fig. 3 gives graphical representation of VAS as applied for the 3G mobile network, in accordance with 3GPP standardized architecture.

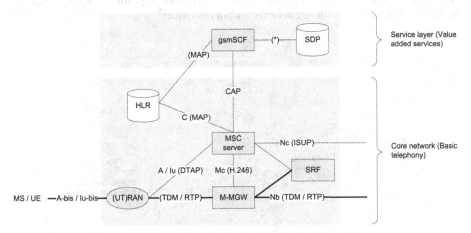

Fig. 3. Core Network versus Service Layer

Legend for Fig. 3			
CAP	CAMEL application part	RAN	Radio access network
gsmSCF	gsm Service control function	RTP	Real-time transport protocol
HLR	Home location register	SDP	Service data point
MAP	Mobile application part	UE	User equipment
M-MGW	Mobile media gateway	UTRAN	Universal Terrestrial Radio Access Network
MS	Mobile station	(*)	Proprietary protocol between SCP and SDP
MSC	Mobile services switching centre		
Refer to 3GPP TS 23.002 for description of the various reference points (A, C, Nc etc.) and for further references to technical specifications (standards).			

Note. Whereas VAS in the 3GPP network architecture is generally realized through a Service control point (SCP), not all deployments of an SCP, with service logic deployed on it, constitutes VAS. An example is the usage of an SCP for carrier selection for long distance calls.

VAS has a long history[3]. A picture like the one given in Fig. 3 does not provide due credit for the comprehensiveness, the powerfulness and flexibility of the toolbox offered through VAS. One main protocol for VAS is the Intelligent Networks Application Part (INAP). VAS and Intelligent Networks (IN) are generally used as equivalent terminology. INAP constitutes the protocol between the core network and the service layer. Specifically, between an Exchange, such as an MSC in the 3G mobile network, and a Service control function (SCF). The SCF is the entity comprising service logic that may be invoked during the establishment of a call through the Exchange. An SCF resides in a Service control point (SCP). I.e. SCP is the *node*, whereas SCF is the *logic entity* within that node.[4]

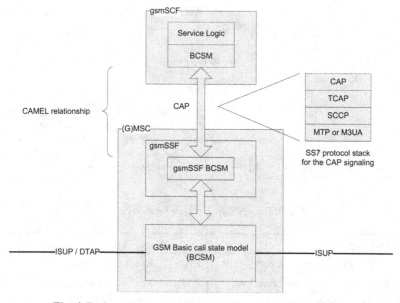

Fig. 4. Basic call state model (BCSM) for value added services

Legend for Fig. 4			
BCSM	Basic call state model; see 3GPP TS 23.018 and 3GPP TS 23.078	SCCP	Signaling connection control part; see ITU-T Q.711 – Q.719
M3UA	MTP layer 3 user adaptation; see 3GPP TS 29.202	SS7	Signaling system #7; see ITU-T Q.700
MTP	Message transfer part; see ITU-T Q.701 – Q.710	TCAP	Transaction capability application part; see ITU-T Q.770 – Q.779

---

[3] And a note here is: there is a thin line between Value added service, Supplementary service and Basic service. They all provide (or add) *value*. The term VAS is introduced to denote a particular category of services, namely the services realized through a designated service platform, allowing the deployment and execution of non-standard services.

[4] In practical deployment, SCF may be located in the same node as MSC and SSF, or other functional entities. Co-location of functional entities in a single node is, where feasible, common practice for e.g. small network deployments.

Fig. 4 is a refinement of Fig. 1, in the sense that it depicts in more detail how an Exchange and an SCF communicate with one another. The figure is specific for VAS as specified in the CAMEL standard.

An MSC or Gateway MSC (GMSC) that is handling a mobile originating or a mobile terminating call, respectively, has subscriber data available that's needed for handling this call. For mobile terminating call handling in GMSC, this subscriber data is obtained from HLR per call. This subscriber data comprises subscription on basic services and supplementary services. The subscriber data may, in addition, comprise CAMEL service trigger data. CAMEL, short for 'Customised applications for the Mobile network enhanced logic', is the 3GPP standard for Intelligent Networks (IN/VAS) for the GSM and 3G mobile network. The subscriber data may also comprise subscription data to non-standard IN services, such as vendor-specific variants of INAP.

The GSM and 3G mobile networks, as well as the ISDN, is a Circuit switched (CS) network. This implies that media transfer, i.e. digitized speech or video, is transferred through the network by means of the establishment of 'communication circuits'. These circuits are traditionally 64kb/s synchronous data channels that allow for the transportation of a voice signal with a nominal frequency band of 3.1kHz (300Hz – 3400Hz) that has been sampled at 8k samples / s and with a sample size of 8 bits[5]. Currently, CS networks support also IP based media transport[6], such as RTP (Real-time transport protocol; refer IETF RFC 3550 and IETF RFC 3551). The control plane used in the CS networks, notably the ISDN and GSM/3G network, is traditionally ISUP, although currently also BICC and SIP-I are used in CS networks.

The ISUP signaling is governed in the exchanges, such as the MSC or GMSC in a GSM/3G mobile network, by Basic call state model (BCSM). The concept of BCSM is not only fundamental for CS networks, but also for Value added services. And we will see that this proven concept of BCSM is in adapted form equally applicable for IP networks, such as the IP multimedia subsystem (IMS)! The BCSM is a finite state machine that describes the states that a call may transit through ('BCSM state transitions'). When a call is established, an instance of a BCSM is spawned in the (G)MSC through which the call is being established. The BCSM will, for a successful call, transit through the states Idle, Collected_Information, Analysed_Information, Call_Accepted, Call_Disconnect, Call_Answer and back to Idle. The 'Idle' state is not a genuine state. When the call is complete (released), the state machine instance is destroyed. Fig. 5 provides an example of gsmSSF BCSM (for CAMEL Phase 1). Later CAMEL phases have a more extensive BCSM definition.

---

[5] When codecs with smaller bandwidth are used over the radio access network, the smaller bandwidth media transfer would be mapped to the 64 kb/s channel.

[6] Although the media transfer is then no longer 'Circuit switched' in the traditional sense of the word.

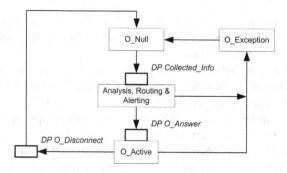

Fig. 5. Basic call state model for gsmSSF in CAMEL phase 1 (source: GSM TS 03.78 v5.11.0, figure 7.2)

It's through the BCSM, and the transition through various states and Detection Points (DP), that VAS may be applied to a CS call (Fig. 5 shows the DPs in the BCSM). As a basic call process transits through the BCSM states, this call process halts execution at defined points in the BCSM, namely the Detection Points (DP). When the basic call processing is halted at a BCSM, signaling is initiated between MSC and the SCP. This signaling enables the service logic in the SCP to influence the call processing, such as providing a different destination for the call, at call establishment.

The subscription data of the subscriber for whom or to whom the call is established may indicate that an IN service shall be invoked. The MSC, in which the BCSM instance of this call is being executed, will then instantiate another process. Namely a Service switching function, SSF. For the GSM/3G mobile network, the SSF is known as gsmSSF, to indicate that it's an SSF specifically for the GSM/3G mobile network. The gsmSSF is a process in the MSC that also comprises a BCSM, as depicted in Fig. 5. When the BCSM of the MSC has instantiated a gsmSSF process, including the gsmSSF BCSM, the MSC BCSM will inform the gsmSSF BCSM of events related to the call establishment or call release. In this manner, changes in the call state result in state transitions in the MSC BCSM, but also in state transitions in the gsmSSF BCSM. The gsmSSF BCSM has fewer states than the MSC BCSM. A result is that not all events of the basic call are reflected in gsmSSF BCSM state transitions.

At various discrete points in the gsmSSF BCSM, namely the Detection Points, there may be interaction with the Value added service. To start off with, at the beginning of a call, the MSC BCSM instantiates a gsmSSF BCSM and the gsmSSF BCSM sends a *Service invocation request* to the required VAS. The sending of a Service invocation request from the MSC towards VAS has the form of establishing a Communication dialogue between the gsmSSF and the gsmSCF. The gsmSCF, GSM service control function, is the counterpart of the gsmSSF. The gsmSCF is a logical entity. It comprises a gsmSCF BCSM. The gsmSCF BCSM is in fact identical to the gsmSSF BCSM. When the gsmSSF transits from one state to another, it informs the gsmSCF BCSM. It does so through the exchange of messages, known as Operations[7], over the

---

[7] Refer to ITU-T Q.880 for description of the concept of *Remote Operations*.

aforementioned communication dialogue between gsmSSF and gsmSCF. In this manner, the gsmSSF BCSM and the gsmSCF BCSM remain synchronized. In that way, the gsmSCF has knowledge of the state of a call (in establishment, active, released). This tight coupling between gsmSCF and gsmSSF (in MSC) enables the gsmSCF to influence the call. The gsmSCF may, for example, alter the destination of the call, monitor the duration of the call (for pre-paid charging purpose), release the call (e.g. when prepaid credit is depleted), disallow the call to be established (call filtering) etc. The capability of the gsmSCF is defined by the Communication dialogue that is established between gsmSSF and gsmSCF. For the GSM/3G network, this dialogue is known as CAMEL application part (CAP). CAP is derived from IN application part (INAP), the principle IN protocol defined by ITU-T in the late 1980's. See ITU-T recommendation Q.1200 series. Successive versions (phases) of CAP were developed over time, CAPv1 up to CAPv4. Each subsequent version of CAP specifies a more extensive BCSM for the gsmSSF and gsmSCF. In addition, each subsequent version of CAP comprises more capability for the gsmSCF to control the MSC BCSM. This increased capability is realized through the specifying of additional CAP Operations and the specifying of additional parameters for existing CAP Operations.

One fundamental characteristic of the manner in which the concept of BCSM is implemented in CS networks is 'single point of control'. This has proven, over the years, to be a very contentious issue! This principle is essentially still prevalent in the contemporary IMS based multimedia communications network. Fig. 6 depicts the implication of this principle in CS (not IMS) environment.

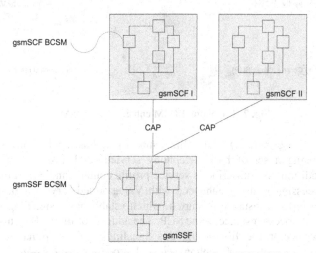

gsmSCF BCSM

gsmSCF I

gsmSCF II

CAP   CAP

gsmSSF BCSM

gsmSSF

Fig. 6. Single/multiple point of control for MSC BCSM

The gsmSSF process instance in the MSC exposes control capability at various points in the Basic call state model. A service logic residing in a gsmSCF could influence the call processing at this point. The concept of state machine does not permit that another gsmSCF would also influence the call processing at this point.

Such influencing of the call processing at this point by a second gsmSCF would interfere with the intention of the first gsmSCF. Keeping the two BCSM instances of gsmSCF I and gsmSCF II synchronized with the BCSM instance of gsmSSF would generally be unmanageable, so such deployment is generally not allowed. Bear in mind that for a call between *calling party* and *called party*, there is independent invocation and execution of BCSM and (optionally) VAS for calling and called party.

The gsmSCF resides in a *higher layer computing platform*. The *node* in which a gsmSCF resides is known as Service control point (SCP). The SCP may be located in the same switching network as the MSC (with integrated gsmSSF) or may be located in another (GSM/3G) network. This will be described further down.

Value added services (VAS) may be considered *an extension* of the basic telephony. The BCSM in the exchange executes *basic telephony logic*. Through the adding of a gsmSSF, including a gsmSSF BCSM, the basic telephony logic can be enhanced with *VAS logic*. The VAS logic in the SCP then becomes an extension of the basic telephony logic. This is reflected in Fig. 7, for basic telephony in GSM/3G network enhanced with VAS logic.

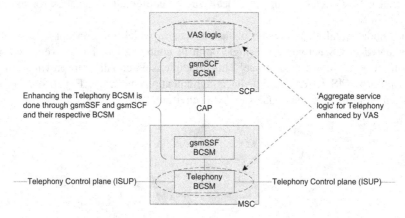

Fig. 7. Telephony BCSM enhanced with VAS

The served subscriber, e.g. the calling subscriber, has a telephony subscription profile comprising a set of basic telephony services and a set of supplementary services. In addition, the subscriber's service profile contains indication that the basic telephony processing shall be enhanced with Value added service logic processing. So, a gsmSSF process instance is started, which establishes a signaling relationship with a gsmSCF process instance in the SCP. The address of the SCP forms part of the subscriber's service profile. It's through this signaling relationship that the VAS logic can act as extension of the Telephony control process, forming *aggregate service logic*. 'Aggregate' in the sense that the Telephony service logic and the VAS logic form a combined 'enhanced call service logic' (albeit that this aggregate service logic is distributed over two functional entities).

In a later section, we're going to apply the principle of VAS in the evolved mobile communication network. We will specifically look at how VAS is applied for IMS and Multimedia telephony.

3   The Evolving Mobile Communications Network

The mobile communication network has undergone major functional enhancements (and is expected to continue to do so). Both the radio access network and the core network, being two of the main functional components of the mobile communication network, are substantially more powerful than when they were first released. We will in this section look at the most relevant architectural aspects of the evolving mobile network.

One main aspect is the gradual transition from 'Circuit switched' (CS) based access network and core network to 'Packet switched' (PS) based access network and core network. Mobile PS network technology was introduced in 1999, under the name General packet radio system (GPRS), as part of the ETSI GSM Phase 2+ specification. The introduction of GPRS opened up the possibility for IP based data applications on GSM terminals. Before the introduction of GPRS, data applications from the mobile phone were facilitated through circuit switched data (CSD) or high-speed circuit switched data (HSCSD). With CSD and HSCSD, a data channel is established through the allocation of one or more time slots, thereby establishing a CS connection. (HS)CSD uses the same core network infrastructure as voice calls through the mobile network. Specifically, (HS)CSD use Mobile switching centre (MSC) for control plane and Media gateway (MGw) for data transmission (user plane). GPRS, on the other hand, comprises dedicated core network infrastructure, comprising Serving GPRS service node (SGSN) and Gateway GPRS service node (GGSN). GPRS is further intrinsically designed to establish IP data sessions with internet applications. I.e. GPRS provides generic IP data connectivity. The radio technology applied for GPRS is identical to the radio technology applied for GSM: Time division multiple access (TDMA).

GPRS, being the *data* enhancement of the GSM (2G) network, allows for one radio access connectivity type at the same time: CS based voice (or data) call or PS based data connection (IP connectivity). This implies a functional limitation in the sense that a Value added service that wants to use the GPRS data connectivity to augment the CS call establishment, can't use the data communication *at the same time* as the CS call.[8]

The 3rd generation mobile network, also known as Universal mobile telephony system (UMTS), is a functional successor of GPRS. UMTS is based on Wideband code division multiple access (W-CDMA). UMTS supports higher data rates than GPRS and it allows for simultaneous CS access and PS access. A VAS may hence augment a voice call with PS data services (or the other way around). One example is Combinational services, as described in 3GPP TS 23.279.

So, both GSM ('2G') and UMTS ('3G') support CS connections. While GSM and UMTS use different radio access networks, the core network UMTS is also upgraded, compared to GSM, considering aspects such as:

- Strict separation of control plane and user plane. In GSM, the core network comprises 'monolithic MSCs', with the MSC handling the control plane of a call

---

[8] A Technique called Dual transfer mode (DTM) facilitates simultaneous CS Access and PS access by a GSM+GPRS terminal. DTM, which requires support by the terminal, access network and core network, is not widely operational.

(ISDN user part, ISUP) and the user plane (the media; TDM circuits, e.g. E1 time slots). In UMTS, the user plane is handled by dedicated MGw's. The MSCs in the UMTS architecture have evolved to 'MSC server' (MSC-S). An MSC-S controls one or more MGw's. One MGw is controlled by exactly one MSC-S.[9]

-   In GSM, a strict 'tree structure' is applied, whereby a group of Base station controllers (BSC) is controlled by one MSC. In UMTS, a Radio network controller (RNC), fulfilling a role comparable with BSC in GSM, may have control relationship with multiple MSCs. This concept is known as 'MSC in pool'. It allows for more flexible allocation of MSCs to subscribers that attach to the network. In addition, it may reduce the number of inter-MSC Location area updates, due to larger geographical area controlled by a single MSC (overlapping with the geographical area controlled by other MSCs in the network).
-   The successor of ISUP, namely the Bearer independent call control (BICC) can be used.
-   The usage of BICC as opposed to ISUP allows, among others, for using other forms of media transport than TDM circuits. For example, media transport may be based on GSM codec, encoded in accordance with RTP.

The PS core network infrastructure in UMTS has the same architecture as the PS core network infrastructure in GPRS.

A next enhancement within the 3G access network is High speed packet access (HSPA). HSPA is *informally* also referred to as '3.5G'. HSPA is the combination of High speed downlink packet access (HSDPA) and Enhanced uplink (EUL). HSPA is essentially a radio technique. It offers higher data speed than UMTS. The HSPA data connection is targeting data *non-conversational data applications*. That is to say, HSPA is generally not used for voice or video (voice over IP, video over IP). Voice & video communication from an HSPA terminal remain CS based. HSPA terminals do, however, allow for simultaneous PS data connection and CS voice / video communication. CS calls established from an HSPA terminal may be subject to the same set of VAS as CS call established from a UMTS terminal (or GSM terminal).

A major development in mobile communication is the 4th generation mobile network. The 4th generation mobile network is heralded especially by the advent of Long term evolution (LTE). LTE comprises fundamentally new radio access network architecture, compared to GSM / UMTS / HSPA. Data speeds up to 100 Mbit/s may be achieved with LTE, depending on circumstance in which the mobile data connection is established. Whereas GSM, UMTS and HSPA offer both CS based services (such as voice calls and video calls) and PS based data connection, LTE offers PS based data services only. This is a significantly different approach towards mobile communication, compared to LTE's predecessors. Specifically, LTE access from a mobile terminal can't be used to establish a communication session via the CS core network[10]. All communication services via LTE access, including voice and video communication, are PS based data services. This means, for example, that voice over LTE access is, by definition Voice-over-IP (Voip).

---

[9] A MGw may be split up in multiple 'logical media gateways', whereby the logical MGw's may be controlled by different MSC-S.

[10] When using Circuit switched fallback (CSFB), some of the signaling related to CS call establishment will be conveyed over the LTE access network.

The LTE access network is directly associated with the Enhanced packet core (EPC). The EPC may be regarded as the functional successor of the GPRS core network infrastructure that was introduced by ETSI back in 1999. The EPC has a 'flat' structure, with data connections established directly from the enhanced Node-B (eNode-B) to a Packet data gateway (PDGw). The eNode-B is the functional successor of the Node-B, the radio transceiver in the UMTS network (base station, covering a cell sector). The PDGw forms the data connection with the internet, for IP data applications. The combination of LTE and EPC is known as Enhanced packet system (EPS).

When LTE, in combination with the EPC, is used for voice communication, video communication or messaging, then the EPC is coupled to the IMS network. The EPS is then taking the role of IP carrier access network (IP-CAN). It facilitates data transmission through a mobile terminal. The actual *voice* or *video* application is executed in the IMS network (including the Multimedia Telephony application server, as will be seen in a next section). Voice over LTE is known as VoLTE and is described in the GSM association (GSMA) permanent reference document (PRD) IR.92[11].

The EPS is, in most deployments, closely related to the (UT)RAN and to the CS core network. Reason is that LTE access will, at initial deployment, not be ubiquitous. And where LTE coverage is available, the LTE infrastructure may not always support the QoS that is needed for *conversational voice*. This implies that a VoLTE capable mobile terminal needs to have the ability to *fall back* to CS access, in cases where no voice capable LTE coverage is available. There are various use cases defined for this *fall back*:

- When no LTE coverage is available, a VoLTE capable terminal will attach to a CS network and establish CS network based communication, as normal.
- A VoLTE capable terminal, or a terminal that supports LTE, but not VoLTE, may be engaged in a data session through LTE. When a voice or video communication session needs to be established through the terminal, the terminal reverts to using CS access, via (UT)RAN. The LTE based data connection is either transferred to (UT)RAN or is suspended, for the duration of the CS based communication session. This methodology is known as Circuit switched fallback (CSFB).
- A VoLTE capable terminal may be engaged in a voice communication session through LTE access and the IMS network. When the terminal moves out of LTE coverage, the call can not be maintained through LTE. The terminal may initiate access transfer for the call: the terminal changes from using LTE as access leg for the call to using UTRAN as access leg for the call. This change in access technology for the call is known as Single radio voice call continuity (SR-VCC). SR-VCC is not to be confused with the Voice call continuity (VCC) that was specified as part of 3GPP release 6! Whereas SR-VCC is a fully integrated solution for transferring an IMS & MMTel based voice call from LTE access to UTRAN access, VCC merely specified how a SIP session (over WLAN) may be transferred to (UT)RAN. VCC does not comprise integration with IMS application such as basic telephony, i.e. MMTel.

---

[11] Video over LTE is described in GSMA PRD IR.94.

SR-VCC is, as its expansion implies, specified for *voice* calls. Access transfer for *video* calls is also specified in 3GPP (release 11). Over and above, *reverse* SR-VCC is part of 3GPP release 11 specification, for transferring from UTRAN access to LTE access.

To facilitate these advanced use cases, especially, CSFB and (reverse) SR-VCC, the EPC and the CS core network are closely connected. For example, functional connection is specified between the Mobility management entity (MME) in the Enhanced packet system (EPS) and the MSC server (MSC-S) in the CS core network. The MME controls the attachment of mobile terminals to the LTE access network and the Enhanced packet core (EPC).

4   The IP Multimedia Subsystem – A Building Block Approach

The IP multimedia subsystem (IMS) warrants a book on its own; a challenge which many authors have successfully embarked on, each publication providing a different angle on the IMS network. In the present section, we will limit ourselves to giving a description of the essential building blocks of IMS. In addition, we place focus on the *Service Layer* within IMS.

It's very easy, and tempting at the same time, to throw you, the poor reader, into the deep end of the pool by presenting the typical 'IMS architecture' found in 3GPP technical specifications and in many text books. Such architecture would comprise a collection of boxes (nodes or functional entities) and interfaces (reference points). Such representation of IMS does not do justice to the modular and functional structure of this technology.

Fig. 8 provides a rudimentary, high-level functional decomposition of IMS.

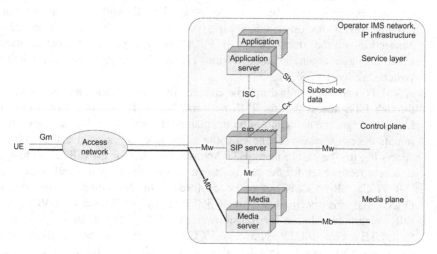

Fig. 8. IMS network – high-level functional decomposition

The IMS network consists of a number of functional entities, located in confined operator-controlled IP infrastructure. The functional entities are essentially IP services, deployed on server platform and connected to IP infrastructure. The labels provided for the connections in the figure are the standardized *reference points*. 3GPP TS 23.002 gives a description of each reference point, including reference to other 3GPP specifications for further description. 3GPP TS 23.228 provides the architecture of the IMS network.

One way of decomposing the IMS network is the division in *Access network* and *Core network*. Fig. 8 does not show 'the intestines' of the access network, whilst this is often shown as part of the IMS network. However, IMS constitutes essentially communications network architecture, allowing for the establishment of a multimedia communication session between two users (end-points) that are registered as *subscribers* of this network; or between a subscriber of the IMS network and an end-point outside the IMS network. IMS is largely *access network independent*. That does not mean that the access network does not play a role. Certain (multimedia) services require access network of particular capability. One prominent example is conversational voice, which generally requires the LTE access network (coupled to the EPC). The *principles* of communication establishment in IMS are, however, independent of the access network. The access network provides IP connectivity for the subscriber. The IP connectivity may be of any form, including (not exhaustive) wireline (e.g. Ethernet), wireless (WLAN) and (cellular) mobile. The mobile IP connectivity may e.g. be the UTRAN + PS core network (GPRS), or LTE + Enhanced packet core (EPC). The combination of LTE and EPC is known as Enhanced packet system (EPS). An IMS terminal may hand over from one IP connectivity type to another, e.g. PS handover between LTE and UTRAN, or the other way around. The access network ensures that the end-user's IP address remains unchanged during such handover. In this manner, the IP service is not affected from the PS handover, apart from the fact that a change from LTE access to UTRAN access results in reduced data transfer speed.

Handover from LTE to UTRAN may be transparent for data applications. However, handover for a *voice call* from LTE to UTRAN requires special mechanism, because of the fact that PS 'conversational voice' service is not available in UTRAN. Single radio voice call continuity (SR-VCC), the required technique for this, will be briefly touched upon in a further section.

Whilst IMS, as communication enabler, is in principle access network independent, the access network, in its turn, may be used for IMS as well as for other IP service, such as HTTP or e-mail. This underscores, once again, the independent roles of IP access network and IMS core network. The mobile IP access network (the Enhanced packet system) may be owned and operated by another operator than the IMS network, albeit that such deployment is not common, for now.

The IMS core network is located in an operator's domain, i.e. IP infrastructure. It comprises a set of functional entities, each entity fulfilling a particular role for the communication. The functional entities are deployed on *hosts*, being computing platform in the IP network. Each host in the IMS network is addressable through IP signaling.

IMS applies a strict separation between *control plane* and *user plane*. The control plane in the IMS network is built up of functional entities engaged in exchanging signaling messages that are needed for session establishment (and termination) and for mobility (including registration with / deregistration from the IMS network). The user plane, on the other hand, comprises the functional entities involved in the media transport (e.g. digitized voice/video). A media session is always controlled by a control plane session; control plane and media plane are hence intertwined.

One prominent functional entity that is located in the IMS core network is the Serving control session control function (S-CSCF). There are a number of *CSCFs* defined for the IMS network, the S-CSCF being one of them. A CSCF is the principal SIP Proxy entity for the IMS network. The functionality of SIP proxy is described in [4]. Or refer to IETF RFC 3261 for further information about SIP and SIP proxies. The S-CSCF, being an IP application deployed on a host in the IP network, acts as *registrar*. The concept of registrar is known from Voice over IP (VoIP) network technology. The VoIP protocol used by the IMS network is the Session initiation protocol (SIP). SIP is described in IETF RFC 3261. SIP is a functional successor of H.323, defined by the ITU. The registrar is the entity where a VoIP subscriber (and IMS subscriber, in the case of S-CSCF) *registers*. This implies that the subscriber of that network deposits his/her public user identity and his/her current contact address (IP address). This depositing of public user identity and contact address constitutes 'binding': as long as this registration is valid, the user's public user identity is *bound* to this contact address. A communication session may be established towards that subscriber's public user identity, such as sip:john.smith@my-company.com. The scheme 'sip' indicates that this subscriber is contactable for communication through the SIP protocol. The remainder of the public user identity, john.smith@my-company.com, constitutes a Universal resource identifier (URI) that is routable through (public) IP infrastructure. This routing is typically done with the aid of Domain name server (DNS). There may be multiple registrars in the IMS network. Within the IMS network that is serving this user, john.smith@my-company.com, a user database may be used to determine in which of the multitude of registrars of that network, this subscriber has deposited his IP address. Within IMS, this user database is embodied in the Home subscriber server (HSS).

When the communication session is established towards John Smith and the session establishment message is routed towards this registrar, the registrar can forward the session establishment message towards John Smith's current contact address.

The IMS terminal is commonly referred to as 'User equipment' (UE). The term UE is also, generically, used for a 3G mobile terminal (connected to the 3GPP cellular mobile network).

Other *CSCFs* defined for the IMS network are:

- Proxy CSCF (P-CSCF): the P-CSCF is a SIP server at the border of the IMS network; all SIP signaling to/from a terminal of an IMS subscriber traverses a particular P-CSCF. The P-CSCF protects the IMS network, especially considering the fact that the communication between UE and IMS network may run over public IP infrastructure. The P-CSCF also removes confidential information from the signaling messages before passing the messages on to the end-user. When an IMS subscriber is roaming abroad, (s)he may register to the IMS network through a P-CSCF in an IMS network in that foreign country. The P-CSCF in that foreign network, the *visited IMS network*, will relay the SIP messages to/from the *home IMS network*, i.e. the IMS network that this roaming subscriber is a subscriber of. Registering to IMS network through P-CSCF in foreign network is known as 'IMS roaming'. VoLTE mandates that IMS roaming is used by roaming subscribers. This is needed to ensure that the media plane can take a local breakout, i.e. be routed in the foreign network, without having to be routed via the home network.

- Interrogating CSCF (I-CSCF): when a SIP message is destined for a subscriber in an IMS network, it needs to be determined in which registrar that subscriber is currently registered (the subscriber can be registered in one registrar at the most). Hereto, when an initial SIP request message enters an IMS network, it is routed through an I-CSCF of that IMS network. The I-CSCF has the capability to interrogate the IMS network's Location server, i.e. HSS, to obtain the information about the registrar in which the subscriber is currently registered. The I-CSCF can then forward the message to that S-CSCF. The I-CSCF is always located in a subscriber's Home IMS network. This implies that a communication session established for a subscriber is always routed to that subscriber's Home IMS network, from where it may be routed to the subscriber's terminal.

- Emergency CSCF (E-CSCF): the E-CSCF is introduced in the IMS network architecture specifically for handling emergency communication sessions. When a P-CSCF in an IMS network (home IMS network of subscriber or foreign IMS network in the case of roaming) detects that a communication session establishment relates to an emergency communication session, it routes the session establishment to the E-CSCF. The E-CSCF resides in the same network as the P-CSCF. The E-CSCF applies specific tasks for emergency sessions, such as obtaining location information of the subscriber. Compare with Circuit switched (CS) mobile network. An emergency call from a GSM/3G handset (e.g. 112, 911) has the effect that most basic telephony functions in the MSC are bypassed. Instead, the call is routed directly to the nearest Public safety access point (PSAP). Analogous to the CS network, an IMS based emergency call is not routed through S-CSCF and is not handled by a Multimedia telephony application server (MMTel-AS). Hence, no telephony service is applied to the call.

4.1 Applications in IMS

Of particular interest is the manner in which *applications* are applied in the IMS network. Let's have a look again at a fundamental functional component in the IMS network architecture: the Service CSCF (S-CSCF). Refer to Fig. 9.

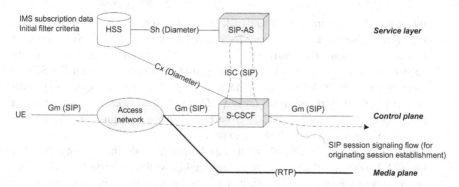

Fig. 9. S-CSCF with SIP application server (SIP-AS)

> *For a description of the various reference points in Fig. 9 (Gm, Cx, Sh), refer to 3GPP TS 23.002 and 3GPP TS 23.228.*

When a SIP session is established by or to an IMS subscriber, control signaling (SIP signaling) is sent through the SIP server of that subscriber (denoted by the dashed line in the figure). The S-CSCF is acting as SIP server for the IMS subscriber. The figure shows that the SIP signaling is routed *through* a SIP application server (SIP-AS), before being routed to the destination, i.e. the called party. The routing of the SIP signaling through a SIP-AS is based on service trigger data. When the IMS subscriber registers in the IMS network, a S-CSCF is assigned to that subscriber and IMS subscription data is sent from HSS to that S-CSCF. The HSS, Home subscriber server, is the persistent subscription data storage. The IMS subscription data may comprise Initial filter criteria (IFC). IFC consists of one or more Service point triggers (SPT). An SPT is a service trigger definition, indication that for particular initial SIP request message, a SIP service shall be invoked. Such *invoking* has the form of routing the SIP initial request *through* the SIP-AS hosting that SIP service. The address of the SIP-AS, typically in the form of a host name (e.g. sip-as2.ims.operator-x.com) forms part of the SPT definition. The SIP-AS is a *functional entity* residing on a *host*, an IP host in the operator's IP domain. It is, according to 3GPP specifications for the IMS network, allowed that the SIP-AS resides in a different network than the IMS operator's network. That is, however, not common.

The SIP-AS now has the possibility to control the SIP session establishment. It may modify data in the SIP message, resulting in the SIP session to be established to a different destination. Or it may bar certain SIP sessions to be established, e.g. to certain destinations. Or it may alter the number presentation of the calling party, e.g. provide an enterprise-specific number (short number) to be used for displaying to the destination party ('short number presentation').

The *user plane* of a SIP session does not traverse the SIP-AS. The SIP-AS can nevertheless control the user plane. The details of the user plane are negotiated, end-to-end, between the respective parties in the call, i.e. between calling party and called party. This negotiation takes place through SIP signaling. More specifically, through the exchange of an SDP (Session description protocol) offer and SDP answer:

SDP Offer: The calling party 'offers' a particular user plane; the offer comprises, among others, a list of media streams and a set of proposed media codecs.

SDP Answer: The called party provides an 'answer' to the SDP offer, indicating which media streams it accepts and which codecs.

Compare the above with Circuit switched (CS) network. In CS network, the characteristics of the user plane, such as speech codec, are defined at call establishment and can't be modified later on. SIP, on the other hand, allows for flexible definition of user plane, through negotiation between calling party and called party. In addition, the user plane may be modified during a call, e.g. adding video media stream to an established voice call.

> **Note** This flexible definition of the characteristics of the user plane of a multimedia session in IMS, based on SIP, places particular requirements on VAS. Traditional VAS (Intelligent Networks; INAP) is not prepared for this capability. VAS in IMS network shall be adapted to be adequately prepared for this (complex) capability.

The SIP-AS may control the user plane through manipulating (modifying) the SDP offer / answer exchange. For example by removing 'video' media stream in the SDP offer.

A particular problem that exists in Value added services (VAS) in Circuit switched (CS) networks is the invocation of multiple application servers for a single call. This dilemma is rudimentarily depicted in Fig. 10.

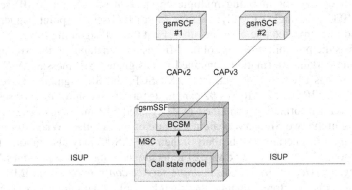

Fig. 10. Multiple point of control in CS networks

According to the CAMEL standard (3GPP TS 23.078), at the most one *subscribed* IN service may be invoked from the gsmSSF in an MSC, for a call to/from a served subscriber. In addition, one (and potentially two) *dialed* services may be invoked in an MSC for a call from a subscriber.[12] A dialed service is triggered for calls to particular numbers. A dialed service has far less control capability than a subscribed

---

[12] In a practical deployment, a <u>single</u> IN service may be invoked from a telephony server, e.g. an MSC, whereby this single IN service constitutes a Trigger management (TRIM) entity. TRIM may invoke two or more IN services. For the core network (the MSC in this example), this deployment is still seen as a single service invocation.

service. This results from the fact that the two services interact with the same basic call state model (BCSM) in the gsmSSF in the MSC. The principle of *single point of control* applies. A single CAMEL service, the subscribed service, may influence the call handling in the MSC. The other CAMEL service(s), the dialed service(s), may be involved only at call establishment, but are not permitted to apply further call control. Reason for this limitation is that integration of more than one additional (gsmSCF) state model with the MSC state model would not be feasible.

In IMS, this dilemma has been resolved (or rather: addressed) by allowing multiple application servers to be invoked sequentially. This is depicted schematically in Fig. 11. Only control plane (SIP signaling) is shown.

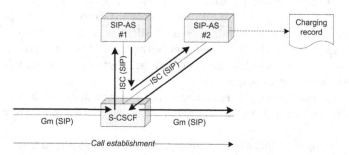

Fig. 11. Multiple SIP-AS invocations for a SIP session

The methodology for invoking multiple application servers for a SIP session is known as 'IFC chaining'. Literally; two (or more) IFC service point triggers (SPT) are 'chained', i.e. invoked one after the other. First the SIP signaling traverses SIP-AS #1, which has the possibility to control the SIP session (manipulate the SIP signaling, e.g. changing certain information contained in designated SIP messages). When the SIP signaling has been routed back to the S-CSCF, the SIP signaling traverses the second SIP-AS, SIP-AS #2. SIP-AS #2 can, in its turn, also control the SIP session by changing certain information contained in designated SIP messages. The respective service logic in the two SIP servers are not aware of one another. When, for example, SIP-AS #1 modifies certain SIP header(s), then SIP-AS #2 may also modify that SIP header, without SIP-AS #1 being aware of it, let alone being able to prevent it! So, the issue of *single service control versus multiple service control* prevails in IMS.

IFC chaining is therefore a method that shall be applied with great care. Let's put it differently, IFC chaining does not provide 'multiple point of control'. The operator shall ensure that the two IMS services don't interfere with one another (or don't have mutual dependency). For example, SIP-AS #1 may be an IMS service that needs to be in control of the entire duration of a SIP session (multimedia call), while SIP-AS #2 merely applies a charging rebate for designated calls. This action by SIP-AS #2 may be done by the generation of a charging record during call establishment. SIP-AS #2 does not assert any further control on the call, i.e. won't interfere with any SIP signaling. The charging record generated by SIP-AS #2 is used off line as input for the charging system that calculates the cost for this call. The charging record indicates to the charging system, for example, that the call qualifies for 50% tariff reduction, since the call is established to a 'friend' (included in a list of numbers).

The sequence of invocation of the two (or more) SIP-AS's may differ per call case. The sequence may e.g. be reversed for terminating call compared to originating call.

Invoking more than two SIP-AS's for a SIP session easily gets difficult to manage, so is generally not recommended. One standardized deployment of <u>two</u> service invocations in IMS is the (sequential) combination of the Service centralization & continuity application server (SCC-AS) and the Multimedia telephony application server (MMTel-AS). The combination of SCC-AS and MMTel-AS is needed for IMS based telephony service for mobile devices, whereby the mobile device may a GSM/3G device, a CSFB terminal or a VoLTE terminal.

5   Multimedia Telephony – The New Communications Standard

The expansion of 'IMS' can be somewhat misleading, which is, in a way, historic. IMS, being the acronym of 'IP multimedia communications subsystem', can easily be interpreted as the network providing the capability for establishing a communication session between two (or more) end users. The exact details of how IMS establishes a communication session between two end-users, that may be residing anywhere in the world and connected to an arbitrary IP access network at the time of call establishment, goes beyond the scope of this chapter. The reader is referred to [4] for explanation of IMS network and SIP session establishment.

Rather than regarding IMS to be 'the communications system' itself, IMS should be regarded to be the 'communications enabler', or a 'communications framework', if you will. This is elucidated through Fig. 12.

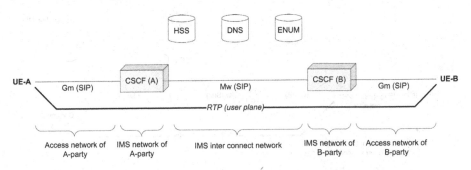

Fig. 12. IMS network as communication enabler

What Fig. 12 depicts is that the IMS network facilitates in the establishment of *communication connectivity* between an A-party (calling party, UE-A) and a B-party (called party, UE-B). The communication connectivity entails (i) that a signaling relation is established between the two parties in the call and (ii) that exchange of media is supported between UE-A and UE-B. The media exchange may typically have the form of RTP message exchange.

Communication connectivity is, however, not the same as *telephony* (further referred to as *basic telephony*). Basic telephony comprises, traditionally, also the following service features (not exhaustive):

- Quality of service control;
- Call progress tones and announcements;
- A basic set of supplementary services (such as Call hold & retrieve, Call waiting, Call transfer and Call forwarding).

A paradigm that's intrinsic to the Session initiation protocol (SIP) is that the IP core network assists in establishing a communication session between two end-points, i.e. calling party and called party. Telephony services are, within this paradigm, handled by the end-points themselves. SIP signaling comprises capability to (un)conditionally forward an incoming communication session to another destination, to place a communication session on hold, to transfer a communication session to another call party etc. This paradigm implies that the end-user (the terminal) 'is in control', placing great dependency on terminal capability and terminal configuration.

It is observed in 3GPP that for realizing a *true* telephony service, the basic call handling should reside in the core network. End-user terminals shall comply with the telephony signaling protocols, including SIP (control plane, for call establishment, call release, mid-call services), RTP (user plane, for media transport) and XCAP (subscribed profile management). The execution of telephony services is done in the IP core network.

The afore-described differentiation between *communication connectivity* and *telephony* is maintained in the implementation of *Basic Telephony* in the IMS network. This is depicted in Fig. 13. Refer to 3GPP TS 23.002 and 3GPP TS 23.228 for description of the reference points (Gm, Mw, ISC).

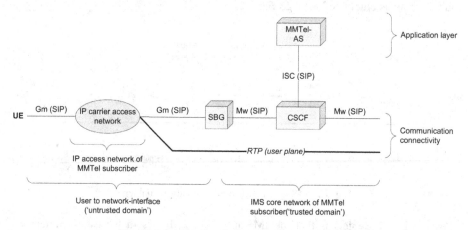

Fig. 13. Multimedia telephony application server

The Multimedia telephony application server (MMTel-AS) acts as SIP application server (SIP-AS) in the IMS network. SIP session signaling traverses the MMTel-AS. MMTel is hence deployed as an *application* of IMS. See Fig. 14.

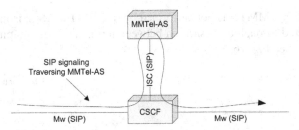

Fig. 14. SIP signaling (control plane signaling) traversing the MMTel-AS

Although MMTel-AS is deployed in the IMS network as *application server*, it's essentially the facilitator of basic telephony. It's trough the combination of IMS core network (comprising CSCF, HSS, MRF, ENUM etc.) and MMTel-AS that a true telephony service is realized. It shall be understood that more functional components are needed, but the mentioned ones are the essential components.

The MMTel-AS contains an extensive, standardized *SIP session state machine*. This state machine fulfills a similar role as the ISUP basic call state model in the MSC. See Fig. 15.

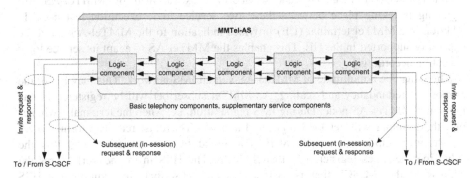

Fig. 15. MMTel application server – functional components

Fig. 15 gives a *logical* (and simplified) representation of the SIP session handling execution model in MMTel-AS. The *logic components* represent service execution of a SIP request or response message.

When a SIP session is established between two communicating parties, the SIP signaling traverses the MMTel-AS of the respective parties (if both parties are IMS subscribers). In each MMTel-AS, an instance of the MMTel SIP session state machine is created. The SIP session state machine comprises a set of *functional blocks*. Each block is responsible for one or more sub sections of the Multimedia telephony, such as destination number analysis & normalization, calling party number presentation check, call diversion (in the case that the call is not established), call hold etc. The SIP messages function as stimuli for the function blocks; the messages traverse the blocks in a defined sequence and lead to taking action like putting a call on hold or retrieving a call from the held state.

Strictly speaking, MMTel is not performed by the MMTel-AS in isolation. Instead, MMTel is realized through orchestration between terminal (User equipment, UE) and the MMTel-AS. See Fig. 16.

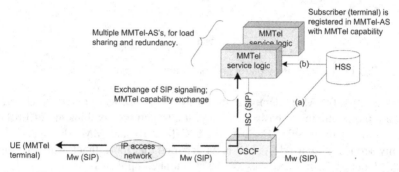

Fig. 16. MMTel functionality distributed between UE and MMTel-AS

Multimedia telephony comprises a combination of service logic execution in the terminal (User equipment, UE) and service logic execution in the MMTel-AS. SIP signaling is taking place between these two service logic execution instances. In addition, the MMTel terminal (UE) provides indication to the MMTel-AS about the capability supported in the UE. This enables the MMTel-AS to adapt its service logic execution accordingly.

There may be a multitude of MMTel-AS's in an IMS network. This may be for the purpose of redundancy and scaling. An MMTel subscriber will be registered in one particular MMTel-AS node. During IMS registration, i.e. when the terminal 'switches on', the terminal will get IMS registered *and* MMTel registered. The former (IMS registration) implies that a S-CSCF is assigned to that subscriber and that the subscriber becomes registered in that S-CSCF. The HSS in the network stores the address of the S-CSCF that is assigned to the subscriber. In addition, the HSS provides IMS service subscription data to S-CSCF (see (a) in the figure). This category of service subscription data is known as *non-transparent data*, since the structure of this data is known to the HSS. The latter (MMTel registration) implies that an MMTel-AS is assigned to the subscriber and that the subscriber becomes registered in that MMTel-AS. The MMTel-AS obtains MMTel service subscription data from HSS (see (b) in the figure). This category of service subscription data is known as *transparent data*, since its structure is not known to HSS. The structure of this service subscription data, the MMTel service subscription data, is known to MMTel-AS.

6   VAS in the Evolved (4G) Communications Network

So, how do we then apply the VAS invocation principles, described in previous sections, in the 4th generation communication network? We consider the 4th generation communication network to be IMS based, with Multimedia telephony

(MMTel) as the facilitator of *telephony*. The IMS based communication network supports a variety of access networks, supports a variety of public user identity classes (e.g. +31161279912 and sip:john.smith@my-company.com) and supports subscribers that have multiple terminals (e.g. a mobile device and a desktop based or PC based SIP phone). In first instance, when operators migrate from contemporary, Circuit switched based communication network such as the PLMN (GSM/3G) to IMS with MMTel, these operators will want to continue to use specific Value added services that are in operation. For example:

- Prepaid service;
- Virtual private network (short number dialing, incoming and outgoing call screening, charging control);
- Location based service (location based tariff, e.g. free calling when in Home zone).

These services are currently deployed within a pure GSM/3G context. That implies that they are grafted on GSM/3G principles such as (i) subscriber has one identity (his mobile number), (ii) subscriber has one terminal (his GSM/3G phone), (iii) access network is restricted to GSM/3G. Practically, when existing VAS is applied in IMS/MMTel context, this VAS will be restricted by the above-identified GSM/3G constraints (one public number, one terminal etc.).

Previous sections have described how the MMTel-AS in IMS network is the *telephony server* and fulfills a role similar to (Gateway) MSC in the GSM/3G mobile network. When reflecting the VAS mechanism of the GSM/3G network on telephony in IMS, we obtain architecture as shown in Fig. 17, as one possible embodiment of VAS for MMTel.

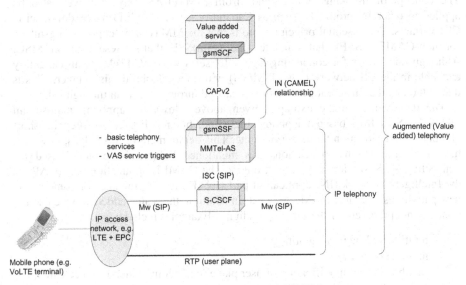

Fig. 17. VAS combined with MMTel

The figure shows a very restricted picture of telephony in IMS. It shows particularly only those functional components (functional entities) that are involved in the invocation of existing VAS from MMTel in IMS.

The MMTel subscription data that the MMTel-AS has obtained from HSS (not depicted) comprises, besides basic telephony service subscription data, also Value added service subscription data. The MMTel-AS applies basic telephony through a defined telephony *state machine* (see previous sections). The gsmSSF that we know from contemporary circuit switched networks, notably the PLMN, is functionally coupled to this state machine. The state machine for MMTel is not identical to the GSM/3G basic call state model (BCSM, see 3GPP TS 23.018 and 3GPP TS 23.078). However, it contains Detection Points (DP) that provide the same interaction capability as the DPs in the BCSM for GSM/3G. In this manner, the same gsmSSF process can be coupled to the IMS telephony service logic execution as to the GSM/3G telephony service logic execution. And the gsmSSF in MMTel-AS can in this manner invoke the same, existing, Value added service.

The figure shows a mobile phone as device in use by the end-user. This mobile phone may be a native SIP phone, such as Voice over LTE phone, but may also be a GSM/3G phone, i.e. a non-SIP phone. The IMS network comprises functionality to connect GSM/3G phones to the IMS network and treat these phones as if they are SIP phones. This methodology is known as IMS centralized services; see 3GPP TS 23.292. For MMTel and VAS, it is largely transparent that the served user is using a non-SIP device.

The Value added service (VAS) shown in the figure is contained in an existing Service control point (SCP) in the GSM/3G network, but is now also connected to MMTel in the IMS network. The functional connection between the gsmSCF (in the SCP) and the gsmSSF (in MMTel-AS) is in the example in Fig. 17 formed by CAPv2. The concept of invoking 'northbound' from MMTel-AS may, however, also be applied to other IN protocols, such as Capability set nr. 1 (CS1) or vendor-specific CS1 variants. The essential principle here is that the MMTel-AS 'exposes' a gsmSSF (or non-CAMEL SSF) that emulates the (gsm)SSF that's present in an MSC. Although this allows for connecting legacy IN services to MMTel, not all capability available in the CS network (e.g. GSM/3G) will be available in this manner. This is due to the fact that different information is carried through SIP than through ISUP.

The deployment in the example given above allows for applying mainstream legacy VAS to IMS based telephony, including, but not limited to, prepaid, short number dialing, location based services etc. This deployment of VAS does, however, have certain functional restrictions. As mentioned before, the protocol used for connecting VAS to telephony service engine, the CAMEL application part (CAP) or the Intelligent network (IN) application part (INAP), is not prepared for some of the new paradigms available in IMS MMTel. In addition, the Value added service itself is typically not prepared for these new paradigms. Examples include:

-   multiple public user identities;
-   multiple devices;
-   flexible, in-call modification of user plane (e.g. adding video to voice call));
-   name calling (sip:john.smith@my-company.com);
-   access transfer (moving from LTE access to UTRAN access during a call)

When VAS is applied to MMTel as described and depicted above, the IMS telephony user may still use these advanced IMS services. However, it will not be possible for the VAS to apply specific control over it. For example, when the IMS telephony subscriber moves from LTE access to UTRAN access during a call, that will not visible for the Value added service.

But, at least, it will be a method for continuing to use existing VAS, with accepted restrictions, to IMS based telephony.

7   Advanced Services

For taking the next step in Value added services for IMS based telephony, we will take a closer look at the MMTel service logic engine. See Fig. 18.

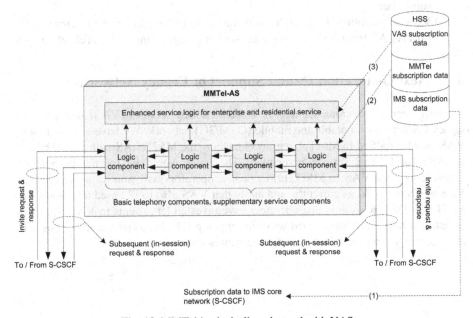

Fig. 18. MMTel intrinsically enhanced with VAS

It was explained in previous section that the legacy concept of VAS, for enhancing basic telephony, is restricted due to the very VAS protocol restrictions. The service logic components shown in Fig. 18 may be handling advanced features like access transfer or voice call to video call upgrade. But such advanced service can't be signaled to the Value added service. One approach to mitigate this restriction is to integrate the VAS with the MMTel service logic, as shown in the figure. The vertical arrows in MMTel-AS represent functional connection between MMTel and VAS. When a designated MMTel service logic component is handling the upgrade from voice call to video call, that service logic component may interact with a VAS component, to verify whether the subscriber's enterprise service profile may possibly disallow such voice to video upgrade. The integration of VAS with MMTel is in this manner not restricted by a VAS protocol like CAP or CS1.

This method constitutes intrinsic enhancement to MMTel. This method is, obviously, not suitable for connecting legacy VAS to MMTel. However, certain legacy VAS would not be suitable for connecting to MMTel through existing (vendor-specific) INAP. This is especially true for advanced services that comprise complicated call leg manipulation, for services like call barge-in, multi-SIM, call hunting.

The service subscription data in HSS may, in this constellation, be divided in three groups:

(1) IMS service subscription data; this is non-transparent subscription data, sent to S-CSCF when the subscriber registers in IMS and a S-CSCF is assigned to that user;

(2) MMTel service subscription data; this is transparent subscription data, retrieved by MMTel-AS from HSS, when the subscriber is registering as MMTel subscriber.

(3) VAS subscription data; this is also transparent subscription data, retrieved by MMTel-AS from HSS, when the subscriber is registering as MMTel subscriber.

8   Next Generation IN and Support of Legacy Networks

We have seen in previous sections how Value added services (VAS) is applied to legacy CS networks, notably the mobile (GSM/3G) network. We have also seen how VAS may be applied to MMTel, e.g. by enhancing the MMTel-AS with a northbound gsmSSF for CAPv2 service invocation. The latter would be for the purpose of applying existing VAS to MMTel. Practically, operators will want to apply existing VAS to CS network, as currently, and apply that VAS *also* to IP based telephony, i.e. MMTel in IMS. Reason is that operators have invested large sums in VAS. And this investment has to be safeguarded when introducing IMS based telephony. A possible architecture that would fulfill such requirement is shown in Fig. 19.

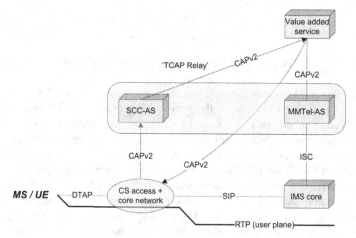

Fig. 19. VAS for MMTel and CS core network

The figure shows the Service centralization and continuity application server (SCC-AS). The SCC-AS takes care of 'anchoring' calls that are established from / to the GSM/3G mobile network, into the IMS network. As explained before, this allows for GSM/3G phones to be used by IMS subscribers, whereby these subscribers may still receive the telephony service, including VAS, from the IMS network.

The SCC-AS has the role of CAMEL SCP; the SCC-AS resides in the home network of the IMS network operator. It may be co-located with MMTel-AS. When a call is established in the mobile network, service logic in the SCC-AS is invoked, fully in accordance with CAMEL service logic invocation. The calling subscriber (the IMS subscriber) may be in home network or may be roaming abroad. The service logic in SCC-AS, will take one of the following actions:

(1) anchor the call in IMS;
(2) do not anchor the call in IMS, but instead instruct the MSC from where the SCC-AS is invoked, to continue call establishment; the call will now be established in GSM/3G network.

When (1) applies, the call is routed to the IMS network and within the IMS network, the call establishment is subject to IMS and MMTel originating call establishment procedures.

When the subscriber is roaming abroad, SCC-AS may, based on configuration, decide to take action (2). One reason for such decision is that the anchoring in IMS leads to additional cost related to signaling (ISUP) and media transmission (E1 circuits). The additional cost is caused by the fact that anchoring the call in the home IMS network entails the establishment of an international call connection. However, when the call from the IMS subscriber, using a GSM/3G phone, would not be anchored in IMS, the call would not receive any Value added service, such as number translation (short number dialing) or pre-paid charging.

TCAP relay is a means to mitigate this shortcoming. TCAP, Transaction capability application part, is the transaction protocol used between two end-points in the SS7 network for establishing a communication relationship. TCAP is commonly abbreviated to TC. A TC relationship is used in the GSM/3G network for, among others, establishing a relationship between MSC and SCP for exchanging CAP operations. When the service logic in SCC-AS is invoked, enabling SCC-AS to anchor the call in IMS, a TC relation is established between the MSC (in the visited GSM/3G network) and the SCC-AS (in the IMS operator's home network). When the SCC-AS decides *not* to anchor the call in IMS, it may *still* get VAS invoked for the call. This may be done by relaying the TC relationship, that was initially established between MSC and SCC-AS, towards the SCP hosting the VAS. This means that the SCC-AS will for this call no longer be the end-point for the TC relationship. Instead, the TC dialogue establishment message is forwarded to the SCP, enabling the SCP to become the end-point for the TC relationship. This forwarding of the TC relationship establishment is known as 'TCAP relay' (depicted in the figure).

The continuation of the TC relationship will be between the MSC and the SCP (as also depicted in the figure). This implies that SCC-AS is no further involved in the TC relationship for this call. Meanwhile, the VAS has gained control over the call.

The call is established in the mobile network, under instructions from VAS. So, prepaid and short number dialing may still be applied for the call.

This is a practical use for a VAS that's connected to both the CS network (GSM/3G) and the IMS network. The reader is encouraged to read [5] for further information on VAS evolution for these network scenario's.

9 Summary and Conclusions

This chapter has provided an introduction into Value added services (VAS) in the evolving multimedia communication network. This is done by first setting VAS in its right perspective, namely a mechanism for augmenting the telephone service logic execution in the telephony server. This paradigm for augmenting telephony is replicated into the IMS domain, i.e. the evolving (mobile) communications network. However, applying the paradigm of legacy VAS into the IMS & MMTel architecture is a solution for transition period. It allows an operator to continue to use legacy VAS when that operator introduces IMS MMTel. This form of applying VAS has the limitation that it has no intrinsic support for advanced use cases such as device transfer, access transfer, multi-device and other advanced cases. To mitigate this shortcoming, VAS for the evolved communication network should be integrated with MMTel.

TCAP Relay may be used for combining VAS for the GSM/3G network with VAS for IMS-MMTel. Such method would be particularly useful for combining IMS-MMTel with roaming.

References

1. Noldus, R.: Camel. Intelligent Networks for the GSM, GPRS and UMTS Network. Wiley (2006)
2. Faynberg, I., Gabuzda, L., Kaplan, M., Shah, N.: The Intelligent Network Standards. McGraw Hill (1997)
3. Black, U.: The Intelligent Network. Prentice Hall (1998)
4. Noldus, R., Olsson, U., Mulligan, C., et al.: IMS application developer's handbook. Elsevier (2011)
5. Noldus, R., Huijsmans, M., Ryde, A., Falkenå, J.: Adding value to IMS multimedia telephony. Ericsson Review 2011-2, pp.28–33,
   http://www.ericsson.com/res/thecompany/docs/publications/eric
   sson_review/2011/Ericsson-Review-2011-2.pdf;

The referenced 3GPP technical specifications can be obtained from http://www.3gpp.org. The reference IETF standards (RFC's) can be obtained from http://www.ietf.org. GSMA documents may be obtained from https://infocentre.gsm.org (restricted access).

NGN Standardization as a Strength

Alain Sultan and Ultan Mulligan

European Telecommunication Standards Institute, ETSI, 650 Route des Lucioles,
06921 Sophia Antipolis, France
{alain.sultan,ultan.mulligan}@etsi.org

Abstract. In the fast changing world of telecommunications, apparently dominated by dynamic downloads of Over The Top applications, one may wonder if standardization still has a role to play. After studying this question and concluding in a positive way, this section provides an overview of who are the active standards bodies and highlights their main "products", such as the Next Generation Network on the fixed side for ETSI TISPAN or 3GPP Release 5 and later for the mobile side. Some explanations are also given on how these bodies work together - or sometimes against each other.

1 Introduction

While, in the second half of the 1980s, GSM was defined, the main challenges were the radio and mobility aspects. The services were almost solely an adaptation of what was then the most advanced available system, i.e. the Integrated Services Digital Network (ISDN). It offered a set of so-called "teleservices", i.e. mainly telephony, fax and "unrestricted data" transport, as well as some "supplementary services" such as call forwarding, call hold, calling line identity presentation, etc [1]. Introducing particularities for the mobiles was not seen as a good thing: it would not only have consumed more time to define the system but would have also introduced extra complexity when interworking with, or transiting on, a fixed network. Even Short Message Services (SMS), a last-minute GSM-specific addition, was seen with suspicion and initially ignored by several operators and manufacturers, leading to years of delay before wide availability and interoperability. However, by introducing services without an ISDN counterpart, SMS proved that mobiles had some great interests to emancipate over fixed telecommunications. This, together with the impressive commercial success of GSM, opened the door in the following decade (roughly 1990 to 2000) to the specification of a series of mobile-specific services - with diverse commercial success- such as Multimedia Messaging Services (MMS), Location-based Services (LCS), CAMEL, etc. On the fixed side, the ISDN was rather static: three-party call would still be seen nowadays as one of the most advanced services if, from the late 1990s, the Internet would not have risen and taken the lead in the service offer. From then, the race in introducing new services has rather been led by the Over The Top, all software, internet approach. The counterpart of this all-software approach is a new time scale, considerably faster, where a life cycle for an application is often reduced to some years. This fast-changing approach is a new challenge for traditional operators, who are not anymore only competing among each

E. Bertin et al. (Eds.): Telecommunication Services Evolution, LNCS 7768, pp. 77–89, 2013.

other but are also facing start-up companies, who invented a successful application, and might become worldwide giants within a few years. At the other end, the users, and younger audience in particular, find this new model attractive : apparent gratuity, fashion-like approach of constantly renewed services, enhanced features.

The question is then to know if standards still have a role to play in this new world.

There are two essential elements that provide a positive answer. The first one is that a key word has somehow been forgotten along the way of the internet approach: interoperability. Indeed, the internet is a battle field where players try to impose their solution by smashing down the opponents. An Apple Face Time user cannot communicate with a Skype user who in turns cannot communicate with a Google Talk user. Interworking solutions could of course be developed, but this is not a priority for the companies in question. On the contrary: their aim is to impose their software over the competitors' ones. This leads to a closed telecommunication world, ending up with a few mega-players - at the opposite of the apparent initial openness of the internet. This shows the limits of the "let the market decide" approach and calls for standardization. The standardized solutions, coming sometimes years after the equivalent proprietary ones - time to reach global consensus - offer the considerable advantage of being interoperable.

The second element of answer is that the Over The Top approach focuses on a certain subset of applications, typically these highly competed multimedia applications mentioned above. They represent however a limited part of what is expected from a mobile telecommunication network. Among the applications ignored by the OTT approach are the ones having a strong impact on the network, such as proximity services, and the ones which do not provide clear flows of revenue, typically (location-enhanced) emergency calls or other services imposed by regulation.

Finally, let's not forget that Standards were initially introduced to benefit from a wide economy of scale on the products: instead of having competing products on the actual market, the competition is done at an earlier stage, i.e. between ideas in a standardization body, so one single technology is chosen at the production time. While the economy of scale has no meaning for OTT software in Smartphones, it will remain a valid criteria on basic devices as Smartmeters, which will more and more also communicate, as covered e.g. by the current specification of Machine-to-Machine type of communications.

So the need for standardization remains, and the standardizations bodies have actually never been so active.

2   The "Traditional" Telecommunication Standardization Landscape

2.1   The ITU

The commercial development of the telecommunications industry has had a direct and immediate impact on the landscape of standardization bodies used by the industry. As the industry developed, it created standards bodies to meet its needs. The process of standardization used in the telecommunications industry has evolved to directly reflect the commercial realities faced by the industry.

Any description of the traditional landscape for telecommunication standardization has to start with the oldest, most official body, i.e. the International Telecommunication Union (**ITU**), created in 1865 in it is original form to deal with telegraphy. It is part of the United Nations and is based in Geneva, Switzerland [1]. Its present standardization structure is articulated around the ITU-T (for Telecommunication) and the ITU-R (for Radio), the former dealing with the network aspects while the later focuses on the radio and transmission aspects. ITU has traditionally a more fixed-network focus. The major success of the ITU in recent history is the specification of ISDN [2]. Nowadays, ITU often plays a role of "framework entity", defining high-level requirements for e.g. fourth generation (4G) mobile networks. ITU-R co-ordinates the allocation of radio frequencies worldwide, setting out global frequency plans, and among other things manages the allocation of orbits of telecommunications satellites. Also, as a governmental body, technology and commercial issues related to international interconnection of telecommunication services remain within the scope of the ITU. In this respect, the ITU is still the place for some detailed technology standardization related to transmission, management and interconnection of services.

The ITU developed during an era of government monopoly on provision of telecommunications services in most countries in Europe, and a period in the US when there was a monopoly in providing long-distance national and international telecommunications services. Therefore it should not be a surprise that the ITU is part of the United Nations, where positions are taken on a nation-state basis. The ITU's interconnection standards were necessary on international boundaries. Internally in each country, the single national operator often worked together with a single or preferred set of national telecommunications equipment providers (sometimes also government owned), together defining the proprietary technical characteristics of the national telecommunications network. The technology foundations were broadly similar in each network, but details were sufficiently different to impede competition.

2.2   ETSI

During the 1980s, a wave of liberalization was experienced in the world of telecommunications on both sides of the Atlantic. National operators and equipment manufacturers were privatized, monopolies broken up, markets introduced and space was made for new entrants. In this environment, interconnection interfaces needed to be defined between operators in one country, as well as on international boundaries. Telecommunications equipment vendors saw new markets open up with new operators entering the market. Thus was born the need for detailed specification and standardization: for operators, to ease their interconnection difficulties and create a level playing field, for equipment vendors, to generate economies of scale in offering similar products in multiple markets. To cater for this need for standardization to meet market liberalization needs, Europe decided to create an institute dedicated to the standardization of telecommunications.

From the early 1980s, work was being organized in Europe for the specification of a pan-European mobile communication system, in the Groupe Spécial Mobile (GSM) committee established in 1982. This would be a second generation digital system, the first generation being national analog systems which have now mostly disappeared. The introduction of GSM -the system was indeed named as the group which defined it- was important not just from a technical point of view, but also from a competition viewpoint: in many European countries the first GSM operators were among the first private telecommunications network operators to compete with the incumbent fixed-line operator, and Europe required that multiple licenses to operate GSM services be granted in each country, on a competitive basis. The introduction of GSM services forced competition on the European telecommunications landscape. It was decided that GSM would become the key topic in the newly created European Telecommunications Standards Institute (**ETSI**), established in 1988 in Sophia Antipolis, near Nice, France [3], [4]. Since its creation, ETSI was open to direct participation of all interested parties: manufacturers, network operators, system providers, regulators and national telecommunications administrations from all countries worldwide. Today more than 700 organizations from 62 countries are part of ETSI. Beside GSM, ETSI has also defined or being particularly active in other key topics such as DAB [5] and DVB [6], TETRA [7], Fixed NGN [8], DECT[9], or recently M2M [10]. Each technology has been developed using the consensus-based approach used in GSM, combining the interests of all parties concerned.

Back to GSM, the first stable version of the full standard was published from end of 1991 until beginning of 1992. From then up to the present days, it has been evolving regularly, each new version been called a "Release". From its first version until early 2012, 14 successive releases of the standard have been published, i.e. an average of one every year and a half. Figure 1 shows the main technologies introduced in the successive Releases, starting by "plain GSM" in 1991, followed by 3G (also known as UMTS) in 2000, then LTE and LTE-Advanced from 2010. As of 2012, GSM and its improvements are the most widely deployed mobile telephony systems in the world, with 5 billion subscriptions for a worldwide population of 7 billion people. In fact, only two countries in the world have never deployed at least one GSM network (Japan and South Korea), but have directly deployed UMTS networks.

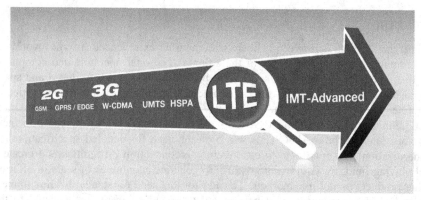

Fig. 1. The technologies defined by ETSI then by 3GPP

2.3   3GPP

With GSM becoming a worldwide success, it was time to create a structure capable of welcoming all the organizations from all over the world with interest in a GSM-based third generation mobile system (3G). After a failed attempt in ITU to define from scratch a 3G network (the Future Public Land Mobile Telecommunications System, aka "FPLMTS"), mostly pushed by the few operators who did not deploy a GSM network, a structure called "**3GPP**" for Third Generation Partnership Project was established [11]. This Partnership was established between ETSI and its equivalent standards bodies in the world, the Standards Development Organizations (SDOs), as shown in Figure 2, on an equal basis. In exchange for giving up a degree of 'European control' over the development of GSM, the European telecommunications industry gained access to new markets thanks to the continued deployment of GSM and UMTS systems. For example, the Japanese market, previously closed to GSM, was the first to deploy UMTS. Today six standards bodies make up 3GPP. In addition to ETSI, there is ATIS from the US, CCSA from China, ARIB and TTC from Japan, and TTA from Korea. 3GPP does not produce any constraining material: after the Technical Specifications have been elaborated in 3GPP, it is up to each standards body involved to approve each and every document produced by the 3GPP. Only then, they become official standards. 3GPP has already completed standardization of Long Term Evolution (LTE) and is now nearing completion of "LTE Advanced" technology, which will enable mobile connections over 1 Gbit/s.

The effort invested in standardization of the GSM family of mobile systems has never ceased to increase. While for many years GSM was the most important and largest standardization activity in ETSI, today the resources committed by industry to 3GPP standardization dwarf all other ETSI standards activities combined, and indeed make many other standards bodies look small. In the case of radio access standardization alone, working groups can have up to 250 delegates per meeting, with 1000 documents and contributions being handled in each week-long working group meeting. Four such working groups, meeting together, can result in 600-700 delegates attending a set of working group meetings – this being repeated up to 8 times per year. In addition to this schedule, one must add the four Plenary meetings per year of the radio access group in 3GPP, each plenary meeting producing and approving updated versions of all specifications subject to change requests. Each year ETSI publishes some 2000-2500 specifications which were developed by 3GPP.

Fig. 2. 3GPP SDOs

2.4   TIA and 3GPP2

In parallel to the development of GSM in ETSI, North American mobile systems were also being standardized. Here, the **TIA**, Telecommunications Industry Association [12], was the focus of work on two competing systems: D-AMPS, sometimes known as TDMA, in the IS-54 and IS-136 standard, and CDMA in the IS-95 standard. The "**3GPP2**" initiative [13], whose structure has been inspired by 3GPP, was established to create a 3G mobile system based on IS-95 CDMA, namely CDMA2000. This group is still active. However, CDMA2000 operators have chosen to migrate to LTE-Advanced as their 4G technology, with the result that 3GPP2 will not develop a separate 4G system standard.

2.5   GSMA

Beside these large-scale projects, there are some groups dedicated to particular aspects of the ecosystem. The GSM Association, or **GSMA** [14], was founded as an association of GSM network operators shortly after GSM entered into commercial service, in the mid 1990s. Initially, its role was to handle the roaming agreements between GSM network operators, which was significant in making GSM a worldwide success. Since this early mission, GSMA has expanded widely both in terms of number of members, with now 800 mobile operators from 220 countries, as well as in terms of its mission: indeed, GSMA now proposes some pragmatic implementation profiles based around existing standards, such as RCS (Rich Communication Suite), a deployment solution for the IP Multi-media Subsystem (IMS) standardized by 3GPP. Beside these operational aspects, the GSMA also organizes the Mobile World Congress, a yearly industry commercial conference and exhibition offering an opportunity for all the actors of the mobile industry to meet.

2.6   NGMN

Another important alliance of network operators which has had an influence on standardization is the Next Generation Mobile Networks Alliance (**NGMN**) [15]. Although this body does not develop standards or specifications, it was formed with an objective to focus attention on operators' requirements for next generation broadband mobile networks, in particular based on LTE and EPC (Evolved Packet Core). Through a series of white papers and similar documents, the operators participating in NGMN provide detailed technical guidance on what they would like to see in future standards for next generation mobile networks.

2.7   OMA

The Open Mobile Alliance, or **OMA**, develops "market driven mobile service enablers that ensure service interoperability across devices, geographies, service providers, operators, and networks" [16]. The creation of the OMA was driven by the fact that several companies, in particular mobile network operators, felt that 3GPP was too centered on aspects such as transmission techniques, network architecture, etc., and was not focusing enough on defining applications or service enablers. This was indeed before the publication of the specification of the IMS. Ten years later, the OMA's success stories are mostly the handling of Digital Rights Management (DRM) or Push-to-talk Over Cellular (POC) and the organization is facing an uncertain future.

2.8   IETF

Back at the time when 3GPP realised that a platform had to be specified for mobile service handling, in the early 2000s, a first consensus was quickly reached: it was not desirable to reinvent such a platform since, as for GSM with ISDN, it would have been time consuming and the interoperability with the fixed network would have been more complex. This being concluded, two approaches were possible: the ITU's Broadband ISDN, using the H.32x series of protocols, or the **IETF**'s internet, based on the Session Initiation Protocol (SIP). After a careful consideration of the two options, it was decided to move towards the IETF/SIP approach. IETF then became a key partner of 3GPP for the specification of IMS, and all the dependencies from IETF were carefully tracked and monitored in 3GPP, asking the IETF whenever needed to take into consideration the specific characteristic of mobile access, as to avoid to have two versions of SIP (an IETF one for fixed access and a 3GPP one for mobile access). There was a successful handling of this challenge, so nowadays there is one single SIP, defined by IETF. The 3GPP's IMS specification provides all the aspects needed for SIP operation, such as the architecture, the operation and maintenance aspects, etc.

2.9   Other Groups

Finally, to close this overview of the telecommunication standardization landscape, two groups have to be kept in mind: the **IEEE** (Institute of Electrical and Electronics Engineers) [17] probably best known for its Ethernet, WiFi (IEEE 802.11 series) and WiMax (IEEE 802.16) standards, and the **W3C** (World Wide Web Consortium) [18] who "develops open standards to ensure the long-term growth of the Web".

3   Collaboration and Competition between Standardization Bodies

3.1   Examples of Competing Standards

When seeking to understand issues of competition between standards bodies, it is important again to look at the makeup of the industry participating in each standards body. While it may appear that some standards bodies compete or have overlapping efforts, in practice it is more common to find competing technologies, usually in different standards bodies, but sometimes in the same standards body. This competition in standards is of course directly driven by competition within the industry.

It is relatively easy to find cases of competing communication standards, and hence, competing standards bodies. Immediate examples spring to mind: IEEE's WiFi vs. ETSI's HiperMAN, USB2 vs. IEEE 1394, IEEE's WiMAX vs 3GPP's UMTS and now LTE, IETF's SIP vs. ITU-T's H.323. But one can also look within a single standards body to find competing standards. WiFi and WiMax can be considered as competing in some markets. ETSI has published four different standards for Mobile

TV, and has three different standards for private mobile radio systems, each targeted at a distinct market. It is therefore the technologies, and their supporting companies, which compete with each other.

3.2   Some Factors of Standard Successes or Failures

Each standardized communication technology is developed with a particular use and a particular market in mind, and has a distinct set of industrial backers. One must examine markets and market players when considering competition between technologies. Among the numerous factors to decide whether a technology is successful, the key ones are: commercial considerations (cost and price), technical performance, market issues, and the strength of supporting companies. This last factor is very important in cases where broad consensus on technology choices is not established: in effect each competing technology has its circle of supporters, those who have either developed the technology or invested in its adoption. The broader the circle, the greater the consensus on the technology choice, and the greater the potential success of the technology. Nowhere is this more evident than in the attempt to develop WiMax as a competitor to UMTS and later to LTE. Most of the mobile telecommunications industry was involved in creating 3GPP to define the network standards it needed. Any new radio interface deployed in mobile telecommunications networks would almost by definition need to be developed by 3GPP, as this was where the operators set out their requirements, where the manufacturers collaborated to meet these requirements, and where the whole mobile telecommunications industry sought consensus on their technology choices in order to achieve economies of scale and cost savings. Any technology developed outside this structure was not going to be developed with these operators requirements in mind, and so would immediately face an uphill task to be adopted by the industry, regardless of its technical qualities. Of course technical and commercial considerations also come into play, but the notion of strength of industry support is very important. Some may see this as proof that 3GPP is the 'right' place or the natural venue for mobile communications standards. Of course, there is no 'right' place to develop a particular standard. There are standards bodies where a particular industry is present or dominates, and there are standards bodies where the same industry is largely absent or at least does not dominate.

3.3   Natural Limitation to the Number of Standardization Bodies

Finally, there is in theory no limitation on the number of standardization bodies: a company judging that none of the present structures is appropriate (e.g. too slow, too big, too controlled by certain competitors) can try to convince other companies to create a new forum. In practice, the success of such an operation is determined by the quantity and the quality of the work but also, and mostly, by the untold "convincing factors" (political/commercial agreements, etc). And, just as new players would support the creation of a new standard group in which they might be more listened, the already established players would not appreciate to see a new group trying to define a new standard. If defined, the new system would indeed compete with the solutions defined/being defined by the established group, challenging some investments and fragmenting the market.

3.4   Collaboration between Bodies

With such concentration of industry interests in certain standards bodies, when industry sectors need to collaborate on new technologies, the standards bodies used by these sectors will also need to collaborate. And examples of cooperation between standards bodies are just as common as examples of competition. This should not be a surprise: many industry players participate in multiple standards bodies, and no company likes to standardize a similar technology twice in two different places. At best, it is wasted effort. At worst, it results in incompatible solutions.

The latest standardized communication systems are comprised of technologies sourced from numerous standards bodies, bundled together into a standardized and interoperable architecture. In this context, it is essential for standards bodies to cooperate. One example of such co-operation include that between ISO, CEN and ETSI for Intelligent Transport System standardization, which also uses technology standardized by the IEEE and the IETF. But the most relevant example to our study is that of 3GPP and IETF co-operating together to develop the IP Multimedia Sub-system (IMS), part of the core network of the 3GPP mobile communications system. This was later extended to a cooperation between ETSI, 3GPP and the IETF for NGN development.

4   The NGN Standardization Process

4.1   The Convergence of Mobile and Fixed Network Needs

From the earliest stages of standardization of 3G mobile systems in 3GPP, the core network was planned to be IP-based. An initial debate was whether to use a H.323 based system for call and session control, or whether to use SIP, as specified by the IETF. Once this question was decided upon in 2000, work began in earnest to develop an IP Multimedia Subsystem (IMS) which was SIP-based. In this particular case, the architectural model was developed by 3GPP. Many of the component technologies or protocols used in the IMS architecture were specified by IETF: not simply SIP but also Diameter, XCAP etc. 3GPP required extensions or modifications to many IETF RFCs in order to meet the requirements of mobile networks. Careful liaison between the IETF management and the 3GPP management ensured that each body understood the development plans of the other, since 3GPP specification which referred to IETF RFCs were in fact dependent on the availability of these RFCs. And in many cases the IETF RFCs were developed by the same individuals (and therefore the same companies) as participated in 3GPP, further ensuring alignment.

In the fixed network community, developments towards an all-IP core network were also taking place. Here the drivers were somewhat different. The fixed network community had already spent a number of years developing Broadband ISDN standards, but there was little interest in the take-up and deployment of these. DSL access was being rolled out instead, providing better IP connectivity to subscribers at a more reasonable cost for operators. Those same operators needed to continue uninterrupted support to legacy PSTN subscribers as part of their universal service obligations, since many of their subscribers would not require or be interested in having internet access via DSL. The operators were also facing requirements of cost reduction: not simply a case of reduced capital and operational expenditure in rolling out a new network, but also freeing up capital tied up in real-estate, since new

IP-based networking equipment would take up significantly less space than legacy circuit-switched network equipment.

4.2   ETSI's NGN

Work on Next Generation Networks (NGN) designed to meet these requirements was started at a later stage to the development of IMS in 3GPP, when 3GPP-IETF liaison was already well established. As early as 2003 the first ETSI specification describing an NGN architecture were published [20], based upon work done earlier in ETSI TIPHON committee, and on 3GPP's IMS and an MSF architecture. NGN as standardized by ETSI is more than simply IMS: it covers a number of other subsystems and needed to include PSTN emulation and simulation, NGN (IP terminal) access, mobile access, and new subsystems for services such as IPTV and ENUM [21].

The development of NGN in ETSI Technical Committee TISPAN was based upon detailed technical requirements which were established as part of the standardization process. These were in turn driven by higher level commercial and organizational imperatives, which did not feature in the standardization process. As a telecommunications network, NGN needed to offer full interoperability of all services across network boundaries – within a country as well as internationally. Operators needed to be able to roll out IP networks which provided full transparent PSTN replacement. These same networks needed to be able to transport all mobile related services, enabling a common backbone network for fixed and mobile services. The NGN needed to support the same types of applications as the mobile network, featuring the same application server technology. Access to the network would be from a diverse range of devices, with different capabilities: mobile devices with UICC cards, legacy PSTN devices, fixed IP terminals, WiFi-enabled devices etc, therefore authentication would be a critical feature. And operators needed to be able to offer new services such as IPTV using as much of the existing NGN functionality as possible to support access and authentication, billing and charging, transport, quality of service etc.

Given the diversity of the requirements and the intention to re-use internet technology where possible, the issue of co-ordination with other SDOs quickly became an issue. ETSI TISPAN needed to track IETF work and sometimes drive it, ensure the ITU-T was kept regularly informed of the progress in ETSI, and most importantly ensure full compatibility between ETSI NGN IMS and 3GPP's IMS. The most efficient means to achieve this co-ordination was to ensure that ETSI NGN referred out to work done elsewhere, when this was suitable. And liaison between bodies was best performed by having individual experts from ETSI TISPAN committee attend other SDO meetings. With this approach, the standardization of IMS was fully devolved to the 3GPP, ETSI NGN requirements being fed directly to 3GPP. And a number of standards delegates took leadership positions in multiple SDOs (e.g. ETSI, IETF or 3GPP) in order to ensure close collaboration between these bodies.

5   What Comes Next

5.1   What Is Already "in the Pipe"

Standardization of NGN is now largely completed in ETSI, but standardization of mobile systems in 3GPP continues at an even greater pace, and a new wave of standardization is developing around Machine to Machine (M2M) communications. Telecommunications standardization, including the development of LTE, is primarily focused on reducing cost and improving efficiency, rather than offering radical new services. New air interfaces such as LTE and LTE Advanced offer higher bitrates, greater throughput, reduced delay, greater energy efficiency and ultimately enable the provision of high data rate communications to more subscribers for less cost. Further initiatives are focused on self-organizing networks, reducing the complexity of deploying and maintaining a network. In the core network, reduced delay, reduced power consumption and traffic offload are also aimed at improved efficiency.

On the service side, rather than offering standardized services, more emphasis is being put on enablers which will allow the bundling of features which may be offered as a service. Even here there may be limited scope for future standardization, given the growth in popularity of what are known as 'Over The Top' or OTT services – services delivered by an external party over a service provider's IP connection. These services tend to have their own critical mass and community and rely on the provision of a reliable underlying IP connection, often finding alternative sources of revenue than connection or usage fees. Indeed interoperability outside the closed community related to each service is less of a requirement than for previous telecommunications services.

5.2   What Comes After

There are different types of challenges that can be foreseen in telecommunications network standardization - and the ones that cannot be anticipated.

A first set of challenges lie in the need to deploy greater capacity in a cost-effective manner. New video formats with definitions much greater than HD (2K, 4K, 8K) have been developed for digital cinema, and these are starting to appear on high-end 'prosumer' devices. No convenient physical medium exists for the transport and delivery of films in these formats (except expensive memory cards), therefore telecommunications networks will be an essential delivery channel. Legal and illegal file sharers are increasingly exchanging HD video content online. New camera and display technologies may enable a greater range of colours to be captured and displayed – colours which the human eye can already see, but which are not offered due to the restricted capabilities of current video systems. And even basic, bottom-end cameras and camera phones now include basic video camera functionality, to enable the capture of video which is intended for sharing online. This is in addition to currently existing applications such as internet TV, catch-up TV (iPlayer) etc. Given these developments, operators can expect an ever increasing flow of video content over their networks, straining already limited network resources and ultimately requiring more investment in capacity.

A second set of challenges concerns the number of users: the tendency is that the users of the telecommunication network will not only be human but also machines, from a smart meter to a fridge, passing by a camera or a car. This will increase the number of "users" from a few billions to hundreds of billions, with a significant impact on the traffic, the addressing, the data storage, etc.

A third set of challenges is for the network to cater with a plurality of natures of traffic: from the remote monitoring of a static food vending machines, leading to send some bits every now and then, up to fast-moving multimedia real time applications.

The less foreseeable aspects include the needs of specific applications of particular fields such as telemedicine or military (drone control, etc.).

So the Over-The-Top approach is definitely complementing the standardization aspects rather than competing with them, and both domains will continue to define new systems and applications in the foreseeable future, with competitions and collaborations within and between each domain.

6   Acronyms

3GPP	3rd Generation Partnership Project
ARIB	Association of Radio Industries and Businesses
ATIS	Alliance for Telecommunications Industry Solutions
CAMEL	Customised Applications for Mobile networks Enhanced Logic
CCSA	China Communications Standards Association
CDMA	Code Division Multiple Access
CEN	European Committee for Standardization
DAB	Digital Audio Broadcasting
DECT	Digital Enhanced Cordless Telecommunications
DRM	Digital Rights Management
DSL	Digital Subscriber Line
DVB	Digital Video Broadcasting
ENUM	Electronic Number Mapping
EPC	Evolved Packed Core
ETSI	European Telecommunications Standards Institute
GSM	Global System for Mobile communications
GSMA	GSM Association
HD	High Definition
IEEE	Institute of Electrical and Electronics Engineers
IETF	Internet Engineering Task Force
IMS	IP Multimedia Subsystem
IP	Internet Protocol
ISDN	Integrated Services Digital Network
ISO	International Organization for Standardization
ITU	International Telecommunication Union
LTE	Long Term Evolution
M2M	Machine to Machine communications
MMS	Multimedia Messaging Service
MSF	MultiService Forum
NGMN	Next Generation Mobile Networks Alliance
NGN	Next Generation Network
OMA	Open Mobile Alliance
OTT	Over The Top
POC	Push-to-talk over Cellular
PSTN	Public Switched Telephone Network
RCS	Rich Communications Suite
RFC	Request for Comments
SDO	Standards Developing Organization
SIP	Session Initiation Protocol
SMS	Short Message Service
TETRA	Terrestrial Trunked Radio
TIA	Telecommunications Industry Association
TIPHON	Telecommunications and Internet Protocol Harmonization over Networks

TISPAN	Telecoms & Internet converged Services & Protocols for Advanced Networks
TDMA	Time Division Multiple Access
TTA	Telecommunications Technology Association
TTC	Telecommunication Technology Committee
UMTS	Universal Mobile Telecommunications Service
USB	Universal Serial Bus
W3C	World Wide Web Consortium
XCAP	XML Configuration Access Protocol
XML	Extensible Markup Language

References

1. 3GPP TS 02.01 Principles of Telecommunication services supported by a GSM PLMN, http://www.3gpp.org/specs/specs.htm
2. http://www.itu.int/
3. ITU-T Recommendation I.120 Integrated Services Digital Network (ISDN) - General Structure, http://www.itu.int/rec/T-REC-I.120-199303-I/en
4. http://www.etsi.org/WebSite/AboutETSI/Introduction/history.aspx
5. Mouly, M., Pautet, M.B.: The GSM System for Mobile Communications. Cell & Sys. ISBN:0945592159
6. ETSI EN 300 401: Digital Audio Broadcasting (DAB) to mobile, portable and fixed receivers
7. EN 301 192: DVB specification for data broadcasting
8. ETSI EN 300 392-1: TETRA Voice+Data (V+D), General network design
9. Sultan, A., et al.: Overview of TISPAN's Next Generation Network Release1, http://portal.etsi.org/docbox/tispan/Open/Information/NGN_Presentations/TISPAN_NGN_Release1_Overview.zip
10. ETSI EN 300 175-1: Digital Enhanced Cordless Telecommunications (DECT); Common interface (CI); Part 1: Overview
11. ETSI TS 102 689: Machine to Machine Communications (M2M); M2M service requirements
12. http://www.3gpp.org/About-3GPP
13. http://www.tiaonline.org/
14. http://www.3gpp2.org/Public_html/Misc/AboutHome.cfm
15. http://www.gsma.com/home/
16. http://www.ngmn.org
17. http://www.openmobilealliance.org/AboutOMA/Default.aspx, http://www.ieee.org/about/index.html
18. http://www.w3.org/
19. 3GPP TS 23.830: Architecture aspects of Home Node B (HNB) / Home enhanced Node B (HeNB)
20. 3GPP TS 25.467: UTRAN architecture for 3G Home Node B (HNB); Stage 2
21. ETSI TS 102 261 V1.1.1 (2003-09): Open Network Services and Architecture (ONSA); Abstract architecture and reference points definition; Mapping of functional architectures and requirements for NGN
22. ETSI ES 282 001 V3.4.1 (2009-09): NGN Functional Architecture Release 3

A Short History of VoIP Services

Dorgham Sisalem[1], Jiri Kuthan[1], and Jörg Ott[2]

[1] Tekelec Germany
Berlin, Germany
{Dorgham.sisalem,Jiri.Kuthan}@tekelec.com
[2] Aalto University
Espoo, Finland
jorg.ott@aalto.fi

Abstract. While starting as an experimental research topic in the early seventies VoIP went through different stages before becoming a commodity service competing with the circuit switched telephony and in some cases even replacing it. In this chapter we give a brief overview of the major developments in the area of voice over IP (VoIP) and look at the major milestones and competing standards. We further give a short look into the latest developments and recent applications and deployment scenarios.

1   Introduction

The discussion about the various aspects of advanced services such as service creation, service platforms and service interfaces have occupied a large share of the research and standardization work done in the area of telecommunications. However, even with the increasing usage of smart phones the plain telephony service based on the selling of minutes still generates more than half of the revenues of telecom operators [1].

Up to the early nineties the voice service used to be the only revenue generating service of telecommunication operators. Since the introduction of telephony services at the end of the nineteenth century most of the innovations in the telecommunication sector were targeted at the operators and not the customers. Hence, the most revolutionary innovations such as the move from manual switching to mechanical switching or the move from analog to digital had nearly no effects on the services used by the subscribers. The service itself did not change, only the comfort of using it, the price and availability have improved.

While the introduction of intelligent networks (IN) and ISDN have surely improved the quality of the telephony services and added a number of additional useful features the first real revolution in telecommunication networks as perceived by the subscribers was the move from fixed to mobile networks in the late eighties. However, even in this case, the service was still plain telephony.

The nineties saw the advent of two major developments. With the rise of the Internet operators started offering dial-up access. Thereby, the phone plug was no longer just the source of calls but also the access point to music, video and chat services and the world wide web. The introduction of the Short Message Service

E. Bertin et al. (Eds.): Telecommunication Services Evolution, LNCS 7768, pp. 90–110, 2013.

(SMS) extended the telephony service of mobile operators with a simple service for exchanging text messages.

The nineties have also seen the first attempts to introduce telephony services on top of the Internet. While mostly a commercial failure these early Voice over Internet Protocol (VoIP) services were the first steps for the introduction of real-time communication to the Internet and the transformation of the Internet into an all encompassing communication platform.

In this chapter we will be looking at the different stages of the development of the VoIP technology over the last thirty years and its effects on the telecommunication market.

2   Pre-VoIP: Voice over Packet Networks

The first papers discussing the possibility of transmitting information using packet switched networks were published in the early sixties [2]. Already at this early stage of the development of packet switched networks the authors were considering the possibility of transmitting voice over packet switched networks [3].

These early considerations were first put into practice with the ARPA (Advanced Research Projects Agency) funded research project under the name of Network Secure Communications (NSC) in the beginning of the seventies. The goal of the NSC project was "to develop and demonstrate the feasibility of secure, high-quality, low-bandwidth, real-time, full-duplex (two-way) digital voice communications over packet-switched computer communications networks" [4].

As part of the NCS project the Network Voice Protocol (NVP) was designed and implemented. NVP specified a control and a data transport protocol. The control part of NVP enabled the establishment and termination of two and multi-party voice sessions and negotiation of capabilities. The data protocol enabled the transport of voice packets between the end systems.

The NCS project resulted in the development of a low bandwidth voice compression algorithm, namely LPC (Linear Predictive Coding) [5] as well an implementation of the NVP protocol and the first demonstration of voice over a packet switched network between different sites connected to the ARPA network.

The NCS project resulted in an innovative communication system supporting a user interface, multi-party communication, voicemail and floor control. However, as only well funded universities and research labs could afford the needed hardware and network links these results can only be seen as a proof of concept showing the feasibility of using packets switched networks for voice communication.

It is probably worth noting that while NVP can be seen as the predecessor of modern VoIP protocols, NVP did not run on IP as the specifications of the Internet Protocol [6] and the move from the then used NCP [7] (Network Control Protocol) to IP did not take place till the beginning of the eighties.

3   First Steps: Proprietary Solutions

In the seventies and eighties most of the work related to VoIP was confined to universities and research labs. There, researches investigated different possibilities for exchanging audio and video data over packetized networks with a high quality of service (QoS). This involved research on compression schemes, scheduling and queuing algorithms, congestion control mechanisms and protocols and operating systems for real-time communication.

It wasn't until the mid nineties that the VoIP technology was allowed to leave the research labs. The 1995 released Internet Phone application by Vocaltec [8] was probably the first VoIP client targeted for commercial use. Based on a proprietary signaling protocol and a proprietary compression technique the Internet Phone application enabled two users using the same application and having similar sound cards to turn their PCs into phones. The Internet Phone offered voice-mail and text chat. To enable the users to communicate with other users the vendor maintained a global directory, which listed other users of the Internet Phone application. Further, one could directly call another user using the email address or IP address of that user –if known.

The voice quality provided by the Internet Phone was lower than that of traditional phones. This was a result of the low bandwidth compression technique used, losses in the overloaded Internet and delays caused when processing the voice at the PCs. However, with the high costs of long distance calls the idea of free calls lured a fair number of users.

Besides the commercial success of the Internet Phone itself, this venture into the VoIP market had two important contributions. On the one side, end users started to become aware that there are other options for making phone calls than what is offered by telecom operators. This awareness paved the way for other companies to roll out VoIP solutions based on standardized protocols and new business models. On the other hand, the technology behind the Internet Phone contributed to a great extent to the development of the H.323 suite of standards, see Sec. 5.

Vocaltec was also the first company to demonstrate a VoIP to PSTN gateway and thereby launch the PC to PSTN services as well as the VoIP trunking business, see Sec. 6.1.

4   Turn of Millennium: Protocol Wars

By the end of the century, telecommunication industry was working hard on standardized solutions. Several competing standards for VoIP communication protocols began to claim their place on the planet. In most of the standardization debates passionate technological and religious arguments played a role. However, it was eventually the market forces that gave conclusive answers.

The battle over centralized control was one of the very first on the VoIP battlefield. Proponents of the telco-leaned paradigm advocated "dumb" telephones controlled by "smart" network elements, frequently referred to in marketing speak as "softswitch". The outcome of this approach was the twin "**master-slave**" protocols MGCP and Megaco/H.248 [9]. These protocols allow network components to control telephones in a centralized manner. The network elements control, when a telephone starts ringing, propagate notifications on answered calls, tear down established calls, and so on. Opponents argued that innovation advances faster in the end-devices and would be impeded by a strict control protocol. Instead they offered the "**end-to-end**" vision based on smart end-devices. Such devices can set up media-rich sessions between each other with the help of application-unaware infrastructure. Eventually, MGCP and Megaco gained noticeable adoption only in the PSTN realm as protocol for decomposed PSTN gateways. Most native IP end-devices followed, however, one of the decentralized end-to-end protocol designs.

The decentralized protocols, ITU-T's H.323 and IETF's SIP, battled bitterly against each other. ITU-T, the telecom standardization body, started off and published the H.323 standard in November 1996. The protocol family defined in this standard largely borrowed from the ISDN protocols for sake of seamless PSTN interoperability. The Internet community in the IETF accepted the challenge and published a competing standard called Session Initiation Protocol (SIP) in March 1999. This protocol mimics Web's client-server HTTP protocol. The most visible and indisputable difference between SIP and H.323 is encoding. H.323 messages are encoded in a binary form whereas SIP messages are textual and human-readable. SIP advocates also maintained that SIP was built with greater extensibility in mind. This argument certainly affected decision-making process of 3GPP, the mobile phone standardization body. As result, in 2000 3GPP adopted SIP for use in all-IP mobile networks. We believe that the most important argument came from the market few years later. It was the ISPs and ASPs who started the mass consumer VoIP services in 2004. As the SIP "language" was easier to understand for ISPs used to deal with HTTP, SIP eventually prevailed in most deployments.

At the same time, conflict between architectural purists and deployment pragmatics caused years of delay. The conflict's origin had been hard-wired in the IP protocol decades ago: too short IP addressing space. 32 bits were simply too short to match with the dramatic Internet growth. Market's answer was Network Address Translators (NAT) that allow multiple devices to share a single IP address. Purists condemned the NATs as evil because they violate transparency of the Internet and have indeed numerous side-effects. One of them is that servers behind NATs are hard-to-reach, a problem affecting every VoIP telephone behind a NAT. That's because such a phone acts as server when it listens for incoming calls and voice. By then purists were hopeful that NATs would disappear with the arrival of IPv6. Pragmatists were concerned about slow IPv6 adoption rate and were trying to find protocols to get around NATs, such as Midcom, UPnP, STUN and TURN.

Market began to be impatient and delivered two answers before tha standardization efforts were concluded. One of them is the notion of a "Session Border Controller (SBC)", a network box that handles the "NAT problem" for both end-devices and other network equipment. The SBCs mediate both signaling and media in a proprietary way which allows VoIP to traverse NATs. Market availability of the SBCs more or less drove the NAT traversal standardization debate in obsolescence. The other market's answer was skype: skype architects didn't bother with debates about IPv6 and created a proprietary peer-to-peer protocol that can traverse NATs and firewalls. We believe it was this capability which made VoIP largely usable for consumers. As a result, skype sky-rocketed on consumer market in years when the standardization bodies were still trying to find an "architecturally correct" answer.

Next to these major battles, numerous other ones took place in standardization bodies and related to addressing (Email-like versus telephone numbers), Internet-ready codecs, encryption protocols (zRTP versus DTLS), QoS control (tied versus loosely-coupled), integration with messaging (SIP versus jabber), and others. In most of these matters practicability for service providers and especially PSTN backwards compatibility often determined the outcome. As a result most VoIP users are reachable today by a telephone number and the most interoperable codec remains the proven but wasteful G.711.

5   Telecom VoIP Standard: H.323

The origins of H.323 date back to 1994, when (at that time) Study Group 15 of the ITU-T decided to extend their perspective on multimedia communication (especially video telephony and conferencing) to include local area networks. SG 15 had, at this point, developed the Recommendations for video telephony over ISDN (H.320), combining 1 – 30 ISDN B channels to create a multimedia pipe of up to 2 Mbit/s and running a bit-oriented multiplexing protocol on top to differentiate between audio, video, data, and control channels. SG15 had already expanded their scope to native support for ATM networks, officially termed "B-ISDN" in H.321 (primarily driven by institutions from Japan) and was looking at video communication over modem connections with H.324. An extension of this is known as H.324M, the low-overhead equivalent for multimedia over circuit-switched cellular networks, which found its application for video calls in early (pre-IMS) releases of UMTS. A parallel (low-profile) activity was also defining how to run video communications over "local area networks with guaranteed quality of service", i.e., isoEthernet (IEEE 802.9), which led to H.322 but remained without practical relevance.

There are several myths about the ITU-T and some of these may hold true to some extent: two prominent ones state 1) that the work progress is slow (because of bureaucracy and long meeting cycles) and 2) that the work is driven by the telecom operators. Interestingly, none of those held for the group designing H.323: Concerning 2), the group was dominated by equipment vendors who, coming from H.320, wanted to build interoperable products also for IP-based local area networks. With a few exceptions, telcos played mostly just an observing role in the beginning. As for 1), the companies were eager (if not required) to move quickly to get their products into the market. This resulted in a tremendous effort put into H.323 and yielded the completion of the first functionally complete specification in about 10 months (just a bit more than a year including the formal voting process, 1996). The strong efforts continued to a functionally enhanced and partly optimized H.323v2 (1998) and subsequent extended revisions H.323v3 (1999) and H.323v4 (2000). With especially video conferencing products being shipped—and with the Session Initiation Protocol (SIP) establishing itself as a (supposedly) more promising solution for telephony—the effort reduced and the group went more into a maintenance mode. At this point, the specification was essentially complete and only rather minor functional enhancements took place, the most notable one being the work on NAT and firewall traversal.

5.1   H.323 Series of Recommendations

The original goal of H.323 was extending H.32x-based multimedia communication to endpoints across (local area) IP networks—so that gateway considerations played an important role. Recall that, at that time around 1994, 56k modems were about to be standardized and the non-academic wide-area Internet was essentially unusable for multimedia communication. Thus, it was not the creation of a new multimedia communication architecture that guided the design but gatewaying and legacy interoperability considerations—paired with the need for a certain "cultural compatibility" to obtain support in the video conferencing industry and acceptance in the ITU-T. One specific consequence of this was that NAT traversal was not an issue: local endpoints would connect to their gateway and then be routed via the telephone network to the target site, where they would be again gatewayed to their final destination. The idea of using H.323 for Internet telephony evolved only over time.

Typically, an H.32x series required multiple specifications, as does H.323:

- the systems framework (H.323) that provides the overview and defines the interactions of the diverse components comprising one endpoint;
- the signaling protocol (H.225.0) that defines the interaction between endpoints (for ISDN and PSTN, H.221 and H.223 would also do the channel multiplexing);
- the media control channel (H.245) for capability negotiation, setup/teardown of media channels, and further control operations; and
- specifications for multiparty conferencing support using central *multipoint control units* (MCUs) (H.239, H.241).

When the H.323 system specification was started, this did not happen in a vacuum:

- H.245 was incorporated as an elaborate—actually: too elaborate, given that many features were generally not used in the end—capability and media control channel since all other systems specifications (except for H.320) were using it as well and mappings to H.320 were already in place.
- With gatewaying to ISDN in mind, Q.931 was chosen as the basis for the call signaling channel. While the protocol state machine could be considered ok for the purpose, the protocol messages required substantial extensions. H.225.0 evolved as the equivalent call signaling protocol borrowing heavily from Q.931.
- The basics for multiparty conferencing operation were adapted and enhanced from the basic conferencing functionality defined for H.320.
- Mapping between the different H.32x systems was defined in H.246.

Moreover, SG15 also standardized audio (ITU-T G.7xx series of Recommendations) and video codecs (H.261, H.263, and H.264). These codecs could be used without changes. Nevertheless, over time, the growing relevance of packet-based communication led to a shift in codec standardization, away from mere bit error tolerance to considering packet boundaries and especially packet losses in the coding process and data representations. The IETF Real-time Transport Protocol (RTP) was chosen as the media transport and so were the established payload formats—followed by a fruitful interaction between ITU-T codec people and the IETF to define appropriate ones for new codecs.

One important difference to all other H.32x series Recommendations was the need for an address resolution mechanism: E.164 phone numbers (as used for H.320 and H.324) would need to be mapped to IP addresses—and a similar approach could be taken for aliases or H.323 URIs for users. Therefore, a *Registration, Admission, and Status* (RAS) channel was added to H.225.0. Endpoints would use H.225.0 to register themselves with an entity called *Gatekeeper* and to ask the Gatekeeper to resolve addresses. When performing address resolution, the Gatekeeper could also police or prioritize call requests, for example for local resource management.

The above specifications were complemented over time by a number of additional one as H.323 grew: for security (H.235 series), *supplementary services* for telephony (H.450 series), media gateway control (H.248), service creation, call reporting, intra/inter-domain gatekeeper communication, and robustness (diverse annexes), broadcast-style conferences (H.332), an extensibility framework (H.460), and directory services (H.350 series), among others. Data communication may be added, e.g., using the T.120 series of Recommendations.

Except for the Real Time Transport Protocol (RTP) used for the transport of media data and the basic PDU formats inherited from Q.931, all H.323 specifications use the *packed encoding rules* (PER) of ASN.1 (X.68x and X.69x) for protocol encoding.

5.2   System Overview

Figure 1 provides an exemplary overview of H.323 system components and their interactions across two domains. Endpoints (EP), gateways (GW), multipoint control units (MCU), and media servers (MS) are the nodes originating and terminating H.323 calls, i.e., call control channels and media streams.

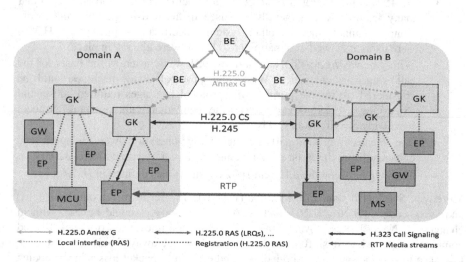

Fig. 1. H.323 system overview

In order to become reachable they register with their local gatekeepers that are also responsible for address resolution and call admission control. Since multiple gatekeepers may exist per domain, they may cooperate to resolve local addresses using an intra-domain inter-gatekeeper protocol. Interaction with other domains (e.g., to exchange call routing information) may happen via dedicated Border Elements (BE) that perform (similar to border routers in IP) policy-based information exchange, but they do not participate in the actual per-call signaling. In practice, albeit implemented, very few people actually use BEs; instead, one rather would find peering relationships directly between gatekeepers with all necessary policies implemented in those.

Media always flows directly end-to-end while the call signaling and capability negotiation channels may or may not through a gatekeeper, depending on the chosen call model.

5.3 Call Models

H.323 defines three different call models: 1) In the *direct call model*, the two H.323 endpoints establish direct TCP connections for call signaling and H.245 (one each). The gatekeeper is (usually) only involved in the beginning and at the end of a call for address resolution and to obtain and release resources. Alternatively, a *gatekeeper-routed call model* can be used, in which 2) the call signaling channel runs through the gatekeeper(s) and the H.245 channels directly end-to-end (this model was not specified and left for further study) or 3) both call signaling and H.245 are routed via the gatekeeper. The calling party's gatekeeper dictates the local model upon address resolution where it either returns its own address or that of the remote peer; it may also decide to target the remote gatekeeper with the call setup (rather than directly the remote endpoint if call routing information demands so). The called party's gatekeeper can take a similar decision and order its endpoint to redirect the call signaling to itself to enforce the gatekeeper-routed call model also on this side. Since the gatekeeper is optional, there is arguably another model: 4) Without a gatekeeper involved there is no RAS channel and endpoint will interact directly, using external mechanisms (e.g., DNS-based) for address resolution; this is, however, mostly limited to environments where devices have fixed addresses so that there is no need for highly dynamic addresses resolution, e.g., in some distance education setups.

Being the ones fully defined, only 1) and 3) were commonly used, but variants of 2) appear to be used in practice when decomposing MCUs into Media Processors (MPs) for media switching/mixing and Media Controllers (MCs) for handling the signaling; in such a case, H.225.0 would be terminated at the MC whereas the H.245 control channel go to the MPs. Figure 1 shows the call signaling and H.245 connections found in model 3).

5.4 End-to-End Design

All video communication Recommendations of the H.32x series treated the network as a bit pipe (as ISDN channel, ATM virtual circuit, or a modem connection):

obviously, since – coming from the telephony domain – the end user would be expected to know the number to call and the network would do the rest. All media multiplexing, control signaling (naturally besides channel setup and teardown), and all media themselves would run in-band end-to-end.

H.323 did not deviate from this concept of assuming a dumb network: assuming IP connectivity underneath, it borrowed the relevant IETF work for transport (UDP, TCP, RTP) to have communication happen end-to-end. And with a packet-based network, H.323 did no longer require to provide its own multiplexing scheme as H.320 and H.324 did. The only infrastructure element (a host from a network perspective) that H.323 relies upon is the gatekeeper. But, of course, the gatekeeper as well as MCUs, media servers, and gateways could be run by operators as well as by enterprises or, ultimately, by cloud service providers.

5.5   Functional Evolution

As noted above, H.323 started out as a system for extending video conferencing into LANs. However, once the basic system architecture and the IP-based signaling standards were in place, the strongest influence came from vendors and service providers interested in Voice-over-IP and video and multiparty communication got out of focus for quite a while [10]. What followed was a rush for adding all kinds of features mimicking telephony services in the IP world and making those "work" within the confines of the architectural framework devised for the original design goals, with the limitations of telephony signaling, and with the burden of extensive multimedia capabilities.

It was this phase—maybe as a result of the success of the early development and the take-up of industry interest—during which the fairly clean architectural design of H.323 got lost. A flood of contributions suggested manifold features often independently that needed to be bolted on mostly one at a time, so that it turned out impossible to maintain the architectural integrity and principles of the specifications and develop a clear structure for extending the system and at the same time keep up with the strong industry demand [11]. The result was a series of extensions in fairly rapid succession, leading to several revisions of the base specification and the development of numerous additional ones (as annexes and separate specifications). It was probably this phase during which H.323 lost quite a bit of its appeal becoming way too complex for the supposedly low-cost telephony world as the specifications grew quickly in size and number.

After 2000, the specifications stabilized and operational and maintenance features (robustness mechanisms, a MIB, NAT traversal, etc.) were added. While H.323 was leading the development, numerous of its features (most prominently probably user registration) were also adopted by SIP. At the later stages the development could possibly be characterized by an inverse "me too" strategy, in which H.323 received suggestions for features developed for SIP before, including presence and instant messaging, among others. But only few, such as the (natural) use of URIs, were actually adopted [12].

5.6   H.323 in Retrospect

As noted above, H.323 has "earned" a reputation as being (too) complex and adoption especially by academia (and thereby future engineers) was quite limited – it took quite a while before open source projects (such as openh323 or opengatekeeper) took up. There are probably many reasons, but four—in the authors' opinion—important ones include: 1) The semi-closedness of the design process and limited access to specifications might have brought an advantage to the (paying) ITU-T members involved in the design, but hurt the specification adoption in the long run. 2) The extensive use of complex data notation for exchange formats and their binary encoding made implementation and manual debugging extremely hard; the de-facto need to buy expensive tools to even start development is a non-started for university and open source projects. 3) The tool-based design also simplified the notation for complex ideas where the connection between a specification and the resulting implementation complexity was lost so that modesty in protocol design was not encouraged. This holds for encodings but also for the implications for protocol state machines. 4) Finally, H.323 had too many cooks dragging the specification to do too many things at the same time, harming architectural integrity and thereby contributing to further extensions getting more and more complex [13].

H.323 has also earned the reputation as being telco technology—which is closer to a fairy tale (or counter-marketing) than reality. Nevertheless, H.323 has clearly been designed coming from a telecom background and clearly missed the opportunity of introducing a paradigm shift in communication that capabilities of which were surely inherent in IP.

To sum up, H.323 has been a tremendous commercial success in the video conferencing market. It solidified the customer base, aggregated the vendors and made the market for IP based video conferencing. While the path was difficult, and many of the decisions were flawed, H.323 provided a platform that provided interoperable video communications for the last decade.

Finally, it is worth noticing that the development of H.323 and experience gained with it surely accelerated the paradigm shift towards IP-based multimedia and the rapid development of SIP (competition is healthy, after all).

In the long run, the specific technology may become immaterial at least for endpoints as we are moving towards a "webby" model in which the end point (i.e., a web browser or equivalent) just downloads the code to interact with a remote peer when engaging on an interaction. This paradigm shift is aggressively pursued by RTC web [14].

6   Internet VoIP Standard: Session Initiation Protocol (SIP)

By the mid nineties the Internet had established itself as a consumer product. The number of users buying PCs and subscribing with an ISP for a dial-up access was increasing exponentially. While mostly used for the exchange of Email, text chatting and distribution of information VoIP services based on proprietary solutions as well as H.323 started to gain some popularity.

While there is no organization that is formally responsible for the Internet as such the Internet Engineering Task Force (IETF) is playing the role of the standards organization of the Internet. The IETF has among others produced the needed specifications for the transport and routing of packets in the Internet as well as the protocols for Email, address resolutions and all other kinds of applications and services running on top of the Internet.

At this stage the IETF has already produced different protocols needed for enabling VoIP. The Real-Time Transport Protocol (RTP), see RFC 1889 [15], enabled the exchange of audio and video data. The Session Description Protocol, see RFC 2327 [16], enabled the description of multimedia data. With the Session Announcement Protocol (SAP), see RFC 2974 [17], it was even possible to distribute the necessary information to watch a certain publicly broadcasted audio and video session. Further, the first applications, mostly open source, for the sending and reception of real-time audio and video data were available.

Those days, the procedure for establishing a VoIP call between two users based on the IETF standards would look as follows: The caller starts his audio and video applications at a certain IP address and port. The caller then either calls the callee over the Phone or sends him an Email to inform him about the IP and port address as well as the audio and video compression types. The callee then starts his own audio and video applications and informs the caller about his IP and port number. While this approach was acceptable for a couple of researches wanting to talk over a long distance or for demonstrating some research on Quality of Service of media compression this was clearly not acceptable for the average Internet user.

The Session Initiation Protocol (SIP), see RFC 3261 [18], was the attempt of the IETF community to provide a signaling protocol that will not only enable phone calls but can be also used for initiating any kind of communication session. Hence, SIP can be used for VoIP just as well as for setting up a gaming session or a control session to a coffee machine.

In general a SIP-based VoIP service consists of user agents (UA), proxies and registrar servers. The UA can be the VoIP application used by the user, e.g., the VoIP phone or software application, a VoIP gateway which enables VoIP users to communicate with users in the public switched network (PSTN) or an application server, e.g., multi-party conferencing server or a voicemail server.

The registrar server maintains a location database that binds the users' VoIP addresses to their current IP addresses.

The proxy provides the routing logic of the VoIP service. When a proxy receives a SIP request from a user agent or another proxy it also conducts service specific logic, such as checking the user's profile and whether the user is allowed to use the requested services. The proxy then either forwards the request to another proxy or to another user agent or rejects the request by sending a negative response.

With regard to the SIP messages we distinguish between requests and responses. The INVITE request used to establish a session between two users is a session initiating request. The BYE sent for terminating this session would be an in-dialog request. Responses can either be final or provisional. Final responses can indicate that a request was successfully received and processed by the destination. Alternatively, a final response can indicate that the request could not be processed by the destination or by some proxy in between or that the session could not be established for some reason. Provisional responses indicate that the session establishment is in progress, e.g., the destination phone is ringing but the user has not picked up the phone yet.

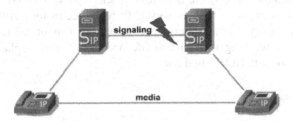

Fig. 2. SIP trapezoid model

As illustrated in Figure 2 the actual topology of a server-mediated call between two SIP phones has the SIP trapezoid in its heart. On the remote sides of the trapezoid, there are the SIP telephones belonging to their respective call participants. Each phone is registered with its SIP server. The registration happens when a phone is turned on and re-registers periodically later to prove it remains reachable. When a caller later decides to dial his peer, his telephone sends a SIP INVITE request through his SIP server. His SIP server looks up the IP address of the server responsible for the destination domain using DNS and forwards the request there. The destination server eventually relays the request to its final destination, the telephone of the previously registered called party.

The initial vision of SIP foresaw a world in which Network Address Translators (NAT) and firewalls were not used, users were more or less trusted and all logic for any type of service was supposed to be located at the end devices. This simplified view of the world led to simple specification and easy implementation. However, with a world full of NATs, firewalls, untrusted devices and subscribers used to some set of supplementary services, this meant that SIP still had to go through endless discussions and a long standardization path before a deployable version was finally available. What started in the mid nineties as a simple solution for session establishment is still a continuing process today and has led to a set of specifications that describe session establishment, NAT traversal, transport of DTMF tones, various addressing schemes, security and application of SIP to various other services such as messaging.

First commercial deployments of SIP-based VoIP services started appearing at the beginning of this century. Internet Service Providers (ISPs) started offering VoIP services as an additional service to Email and messaging on top of their broadband access lines. Unlike the VoIP deployment 10 years before, the availability of moderately priced broadband access lines and the seamless integration of SIP into DSL and cable access devices enabled the ISPs to rapidly increase the number of SIP-based VoIP users from a couple of thousands at the beginning of the century to millions today [19].

6.1   Trunking and SIP-I

SIP was originally designed with an end-to-end VoIP model in mind with the caller and/or the callee being connected to the Internet. While this model is popular with ISPs offering their customers broadband Internet access, large telecom operators have been more reluctant to replace their classical PSTN-based service with a VoIP service. With the classical telephony minutes still making up the largest part of the operators' revenues there is no clear need for replacing one voice service with another one –even if it was based on SIP. However, IP based technology still has different advantages for large operators; namely in reducing the costs of the backbone. With telephony switches reaching their end of life operators started replacing their SS7 based infrastructure with an IP based one.

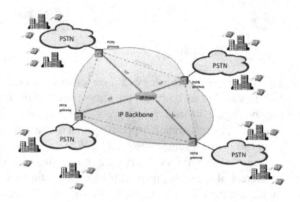

Fig. 3. SIP trunking scenario

In the SIP trunking scenario the original PSTN signals are attached to SIP messages and preserved across the Internet haul. The SIP-based tunneling is known as "SIP-T", RFC 3372 [20], its ITU-originating version as "SIP-I" [21]. Choice of bandwidth-saving codec is important, since with trunking volume bandwidth cost is considerable.

SIP trunking has been from historical and volume point of views the most successful use case so far. With SIP trunking, see Figure 3, the actual calls are both originated and terminated in the PSTN. Only in the middle of the path the call traverses the Internet (or sometimes a private IP network) through SIP-to-PSTN gateways. Call participants remain frequently unaware of the fact that they are using SIP. A particular reason for success of this scenario is twofold. First, it is economically viable: with large traffic volume the VoIP saving can return the investment quite quickly. Secondly, it is easy to integrate. In many cases it takes PSTN gateways from a single vendor, all configured very similarly and interoperating with each other smoothly. The different gateways can be connected with each other in a full-mesh topology or a star topology as depicted in Figure 3.

Proprietary solutions for trunking began to be in operation from about 1995 on. Competing solutions to SIP-based trunking are based on transporting of PSTN signaling using the Sigtran, see RFC 2719 [22] or BICC [23] protocols, remain, however, out of scope here.

6.2   IP Multimedia Subsystem (IMS)

A great push for SIP was its endorsement by the mobile-phone standardization body, 3GPP, as part of its strategy for deploying Internet in mobile networks in the beginning of the millennium.

The Third Generation Partnership Project (3GPP) is a collaboration agreement that was established in December 1998 between a number of telecommunications standards bodies; namely ARIB, CCSA, ETSI, ATIS, TTA, and TTC. Mainly looking at the needs and requirements of mobile operators, the 3GPP first specified the IP Multimedia Subsystem (IMS) as a service architecture combining the Internet's IP technology and wireless and mobility services of current mobile telephony networks. Through the work of the TISPAN, the IMS architecture was extended to include fixed networks as well. The Telecoms and Internet converged Services and Protocols for Advanced Networks (TISPAN) is a standardization body of ETSI, specializing in fixed networks and Internet convergence and was formed in 2003.

IMS [24] builds on Internet Engineering Task Force (IETF) protocols like Session Initiation Protocol (SIP) and Session Description Protocol (SDP). However, for a SIP based solution to replace the current mobile and fixed telecommunication infrastructure it needs to offer the same capabilities; namely secure and efficient access to high quality multimedia services regardless of the user's location. The IMS specifications are, hence, mainly based on the IETF SIP specifications but add some new architectural and functions extensions:

- Functional distribution: The IETF SIP specifications mainly foresee a SIP proxy for the routing of SIP messages. The IMS specifications define different instances of so called Call Session Control Functions (CSCF):
    o P-CSCF (Proxy-CSCF): The P-CSCF is the first point of contact between the IMS terminal and the IMS network. All the requests initiated by the IMS terminal or destined to the IMS terminal traverse the P-CSCF.
    o *I-CSCF (Interrogating-CSCF):* The I-CSCF retrieves user location information and routes the SIP request to the appropriate destination, typically an S-CSCF.
    o *S-CSCF (Serving-CSCF):* The S-CSCF maintains a binding between the user location and the user's SIP address of record (also known as Public User Identity). Like the I-CSCF, the S-CSCF also implements a Diameter interface to the HSS.
    o *HSS (The Home Subscriber Server)*: contains all the user related subscription data required to handle multimedia sessions.
- QoS control: One of the major differences between VoIP and traditional telephony services is the decoupling of the media and signaling paths. On the one hand, this decoupling allows for the establishment of new business models in which a service provider can offer VoIP services without having to own the physical network itself. On the other hand, this implies that the provider will not be able to support any kind of traffic prioritization or resource reservation that would be needed to offer VoIP services with a predictable quality of service level. In the IMS the session establishment process is coupled tightly with the reservation of resources required for achieving the desired QoS level [25]. Further, certain IMS SIP components have an additional interface that allows them to control and communicate with the underlying physical infrastructure.

- Roaming support: The IMS introduces the concept of home and foreign service providers in a similar manner to the current mobile telephony system. A home service provider maintains a contractual relation with the user as well as various user related information required for authenticating the user and offering him certain services. A foreign provider is the provider offering access to the IMS services in geographical locations not covered by the home provider. In order to enable a user to roam to geographical locations not covered by his own provider and still get access to IMS services in a simple and transparent way, roaming agreements between the home and foreign providers are established. These agreements govern whether a user is allowed to access IMS services in a foreign location and the costs of such access.
- Security: The native security mechanisms of SIP enable the service provider to authenticate the users using HTTP Digest, see RFC 2617 [26]. In case the user wants to authenticate the components of the service provider then the Transport Layer Security (TLS), see RFC 5246 [27] should be used. In order to support roaming, the security model in IMS requires also the establishment of a trust relation between the user and the foreign service provider as well as a trust relation between the foreign provider and the home provider. IMS supports similar authentication mechanisms to those used in current mobile networks as well as digest-based authentication. Further, with the extension of IMS to support fixed networks, additional security mechanisms were specified for IMS that reflect the specific needs and characteristics of these networks [28].
- Network-Centric Call Control: Current mobile telecommunication networks provide different capabilities that enable the operators to terminate a user's active communication session when the pre-paid account of a user becomes empty or terminate his subscription if he did not pay his bill for some time. To offer similar capabilities, the SIP components used in an IMS network maintain sufficient dialog and registration information so as to be able to terminate a running session by sending a BYE request to the caller and callee.

While the IMS was initially designed for mobile operators it was first deployed by fixed-line operators. With a profitable business of selling telephony minutes the incentive to replace one technology that provides telephony services with another one was not high. This is especially the case if the new technology is even less efficient in utilizing the limited frequency spectrum and requires all subscribers to either install new applications or even buy a new mobile phone. Fixed operators are on the other hand facing stiff competition from service providers offering bundled packages of high speed Internet access and telephony services. With sufficient access bandwidth and the VoIP clients already integrated into the access devices, IMS offers fixed-line operators a natural solution that reduces the costs and enables a better positioning of the operators.

The advent of the Long Term Evolution (LTE) technology and the all IP Enhanced Packet Core (EPC) networks [29], is changing this. With the increased importance of mobile data services and the availability of high bandwidth wireless networks the number of users moving to more powerful smart phones in increasing together with the interest in VoIP and IMS. IMS is now being considered as the appropriate solution for providing Voice over LTE (VoLTE) services.

7   Reality Beyond Standards: SKYPE

SIP services are based on a client-server model with the servers being operated by a service provider. Hence, similar to PSTN networks, the provider operates a centralized infrastructure that is responsible for user authentication, routing of the signaling traffic and providing additional services. Skype is based on a more distributed architecture based on an overlay peer-to-peer (P2P) network, similar to its file sharing predecessor KaZaa [30]. There are three main components in the Skype network [31]:

- The Skype login server (LS) is one of the few central components of the network. Every user is authenticated through the login server to gain access to the network.
- A Skype client (SC) provides all user functionality to access the network, that is login, initiating and receiving calls, instant messages and file transfer.
- Super Node (SN). A super-node is an SC that is well connected to the Internet and provides additional functionalities to other SN and SC. A super node performs routing tasks such as forwarding requests to appropriate destinations and answering to queries from other SCs or SNs. The SN can also forward login requests in case the login server is not directly reachable from an SC. Additionally, the SN provides media proxying capabilities for other SCs that have only restricted internet access, be it through Network Address Translation (NAT) or restricted firewalls.

To log in to the network, an SC tries to contact one or more Super-Nodes (SN). The code of the clients already contains a list of possible Super-Nodes that are provided by Skype itself. These bootstrap SNs are contacted upon first launch of the client to gather an updated and more extensive list of currently available SN.

Except for some dedicated operations like authentication, user list storage or Skype-to-PSTN connectivity, there are no further central servers in the Skype network. All other operations, e.g. user searches or message forwarding are performed in a decentralized way by the super-nodes.

Skype is arguably the most successful VoIP service. Skype has taken a different approach than most of other VoIP players. Skype invented its own protocol, which is highly proprietary. It is secured against common security threats as well as reverse engineering.

Probably the main reason for the success of Skype is the approach it has taken for rolling out its VoIP service. In the case of SIP and H.323 a lot of energy went into the specification of the signaling protocols. Aspects of deployability and user interface were only considered in the second round. Skype rolled out a complete service with an easy to install and use application, low bandwidth and high quality voice encoding and a highly flexible firewall and NAT traversal solution.

The proprietary mode in which Skype has gotten traction is, however, its greatest weakness too. Many technological companies are reluctant to support closed walled-

garden environments and prefer open standard instead. It remains to be seen how the
success is split between open SIP and proprietary Skype over the coming years.
Further with less than 2 USD average spending per subscriber [32] the business plan
of Skype might not be attractive for operators used to much higher margins.

8   Converging VoIP and Web: WEBRTC

While first designed as the interface to display information provided by web servers,
web browsers are now used as the access to social networks, the interface to online
games and for exchanging emails and messages as well as streaming audio and video
content. Thereby web browsers have become the main access interface to the Internet
and have actually become synonymous with the Internet itself for a large portion of
the Internet users.

Up until recently the communication capabilities of web applications were limited
to either text-based communication such as messaging or email or non-real-time audio
and video, e.g., streaming. The combination of real time services such as a voice call
or a video conference with a web application was only possible using either a separate
application or proprietary plug-ins that lack open specifications, interoperability and
are often limited to certain platforms [33]. Using a separate application would mean
leaving the browser and launching a new application. Thereby there can be no real
integration of the content presented by the browser and the real time content.
Solutions based on plugins provide tighter integration between the real-time content
and the provider's web pages. However, plugins such as Flash are proprietary and do
not work in all environments. In particular Flash does not work over IOS used for
iPhones for example. Another issue with the Flash technology is its centralized
model. A Flash plugin that was downloaded from domain X can only communicate
with a server in domain X. This means that an application provider that is offering a
number of applications in the form of Flash pluging will have to deal with all the
signaling and media traffic generated by the plugin. This restriction was introduced to
prevent a malicious application from sending traffic to some destination and hence
attacking that destination.

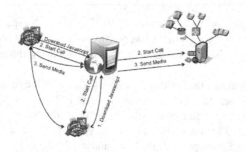

Fig. 4. High Level WEBRTC Framework

The major standardization groups responsible for the advancement of the Internet protocols and applications have launched the HTML5 and real-time web (WebRTC) initiatives to complement web applications with real time media features. New browser capabilities are being defined in HTML5 [34] for video conferencing and peer-to-peer communication. New working groups have been created in W3C and IETF to define elements of real-time communication in the browser[35,36,37]. The specified WebRTC framework is based on the following main parts:

- Browser API: To provide application developers with the ability to send and receive audio and video streams directly from a browser, browsers must be enhanced with capabilities for controlling the local audio and video devices at the computing device at which the browser is running. These capabilities will then be exposed to the application developers through a well-defined application programming interface (API).

- Web application: The typical mode of running a web application is for the user to download a Javascript from a web server. This script runs then locally at the user's system but interacts with the web server for executing the application logic. The web server can instruct the Javascript to conduct certain actions and the script can send feedback information to the web server.

- Web server: The server provides the Javascripts for the users and executes the application logic.

With such a framework a web telephony application would be developed as a Javascript that is provided at a web server, see **Figure** 4. A user wishing to use this application downloads the script. When making a call the Javascript then informs the web server about the call destination and the web server contacts the final destination. Once the callee answers the call the web server forwards the response to a Javascript running at the caller's system. The Javascript now instructs the browser to use the local audio and video devices to exchange audio and video content with the callee.

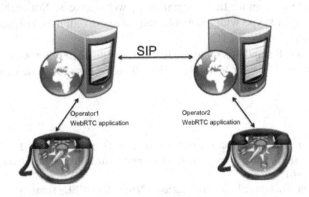

Fig. 5. WebRTC Trapazoid

In order to ensure that the type of applications that can benefit from the integration of real-time services with the browser is only limited by the imagination of the developers, the WebRTC framework is only defining the API to be provided by the browser as well minimal security requirements needed to avoid the misuse of WebRTC applications for initiating denial of service attacks.

In order to avoid the restriction of a centralized model that is used with the Flash technology, the WebRTC framework indicates that a browser can send data to a host other than the one from which the application was downloaded if that host consents to receiving the data.

To enable browsers using different application providers to communicate with each other (e.g. a user logged in to Facebook wants to call someone that is logged in to linkedin) a so called RTC trapezoid, see **Figure** 5, can be used. In this case the two providers use a widely used VoIP signaling protocol in between such as the Session Initiation Protocol [38] to federate between them. However, each of their respective browser-based clients signals to its server using proprietary application protocols built on top of HTTP and Websockets.

WebRTC technology should not be mistaken for yet another telephony service. Dedicated applications and devices based on Skype and SIP will continue to be the preferred way for making phone calls. WebRTC will, however, turn telephony to become one of the many features offered by a web application instead of being a dedicated service.

9   Summary

It is obvious that there is no clear winner in the VoIP arena. While not becoming the next PSTN, H.323 continues to exist, especially in video-oriented installations. SIP dominates the trunking deployments and is the first choice for ISPs and ASPs. Skype uses its proprietary protocols for on-net calls and SIP to reach PSTN, and is reportedly the largest provider of cross-border voice communications [39]. Latest efforts concentrate on a more tied integration of web services. Noticeable examples include integration of skype with facebook, and standardization of VoIP embedded in web browsers known as WebRTC.

The different VoIP standards continue to exist next to each other as well as next to PSTN technology and it is our belief that this will be the case for some time to come.

References

1. http://www.ctia.org/advocacy/research/index.cfm/AID/10323
2. Kleinrock, L.: Information Flow in Large Communication Nets. RLE Quarterly Progress Report (July 1961)
3. Baran, P.: On Distributed Communications Networks. IEEE Trans. Comm. Systems (March 1964)
4. Cohen, D.: Specifications for the Network Voice Protocol (NVP), RFC741(1977)

5. Rabiner, L.R., Schafer, R.W.: Digital Processing of Speech Signals. Prentice-Hall(SignalProcessingSeries) (1978)
6. Postel, J.: Internet Protocol. RFC791 (1981)
7. Crocker, S.: Protocol Notes. RFC 36 (1970)
8. http://www.vocaltec.com
9. International Telecommunication Union. Gateway control protocol: Version 1. ITU-T Recommendation H.248.1 (March 2002)
10. Interestingly, a similar observation could be made during the evolution of SIP in the late 1990s and early 2000s
11. SIP also shared this fate: a flurry of proposals came about just after the initial revision of SIP became RFC in February 1999 and strong arguments were needed to maintain some architectural integrity—only to be given up later with the demand for operator-administered middlebox control
12. H.323 did not adopt presence and instant messaging, though, leaving those to XMPP
13. In the end, quite a few of the specifications published did not matter in the real world because they were not implemented—yielding another similarity to SIP
14. https://datatracker.ietf.org/wg/rtcweb/charter/
15. Schulzrinne, H., Casner, S., Frederick, R., Jacobson, V.: RTP: A Transport Protocol for Real-Time Applications (RFC1889). IETF (1996)
16. Handley, M., van Jacobson: SDP: Session Description Protocol (RFC 2327). IETF (1998)
17. Handley, M., Perkins, C., Whelan, E.: Session Announcement Protocol (RFC2974). IETF (2000)
18. Rosenberg, J., Schulzrinne, H., Camarillo, G., Johnston, A., Peterson, J., Sparks, R., Handley, M., Schooler, E.: SIP: Session Initiation Protocol (RFC 3261). IETF (2002)
19. http://www.ilocus.com/content/report/global-voip-market-2010-11th-annual-update
20. Vemuri, A., Peterson, J.: Session Initiation Protocol for Telephones (SIP-T): Context and Architectures (RFC3372). IETF (2002)
21. Interworking between Session Initiation Protocol (SIP) and bearer independent call control protocol (BICC) or ISDN user part (ISUP). ITU-T Rec. 1912.5 (2004)
22. Ong, L., Garcia, M., Schwarzbauer, H., Coene, L., Lin, H., Juhasz, I., Holdrege, M., Sharp, C.: Framework Architecture for Signaling Transport (RFC2719). IETF (1999)
23. Bearer Independent Call Control Protocol (BICC). ITU-T Rec. 1902 (2003)
24. 3GPP, TSG SSA, IP Multimedia Subsystem (IMS) – Stage 2, TS 23.228
25. 3GPP, TSG SSA, End-to-end quality of sevice (QoS) signaling flows. TS29.208
26. Franks, J., Hostetler, J., Lawrence, S., Leach, P., Luotonen, A., Stewart, L.: HTTP Authentication: Basic and Digest Access Authentication (RFC2617). IETF(1999)
27. Dierks, T., Rescorla, E.: The Transport Layer Security (TLS) Protocol. Version 1.2 (RFC5246). IETF (2008)
28. Sisalem, D., Floroiu, J., Kuthan, J., Abend, U., Schulzrinne, H.: SIP Security (2009)
29. Lescuyer, P., Lucidarme, T.: Evolved Packet System (Eps): The LTE and SAE Evolution of 3G UMTS. Wiley Publishing (2008)
30. Ross, K.W., Liang, J., Kumar, R.: The kazaa overlay: A measurement study. Computer Networks 49, 6 (2005)
31. Ehlert, S., Petgang, S., Magedanz, T.: Analysis and signature of Skype VoIP session traffic. In: 4th IASTED International (2006)
32. http://www.sec.gov/Archives/edgar/data/1498209/0001193125110 56174/ds1a.htm

33. http://download.macromedia.com/pub/labs/flashplayer10/flashp
    layer10_rtmfp_faq_070208.pdf
34. Hickson, I.: HTML5. Web hypertext application technology working group,
    http://whatwg.org/html
35. Web real-time communications working group charter. W3C (December 2010),
    http://www.w3.org/2010/12/webrtc-charter.html
36. RTC-Web IETF working charter proposal (March 2011),
    http://rtcweb.alvestrand.com/ietf-activity
37. Rosenberg, J., et al.: An architectural framework for browser based real-time
    communications. IETF Internet draft. Work in progress (February 2011)
38. Rosenberg, J., et al.: SIP: Session Initiation protocol. IETF RFC 3261 (June 2002)
39. Financial Times, Skype's changing traffic growth (May 10, 2011),
    http://www.ft.com/cms/s/2/e858ad1c-7b1f-11e0-9b06-
    00144feabdc0.html#axzz1uyxE2aNp

NGN Shortcomings

Luc Le Beller[1] and Sébastien Cubaud[2]

[1] France Telecom - Orange Labs, Networks and Carriers,
2 Avenue Pierre Marzin 2307 Lannion Cedex
luc.lebeller@orange.com
[2] France Telecom - Orange France
3 Avenue Francois Château 35000 Rennes
sebastien.cubaud@orange.com

Abstract. Trying to analysis why some standards did not fulfill all the operators and vendors expectations constitutes the objective of this chapter. NGN was supposed to be the network ecosystem for fixed access on which operators will develop services, while IMS was expected as the universal one for mobile and fixed access. Both NGN and IMS have benefit of a huge manpower investment in standardization bodies. A clear understanding of what happened can greatly contribute to better foresee the architecture for the next generations networks ...

1 NGN Deployement

ITU-T defines Next Generation Networks and its fundamental characteristics as follows [1]:

"A packet-based network able to provide telecommunication services and able to make use of multiple broadband, QoS-enabled transport technologies and in which service-related functions are independent from underlying transport-related technologies. It enables unfettered access for users to networks and to competing service providers and/or services of their choice. It supports generalized mobility which will allow consistent and ubiquitous provision of services to users.

The NGN can be further defined by the following fundamental characteristics:

- *packet-based transfer;*
- *separation of control functions among bearer capabilities, call/session, and application/service;*
- *decoupling of service provision from transport, and provision of open interfaces;*
- *support for a wide range of services, applications and mechanisms based on service building blocks (including real time/ streaming/ non-real time and multimedia services);*
- *broadband capabilities with end-to-end QoS (Quality of Service);*
- *interworking with legacy networks via open interfaces;*
- *generalized mobility (see 3.2 and 8.7);*
- *unrestricted access by users to different service providers;*
- *a variety of identification schemes;*
- *unified service characteristics for the same service as perceived by the user;*

E. Bertin et al. (Eds.): Telecommunication Services Evolution, LNCS 7768, pp. 111–117, 2013.

- *converged services between fixed/mobile;*
- *independence of service-related functions from underlying transport technologies;*
- *support of multiple last mile technologies;*
- *compliant with all regulatory requirements, for example concerning emergency communications, security, privacy, lawful interception, etc."*

It is quite difficult to estimate at which level of conformity to NGN do fit deployed networks. Obviously, if we consider the 2000 -2010 decade, almost all deployed networks do comply with more than one feature of the list, but no one comply with all bullets. Packet-based transfer and interworking with legacy networks are common features but what about generalized mobility and converged services between fixed/mobile? Some people might shorten NGN as a triple-play access (Internet, phone and TV) but this feature was already required for the B-ISDN as presented bellow. Here we will start by considering one re-wording of the initial concept of NGN made by one of the most emblematic figure of telco activities during the 2000-2010 decade, Viviane Reding, former European Commissioner for Information Society and Media from 2004 to 2009.

In 2006, Viviane Reding presented NGN as follows :

"Now when we talk about Next Generation Networks we generally mean two things: very fast access networks pointing towards fibre optic very near premises; and – most important – an end to end Internet network."

The stress put on optical fibre is consistent with ITU-T definition: although NGN aims to cover also radio cellular access, it was defined by an SDO focusing on fixed networks as explained in the chapter "NGN Standardization as a Strength". On the opposite, considering NGN as an end to end Internet network is at the opposite of what NGN aimed to be. But the fact is that Viviane Reding definition perfectly fits with fixed networks deployment in the 2000 – 2010 decade. And the question is why such divergence has occurred.

2   One Step Beyond NGN: B-ISDN

NGN is the direct continuation of B-ISDN that was the 1990 – 2000 fixed network standardization model, and most of NGN flaws were already present in the B-ISDN. B-ISDN, as the continuation of the (narrow-band) ISDN, aimed to integrate data and TV/Video services to the phone service on a unique broadband network built on ATM technology. Coming back to Viviane Reding speech and the fibre optic very near premises, one must know that B-ISDN access were initially defined only as a fibre to the home access at a minimum bit rate of 155 Mbit/s. In a second step (late 90's), new access interfaces were standardized at lower bit-rates (51, 21 and 2 Mbit/s) and on metallic wire-line but xdsl technology that was also standardized during the same time had been totally ignored by B-ISDN ITU-T recommendations.

What has been very detrimental for B-ISDN is not related to bit-rate capabilities nor to physical medium characteristics but to the fact that, by reusing the copper infrastructure, xdsl has permitted a very fast deployment of broadband access in the 2000's, much more faster than the other blocks of B-ISDN (QoS, traffic engineering, control plane...). In the early 2000s, the adsl deployment driven by the World Wide Web emergence and the competitive market between operators has created the pre-NGN ecosystem, on which we continue to live. Without adsl technology, optical fiber to the home would have been the legacy broadband access interface and it would have taken many years to deploy it: a timescale much more appropriate to create a better ecosystem for operators, much more close to the B-ISDN principles. In 2012, when the question of fiber to the home is addressed again (and for real this time), this bad timing of the 2000's should be kept in mind.

If B-ISDN ignored xdsl technology, the opposite was not true : the inherent packet technology of xdsl was ATM, and the deployment of xdsl contributed to the deployment of an national wide ATM backbone network. This packet based transfer network was expected to be the cornerstone for the NGN deployments and did in fact permit to offer multi-play on adsl.

3   Pre-NGN towards Some NGN

Around 2004, some European operators started to offer multi-play on adsl: in addition to the Intenet access, the customer could benefit of IPTV services (live TV channels and VoD) and VoIP (a second phone line). What is meant here by IPTV and VoIP is services bundled within a given operator access offer on adsl; IPTV and VoIP line are commonly referred to managed services, by opposition to Internet best effort services that can also include TV/VoD and voice services. Were those evolutions towards IPTV and VOIP compliant with NGN principles?

Chapter XX "A Short History of VoIP services" describes in details the two main protocols that have been deployed by networks operators for VoIP services: first H.323 and in a second time SIP/IMS. As stated in this chapter H.323 (which has often been the first VoIP operator implementation) was coming from a telecom background (ISDN and B-ISDN) and fitted well with NGN fundamental requirements: the separation of control functions among bearer capabilities, call/session, and application/service, or the interworking with legacy networks via open interfaces.

IPTV architecture has almost nothing to do with NGN principles, except the packet-based transfer capabilities. For instance control functions on network resources which is a key feature on all NGN services is almost fully missing in IPTV architectures: the services (live channels or VoD) can be activated without dynamic end-to-end bandwidth reservation. If interworking with legacy networks has a meaning for IPTV, one could say that it was done trough multi-access capabilities of the terminal (i.e. some STB could also be connected to DVB-T or DVB-S antennas for live channels).

One of the most important consequence of IPTV services on some operator network architecture was the progressive replacement of ATM by IP in the backhaul (for reasons of cost and for the multicast capabilities of IP). It thus created an end to end IP network for almost all services available on adsl, with on one hand managed services (IPTV and VoIP) and on the other hand the Internet channel with OTT services. And in fact since the middle of the 2000s the most attractive for customers was the Internet channel rather than the managed services, no operator could have sold adsl access with only managed services and no Internet channel: maybe this is why Viviane Reding only retained "end to end Interne network" as the most important feature of the NGN...

So one could expect that the mandatory coexistence of managed services and OTT services on a single adsl access would have been the starting point to further consider network architecture evolutions, and how network operators could combine both possibilities to extend their business activities. But in fact in the second half of the 2000's operator strategy in standardization mainly focused on managed services and how to unify through the IMS architecture all possible managed services, without paying attention to what could exist in the Internet channel because the best effort mode was never expected to reach the required operator QoS ... but in fact it did reach customer QoS expectations !

4   Post NGN: IMS

As stated in chapter XX "A Short History of VoIP services", IMS was first defined by 3GPP for mobile networks and for various services, then endorsed by TISPAN for both fixed and mobile networks, and still more services. At that time (mid 2000s), mobile operators control on their business activities was much better than fixed operators control on their business activities: mobile phones were used almost exclusively for operator managed services (phone calls, SMS, TV/VoD, ...), the Internet channel was not present on cellular networks or of very bad quality ; only devices with a WiFi interface could browse on the Web. It was an opportune context to try to impose IMS for all services on wireless access but already too late on wireline access as explained before.

In fact the very fast development of VoIP services on adsl access in the second hald of the 2000s have lead to the first IMS or IMS like implementations with SIP VoIP. But the extension to other services like IPTV failed and today it seems recognized that IMS will not cover more than conversional services on fixed and mobile access. The main reasons for such drawback find their roots in technical shortcomings, in the IMS deployment model, the IMS cost structure, and in the current standardization processes

4.1   Technical Shortcomings

Firstly, **architecture-wise**, the IMS has chosen to adopt the traditional architectural methodology used in the PSTN consisting in starting from the service requirements, and then defining the functional entities, the procedures for data exchange between those entities and finally the protocols to allow these exchanges. This approach presents the major drawback that the non-functional properties of the architecture (e.g. availability, security, extensibility, scalability) – very dependent of the protocols choice- are seen of secondary importance. This creates constraints on the organic elements which are forced to provide these functionalities: for instance, to embed a master/slave mechanism to enhance availability. This explains why when two service require different availability levels, the platforms used may not be the same; as in the case of a low-cost free residential service and a business mobile telephony service (e.g. for MIPC and RCS). In addition, the IMS has also chosen to define non-atomic generic stateful functional entities, forcing them to get crossed for the duration of the service when only a subset of these functional blocks are needed to offer a service whilst forcing them to evolve when potentially required by various services[1]. Finally, the IMS has taken the original assumption that different roles would be handled by the same operator: access transport network provider, core network transport provider, core service provider. This assumption creates rigidity to create new business opportunities, should these roles be separated.

Secondly, **protocol-wise**, unfortunately, the aforementioned choice of protocols (e.g. SIP, Diameter) hampered a few non-functional properties of the IMS architecture, even if multiple evolutions of those protocols have been done to enhance them. Beyond the protocol complexity that it created – having consequences on the operational cost (e.g. end to end interoperability testing) – the most impacted remaining non-functional property is certainly extensibility. This is partly due to the SIP entities acting as both client and server, creating grips between the evolution of the devices and of the core infrastructure. This is also partly due to the unclear separation between service-related information and protocol standardized elements within SIP, Diameter or H.248 messages. This is also partly due to the lack of graphical rendering framework in SIP, thus preventing service provider from having a complete control on the graphical representation of its service on the various devices. This latter lack creates for instance constraints on the ability to manage an unified branding for a service in heterogeneous devices (in particular when a user can use multiple devices to get this service).

These reasons affect directly the ability of the IMS to pursue the following strategies in regard to direct revenues: reduce OPEX, extend the footprint of existing services, and develop attractive services.

4.2   Deployment Model

The IMS deployment model followed by operators consist in buying solutions from vendors in a complete dependence: while standards propose more and more technical options due to the required trade-offs of parties with different interests, **operators are tied and bound** with customized, potentially non-interoperable vendor solutions. This dependence is particularly present in a context when operators try to differentiate between themselves, when they inherit from legacy networks and when standards have to take a few years before stabilizing. Within Orange, this dependence has even shaped the organizational structure (e.g. the vendor-specific Skill Centers, vendor-specific testers ...).

---

[1] For instance the S-CSCF function embedding among others registration, security filtering and route forwarding functions, will be crossed at the registration phase, for inbound service session as well as outbound service session, and should a crash occurs, all these phases will be impacted.

While providing many advantages (e.g. industrial products, externalization of development risks ...), this dependence has multiple adversarial consequences: firstly, the costs – either CAPEX or OPEX depending on vendors' strategies- of the platforms are important, secondly, features evolution has to get integrated in the vendors' roadmap – not necessarily compliant with expected services or market demand -. It affects then the ability of the IMS to pursue the following strategies in regard to direct revenues: reduce costs and develop attractive services while in regard to indirect revenues limits the ability to provide differentiated services to subscribers.

4.3   Cost Structure

Concerning the IMS cost structure, the **huge initial investments** needed on each IMS platform (CAPEX and even more OPEX) as well as the licensing policy of IMS vendors (per user costs) prevent a quick amortization. This is an issue to compete on a more and more cost-driven market, especially for services whose success as well as business model are not stabilized.

4.4   Standardization Process

Finally, the current services standardization processes require **time** – in the order of magnitude of years - and **consensus** within the ecosystem, relying on complete alignment of the different actors, which was certainly not a problem in the early days of GSM, but maybe not accurate today with the empowerment of different types of actors. This affects the ability of the IMS to pursue the following strategies in regard to direct revenues: develop attractive services.

These four reasons explain why the IMS requires a complete control of the ecosystem (user device, service provider, service developer, network providers) and why it makes it not ideal within the current heterogeneous ecosystem of the conversational services.

Still, the IMS is today the most accomplished technical solution to provide enhanced telephony services over IP and present **at short-term** the undeniable **advantage** to permit coexistence with circuit-switched technology to offer these services as well as to allow a fine-grained control of the network usage. This permits the IMS to pursue the following strategies in regard to indirect revenues: provide a sufficiently differentiating quality/price ratio on access networks (i.e. while no broadband IP technologies have sufficient mobile access coverage).

5   Conclusion

Whatever the network architecture achievements compared to the initial expectations, we must be able to derive from the gap the inputs to build next generation networks. It is very surprising that for instance on the topic of fixed mobile network convergence, many people still think, that as initially stated by 3GPP:

- WiFi constitutes a secondary access to operator mobile services in comparison to the primary one, radio cellular access,
- Wifi access must be enhanced to reach the same level of functionalities (identification, accounting, QoS, mobility, ...) than what is existing on cellular networks.

We think that the opposite is much more appropriate to consider at first fixed mobile network convergence:

- WiFi constitutes the primary access for Internet based services on personal devices, 4G radio cellular access will constitute a secondary access,
- 4G radio cellular networks functionalities must be adapted to the level of fixed access.

In other words for Internet based services on personal devices, in geographical areas where WiFi is abundant, it could rather decrease the value of mobile operator access rather that enhancing it.

When we consider today what will be the future networks architecture in 5 – 10 years, the most noticeable thing is that we do not have any longer models (big pictures) like we had in the past with B-ISDN,NGN and IMS. As stated in different chapters of this book, in the end-to-end value chain of telecommunication, network operator represent now just one segment, with variable extensions on contiguous segments (content services, devices, IT capabilities, M2M, ...). It seem unlikely that a new network architectural model could accommodate with all the variable network operator profiles that will exist in the future. This should not be considered as a threat but as the new starting point for a very challenging and exciting project for network architect.

References

1. ITU-T recommendation Y.2001 General overview of NGN (December 2004)
2. Conecting up the Global Village: a European view on Telecommunications Policy ITU-T ConferenceTelecom World 2006, Hong Kong (December 2006)

An IT Perspective on Standards, Service Architectures and Platforms

John O'Connell

Hewlett-Packard, Grenoble, France
john.oconnell@hp.com

Abstract. Telecom services and internet services have traditionally been deployed using very different service architectures, conforming to different sets of industry standards. With the evolution of the network infrastructure to NGN and with the migration of both IT and telecom services to the cloud, there is an increasing harmonization of service architectures and an increasing adoption of IT technology within telecom environments. In this chapter, we describe how standardization activities in the IT industry have helped to transform the internet into a global service infrastructure and how a combination of standard technologies, open APIs and common platforms has helped to drive the growth of web services. We also highlight some of the emerging standards and platforms that are shaping the mobile application and cloud computing spaces.

1   Introduction

The convergence of IT and telecoms has been a major topic within the communications industry over the past decade. With the roll-out of packet-based Next Generation Networks (NGN), as described in the previous chapter, that convergence has now become a reality and it is impacting all layers of the network. The latest generation of smart phones and tablet computers are designed for both communication services and data services, a common network backbone transports both voice traffic and data traffic, telecom applications which previously ran over dedicated telecom protocols are migrating to IP, and with the evolution to cloud services, the boundary between telecom service providers and data service providers is disappearing. Indeed, with the emergence of Twitter, Facebook, YouTube and other social networking and content sharing services, it is no longer meaningful to classify services as either communication services or data services.

The software stack that will be used to deliver a diverse range of services over this converged infrastructure is taking shape and it will be quite different from the traditional telecom software stack for a number of reasons:

- Users expect ubiquitous access to services, from any device, via any access network. Mobility must be enabled by default, as devices become network agnostic, capable of connecting to any available wireline or wireless network. This is a significant shift away from yesterday's model where mobile services were designed for and deployed on dedicated mobile-enabled infrastructure.

E. Bertin et al. (Eds.): Telecommunication Services Evolution, LNCS 7768, pp. 118–137, 2013.
© Springer-Verlag Berlin Heidelberg 2013

- The demand for ubiquitous access is accelerating the separation of the service layer from the network layer. While services can still take advantage of network capabilities such as messaging, location, device information and billing services, the services must be designed to run over any network, using open network interfaces, irrespective of whether those services are operated by the telecom service provider or provided by over-the-top (OTT) players.
- While some core services will continue to be deployed within the control layer of the network, the migration of both IT services and telecom services to the cloud is driving more IT and internet technology into the service software stack. Economy of scale gives those IT/internet technologies a competitive advantage over equivalent telecom-specific service platforms or telecom-specific software stacks.
- Smart phones and tablet computers are bridging the gap between mobile phones and personal computers. These devices are also being more widely adopted in the enterprise environment, as "bring your own device" (BYOD) becomes the norm. These powerful personal devices provide rich client environments, with the result that some application functionality is moving out of the network, from the server side to the client side.

As IT/internet standards and technologies become more widely adopted in the telecom services space, it is important to understand the role that standardization has played in shaping the internet and in harmonizing the architecture of web services[1]. Those web services have been able to take advantage of the global reach of the internet and of the availability of open platforms and standard browser features on the device. We also need to recognize the important role that open APIs and open platforms have played in shaping the IT industry. As we will see in this chapter, standardization is just one of the approaches used by IT industry players to drive adoption of their technology.

2   IT Standards Landscape

There can be no doubt that standards are important in the IT industry, and that standards have played a major role in driving the growth of both IT technology and the internet on a global scale. Just think about the many standards that we use when performing everyday tasks with our computer or on the internet – from using WiFi to connect to the internet, using USB to attach external devices such as printers and storage devices to the PC, using HTTPS to make secure credit card payments over the web, and downloading HTML or MPEG content when browsing the web. Indeed, the history of those different standards illustrates very well the different ways in which standards are defined and adopted in the IT industry.

---

[1] We use the term "web service" to refer to any service that is delivered over the internet irrespective of whether it is accessed from a web browser or from a native application on the device, since many services now offer both browser-based interfaces and native applications for smart phones and tablet PCs.

The original version of Wifi was developed over 20 years ago by NCR corporation/AT&T for wireless cash registers [1]. In 1999, IEEE released the 802.11a and 802.11b standards. Today, Wifi implies compliance with the IEEE 802.11 family of protocols as defined by the IEEE Wireless LAN working group [2], while an industry consortium, the WiFi Alliance [3], owns the Wifi trademark and is responsible for promoting the technology.

Over the past decade, the Universal Serial Bus (USB) has replaced the multitude of interfaces that had previously been used to connect different types of peripheral devices to a computer. USB 1.0 was published in 1996 [4] and was the result of a joint specification work by Compaq, DEC, IBM, Intel, Microsoft, NEC and Nortel. The USB 2.0 specification brought higher data transfer rates and it was the result of a joint initiative by Hewlett-Packard, Intel, Lucent Technologies, NEC and Philips, before being ratified by the USB Implementers Forum [5] in 2001. The family of USB standards has since been expanded to include mini-USB and micro-USB to support smaller form factors.

Netscape Communications created HTTPS in 1994 for its Netscape Navigator [6], to enable secure data exchange between a browser and a web service. The current version of HTTPS was formally published by the IETF as RFC 2818 in 2000 [7].

The Hyper-Text Markup Language (HTML) was created by the W3C [8] and published as an IETF RFC [8] before being ratified as an international standard by ISO/IEC Joint Technical Committee (JTC-1). The MPEG standard for encoding moving pictures and audio was the result of a joint industry initiative [10] and it is also now recognized as an ISO/IEC standard.

2.1   IT Standards Bodies

Given the diversity of IT standards, it is not surprising that the IT standardization landscape is quite fragmented, made up of many formal standard bodies and industry consortia. For example, no one standards organization is responsible for all internet standards and there is no overarching reference architecture for the internet that could be considered equivalent to, say, the GSM, LTE or IMS standards in the telecom world. However the combined efforts of groups such as IEEE, IETF, W3C and ISO/IEC have resulted in a set of core protocols, languages and APIs that bind everything together. Some of those organizations' standards have been defined through a structured standard defintion process while in other cases, as highlighted in the previous section, these organizations have adopted and ratified the results of vendor-led industry consortia.

The International Standards Organization (ISO) [11] was founded in 1926 as a network of national standards bodies, such as the American National Standards Institute (ANSI), British Standards Institute (BSI) and National Standards Authority of Ireland (NSAI). With 163 member organizations, ISO has a very broad scope and publishes standards in many areas, but through its joint work with IEC, all international IT standards are managed by the ISO/IEC JTC-1 sub-committee [12].

The Institute of Electrical and Electronic Engineers (IEEE) Standards Association [13] is responsible for over 900 active standards, covering all engineering disciplines.

Key standards in the computer networking area include the Ethernet and 802.11 (80 series), reflecting the IEEE's strong focus on networking and network-level interoperability.

The Internet Engineering Task Force (IETF) [14] was established in 1986, with the mission to make the internet work better. Since then, it has published more than 6000 RFCs and has approved more than 70 Internet Standards, including many that specify the basic internet protocols and services, such as DHCP, TCP, FTP, SMTP and HTTP. Unlike formal standards organizations, the IETF has adopted a very open structure, with no formal membership, no membership fees, and very clear rules on copyright and patents which help to avoid IP issues. The low entry cost is attractive for innovators and innovative startups, which in turn has helped to create a very diverse set of standards, with ad-hoc groups collaborating on topics of common interest.

The World Wide Web Consortium (W3C) [15] was founded by Tim Berners-Lee in 1994, and it has since emerged as one of the key organizations that has shaped the web as a global platform for publishing digital content and exchanging information. By focusing more on languages rather than protocols, such as the XML family of languages, the work of the W3C has facilitated the easy exchange of information both between user devices and web services and between web services.

Other important IT standards organizations include OASIS and ECMA. OASIS [16] is responsible for a set of standards for web service discovery (UDDI), publication (WSDL) and interaction (SOAP). ECMA [17] was originally established as the European computer manufacturing association, but it is now open to all. It recently celebrated its 50th anniversary, it has worked with ISO/IEC to define a fast track approach, and it has ratified standards such as NFC (ECMA-340, ISO/IEC-18092), ECMAScript (which is the basis for JavaScript) and the Office OpenXML formats.

The work of these various IT industry standardization bodies has helped enormously to harmonize and commoditize IT technology on a global scale. There is strong recognition within the computer industry of the importance of having global standards and of the economic benefits that have resulted from the globalization of the digital economy. IT is now widely recognized as a source of economic growth, and the globalization of IT, through standardization, is an important driver for that growth.

2.2 The Importance of IT Standards for Telecom Services

With the convergence of IT and telecoms, the standards that dominate the IT/internet landscape have become more relevant for telecom networks and telecom services. In the past, many telecom services were developed on top of industry-specific software stacks and deployed on carrier-grade telecom platforms, which in turn were designed to operate in NEBS-compliant central offices. As IT and telecoms converge, the next-generation of service platforms will leverage more IT technology. Users now expect to be able to access services and to consume content on a wide range of personal devices, irrespective of whether those devices come from the telecom, IT or consumer electronics industries. To meet that goal, the interaction between client applications and network services should be based, when possible, on SOAP, REST and other standard client-server technologies, while content should be defined using standard formats such as HTML, MPEG and JavaScript. As the industry moves to a converged infrastructure, all services, including communication services, are expected to run on a common data network, with IP at the core. At the service layer, the protocols, languages and APIs from the IT/internet industry cannot be ignored as services migrate to the standard client-server reference architecture. The mobile application revolution implies that a more IT-like software stack will be used on the client device, with support for standard data formats, scripting languages and web browser functionality. Exceptions and telecom-specific extensions may continue to exist to handle smaller form factors, real-time requirements and interworking with legacy systems. But the trend will be to adopt more rather than less IT and internet technology within the telecom service provider's environment.

3   The Internet as a Global Service Platform

One of the primary reasons for the phenomenal growth of web services is the global reach of the internet. Originally a collection of interworking networks, based on different networking technologies, the widespread adoption of IP and other IEEE and IETF standards has helped to harmonize the network infrastructure and to create a global network with end-to-end connectivity. Many of the popular web services that people use on the internet would not have grown as quickly, nor on such a global scale, without standards such as IP, DNS, HTTP, HTML, UDDI and WDSL.

The result is that the internet and associated web standards have become the default global platform on top of which companies can easily role out innovative services. While each individual web service is designed for a specific purpose, often with its own proprietary architecture and interfaces, all web services benefit from a common underlying set of internet standards and web service standards. The combination of standard protocols, standard services and standard content formats has created an extremely powerful foundation which can be leveraged by all web services.

The internet has fuelled innovation by creating a global network with end-to-end connectivity. Standards have helped to resolve many of the client-server interoperability issues, and this in turn has lowered the entry barrier for companies who want to roll out new services on a global scale. Web services are by default global services. Services such as Facebook, Twitter and Skype are available from any internet-connected browser, and that same global characteristic applies to any web-site such as personal web pages, e-commerce sites and company web-sites. Any web-site with an internet domain name can be reached from anywhere in the world, except in cases where local regulation may prevent access.

The internet is global, not regional or country-based. Even if Internet Service Providers (ISP) are regional or country-based, there is a common set of core network services, such as DNS and DHCP, that is provided by all ISPs. This is a critical enabler for ubiquitous access to services. In contrast, this has not always been true for telecom networks where the set of services that is available to a user depends on the network that they are connected to. Certain telecom services are only available on the local network. Examples include short-dial services, premium-rate SMS services, and free-phone and premium rate voice services. As a result, for example, in order for a new enhanced voice service to be available on every network, each telecom operator was required to deploy its own instance of that service and to ensure interoperability with peer services in adjacent telecom networks. Fig. 1 below highlights the different relationships that exist between clients, servers and the network layer for both internet services and telecom services.

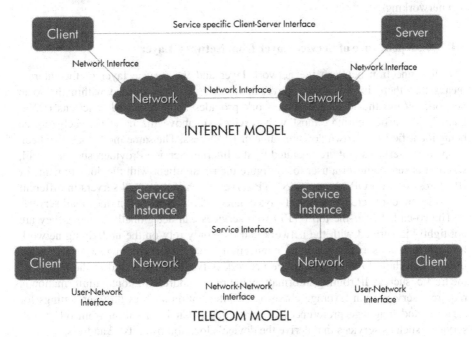

Fig. 1. Comparison of Internet and Telecom Service Models

With the internet model, the service is typically depicted as being deployed on a single server, accessible from clients that may be distributed across multiple access networks. The interface from the client to the network is open and standardized, while the interface between the client and server will often be service specific, even if based on standard protocols, as we will describe later. With the telecom model, the service is typically implemented as a set of interworking services, with an instance of the service deployed in each network. A user-to-network interface specifies how a client interacts with the network and with services running in the network, while the network-to-network interface ensures end-to-end connectivity and interworking between peer networks. The network also exposes an interface to the service layer, both to invoke services in response to client requests and to enable communication between service instances. Although the differences between the two models may seem trivial or academic, there are some unique and powerful characteristics of the internet service model that are worth highlighting:

- In the internet model, the service layer is independent from the network layer
- Each web service is accessible from any access network, with the possibility to deploy multiple instances of a given service at different locations, if required
- The part of the service logic that runs on the client side can take advantage of open platforms, and in particular standard browser features, on the device
- The implementation of each web service is unique and specific to that service, although most web services have adopted similar software reference architectures
- Web services interfaces provide a common methodology for web service interworking.

3.1   Independence of Service Layer from Network Layer

The disconnection between the network layer and the service layer of the internet means that there is no need to have an instance of each service within the local network. While the local access network provides some standard functions (DNS, DHCP, IP traffic routing), most web services sit above the network, each service being identified by its own domain name or IP address. The same model has also been adopted for services that are operated by the Internet Service Provider, such as email, where it is sufficient for a user to configure their mail client with the domain name or IP address of the POP server and SMTP server. Even if the email servers in different networks are connected, the user always connects directly to their home email server.

The so-called over-the-top (OTT) web services can act globally because they are not tightly integrated with the network and they only rely on the underlying network for some basic services such as connectivity and traffic routing services. What information they do require from the network is typically delivered in the header of the traffic, such as IP routing information and return address. If context information is required, services can leverage client-based information such as browser settings for regional and language preferences or can request that information from other web services, such as services that derive the device's location from its IP address.

3.2   Service Accessibility from any Access Network

In the internet model, all traffic for a given web service is routed to an instance of that service, and in the simplest case, there may only be a single instance of the service serving all users from across the globe. In the past, this model was considered an obstacle for the roll out of real-time services over the internet, such as VoIP services and other communication services, because of concerns with respect to latency. However, with higher network bandwidth and the reduction in round-trip times, this model is also now being adopted even for real-time services. Hybrid approaches are possible where multiple instances of a service are distributed across the internet if there are technical reasons to deploy the service close to the end-user. In that case, user traffic can be directed to the closest regional server. If those multiple service instances need to communicate with each other, for example in the case of content distribution networks, then dedicated overlay networks can be deployed to avoid overloading the core network.

This model for ubiquitous access has not stopped services from offering regional or language-specific variants. Services such as Facebook and Skype have their own regional variants, or at least, language-specific variants. For example, connecting to http://www.facebook.fr provides access to the french language version of Facebook. Each language-specific or region-specific variant is itself available globally and all variants are provided by a single service provider. While the service will typically direct the user traffic to a given variant based on the regional and language settings of their browser, all well-designed services will provide the ability for the user to switch to a different variant and to select their own default variant.

While the internet has been designed to enable ubiquitous access, the industry has not seen the emergence of roaming agreement between ISPs, equivalent to the roaming agreements that exist between mobile operators. One side-effect of this is that users can choose to connect to any available network, since the right to connect does not need the approval of their home operator, and users are not subject to home operator's roaming fees. On the other hand, connectivity when roaming is not automatic. While the computer can automatically detect all available local access networks and can attempt to establish an internet connection, the user will typically need to register and to pay access fees to the local ISP or access network operator before internet access is granted. Despite those limitations, this model supports the ability to connect anytime and anywhere, as long as the user is willing to pay local access fees.

3.3   The Browser as a Common Platform

The availability of common platforms on the device has also facilitated the development of global internet services. The emergence of the browser as an open platform on client devices has contributed greatly to the growth of rich web applications. Prior to the browser, each service came with its own client application which had to be downloaded and managed on the device, and client applications that wanted to run on different hardware platforms had to be aware of the different host operating systems.

While there had been some attempts, with varying degrees of success, within the industry to define common APIs across different operating systems, it has been the browser which has greatly simplified the development and deployment of client application logic, particularly with its plug-in model. While there is no standard specification for a browser, there is enough commonality across the different browsers on the market that the browser has become the de facto platform for client applications. Common features supported by all browsers include cookies, history, plug-ins, rendering of standard content types, automatic launching of local applications, regional and language preferences, local time/date, etc. As a result, those functions do not need to be redeveloped for each application. Some application developers still choose to develop and deploy native client applications, but users increasingly expect to be able to access and use applications from a browser, even if native applications may offer richer functionality.

3.4   Silo Web Services

Services such as Skype, Twitter and Facebook are phenomenally successful despite not being standardized. While they have all taken advantage of the internet and browser as common platforms, each service has adopted its own proprietary architecture. However this lack of standardization of the service definition has not hindered their growth. They have benefitted from a network effect to grow their business where millions of users see value in registering with and communicating via those services. As the number of users grows, so does the value of the service and so too does its attractiveness as a platform for 3rd party applications and advertisers. In the case of social networking services, the value of a service is deemed to grow exponentially with the number of users. The fact that the service definitions are not standardized and that each service is a silo has clearly not hindered their popularity.

This silo model has helped to stimulate innovation in a rapidly-growing space where services are competing for users' attention and for advertisers' revenue. Each service can be developed and managed as a standalone entity, and the service developers do not need to get the approval of a standards body before adding new features and rolling out new versions of the service. As with any software development activity, the service developers must always ensure backward compatibility on features and external interfaces when they deploy new versions and must ensure compatibility with the latest devices and browser versions. However they do not need to reach agreement on the specifications of new functionality and features with competitors or with other companies offering similar services.

It must also be recognized that not all internet services are successful or have become as popular and global as Facebook, Twitter and Skype. The brief history of the interest has also been marked by web services that have grown rapidly in terms of number of registered users, only to fade again just as quickly. Reasons for that stalled growth are various – lack of a sustainable business model, competition from disruptive or more innovative competitors, inability to compete or to attract partners in a highly competitive space, or non respect for copyright laws in the case of illegal file sharing services. In some cases, the lack of standards can also be cited as one of the reasons for the failure. The lack of interoperability and the lack of an agreed interworking standard between Instance Messaging systems hindered the growth of that market, in the absence of a dominant player who could impose a de facto standard. A similar pattern appeared in the VoIP space which also quickly became a very fragmented space, with no dominant player. This resulted in a high cost in terms of interoperability as interworking was addressed in a case-by-case basis. By the time that VoIP interworking standards did emerge, Skype had become the dominant player, despite its proprietary technology, thanks to its disruptive and innovative approach compared to earlier players in the VoIP space.

3.5   Software Reference Architecture for Web Services

Although each web service is unique, most web services have adopted very similar software architectures. As shown in Fig. 2 below, the high-level architecture of most web services is made up of these 3 components:

1. Some application logic runs on the client or device side. This client-based application logic may be implemented as a standalone application that is downloaded and installed natively on the device or it may run as a browser-based application. In the latter case, the application logic may be a thin client that just manages the user interface or presentation layer of the application. Alternatively, the application logic may be a thick client that also includes some processing logic which is implemented as a browser plug-in.

2. The core of the application logic or business logic runs on the server side, where the 3-tier software architecture is very common. The 3 tiers are comprised of a front-end web server, an application server in the middle tier, and a back-end database layer. The web server is responsible for handling incoming web requests, load balancing traffic across multiple application servers or routing traffic to the correct application server instance. The application server hosts the server-based application logic.

3. The exchange of information between the client-based application logic and the server-side of the application is based on one or more IP-based standard protocols, such as HTTP, SOAP or REST, and standard content formats, such as MPEG, HTML, CSS, Flash, JavaScript, etc.

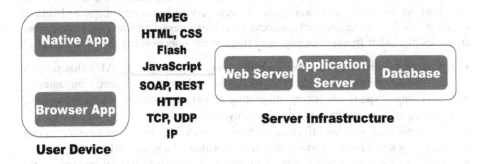

Typical Client-Server Architecture for Internet Services

Fig. 2. Web Service Reference Architecture

This standard client-server architecture puts more emphasis on portability and openness, than on interoperability. At the application layer, the primary concern of the application developer is to ensure portability of the client application logic across a wide range of devices. The application developer does not need to be concerned with the interface between the physical device and the network – rather, it is sufficient for the application developer either to provide a browser plug-in or to provide a native application that can execute on a wide range of devices.

For the interaction between the client-based and server-based parts of the application, each service can define its own set of web service APIs or REST APIs, and can exchange data that is defined using a standard data format, typically defined in XML. By defining an open and stable set of APIs on the server side, with backward compatibility across versions, new client applications can be developed and deployed easily. A single server instance can support multiple variants of the client applications, where each variant of the client application can be targeted at a different type of user or optimized for a different type of usage.

3.6   Web Service Interworking

Although each web service can be viewed as a silo, it is becoming increasingly common for services to interact with each other and it is now relatively easy to re-use existing services to create more complex services. This is largely thanks to industry standard web service technologies such as SOAP and REST which allow any service to publish and expose open APIs, to XML which can be used to define standard data exchange formats, and to JavaScript which can be used to define application logic that is executed by the calling web service.

In the simplest case, the interaction between two services requires one service to invoke the web service API that is exposed by the other service. In the more general case, any service can publish a web service API so that it becomes a building block or enabler for other services, subject to acceptance of the terms and conditions defined by the service owner. One very familiar example of this approach is the Google Maps API [18] which allows any web page or web service to embed maps and related location-based information, such as local places of interest and driving instructions, from Google. Other frequent examples of this service interworking model include:

- Embedding online payment in e-commerce sites by integrating APIs that provide access to payment services provided by PayPal and major credit card companies
- Embedding 3rd-party adverts by integrating APIs that connect to online advertising networks and that retrieve and display relevant adverts
- Displaying local weather information that is provided by a national weather service
- Displaying stock price information that is provided by a stock trading company
- Displaying user-generated feedback on hotels and tourist sites by integrating the TripAdvisor API [19]
- Embedding widgets or plug-ins from popular social networking services such as Facebook and Twitter. In those cases, the plug-ins expose instantly recognizable icons, and users who click on those icons are connected directly to their Facebook or Twitter accounts.

By exposing open APIs for application developers, an individual web service can itself become an application platform. Facebook is a primary example of how a social networking service can become a platform on top of which 3rd party software developers can add value. Via the Facebook Platform API [20], 3rd party developers can build applications that are tightly integrated with Facebook, both leveraging services that are provided by Facebook and allowing users to invoke those 3rd party applications from within the Facebook environment. As social networking services become application platforms, this raises the question of standardization of those APIs. While many social networking APIs remain proprietary, there have been attempts in the industry to categorize services and to define common service features. The OpenSocial API [21] is one example from the social networking area.

3.7   Comparison with the Telecom Service Model

When deploying a web service and growing it to operate on a global scale, the provider of that service must deal with many of the same issues as telecom services providers, such as scalability, end-to-end connectivity, interoperability across a range of devices and client environments, interworking with other services, etc. However, the deployment model for internet services means that those issues have been addressed differently. The successful internet services have benefitted from the internet as a global network, with limited dependency on the underlying network and with global standards that ensure ubiquitous access and end-to-end connectivity. They have also benefitted massively from the emergence of the browser as a common platform. The low entry barrier means that the internet can act as a test-bed where new services and new service features can be rolled out and tested quickly, before being designed and deployed for massive scalability.

Compared to the deployment model for telecom services, there are some notable differences. Although there are global telecom standards, the telecom network is structured as a set of interworking networks, rather than as global network. There is a strong dependence on the local network, implying that global reach may only occur for a given service once all service providers support that service. Furthermore, although the interface between the phone and the telecom network has been standardized, via the user-to-network interface, this has not fully addressed all of the challenges with device interoperability due to the lack of a single widely-adopted client environment on the phone. This lack of a single industry standard or dominant industry player has resulted, for example, in a very fragmented landscape for mobile client environments. Service interworking has also been a challenge for the telecom industry. While the definition of many telecom services has been standardized, service interworking has often been dealt with on a case-by-case basis and there is no industry-wide framework or methodology for combining telecom services.

4   The Importance of Common Software Platforms

In the previous sections, we have made a number of references to the importance of open platforms in shaping the web services landscape. Indeed, it is important to recognize that while industry standards have played a key role in globalizing the IT industry, some of the major evolutions in the industry have also been due to the adoption of common platforms. The widespread adoption by application developers of software platform such as Windows, Linux and Java have helped to harmonize the lower layers of the software stack, where these platform technologies have become de facto standards, offering a rich set of functionality that has helped to spawn new generations of applications.

The most successful platform technologies have leveraged an open approach, enabling an ecosystem of partners, typically Independent Software Vendors (ISVs), who create additional value by developing applications on top of those platforms. Being open does not necessarily mean being standard. The platform interfaces may still be proprietary where the API definition is controlled by one vendor. Openness does imply though that the platform interfaces are public, in that the definitions of the interfaces are clearly documented and have been published. Furthermore, all successful platform providers have understood the importance of providing backward compatibility of their interfaces when introducing new versions. As well as openness and backward compatibility, other important aspects of a successful platform strategy include:

1. Establish a broad ecosystem: Make the platform attractive to a large community of developers by offering a rich set of APIs, with SDKs and other developer support tools. Do not optimize the platform, or restrict the platform API, for a single category of application.
2. Provide portability across hardware systems: Ensure that the software platform is available on a wide range of hardware systems from multiple vendors. If a software platform is only available on a single hardware system or on hardware systems from a single vendor, this increases the perception of vendor lock-in.
3. Adopt multi-vendor APIs: Supporting the same APIs as your competitor is not a problem as long as you can compete on the implementation features. Common APIs across multiple vendors' platforms allows applications to be more easily ported across platforms, increasing the number of applications that are available on each platform.
4. Create a balanced ecosystem: In order to grow a successful ecosystem of ISVs and application developers, the platform technology must also allow each partner to create their own value on top of that platform. In a balanced ecosystem, each participant in the ecosystem needs to be able to create value and generate revenue.

One simple way of measuring the success of any platform technology is by the number of instances of the platform that have been deployed. However, software platforms are also meant to be general purpose, not dedicated to one application or class of application. For that reason, a more meaningful measure of the success of a software platform is the number of ISVs or application developers that have adopted the platform. Indeed, for an enterprise customer who is purchasing a software platform, the value of a platform is often directly related to the number of ISVs who use the platform. Enterprise customers are more likely to purchase the platform and to train their staff on the platform if they see that the platform can be used for many different purposes and if they see that there is a large community of ISVs who have expertise in using the platform. While vendor lock-in is always a concern with non-standard platforms, the fact that a platform can be re-used for multiple purposes can minimize the risk associated with a platform investment.

There is also an important network effect within ecosystems. As the number of ISV partners grows, and as the number of applications that are available on the platform grows, opportunities emerge to create new solutions that leverage or extend existing applications. ISVs within the ecosystem can work together to leverage each other's applications, and it becomes possible to create new solutions that simply integrate and bundle existing application. Because of this network effect, the business value of a platform can grow exponentially with the number of ISVs or applications that use the platform.

One implication of this network effect is that a software platform with no applications and no ISV partners is of limited value and can be difficult to sell. As a result, for vendors of software platforms, it is more important, at least initially, to establish a broad ecosystem of application partners and to make their platform available on a wide range of hardware systems, rather than to get the platform specification approved by an industry standards body. This does not mean that platform vendors can completely ignore the standardization process because, conversely, application developers are more likely to be attracted by platforms where the API definition is not controlled by a single vendor or where the same platform API is supported by multiple vendors.

In order to address this dilemma, some platform vendors have adopted an open source approach, and there are many examples within the IT industry where open source platform technology, such as JBOSS, MySQL and Linux, has become widely adopted and has been able to compete successfully for market share with equivalent commercial offerings.

The open source approach relies on a community of interested parties collaborating to define, maintain and enhance a common platform or technology that meets their needs. Open source encourages an open approach, with no one vendor having complete control of the technology. Since the development effort is shared, with platform extensions and bug fixes being fed back into the community, the resulting platform benefits from the input of multiple companies and individuals. Although the open source software licensing policies usually prevent companies from charging a fee for the software itself, companies who invest in open source technology can still build a revenue-generating business by offering developer support services, production support services, hardware certification, training and other professional services.

The open source approach is not incompatible with formal standardization. Open source technology can be standards-compliant. Indeed many open source projects have started as reference implementations of existing standards. Standards define specifications, but as seen in both telecom and IT industries, there is a strong risk that different implementations of those specifications will be incompatible, either because developers make different design choices or because vendors provide additional, non-standard features, to add value or to differentiate themselves from their competition. Providing a reference implementation as open source software can help limit this risk of incompatibility implementations, by providing guidelines on how the specifications should be implemented and by acting as a vendor-independent implementation against which other implementations can be tested and benchmarked.

4.1   Software Platforms for Web Services and Mobile Applications

For most of the history of the software industry, software platforms have primarily been designed to offer a rich abstraction layer on top of multiple vendors' hardware systems. The value of such platforms was two-fold. Firstly, for application developers, these platforms provided a common set of features that could be re-used across multiple applications, meaning that there was no need to re-implement those features as part of each application. Secondly, availability of the software platform on multiple hardware systems meant that applications that were developed on top of the platform could be deployed on a range of hardware systems, and for enterprise customers, those applications could be easily migrated from one hardware vendor's systems to another vendor's system, if required.

The growth of the internet, the evolution to client-server architectures and the emergence of mobile apps are now changing the nature of software platforms. While the original model for software platforms will continue to exist, two important new trends are worth highlighting – one is the physical decoupling of the application layer from the platform layer, the other is the emergence of common software platforms on the mobile device.

With the physical decoupling of the application layer from the platform layer, the application logic no longer needs to be collocated with, or to run directly on top of, the software platform. In this decoupled model, the value of the platform still resides in the rich, application-independent, set of functionality that it provides, but some or all of that platform functionality is now exposed via web service APIs that are accessed remotely. The application logic will typically be deployed on a separate hardware system, and will use the platform's web service APIs, rather than local function calls, to either invoke the functions of the platform or to be invoked by the platform via callbacks. This web service API model still allows the application logic and software platform to be collocated on a single hardware system if required, but it is obviously designed for the case where application logic is distributed across multiple systems, either for massive scalability or to ensure a clean separation of multiple independent applications. The exposure of web service APIs by social networking platforms is a primary example of this evolution, where a single instance of a social networking service can offer a common set of functions to multiple applications, and where those applications can be launched and invoked from within the social networking service, for example in response to user actions. Cloud computing is expected to accelerate this trend within the industry, where software platform vendors will deploy some or all of their platform functionality on a cloud infrastructure, delivered to enterprise customers as a software-as-a-service (SaaS) or platform-as-a-service (PaaS) offering.

The other important trend in platforms is the emergence of mobile platforms. The mobile revolution over the past few years has seen an explosion in the number of data-enabled mobile devices, such as the newest generation of smart phones and tablets, and the roll-out of 3G and 4G networks means that "always-connected" has become a reality. With better connectivity, and as more functionality, processing power and storage becomes available on the mobile device, it is natural that application logic shifts from the server side to the client side. This in turn raises the question of common software platforms on the mobile device. For many years, the fragmentation of the mobile operating system landscape meant that the various mobile browsers all strived to become the de facto common platform, similar to what had happened on desktop PCs and notebooks. However those mobile browsers typically offered more limited functionality compared to the web browsers on PCs, and they were typically optimized for thin clients, where only the presentation layer ran on the device, while the business logic remained on the server side. The arrival of the Apple iOS [22] and Android [23] mobile operating systems, capable of running on both smart phones and tablets, has radically changed the landscape as those two platforms provide more complete run-time environments for client-based application logic. In both cases, their rapid success has been due to a large extent to their ability to establish large ecosystems of application developers, which in turn has spawned a diverse and innovative range of mobile applications. As a result, these two platforms have quickly established themselves as the dominant client environments for mobile devices. It is the emergence of these de facto standard mobile platforms, backed by a large ecosystem of application developers, which is now driving the shift of application functionality from the server side to the client side.

The success of these two mobile platforms illustrates once again that the success of a software platform, in terms of its adoption by the industry, is directly related to the availability of a wide range of applications on the platform. Establishing a broad ecosystem of ISVs and application developers, and making the platform available on multiple vendors' devices, at least in the case of Android, have been the critical success factors. While both iOS and Android support many existing IT/internet standards, the lack of a common standard for mobile platforms has not hindered their success.

4.2   Cloud Standards and Cloud Platforms

As highlighted previously, the evolution to cloud-based service architectures will be one of the main drivers for harmonization of service architectures, as both telecom communication services and IT data services migrate to cloud infrastructure. In this section, we highlight why standards and platforms will be important in shaping the cloud computing space.

Moving a service to the cloud is not simply a question of moving the software, including both application logic and application data, from the telecom central office or IT system room to a large data center in a remote location. Rather, moving a service to the cloud implies re-designing the service to support the following features:

- The service must be accessible over the web, such as from a web browser in the simplest case. Via this web interface or web portal, users of the service must be able to subscribe to the service, to manage their subscription, to monitor their usage of the service, and to configure their instance of the service just as if the software was running on their desktop or in their local premises.
- The capacity of the service must be elastic, allowing it both to scale up and to scale down – scaling down not just in terms of the number of transactions that it can process, but also in its ability to support customers who require very little capacity.
- The service must be multi-tenant, capable of supporting multiple customers on a single instance of the service. When multiple customers, and their data, are hosted on a single instance of the service, this requires the service to support additional data privacy, encryption and security features.

- The service must support a utility payment model, where users of the service are charged on a pay-per-use mode, whether per user, per month or per unit of capacity.

Example categories of cloud services include Infrastructure-as-a-Service (IaaS) where server processing and storage capacity are offered as cloud services, Platform-as-a-Service (PaaS) where development tools and runtime platforms, exposing open APIs, are made available to software developers as cloud services, and Software-as-a-Service (SaaS), where any software application, such as messaging software, collaboration software, business applications, industry-specific vertical applications, etc. can be offered and delivered to customers as cloud services.

At a service architecture level, a cloud service exhibits many of the characteristics of a web service. A cloud service will typically expose an application-specific interface as a web service API or RESTful interface. While the default access to a service will be via a web browser or web portal, mobile apps can also be developed on top of those APIs, where, for example, different users of a given service may be provided with different mobile apps to meet their specific needs. These open APIs will also allow cloud services to be combined, to create richer offering.

For telecom service providers, this evolution to cloud services raises many opportunities. For example, the business support systems that telecom service providers use to run their business can be made available as cloud services. In this case, the telecom service provider becomes a cloud service consumer, using OSS and BSS services that are offered as cloud services by equipment vendors. In addition, telecom service providers can also become cloud service providers, expanding the set of services that they offer beyond the traditional voice and data services to also now offer IaaS, PaaS and SaaS services to their customers. Finally, telecom service providers can migrate their existing communication, messaging and managed data services to a cloud infrastructure, to leverage the scalability and capacity flexibility that cloud offers. A private cloud infrastructure could be used to support this migration to the cloud, or a hybrid cloud model may be required where public cloud infrastructure handles traffic peaks and unexpected demand.

Given this broad range of opportunities, it is clear that moving everything to the cloud is not a simple task, as it involves a combination of migrating application logic and data to cloud infrastructure, integrating new cloud service models, and managing new cloud service offerings. Not surprisingly, in this context where the cloud becomes the default platform for both legacy services and new services, this raises many questions on the standardization of cloud platforms, of cloud services and of cloud service management models. For example:

- How to avoid vendor lock-in, so that a service provider can deploy their cloud services on multiple cloud platforms, or can easily migrate a service from one cloud platform to another ?
- How to ensure that a customer of a cloud service, or tenant, can easily migrate their data from one cloud service to another? For example, as cloud-based messaging systems become more popular, enterprise customers will expect to be able to migrate mailboxes from one cloud-based messaging system to another cloud-based messaging system, if they decide to switch to a different cloud service provider.

- How to ensure that a cloud infrastructure provider can deploy and manage a multi-vendor cloud infrastructure, rather than being locked-in to one infrastructure vendor ?
- How to manage a portfolio of cloud services in a homogeneous way, and to avoid having to purchase and deploy a separate cloud service management platform for each cloud service ?

In this context, portability and interoperability between different vendors' cloud platforms will be key. A recent report from the ISO/IEC study group on cloud computing [24] highlighted many of the cloud-related areas where standards for portability and interoperability were required. That report also listed more than 20 industry initiatives related to cloud computing, illustrating the large amount of industry collaboration that is already taking place. The cloud-standards.org wiki [25] provides a detailed list of cloud standards activities within established standardization bodies such as ETSI, DTMF, TMF, OASIS and other industry groups, while the US National Institute of Standards and Technology (NIST) maintains a cloud computing collaboration site [26] which keeps an inventory of all standards that are relevant to cloud computing, even if some of those standards are not specific to cloud computing.

As we see from those various lists, the current industry activities on cloud cover a broad range of topics, from cloud computing technologies and cloud platform APIs to cloud management and cloud-related security and privacy issues.

As applications migrate to the cloud, one immediate question is what platform or software stack should be used to host that application. Initially all cloud infrastructure vendor proposed their own proprietary APIs to enable the deployment of applications on their infrastructure. However, given the range of virtual machine (VM) technologies, hypervisor technologies, VM controllers and cloud platform APIs that already exist within the industry, many vendors now recognize the need to have common set of APIs that work across different vendors' infrastructure. Such an API would allow the same application to be deployed on different vendors' infrastructure, and on different types of clouds, whether public, private or hybrid. To address this requirement, OpenStack [27] is an open source initiative, supported by infrastructure vendors, service providers, data center operators, researchers, etc. with the aim of producing an open source platform that can act as a common application platform or software stack across heterogeneous cloud infrastructures. The current version of the OpenStack platform includes functionality for controlling compute, storage and networking resources in a cloud environment.

As the number of cloud-based services grows, this raises the additional question of cloud infrastructure management and cloud service management. Consistent management interfaces and models will be required, while for telecom service providers, it will also be important to align with existing telecom management standards and frameworks. As cloud services are hosted by service providers and typically offered on a pay-per-use basis, it is not surprising that standards for cloud service management will need to deal with many topics that are familiar to the telecom industry, such as service assurance, SLA management, usage collection, billing, etc. The DMTF's Cloud Management Working Group [28] are defining interfaces and common information models for managing compute, storage and networking resources within a cloud infrastructure, focusing on all of the management aspects that are important to a consumer of public or private cloud infrastructure resources, such as SLA management, QoS management, monitoring/reporting, auditing, etc. In parallel, with its strong focus on the telecom service provider industry, the TeleManagement Forum (TMForum) are enhancing their eTOM business process framework to cover service assurance, billing, usage collection, etc. for cloud services.

As these different industry initiatives show, there is widespread recognition within both the IT and telecom industries of the importance of standards to address the many cloud-related portability and interoperability issues. Given the complexity of a cloud environment, it is unlikely that one single standard will dominate. Rather, the shape of the emerging cloud computing space will be heavily influenced by a combination of standardization efforts and platform technologies, including open source platform initiatives.

5   Conclusions

Standardization has played an important role in driving the growth of both the IT industry and the internet as a global service platform. With the convergence of IT and telecoms, standard IT technologies will become more pervasive within all layers of the telecom environment. The software stack that will be used to deliver services over next-generation networks to the new generation of smart phones, tablets and consumer electronic devices will rely heavily on standard web service technologies.

The adoption of common platform technologies has also played an important role in harmonizing the IT software stack, and the history of the software industry shows that the most successful platform technologies are those that have managed to establish a broad ecosystem of ISVs and application developers. The nature of software platforms is changing, in response to the mobile application revolution, the phenomenal success of some social networking services, and the ongoing migration of data services and telecom services to the cloud. New platforms are emerging, but in all cases, the combination of an open platform and an active ecosystem will be required to be successful, irrespective of whether the platform is standards-compliant, proprietary or the output of a collaborative open source community.

References

1. History of WiFi, http://en.wikipedia.org/wiki/IEEE_802.11#History
2. IEEE Wireless Local Area Networks working group,
   http://www.ieee802.org/11/
3. WiFi Alliance, http://www.wi-fi.org/
4. History of USB, http://en.wikipedia.org/wiki/USB#History
5. USB Implementers Forum, http://www.usb.org/
6. History of HTTPS,
   http://en.wikipedia.org/wiki/HTTP_Secure#History

7. IETF HTTPS specifications, RFC 2818,
    `http://www.ietf.org/rfc/rfc2818.txt`
8. History of HTML, `http://www.w3.org/MarkUp/historical`
9. IETF HTML specifications, RFC 1866,
    `http://www.ietf.org/rfc/rfc1866.txt`
10. History of MPEG, `http://en.wikipedia.org/wiki/MPEG-1#History`
11. ISO, `http://www.iso.org`
12. ISO/IEC Joint Technical Committee, `http://www.iso.org/iso/jtc1_home`
13. IEEE Standards Association, `http://standards.ieee.org`
14. IETF, `http://www.ietf.org`
15. W3C, `http://www.w3.org`
16. OASIS, `https://www.oasis-open.org/`
17. ECMA, `http://www.ecma-international.org`
18. Google Maps API, `https://developers.google.com/maps/`
19. TripAdvisor API, `http://www.tripadvisor.com/help/what_is_an_api`
20. Facebook Platform API,
    `http://developers.facebook.com/docs/reference/apis/`
21. OpenSocial, `http://www.opensocial.org/`
22. iOS, `http://www.apple.com/ios/`
23. Android, `http://www.android.com/`
24. ISO/IEC JTC1/SC38 SGCC: Study Group Report on Cloud Computing (September 2011)
25. Cloud-standards.org wiki, `http://cloud-standards.org/wiki/`
26. NIST Cloud Computing Collaboration Site,
    `http://collaborate.nist.gov/twiki-cloud-computing/`
27. OpenStack, `http://www.openstack.org/`
28. DTMF Cloud Management Working Group charter, `http://dmtf.org/sites/default/files/CloudManagementWGCharter.pdf`

A Review: What Matters
for Ecosystem Business Strategy

Quoc-Tuan Nguyen and Nicolai Schultz

T-Systems International GmbH, Germany
Nicolai.Schultz@t-systems.com,
Tuan-Quoc.Nguyen@telekom.de

Abstract. Ecosystem is probably one of the most discussed terms in recent telco discussions. But are the common questions about new APIs and industry
standards enough to lead telcos towards a telco ecosystem? This chapter discusses, which other elements are essential for an ecosystem and which aspects
might be missing in the current discussion of telcos. The model of the shaping
strategy is introduced to describe successful ecosystems such as Apple, Google
or i-mode, which typically requires three essential components: First the *shaping view*, second *shaping platform* and third *shaper acts and assets*. This leads
to a better understanding where the shortcomings of telcos are so far and where
still potential opportunities are.

Keywords: Ecosystem, Shaping Strategy, Apple, Google, i-mode, Telco Ecosystems.

1 Introduction

"Ecosystem" is possibly one of the most frequently used words in strategy depart-
ments of telcos organization in the time between 2007-2009, often in controversial
discussions and it even keeps its high popularity in these very days. The main and
most popular reason for that leads back to two names: Apple and Google, the two
most popular representative of the so-called Over The Top Players (OTTs). The two
companies entered into the mobile industry in 2007/2008, creating two ecosystems
around their Apple iPhone and Google Android triggering a strong innovation wave
that revolutionized the industry and deeply disrupted telcos' business. For telcos, that
innovation wave has its attraction from its tremendous dimension und success on one
hand and from the threatening disruption it created for telco business on the other
hand. This attraction, in our view, is the trigger of "ecosystem talk" within telcos
organizations.

In those "ecosystem talks" among telcos research and analysis community we saw
a number of (re-) new approaches like: "telco enabler", "telco SDKs for developers",
"telco app ecosystem" or new telco open standard for telco service ecosystems, etc.
Many of them are focusing on two essential concepts that are relevant in every ecosystem:

E. Bertin et al. (Eds.): Telecommunication Services Evolution, LNCS 7768, pp. 138–154, 2013.

- Structuring certain telco assets/resources (networks) in open and flexible architecture to create more flexible and effective service platform and
- Enabling innovators and partners to access to those assets, combining it with their assets to create services

However these two concepts, despite their essential in the ecosystem concept, are only a part of the ecosystem approach, a kind of, what we call the *engineering view* on the matter. It often drives to a miss-leading interpretation of "ecosystem" as a sort of architecture because its lack of the *business view*.

"Ecosystem", including the business view, is a (usually aggressive) comprehensive business strategy that is often applied by a market player who wants:

- To disrupt a large business area or even in an industry in order to shape a new structure (or reshape the old one) in its interest [1] [2] or
- To develop a new business/industry in large scale.

It is not only about opening assets or enabling innovators/partners but rather about owning and controlling key assets to become the leader and mobilizing key innovators/partners to form a force that is able to disrupt and change an "old" business/industry structure. Two of the most popular examples for successful ecosystems related to the telecom industry are the DoCoMo i-mode at the end of 90s [3] and the Apple iPhone and the Google Android recently.

In our view, a suitable discussion about "telco ecosystem" should be starting with a clear understanding about:

- Ecosystem as a business strategy and its purpose (not an architecture)
- Telcos capability and assets to implement such a strategy
- The competitive advantage/disadvantage of telco comparing to others ecosystem shapers in the industry, especially the OTTs like Apple and Google.

This paper will give an introduction into these issues by analyzing the current general structure of the mobile industry in Western Europe where the situation shows a very comprehensive and clear picture about how ecosystem shapers like Apple and Google have been disrupting the mobile industry and how telcos significantly lost their competitive position to those ecosystem shapers.

The first part starts with the analysis of the recent smartphone disruption with the focus on the fundamental changes of the product *smartphone* as well as of the balance of power within the mobile industry in Western Europe. The current facts are:

- The "telco industry" as such with clear borders doesn't exist anymore. The last disruptions and the entrance of new powerful players like Apple, Google had radically changed the balance of power in the mobile industry.
- In the newborn smartphone industry, the telcos' role is no longer the dominator but the supplier of network transport service and distribution partners. Device and OS vendors like Apple and Google are the new dominators.

The second part discusses about the key facets of "ecosystem" as a business strategy with two examples of successful *ecosystem shapers* Apple and Google. In our view, there are three essential components of an ecosystem strategy: first the *shaping view*, second *shaping platform* and third *shaper's acts and assets*. It will (hopefully) show what is missing in recent "ecosystem talks" by telcos.

The third part will put the "telco ecosystem" back into the discussion. We are going to review some essential issues in the question: What does matter to telco if we discuss about ecosystem?

2   The Smartphone Disruption

It was the iPhone 2G in 2007 that triggered the first wave of the "smartphone movement", illustrated by the memorable pictures of people queuing in front of shops waiting for the opening to buy an iPhone. In the meantime that "smartphone movement" has developed into one of the prime examples for disruptive industrial evolution. To get a picture of this disruption, one only needs to look at the four phenomena that are still very present in developed markets around the globe:

1. The continuously high enthusiasm of consumers for new generations of smartphones in the last 5 years.

2. High investment spirit and flourishing and strong growth in the segment of service providers, publishers and marketers who have been intensively investing into smartphones as a new screen and channel for their service/content/campaign.

3. The breakthrough of the telcos' mobile data business.

4. The telco's paralyzing perplexity regarding the strong substitution of their other core businesses (especially voice and messaging) that has been emerging from the new smartphone platforms.

Let's take a look at the drivers behind those phenomena to understand the smartphones disruption.

2.1   The Disruption in Customer Value Triggered by Usability and Apps — The Source of Customer's Enthusiasm

In terms of money, people in Western Europe used to pay for a high-end smartphone around 500-600€ since mid of 2000. What had been changing in term of customer value of a smartphone?

Comparing the "smartphones" in the time before birth year of the iPhone at 2007 (like the Nokia Communicator, Windows Mobile Phones, etc.) and first smartphones of generation iPhone and Android in the earlier stage 2007-2008, there are no significant difference in term of functionalities: phone, calendar, address book, internet browser, touch screen, etc. Furthermore, many Nokia and Windows Phone even had the apps concept on board at that time. However, people who struggled to surf on a Nokia Communicator or Windows Mobile can hardly say that those devices are valuable as Internet devices.

The principle is quite simple: a function is hardly valuable if users cannot use it. The simplified mathematical illustration of this principle is described in the Fig. 1.

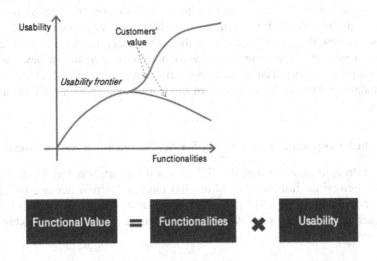

Fig. 1. The link between customer value and usability [4]

Usability is in general the most decisive factor that determines how much "customer value" can be exploited from a "function". That is the reason why the comprehensive and revolutionary leap of usability on iPhone and Android had radically been leveraging the value of "functions" and consequently the customer value of today's smartphones.

What about the component "functionalities" in the equation? The combination of better usability, powerful hardware platform and the "functionality delivery system" (in form of the app) creates a strong fundament for "functionality" to flourish.

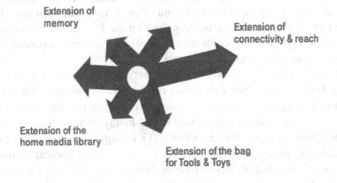

Fig. 2. A user's definition of smartphones

The core value that a "classical" phone delivered is simply the *voice/SMS connection* and few standard *"memory extension"* applications such as address book and calendar. A today smartphone of the iPhone, Android, Windows Phone generation gets far beyond that classical value of a phone and became *"the digital Swiss army knife"*. From the consumer point of view, each app turns the hardware of a smartphone into a new devices or a new tool: the calendar app turns a smartphone into a calendar, a navigator app turns the smartphone into a navigator, a newspaper app turns it into a newspaper, a baby phone app turns it into a baby phone, etc. Nguyen [4] called today smartphone the extension of the bag of modern man for tools and toys (See **Fig. 2**).

2.2   The Disruption of a New Media/Service Screen and a New Channel

Based on strong customer value, the diffusion of the smartphones of the new generation has been pretty fast since its birth (400 million Android devices, 365 million iPhones activated in June, 2012 [5]). That makes smartphone very attractive for content & service providers, publishers and marketers. From their view, today smartphones are:

- An excellent service/content delivery platform and
- A new and very personal channel to consumers.

This view is the driver for high investment spirit and strong growth in this segment. The result is: smartphones have been quickly developing to *the fourth screen* added to the three classical screens (cinema, TV and computer). Newspapers, books, videos, movies, TV and ads have been quickly brought to smartphones and its brother tablets. For publishers, content providers and marketers, smartphones and tablets are a new and pretty high stake opportunity. On one side they bet on a new channel through that they could reach consumers better and differently compared to traditional channels. On the other side they hope to get a way out of the mass pirate copy and the freemium culture against that they have been struggling on the PCs for the last decade. Today, one can find few, if any, key publishers in Western Europe that do not utilize smartphones and tablets as an important channel in their strategy.

Similar to the players in media segment, service providers have also been intensively investing to bring their online and offline services on smartphones. Those are airlines, travel companies, car sharing companies, large retailer chain, online shops, etc. who see smartphones as a new mobile and handy *service delivery platform, customer touch point* and *marketing channel*. Ticketing, boarding cards, product catalogs, shop search, payment, loyalty cards, etc. are the most popular examples for services on smartphones today. Beyond the *mobility* aspect, services on smartphones are characterized by low cost of usage, highly personal and potential for innovation in service process design.

Revolutionary usability leap, strong app/functionality ecosystem, the birth of a new media screen and marketing channel, evolutionary service delivery platform and customer touch point concepts, those are the core elements of the smartphone disruption that has been dramatically changing the telecom industry since 2007.

2.3   The Emerging of New Industry around Smartphone and the Role of Telco

In our view, the development around the new generation of smartphones in the last 4-5 years had crossed the boundary of the telecom industry to become a new industry that we call *smart mobile industry*.

Despite its very close link to the telecom industry smart mobile industry is a totally new playground. In that industry the telephone is no longer the only key service. The same applies for the role of telcos. They are no longer the "dominating force" but became "participants" in the value chain of the smart mobile industry. How did it come to that point?

Looking back at the development *until* 2007, telcos were - as the gatekeeper to mobile networks, the most powerful distributor of mobile devices, and the supplier of data transport service - still the dominator in the game. However, the intense competition among telcos and the IP-dilemma were the drivers that step by step weakened these positions of telcos. Device subvention is the only instrument that more or less holds telcos on the position of a strong distributor. But this instrument is a very expensive one. On the other side, telcos organization was too heavy to keep step with the fast developments in the app and media screen/channel segments.

The introductions of services like WhatsApp, Skype, Facebook, etc. (which are direct substitutions of the core SMS and voice products of telcos) into the two most popular smartphone platforms Android and iPhone shows a clear picture about the power of balance in the new game with four strong forces:

- OS and device vendors in 2 groups: 1) Apple 2) Google & Co (HTC, Samsung, Sony Ericsson, Motorola Mobile, etc.).
- Media and service companies
- Developers
- Telcos.

(The first three are called Over-the-top players or OTTs)
Telco-friendly strategists often had (and have) a negative view on this picture narrowing the development down to discussion "Telcos against OTTs". But is that a right view on the matter?

The fact is telcos were (and still are) stuck in a dilemma for the last decade. That is:

- The IP-dilemma,
- The intense competition among telcos and
- The regulation in the telecom industry

Innovators like Apple, Google have exploited this dilemma and their innovation to trigger a strong disruption in the industry. Together with other forces (developers, media and service providers), they have been shaping a new industry structure that is in their interest and pushing telcos in a role with much less power.

How did Apple and Google successfully carry out this revolution? The short answer is: ecosystem business strategy.

3   Ecosystem as Business Strategy

The term "ecosystem" comes originally from biology. Biological ecosystems consist of all living things, but also resources and environmental conditions that all affect each other in one specific region, niche or habitat. All these elements of an ecosystem influence each other and are highly dependent on each other. If one crucial element of the ecosystem fails, the whole ecosystem is in danger.

On the industry level the "ecosystem" is a popular approach to describe the structure of an industry or of a large business area. Transferred to the business world, every company is part of a business ecosystem. A company's ecosystem may consist of all suppliers, employees, customers, other stakeholders and resources that have an effect on a company's business. For most companies, this initial list will consist of hundreds or more likely thousands of participants and factors that shape this specific ecosystem.

"Ecosystem" on the corporate level is a (usually aggressive) comprehensive business strategy that is often applied by a market player who wants:

- To disrupt a large business area or even in an industry in order to shape a new structure (or reshape the old one) in its interest [1] [2] or
- To develop a new business/industry in large scale.

Those players are often called *ecosystem shaper* [1]. In the core of an ecosystem are the mutual relationships and mutual incentive between the ecosystem shaper and the key participants, targeting a win-win partnership.

The growth mechanism of an ecosystem focuses on generating positive feedback between customers and product/service providers within the ecosystem. The rich providing of products/services attracts customers, and the growing number of customers leads to the creation of more product/service, in a virtuous circle that, at every iteration, keeps the system growing [3].

Additionally, ecosystem shapers need to take the so-called *incumbents* into consideration. Those are basically established companies who are dominating the existing business/industry structure. In common cases, incumbents have very strong positions and are difficult to disrupt. The most common approach for shapers is to find and exploit incumbents innovation dilemma to put them in a paralyzing perplexity that make incumbent difficult to react.

By a successful implementation of ecosystem strategy, a new structure of business/industry is usually shaped in the way that shapers and its partners become the new dominators of the core components of the value chain and of the profitable parts of the business while incumbents often stand in the offside of the development.

Some of the most popular examples for successful ecosystem strategies related to the telecom industry are the NTT DoCoMo i-mode at the end of 90s, the Apple iPhone and the Google Android recently.

There are several models that describe the ecosystem strategy. For the purpose of this paper we used an adapted version of the *shaping strategy* of Hagel, Brown and Davison [1] which is in our view a very suitable option to explain the recent developments in the telco industry. In the core of a well-designed ecosystem strategy is a set of three closely interrelated elements:

1. *The shaping view* that is a long-term view of the shaper that helps to attract and to provide focus for other participants.
2. *The shaping platform* provides leverage to reduce the investment and effort participants need to make while increasing the opportunities to serve several niche markets.*The shaper's Acts and Assets* assure participants that the shaper is trustworthy, committed to the ecosystem and able to lead the ecosystem to success.

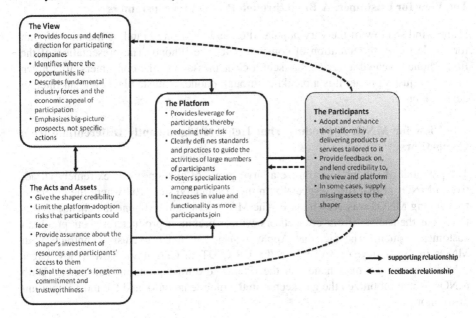

The View
• Provides focus and defines direction for participating companies
• Identifies where the opportunities lie
• Describes fundamental industry forces and the economic appeal of participation
• Emphasizes big-picture prospects, not specific actions

The Acts and Assets
• Give the shaper credibility
• Limit the platform-adoption risks that participants could face
• Provide assurance about the shaper's investment of resources and participants' access to them
• Signal the shaper's longterm commitment and trustworthiness

The Platform
• Provides leverage for participants, thereby reducing their risk
• Clearly defines standards and practices to guide the activities of large numbers of participants
• Fosters specialization among participants
• Increases in value and functionality as more participants join

The Participants
• Adopt and enhance the platform by delivering products or services tailored to it
• Provide feedback on, and lend credibility to, the view and platform
• In some cases, supply missing assets to the shaper

→ supporting relationship
◄-- feedback relationship

Fig. 3. The shaping strategy model

The purpose of such a strategy is to help the disruptors to quickly attract and mobilize a critical mass of participants involving in their ecosystems. Once the powerful network effect occurs it will gain enough power to shape and often dramatically change the industry around it.

Let's take a look at the Apple iPhone strategy as an example.

3.1   Apple's Mobile Ecosystem

How does the Apple iPhone ecosystem strategy look like? How did Apple implement and shape the iPhone ecosystem? It is to mention that Apple is a very experienced ecosystem shaper. Since 2003, Apple establishes and runs a very successful digital music ecosystem around its iPod and iTunes Store. By 2010 the iTunes music store has become the single biggest music retailer not just online but worldwide with 10 billion songs downloads by February 2010 [6].

Let's have a look at the 3 components of the iPhone ecosystem strategy:

3.1.1 Apple Shaping View

From day one, Apple had been intensively focusing on creating a view around its iPhone that compels and mobilizes the key participants for the iPhone ecosystem. Those are, at the beginning, customers and MNOs, and later on, developers, publishers and service providers.

The View for Customer: A Breakthrough Product for Customers

In the wind shadow of the very popular iPod and its strong brand, it was not difficult for Apple to get the attention of consumers for the iPhone. The presentation of the first iPhone revealed a device that sent a clear message to the consumers: it is much more than just a phone. It is a breaking through phone, a music player and an Internet device in once.

The View for MNO: A Product That Helps to Significantly Differentiate from Competitors

The potential of iPhone to mobilize a large group of customer was extremely attractive to MNOs at that time, especially in the US and Western EU where the competition among MNOs was very intense. The MNOs saw in the iPhone the chance to differentiate themselves from competitors with a premium product for their premium customer segment. The fact that Apple managed to make exclusive contracts with MNOs in the first years (AT&T in the USA, DT in Germany) showed how eager MNOs were to get their hands on the iPhone to attract premium consumers. With MNOs, Apple mobilized the gatekeeper in the mobile network and the most important distributor.

The View for Developer: The Chance to become go from "Rags to Riches"

About a year after the launch of the iPhone 2G, as the iPhone was establishing itself as a very popular product on key markets, Apple started to address and to integrate the third key participant into the iPhone ecosystem: Developers and service providers by launching the iOS SDK and App Store together with the new 3G iPhone. The iOS SDK is basically *the production infrastructure* for developers and service providers to develop apps for iPhone while the App Store offers the *essential business infrastructure* to selling apps and services (see more details in the next chapter 0).

Important is, that Apple did not just hand over the SDK to developers and service providers but also intensively invested to create a *compelling perspective* for them. Apple made sure, that developers heard early success stories of other developers who sold apps for the iPhone and stories of developers who went 'from rags to riches' [7] by selling an iPhone App or about the 'App Store Millionaires club' [8] sent out powerful messages about potential financial benefits for developers. The strong customer need for apps and development of the App Store had been regularly being published through the impressive numbers of iPhone sales and app download.

3.1.2 Apple Shaping Platform

There are two essential product elements that have substantial influence and drive the customer value of the iPhone, and consequently the growth of the Apple iPhone ecosystem:

- The iPhone itself and
- The innovative apps/services/contents on the iPhone.

The first element is in Apple's hand while the second element depends on developers, content/service providers and theirs innovation in form of apps/services/contents. In other words, on key shaping activity Apple needs to do is mobilizing and organizing developers and service providers for its iPhone ecosystem. The platform of the iPhone ecosystem is designed for this purpose focusing on two matters:

- To shape an effective and large scale "pipe" from app/service/content production to app consumption on the iPhone that organizes, on one end, hundred thousands of developers and service providers who bring innovative apps/service/content into the iPhone ecosystem and, on the other end, hundred million of iPhone users who consume them and pay for it.
- To provider leverage for developers and service providers to effectively runs theirs business within the ecosystem and to reduce their investment and risk.

Ready-to-use Business Infrastructure, Costs Covered by Revenue Share to Reduce Investment Cost & Risk for Participants

In the core of the *platform* is the combination of the iOS SDK, the iTune Store, the App Store and the iPhone device that facilitates a number of essential business infrastructures: storage, customer touch points (the store itself and device), distribution, billing, channel, marketing (e.g. App Store marketing, customer rating) and customer relationship (e.g. customer feedbacks), etc. These infrastructure form the "pipe" that forwards innovative apps/service/content from developers and service providers to consumers within the iPhone ecosystem. It enables developers and service providers to focus on their core business: developing innovative apps/content/services.

The cost for using this business infrastructure is accounted as revenue share (70/30) meaning it only occurs if developers or providers have sold something. The only investment developers and service providers need to make is the development investment.

Exploiting Customer Value from Innovation and Quality Assurance

Regarding the development, beyond the SDK for app development, Apple sets strong rules for app design and usability and carries out "app check-in" to evaluate apps quality before publishing in Apps Store. What looks like a "barrier" is in reality a standard quality management process and more important a framework to push developers using iPhone usability standard to effectively exploit customer value from functionalities.

3.1.3 Apple Shaping Acts and Assets

Additional to a compelling *shaping view* and a strong *shaping platform,* the third component of the ecosystem business strategy is *the acts and assets of the shaper,* that constitute the shaper's image in participants' view answering two questions:

- Is the shaper capable to lead the ecosystem to sustainable success in the long-term?
- Is the shaper a trustful business partner?

At the start of the iPhone ecosystem, the popular and successful iPod ecosystem since 2003, as well as the financial strength of Apple and the strong Apple brand, formed a persuading image of Apple as a powerful shaper who is capable to lead the iPhone ecosystem to success.

Bold Commitment for Innovation of iPhone

With the acquisition of PA Semi[1] (for $278 millions in 2008 April) and Intrinsity[2] (in 2010 April), Apple aimed to take design of CPU for its mobile devices under its own control. The successful Apple A4 chip (on iPad and later on iPhone 4) is the first Apple-designed system-on-chips showing the intension of the company to build its own version of ARM chip. With this move, Apple runs counter to and also its own strategy in computer area and the common trend of other mobile device makers who usually buy their primary chips from processor specialists/manufactures. The message to the participants of the iPhone ecosystem was clear: Apple is strongly committed to the long-term innovation and success of the iPhone. Beyond the chipset, there were a number of Apple's acquisitions in area of software, material, etc. that strengthen this message.

In some cases, it seems to be controversial as Apple keeps its real intentions behind investments often hidden. But the rumor mills around Apple's investments, seem to rather create excitement about the iPhone among user and innovators that build up more trust than doubt about Apple's commitment.

Apple as Trustworthy Business Partner for Developers

Except few own apps for the iPhone (e.g. iTunes, iPhoto, iMovie, Keynotes, Pages, etc.) Apple stayed away from apps. This act is essential to show the developers that Apple is not going to use the power of the shaper to compete against its partners within the ecosystem.

In its common communication, Apple represents and treats developers as *the innovator* of the iPhone ecosystem. The term "developer" no longer linked to the image of "boring engineers who're coding in basement" but to " Apple's business partners" who have been contributing hundred millions of innovative apps. A look at strategic moves

---

[1] A specialist in making fast, low-power chip.
[2] A specialist in high-speed implementation of ARM architecture.

around 2008-2009 of other key players in the industry (e.g. Google, RIM, Nokia/Microsoft) aiming to gain developers for their value chain shows that change of the role of developers within the industry.

3.2   Google

The starting point of Google was different from the one of Apple since its business model was focusing on online advertisement but not on mobile device selling. The core of this business model is to reach people by offering everyday useful online services and use them as ad platform on consumer's screens. Google had recognized very early that smartphone will become an important consumer screen and this is the very reason to start the Android project. Google launched its Android ecosystem with the Open Handset Alliance (OHA) in 2007 and the first commercial Android smartphone in October 2008.

3.2.1 Google Shaping View

For consumers and developers, Google's platform has similar opportunities like Apple's iOS platform.

But when Android was introduced, the monetizing possibilities for developers were still little due to small user numbers. Google overcame this initial weakness by attracting developers with multi-million $ contests. As early as 2007, they announced a $10 million developer contest [9] in which the best Android apps in various categories would be rewarded. Similar to Apple that produced very early success stories among developers even before the user base grew enough to be profitable for developers. At the same time this made sure, that users had access to a variety of apps from the very beginning.

In 2009 a second developer contest followed with about $2 Million in total prices [10]. Today, Android is the biggest smartphone platform in the world and can therefore attract developers with the sheer number of users, which reached 500 million in 2012 [11]

Winning Hardware Manufacturers for the Android Platform

In addition to these participants, Google had to provide a view for another key participants for the Android platform: Third party hardware vendors. Since Google has no history as a hardware vendors, HTC, Samsung, Motorola and others had to provide the missing component in the Android ecosystem.

Google showed hardware vendors that Android was a good chance to make a breakthrough in smartphone OS and to catch up with the iPhone development. Google wasn't the guru in mobile OS device but a strong and successful innovator with a large portfolio of attractive online services (e.g. maps, search, etc.) for their devices and its business model is not conflicting with vendors' business model.

3.2.2 Google Shaping Platform

Even though Google's Android platform looks similar to Apple's iPhone platform from a consumer's point of view, it is quite different for developers and in regards to its business model that focuses on advertisement. Consequently, Google provides developers not only with the tools to develop apps but also to implement advertisement into their apps as a second way of monetizing them besides the selling price. Since Google has the biggest advertiser network online with more than 1 million advertisers, this opened huge opportunities for advertisers and developers alike.

3.2.3 Google Shaping Acts and Assets

While Google is giving Android away for free, they are clearly communicating that Android is a long-term business for Google. Eric Schmidt made two points clear in an interview with Wall Street Journal: First, Google sees Android as a potential 10 plus Billion Dollar business and second, that Google plans to keep betting on its "one trick pony", the advertising business [12]. This sends a clear message, that Google is highly motivated to further push Android and at the same time, Google stays focused on advertising as a way for developers to monetize apps.

3.3   Telco Ecosystems – Success Examples, Issues and Outlook

The two examples of Google and Apple show that common ecosystem business strategy is constituted from 3 essential components: the *shaping view*, the *shaping platform* and the *shaper's acts and assets* with the goal to *quickly mobilize* a critical mass of key Participants.

3.3.1   i-Mode – A Successful Example of Telco Ecosystems

One may be surprised about the fact that the prime example for ecosystems strategy in modern time was carried out by a telco at 1999. That is NTT DoCoMo who set up and developed in Japan a Wireless Internet Service on mobile phones named *i-mode* that within 3 years (1999-2002) become the World largest wireless Internet Service with a customer base of 30 millions. The i-mode is probably the most popular successful ecosystem in the telecom industry until today with a telco in the position of an ecosystem shaper.

A look at the i-mode strategy[13] described by Takashi Natsuno (who is well known as the managing director and the founder of i-mode) reveals, that the term "ecosystem strategy" and all the essential components of the concept (view, platform, acts and assets) had its origin from the i-mode movement, at least within the boundary of the telecom industry. The strategic components and strategic moves of Apple by implementing the iPhone ecosystem are very similar to what once can learn from the strategy of i-mode. Some sharp tongues even said that the "i" of Apple looks exactly like the "i" of NTT DoCoMo.

3.3.2   Issues in Telco Ecosystem Talks

As mentioned above, we often experienced in "ecosystem talks" among telcos research and analysis community a number of (re-) new approaches like: "telco enabler", "telco SDKs for developers", "telco app ecosystem" or "new telco open standard for telco service ecosystems", etc. Many of them are focusing on two essential concepts that are relevant in every ecosystem.

- Structuring certain telco assets/resources (networks) in open and flexible architecture to create more flexible and effective service platform and
- Enabling innovators and partners to access to those assets, combining it with their assets to create services

Where do these concepts lead the development? Do telcos want to build telco ecosystems competing against the strong OTT like Apple and Google?

3.3.3 The "Telco-Against-OTT" Discussion is Out of Date

One thing we often experience in the Telco-against-OTT discussion is the idea of enabling developers resulting in initiatives, such as BONDI, GSMA OneAPI, etc. The concept is to provide developers with access to certain network assets. The intention of telco is to build up a platform for service innovation. But the question telcos have to face here is: can telcos really offer an alternative for developers and service providers?

Comparing SDK/APIs like BONDI, GSMA OneAPI with the SDK/APIs from OS vendors like Apple, Google or Microsoft, one will quickly recognize that those initiatives hardly offer a real value-added alternative to developers since they are quite behind in term of value for developers (especially *potential value*[3], *actual value*[4]), not to mention the fact that it will be a tough job for telco to get them as an integrated component on devices (high *offering cost*[5]).

The often-mentioned argumentation that developers can *"access the global mobile consumer market simply & quickly with rapid deployment across many operators"* [14] via APIs (like GSMA OneAPI) is not attractive since this is already the everyday business in OTT ecosystems like iPhone and Android, which are available worldwide across many operators. Another argumentation is *"reducing industry fragmentation and drive growth of applications"* [14] which is also misleading. There are two things in this context: *fragmentation* is the nature of competition and there is nothing wrong about it. Its "opponent" *standardization* is necessary in two cases: 1) to form a large alliance or 2) have an agreement among competitors for business with need of long and heavy investment like network infrastructure. Apps business is not the case. Developers do not have a fierce need to ally with telco nor they have painful investment cost to adapt apps from iOS to Android or even for other platform. The wish of reducing development cost for multi-platforms is always there. But as long as the profit developers can make is reasonable there is very little motivation for paying too much attention on fragmentation.

---

[3] The potential value of an asset is the contribution of this asset in the value chain.

[4] The actual value is the relative value of an asset for its user. It is dependent on the substitution/alternative to this asset. An asset can have high potential value but low actual value if there are alternatives/substitutions.

[5] Offering cost of an asset is cost the asset owner needs to account by offering this asset to its users.

Those initiatives could possibly have had the potential to become relevant would they have been introduced in the time *before* the smartphone disruption. But after 2007-2008, they are a kind of "talks about the past". The above mentioned argumentations shows how the incumbent culture still holds some part of telcos away from acknowledging that there is a new industry structure and a new competitive environment. It drives the discussion towards the "telcos against OTTs" direction but the fact is: As we discussed in 0, the *smart mobile industry* is a new one in which telcos no longer the "dominating force" but "participants". The good news is that the participant role that telcos play in the smart mobile industry as the main distributor and the transport service provider is still a profitable one, at least for now. The bad news is that the structure and the dominating forces in this new industry are very strong and difficult to change, not to mention to disrupt.

There is no question about the necessary of telcos' initiatives to signal and to push allied interest of telcos in the time as telco business is under threats that came from the smartphone evolution and other OTT apps. However, these kind of initiatives need to have a clear view and business purpose. Otherwise they will send out a misleading message to other market participants.

Putting these initiatives in the context of ecosystem business strategy they clearly address only a facet of the whole concept: The one of the shaping platform. There is no business vision and opportunity as shaping view and acts and assets are often more misleading than convincing. Without these two components, one cannot have a true "ecosystem" discussion.

3.4   An Outlook for Possible Telco Ecosystems

So what is to do? Where is the next chance for telcos in the smartphone segment and beyond the smartphone segment?

Entering the Smartphone Segment as a Second Mover Is a Tough Task But Possible

Entering the end device segment as second mover is a tough task. A quick look at Microsoft and Nokia, two giants in the mobile device and IT industry, who lost significant shares to Apple and Google, shows the difficulty of introducing yet another completely new ecosystem to this market. Windows Phone is still struggling to gain market share despite vast investments and a strong market share in the PC/laptop market by Microsoft and a full commitment by mobile phone giant Nokia.

However, there are still some opportunities for telcos for allying with other *second movers* or *hedgers* (who have multiplatform strategies, e.g. Samsung, HTC) since the competition in the smartphone segment is getting fiercer.

There Are Business Areas That Are Still Open for Innovative Telco Ecosystems

Telcos have to refocus on assets they still can control or regain control over assets that are not 100% opened yet. Some recent developments show positive signals, that telcos could establish a new ecosystem around big industrial scale services such as

- Mobile payment
- Smart energy
- Logistics

The reason behind this is that these services have such a big scale but requires more national than international competences so that neither global OTT innovators nor small national OTT innovators can easily gain access. This makes them candidates of business for telcos. But in order to build an ecosystem around these opportunities, telcos would have to refocus all assets and stop activities in non-related areas. In some cases this might lead to inconvenient decisions where telcos have to disrupt into their own portfolio structure and may need to "sacrifice" some old businesses in order to create a new ecosystem.

Serious shapers of ecosystems need to mobilize key market participants by offering business visions, platforms that can shape a strong, growing ecosystem structures. They need to show they are capable and creditable partners through their acts and assets. They need to do all that faster than their competitors. And they need to shape and shape again.

References

1. Hagel, J., Brown, J.S., Davison, L.: Shaping Strategy in a World of Constant Disruption. Harvard Business Review (October 2008), http://hbr.org/2008/10/shaping-strategy-in-a-world-of-constant-disruption (accessed September 1, 2012)
2. Iansiti, M., Levien, R.: Strategy as Ecology (March 2004), http://www.uapa533.com/uploads/8/4/4/9/8449980/strategy_as_ecology.pdf (accessed July 20, 2012)
3. Natsuno: The i-mode Wireless Ecosystem (2003)
4. Nguyen, Q.-T.: The iphone, android and the disruptive evolution in the german moble industry. HHL - Leipzig Graduate School of Management, Leipzig (2010)
5. Dillon, N., Cripps, T., Leach, A.: OTT and Smart Device Player Roundup: Second Quarter 2012. OVUM (2012)
6. Roth, J.: iTunes Store Tops 10 Billion Songs Sold. Apple Press Info. (2010), http://www.apple.com/pr/library/2010/02/25iTunes-Store-Tops-10-Billion-Songs-Sold.html (accessed July 1, 2012)
7. Chen, B.X.: iPhone Developers Go From Rags to Riches. Wired (September 2008), http://www.wired.com/gadgetlab/2008/09/indie-developer/ (accessed September 1, 2012)
8. O'Grady, J.D.: The App Store Millionaire Club. In: ZDNet (December 2008), http://www.zdnet.com/blog/apple/the-app-store-millionaire-club/2649 (accessed May 26, 2012)

9. Horowitz, S.: Calling all developers: $10M Android challenge (November 2007), `http://googleblog.blogspot.de/2007/11/calling-all-developers-10m-android.html` (accessed June 15, 2012)

10. Google, Android Developer Challenge 2 (2009), `https://developers.google.com/android/adc/` (accessed August 12, 2012)

11. Shankland, S.: Google: 500 million Android devices activated. CNET (September 2012), `http://news.cnet.com/8301-1035_3-57510994-94/google-500-million-android-devices-activated/` (accessed September 1, 2012)

12. Efrati, A.: Eric Schmidt on Google's Next Tricks. The Wall Street Journal (July 2010), `http://blogs.wsj.com/digits/2010/07/28/eric-schmidt-on-google%E2%80%99s-next-tricks/` (accessed June 27, 2012)

13. Natsuno, T.: i-mode Strategy. Wiley (2003)

14. GSMA, One API - Open Network Enabler APIs, GSMA (2012), `http://oneapi.gsma.com/` (accessed September 1, 2012)

New Regulatory Approaches
in an Evolving Market Structure

Nadia Trainar

Head of Network Economics, Forward Planning and Universal Service
ARCEP (Autorité de Régulation des Communications électroniques et des Postes
is the French telecom regulatory authority)
nadia.trainar@arcep.fr

Abstract. This chapter reminds the key regulation principles of the telecom
market and the challenges posed in this area by the new business context. The
evolution of objectives and tools guiding regulatory action are presented in parallel with the transformations of the sector, from the initial steps of liberalization in the nineties to the 2009 framework review and the questions triggered by
its application. The chapter more specifically examines the consequences on
regulation of the *convergence* phenomenon – including how public policies'
scope and aim are modified by the new, complex models of relationship between players of the wider ecosystem, and what type of innovative regulatory
approaches may hence be required, as illustrated by the recent works on the net
neutrality topic.

1   Introduction

In the recent years, more than ever, policy makers (institutions at and national European levels, nonprofit organizations active in the sector, etc.) have entrusted regulation in telecommunications with a high level of expectations. This is due to the major
contribution of electronic communications networks and services (thereafter ECNS)
to the dynamics of the digital revolution, and therefore to the potential of growth and
social evolution in our modern societies. This is not only because they support the
distribution of information and communication signals (like railways transport people
and merchandises), but most importantly today, because electronic communications
are the platform where are generated all the innovation processes that build the new
knowledge society. In this respect, ECNS differ from most network infrastructures,
because they can be considered as public goods. This explains the high level of ambi-
tion for regulatory policy in telecommunications, which principally deals with two
types of concerns. The first one relates to the promotion of effective competition in
the markets (in close interaction with competition law), which is sought to replace the
previous monopolistic situations. The second reflects the will of public authorities to
maintain a control on products offered in these markets, notably in order to protect
users and ensure they benefit from an easy access to a good quality of service.

The main difficulty in the first mission is to find the right balance between sectorial
regulation, which consists mostly in ex-ante rules, and classical antitrust policy,

E. Bertin et al. (Eds.): Telecommunication Services Evolution, LNCS 7768, pp. 155–181, 2013.

which is based on ex-post intervention. The latter features a significant probability of mistakes (e.g. unaddressed problems), whereas the former bears a risk of over-intervention, or measures that may be more costly than their benefits[1]. We will discuss later on that, in a context of increasingly oligopolistic structure of the markets, it can be all the more difficult to justify a specific sectorial regulation. On the second aspect, since the early days of the telecommunications liberalization process, European and national laws assigned to the regulation system what could be called a "redistribution" objective, i.e. supervising that opening to competition would not result into excluding the poorest consumers. This risk was to be annulled thanks to the setting of a universal service (a set of activities and obligations at a reasonable price), originally guaranteed by the incumbent, and now open to other providers. Regulation is thus inhabited with a concern of social justice, which moves away from a purely economic and competition conception of its role. This is even truer now, since other redistribution tasks have developed, such as the reduction of the digital divide between territories, which is now a relevant objective for regulators.

This needed balance between economical and social requirements is a major foundation of the regulatory system in Europe. These high level objectives correspond to a more detailed set of principles, some of them having founded the early days of European regulation, others having gained importance in the recent years. This evolution will be described in a first section of this chapter that will go through the three main "ages of regulation", whereas the second part will shed light on the current challenges facing public authorities, especially due to the consequences of "convergence" (understood in a broad meaning). In a last section, the "net neutrality debate" will be further detailed, since it is a good illustration of possible regulatory approaches in the near future.

2   Ages of Regulation

There is a reciprocal influence between policy implemented by the regulator and the regulated market. In the electronic communications sector, one can distinguish three main approaches to regulation, which correspond to successive transformations of the regulated market. Indeed, regulation of ECNS must be a dynamic process adapted to market evolutions and the needs of citizens. The activities of national regulatory authorities (thereafter NRAs) must reflect this dynamic, and this is also the case for the legal frameworks that determine the conditions of this regulation. Regular reviews of the European Union (EU) framework are thus a foreseen opportunity to both adapt legislation to sector evolution, and to enhance mechanisms that will strengthen the electronic communications internal market. In this section, we will therefore attempt to present jointly all the simultaneous trends (legal evolutions, regulatory actions and market transformations) observed in the ECNS environment.

---

[1] On the difficulties associated with industry specific regulation, see in particular: Armstrong and Sappington, 2005, *"Recent Developments in the Theory of Regulation"*.

2.1   Liberalization (from the Nineties to 2002)

Regulation as we know it today for many "public utilities" sectors was born in the eighties in the United Kingdom, when the movement of privatization initiated by Prime Minister Thatcher required a system to be put in place in order to facilitate the entry in the market of new operators. In order to ensure a smooth transition from a monopolistic situation to a competitive market environment, more favorable to consumers, regulatory bodies were set up, notably to ensure access by newcomers to the different markets. This logic, supported by article 86.3 of the EC treaty, founded the approach of the European Commission afterwards, which launched a large program to progressively dismantle monopolies in the telecommunications sector: satellite communications, television cable networks, mobile telephony and, finally, the public fixed networks (from 1998). An OECD study from 2001 (Boylaud, Nicoletti) tried measuring the impact of this liberalization initiative, based on data from 24 member countries during the 1991-1997 period. The conclusions emphasized that liberalization resulted in a growth in productivity, a drop in prices, and a better quality of service.

This evolution was insufficient however to guarantee the development of effective telecommunications markets in the European markets, let-alone a European internal market, because of the diversity of network types, of technology used, of interconnection arrangements, etc. More harmonization was necessary in this respect, which lead to the first set of sectorial directives, meant at guaranteeing the development and provision of an open network of telecommunications. This first framework is thus usually referred to as Open Network Provision (ONP) and is composed of a framework directive[2] and a series of related provisions. At the same time, a system of authorizations and licenses was put in place for the various parts of the market, in order to avoid the entry of actors without appropriate technical or financial resources. Although limited, these authorizations or licenses were a threat to the incumbent operator (often owned by the State), which justified the need for independent regulators. These bodies were meant to ensure the application of the ONP framework, i.e. to avoid that the incumbent operator abuses its dominant position, in particular regarding the access to its network (considered as an "essential facility").

A fundamental relationship between regulation and antitrust policy...

Regulation in telecommunications is heavily inspired by antitrust policy principles, which could lead to question whether there are fundamental differences, apart from intensity and precision (ex ante policy is generally handled with larger human and financial resources). One major difference is the following: antitrust policy is based on probabilities and thus includes some risks (mainly two types: prosecute innocent firms, or let some companies pursue unlawful activities), whereas sectorial regulation is rather "determinist" (it is almost impossible to escape from NRAs' surveillance) but bears the concern of over-intervention. In other words, ex ante regulation surely presents some risks of inefficiency (some interventions are more costly than the results they achieve).

---

[2] Directive 90/387/CEE of the Council of 28 June 1990.

Compared with antitrust policy, this higher risk derives in particular from the larger latitude of action for ex ante regulators. Indeed, they possess a large set of tools to intervene on the market structure (e.g. licenses to entry), the organization of firms (e.g. functional separation) and their market choices (requirements of quality, price, coverage…) In addition, the sectorial regulator can fix its own agenda and priorities, whereas competition authorities must be attentive to their positions' coherence with, on the one hand, other courts applying competition law, and, on the other hand, similar positions they have taken in other sectors.

Thus, there is a real danger that sectorial regulation "shapes" market evolution. This concern was one of the main aspects underlying a debate at the beginning of the years 2000, about the interest to maintain such a costly and restrictive sectorial regulation, considering that markets were generally not monopolistic anymore. The level of concentration was arguably very high, but this existed in various other markets where no ex ante regulation was in place. In the short term, for some markets with particularly high barrier to entries and possibilities for the dominant operator to abuse its market power, regulators maintained a strong legitimacy, notably given the technically complex problems to be addressed. By contrast, in the longer term and for markets were effective competition could be reached, it is possible to imagine that classical antitrust tools could suffice to treat anticompetitive practices. In any case, it's a challenge in all the network-type sectors to find a right balance between efficient regulation, on the one hand, and maintaining uncertainties on the market, on the other hand.

But it was never only about competition and antitrust…

As soon as telecommunication networks started being liberalized, European and national legislations incorporated within the regulatory system some specific objectives in addition to the promotion of competition. They addressed in particular the following fields: on the one hand, some form of control of the "production side": technological policy, interoperability of network and services… and, on the other hand, various forms of "redistribution" to ensure a certain equity between citizens and between territories (to avoid the so-called "digital divides" – between social groups, rural and urban, etc.)

Efforts in standardization were undertaken very early in the liberalization phase, since they rightly appeared compulsory for the setting of a competitive environment, which could not function properly with, for instance, too many problems of compatibility between terminals, or with high technical barriers making interconnection or interoperability of networks too costly or even impossible. Having fulfilled this standardization prerequisite, it is interesting to note that national and European public authorities have not left the market pursue the selection of further standards (through competition or cooperation between firms), but have on the contrary maintained an important control over the technological and industrial evolutions in the telecommunications sector. At Community level, these powers are reflected in the primary legislation (article 17 of Framework directive 2002/21/CE), which provides for normalization procedures, potentially restrictive. This has triggered certain critics in the academic and professional circles: although standardization is welcome from the consumers' point of view, since it increases the network effects, various authors (see for instance Gandal et al. (2003)) underline the limits of a regulatory and restrictive standardization, which can lead to inefficient technological choices. One well-known example in the field of telecommunications is UMTS, whereby Europe chose a standard through regulatory procedures, which several analysts have since then noted its complexity and delayed adoption with regards to third generation mobile telephony in American or Japanese markets (although other factors than normalization should also be taken into account to explain the observed evolutions).

Already at the time of the initial opening of the sector to competition, other policy objectives were assigned to regulation. These corresponded to a politic will of redistribution (to all users and all localities), and resulted in two concrete regulatory settings. First, a universal service was created, in order to guarantee a minimum level of services to consumers, complying with principles of easy access, equality and affordable price. Second, both regulators and local communities were entrusted with certain powers and responsibilities, in order to reduce the territorial discrepancies in ECNS.

First results and first questions...

Before looking at the provisions in details, it may appear that the setting of a regulatory environment was quite straightforward in the first years of liberalization: end up the monopolistic rights (including the collateral situations such as the compatibility of terminals etc.) and ensure, through access obligations, that alternative operators will be able to progressively climb the ladder of investments.

All things considered, the system was very early designed in a much more sophisticated way, adding, beyond the antitrust-like policy objectives, various principles and provisions promoting spatial planning and standardization, as well as protecting consumers.

However the environment remained quite simple in that age, with the incumbent operator being strongly dominant, usually vertically integrated, with clearly identified activities. Regulation is mostly asymmetric and prescriptive, turned towards incumbent operators to try to avoid any external discrimination (against alternative operators), as well as internal (this form of discrimination could happen e.g. if the incumbent favored its own subsidiaries).

When the "liberalization" age ends, the movement conducted under the surveillance of regulatory authorities has enabled to create suitable conditions for the development of competition in the telecommunications sector. However, in most cases, incumbent operators remain dominant, and the companies having been able to establish a sustainable presence in the market are very few. On the one hand, the persisting dominance of the incumbent on the "historical" markets raises questions regarding the necessity to regulate the "new markets" and innovative services. This is due to the possible leverage effect that the dominant firm could exert in a new market which is connected to the historical one. This has justified in particular the introduction of specific provisions in the European framework. On the other hand, some markets are moving from a monopolistic to an oligopolistic structure, triggering other aspects of the economics theory and of the legal environment. One way to address such market structure, and avoid in particular price collusions, is to transpose in ex ante regulation concepts such as joint dominance. In practice, such concepts have not proven easy to use by regulators. Instead, this has triggered a new approach by the Commission in order to regulate resulting prices, based on the definition of relevant markets. This was materialized in the new framework for telecommunications adopted in 2002.

2.2   Regulate Competition (from 2002 to 2009)

In 2002 were adopted new European directives[3], constituting the so-called "telecom package", setting up "a new Community framework for the regulation of electronic communications". Various important principles founded this reform, particularly the reference to economic analysis and competition law, in order to ensure technological neutrality and to address the growing concerns related to oligopolistic market structures.

Indeed, as mentioned above, several European countries had seen the transformation, in a few years, from a regulatory context centered on the access from third parties to the incumbent operator's network, to policy questions related to oligopolistic market structures. Therefore, it was now demanded from regulators to identify the various forms of market dominance, after having defined and delineated the exact market on which this market power should be measured. In this matter, the new framework is inspired by the case law related to dominant position abuse (art. 82 of the EC treaty), although obviously the scope here is not to address abuses ex post, but to impose obligations ex ante.

Regulation in the 2002 framework should primarily focus on the 18 "relevant markets" (both wholesale and retail markets) identified by the Commission as susceptible to sectorial regulation. These markets are defined in terms of products/services (according to an analysis of substitutability of offer and demand) and in geographical terms (aiming at defining the boundaries inside which the competitive conditions are homogeneous). A crucial aspect of this methodology is its neutrality with respect to the various technologies being used in the market, which is a big difference compared with the ONP system and also, for example, the regulatory setting in the United States of America (where typically cable networks were not submitted to the same obligations than copper networks). Regulators are thus equipped with the ability to define and impose specific ex ante "remedies" to companies considered as holding market power, on products that the regulator would define upon market analysis (and not predefined by a technological categorization). In the view of this great power, a strong concern was voiced by certain stakeholders at that time, about the risk for nonproportionate regulation. The directives partly addressed this by specifying in details the types of remedies that could be imposed (e.g. publication of a reference offer, price control...), and by establishing a mechanism whereby regulatory authorities should justify their decision.

Other guiding principles were useful to ensure proportionality in regulation. A first important idea was to promote infrastructure competition following a progressive approach, i.e. stimulating alternative operators to climb the "ladder of investment". This is translated into remedies, which refrain from providing immediately very cheap access to complete wholesale products, ensuring that there is a true economic interest for new

---

[3] In particular the four directives adopted on 7 March 2002, named "Framework", "Access", "Authorization" and "Universal Service", as well as the directive "Privacy" adopted on 12 July 2002.

entrants to replicate part of the architecture themselves, and thus become more autonomous. This stimulation policy is reflected in the preference given to wholesale regulation with respect to retail control, and was further materialized in 2007 when, at the time of reviewing its recommendation on relevant markets, the Commission removed from the list most of the retail markets, inviting regulators to focus on wholesale obligations, that would induce reinforced competition at retail level.

The outcome of this approach can be seen as generally successful in a number of EU markets. Indeed, this second cycle of deeper regulation has allowed, in several European countries, for the setting of a sustainable competition, with multiple players and more balanced market shares between the incumbent and the alternative operators. Given this evolution of market structures, some forms of regulation, not solely focused on the incumbent position, gained importance anew: rules to preserve a fair competitive environment need to be applied more symmetrically to all main actors in the market, whereas other objectives than antitrust or competition come stronger at the forefront of regulators' preoccupations. These aspects will prove central in the framework review of 2009.

Already before this latest review, regulators have in practice reflected this evolution to a certain extent. On the one hand, they developed more symmetrical, often indicative, regulatory measures, which are to be followed by all operators (for instance, similar expectations in terms of security and data protection, integrity of networks, quality of interconnections, etc.). A first example below (from ARCEP[4] regulator in France) describes this type of symmetrical decisions. On the other hand, besides strengthening the competitive environment to support a plurality of best-priced offers, regulators have increasingly supported other objectives: efficient usage of spare resources such as numbering or spectrum, promotion of services adapted to special social needs (e.g. for disabled people). To illustrate this "branch" of regulation, below are detailed two further examples of ARCEP activities.

2.2.1   Examples of Symmetrical Regulation

Ex. 1: the roll-out of new high speed networks

An important part of ARCEP's activity in the recent years has been devoted to regulating the so-called "next generation access" (NGA), in order to set the conditions for a balanced (meaning in particular: both efficient and competition-friendly) deployment of very high speed access networks (fixed and mobile) on the whole territory. This regulation is based primarily on a specific law ("loi relative à la lutte contre la fracture numérique"), which gave public authorities (local and national), as well as operators, the tools to rollout fiber optics technology.

---

[4] ARCEP ("Autorité de Régulation des Communications électroniques et des Postes") is an independent national regulatory authority, created on 1st January 1997. Its competences are fixed in the main telecommunications related laws ("loi n° 96-659 du 26 juillet 1996"; "loi n° 2004-669 du 9 juillet 2004"), whereby ARCEP exercises, in the name of the French State, the function of regulation of the electronic communications and postal sectors in France.

Leveraging on this legal background, and on the existing competitive structure of the French broadband market, ARCEP elaborated a symmetrical regulatory framework. This was made possible because alternative operators have climbed up the ladder of investments in the fixed market, which renders credible the possibility to duplicate at least part of the local loop, therefore avoiding the reproduction, with fiber, of the copper access monopoly. ARCEP's framework thus promotes, when economically viable, infrastructure competition, which is a guarantee for innovation. At the same time, it intends to favor sound investment mutualizing when needed.

Ex. 2: national coverage of networks

Digital land settlement is an important objective to be pursued by ARCEP – in particular by promoting the extension of broadband coverage, both fixed in mobile.

For instance, ARCEP lead various processes to attribute frequencies to mobile operators (the latest operation concerning the 2,6 GHz spectrum band and the so-called " golden frequencies" of the digital dividend, in the 800 MHz band, for mobile very high speed services (4G)). In this scope, ARCEP sought after land settlement as a priority objective, as required by the French Parliament in the above-mentioned law. This objective was implemented through the definition of the selection criteria of operators applying for these frequencies. More generally, this is a key aspect that regulators must take into account both when fixing the rules for entering a market (in particular in the case of selection or bidding processes, for spare resources), and then when supervising whether these rules are respected. With this aim, ARCEP implements regular coverage measurements of mobile networks.

Ex. 3: consumer protection

In the recent years, ARCEP has reinforced its action in favor of consumers. This means that it no longer considers sufficient to promote the development of innovative and affordable offers through fair competition between operators. It also intends to make sure (in collaboration with other administrations in charge of consumer protection) that consumers -private individual or body corporate- can access these services in satisfying conditions. This second dimension requires that users can make an informed choice when they subscribe to an offer – on the nature and quality of the services as well as on their price. Hereafter are some examples of subjects covered by this activity.

In many cases, new offers are innovative but hardly understandable by users. For instance, the exact scope of the "unlimited" notion (very common for telephony or internet access services in France) is blurred, ambiguous, or even sometimes misleading, not to say dishonest. Many are the consumers that do not understand the meaning of "unlimited" offers until they receive exorbitant bills.

Similarly, most offers of access to Internet via mobile networks remain silent on the bandwidth offered in reality, which differs from the maximum speed that technologies enable. Limiting the bandwidth is, most of the time, legitimate in order to reduce production costs and thus prices. But lack on transparency on such limitations is not acceptable in regulators' view.

Easy switching of providers is another crucial aspect, since it determines the exercise of choice by the end user, and thus the full expression of competition. It is a multifaceted topic, which encompasses various requirements. The first are number porta-bility (as well as the possibility to retain an email address for a reasonable period), as well as the option to dissociate services when changing operators (important with the rise of triple and quadruple play offers). Also, continuity of services should be en-sured, by reducing as much as possible service interruptions when moving to a new provider. Furthermore, switching costs should not be excessive and represent a de facto barrier to benefiting from competition. This applies in particular to abusive con-ditions for terminating contracts.

The growing importance of symmetrical tools and new objectives was confirmed during the review of the European regulatory framework for electronic communica-tions, which stemmed from 2007 to 2009 and materialized these new trends in regula-tion.

2.2.2   EU Framework Review (2007-2009)

Texts adopted in 2002 have paved the way for powerful rise of competition in several European countries, leveraging on a regulatory system of generally recognized effec-tiveness, and still considered fully relevant today. The model of regulation defined in the texts adopted in November 2009 by European legislators fits in the line of the 2002 framework, in making regulatory authorities the instrument of a progressive bridging between sectorial legislation and competition common law. Hence, although the framework adopted on 25 November 2009[5] marks a new important phase, it represents an evolution rather than a revolution, providing new tools to regulators whereas better securing their independence and cooperation, creating some new in-struments for emerging markets, and providing new guarantees for consumers. It therefore achieves both an institutional and practical modernization of the legal back-ground in the ECNS sector.

In order to take into account the evolution of markets (as mentioned above), the 2009 "telecom package" adapts a number of powers from NRAs and the European Commission, with the objective to increase harmonization and efficiency (e.g. a better management of spectrum resources). A progressive relaxing of asymmetrical regula-tion is foreseen, though some powerful tools are included (such as functional separa-tion). In parallel, symmetrical regulation is reinforced, in particular provisions ad-dressed to consumers (e.g. transparency obligations, numbers portability, maximum duration of engagement periods, etc.). Lastly, European legislators have recognized the upcoming challenges for regulators in the modern ECNS environment dominated by IP-based technologies and universal connectivity to Internet. In this context, they have notably emphasized the following objectives: promoting the access to content, ensure network security and protect private data. These will prove utmost important in the third age of regulation which has now started.

---

[5] This « telecom package » includes two amending directives and a regulation (see References).

2.3   New Business Models (from 2009)

In parallel to the evolutions of the ECNS framework, which have been presented above, EU and national legal backgrounds have been progressively enriched by taking into account new roles and stakeholders in the Internet ecosystem. For instance, the concept of "intermediaries" between content and networks, and the (limited) obligations attached to providers of information services, were detailed in the Directive on electronic commerce[6]. More generally, the purpose of this directive is to improve the legal security of relationships in electronic platforms, in order to increase the confidence of Internet users. It sets up a stable legal framework by making information society services subject to the principles of the internal market (free circulation and freedom of establishment).

Interaction between those actors and telecommunication operators is a central challenge for electronic communication regulators: with the powering up of "convergence" (see hereafter), such new stakeholders indeed have a growing impact on the ECNS sector, and induce a redefinition of operators themselves, and of their strategies. Yet, many of these emerging issues fall outside, or at the limit, of the core competencies of electronic communications regulators. To grasp this problem, one must visualize that new ecosystems such as the Internet platform are two-sided markets, whereby networks interconnect CAPs[7] (content editors and/or applications and services providers) with all users of these contents, applications and services.

Historical activity of EC regulators has consisted in setting rules for operators, in the benefit of end users, with an explicit focus on "networks" (including how different operators' network interconnect). However, the experience offered the end user is in fact composed of various layers, which bear various names in the public debate, but can be divided into: infrastructure, "infostructure", and services[8]. Nevertheless, "in the telecommunications sector, it is quite difficult to draw a clear separation, upstream, between infrastructure and infrastructure, and downstream, between infostructure and services." What can be purely considered as the infrastructure part of the networks nowadays? Probably only copper or passive fiber, since other types of equipment are increasingly "intelligent" – such as routers, which are much more sophisticated than in traditional switched networks. What about the other side of the system? Here also, the actors of the infostructure layer interfere, notably by exploiting data servers, with the traffic flows injected in the networks. As an illustration,

---

[6] Directive 2000/31/EC of the European Parliament and of the Council of 8 June 2000 on certain legal aspects of information society services, in particular electronic commerce, in the Internal Market.

[7] Derived from the framework directive reference to « *content, applications and services* » providers, the label « CAP » is increasingly used by European regulators, with a similar but wider sense than the term « OTT », also often used in the public debate. CAP indeed includes content producers, whereas the term OTT rather designates, in general, providers of service and of platforms of access to services.

[8] The cleavage used here, and various related quotations, are based on the model introduced by Michel Gensollen and Nicolas Curien –the latter is a previous member of ARCEP board. See for example in Flux 2012: « *La régulation des communications électroniques en France et en Europe Entretien avec Nicolas Curien* », May 2012, Géraldine Pflieger. English translation of N. Curien's quotation by the author of this article.

"Google is both the biggest infostructure manager in the world and the number one search engine in the service and applications market". This growing importance of the infostructure is not ony a feature of the telecommunications sector, and can also be observed in other networks. An example is the development of "smart grids", which electricity stakeholders intend to use both for optimizing (upstream) the usage of production facilities, and guiding (downstream) the consumption behavior of customers (in particular of large companies or local public authorities).

The landscape is therefore, more and more, one of a continuum of interaction between actors present at various levels of the networks value chain. Furthermore, the increasingly important role of terminals (smartphones, set top boxes, tablets, connected TVs and all sorts of devices) must also be taken into account. For instance, the parameters set in a handset indeed have a strong impact on the ability to use certain services in certain network conditions. Even more important is the crucial position, which is now being taken by the application platforms related to such devices (e.g. iOS and App Store, Androïd, etc.). These stakeholders can't be omitted when analyzing the whole chain of interactions resulting into the end users' experience.

Beyond the complexity of relationships and variety of actors, new business models also trigger regulatory questions that go beyond traditional economic considerations. Two areas are of particular interest here. First, it is increasingly demanded that public authorities take care of ensuring "open" relations between operators and CAPs (here lie typically some central issues of the net neutrality debate, which will be discussed below). There is, secondly, a growing attention to the substance of relations between editors and consumers of content: respect of copyright, protection of individual freedoms, pluralism of expression, cultural diversity, fight against « cyber-crime », etc.

Missions of the sectorial regulator have been enlarged to take those aspects into account, with the 2009 framework adding the following objective: « promoting the ability of end-users to access and distribute information or run applications and services of their choice »[9]. In other words, regulators must make sure that the development and functioning of ECNS support the access to content in a smooth and effective manner, but they do not regulate the provision of contents in itself. This is often a delicate position, which explains why new forms of regulation are increasingly called upon in this sector. This includes various approaches, inter alia non-binding guidelines, advise to policy makers, informing consumers, and setting up co-regulation processes, whereby the different stakeholders are invited to actively participate in the definition of rules applying to their activity.

Co-regulation is firstly needed with actors in the market place (operators, CAPs, users' associations). Solving problems requires a collective and concerted approach (auditions, working groups, publishing best practices, animation of forums, etc.). To a certain extent, the regulator becomes a "facilitator". Success in such approach can only happen if there is trust – in the regulators' capacity to understand and synthetize concerns, stimulate action and control the efficiency of initiatives taken.

The second level is a closer collaboration with other NRAs and the European Commission. On such complex matters, exchanging experience, designing and recommending common methodologies, are of utmost interest. This need for reinforcing cooperation between regulation authorities was recognized in the 2009 frame-

---

[9] Article 8.4.g of the revised Framework directive.

work, and gave birth to the Body of European regulators of electronic communications (BEREC). It is aimed at deepening the dialogue between national regulators, and between those regulators and European institutions, as well as providing them, when necessary, some assistance. In parallel, the Commission sees its harmonization capacity extended via a power to impose general decisions on the regulation deriving from market analysis, and a reinforced control on « remedies » (obligations on providers) planned by NRAs. These measures are aimed at bridging the analysis methodologies and remedies selected in Members States, thus ensuring a better predictability, especially for operators.

The third level of co-regulation, or at least increased collaboration, relates to authorities from other sectors. As stated previously, the missions of the regulator increasingly require to take into account, beyond competition and antitrust considerations, other policy objectives: support to innovation and investment, issues linked to fundamental rights and freedoms (as in the net neutrality debate). In these domains, various other institutions are concerned (for instance in France: the audiovisual sector regulator - « CSA », the regulator for the protection of private data - « CNIL », a recently created institution that looks after the respect of copyright - « HADOPI », etc.). All those bodies must ensure that their doctrines are coherent.

These close interactions with other institutions and public authorities, both at national and supranational level, appear particularly important in the context described above of complex layers overlapping. For most of these evolving types of relationships, there are little guidelines for regulators today (for example, the recent revision process of the R&TTE directive resulted in quite minimalistic updates, far away from the considerations of interoperability at software platforms level). Some of the questions posed to regulation by this cross-sector convergence will be further examined in the next part, since they are expected to gain momentum in the next years. They may in particular be considered in the scope of the next revision of the EU regulatory framework. Although it is of course a very early stage of the procedure, there are indications thereof in the recent study on "Costs of non-Europe" delivered by Ecorys to the European Commission.

3   The Effects of Convergence

The previous section has introduced the various transformations in the roles and relationships of actors involved in the delivery to end users, through ECNS, of services from the information society. The term "convergence" is used in this paper in a wide sense, and refers to the growing overlap between the activities of a large array of stakeholders, including telcos, CAPs and terminals suppliers. The consequences of these complex models for regulation are examined in the following parts.

First of all, the extension of convergence leads to a concentration of actors and the formation of an oligopolistic market structure covering larger parts of the ecosystem. For regulators, this raises questions regarding the relevant area that they should regulate, within their traditional zone of competence but also beyond, taking into account incentives and consequences across markets. In this respect, convergence may imply going from a market-by-market regulation to a transversal regulation, across markets.

The second aspect of convergence, which derives from the growing interpenetration (as described above) of infrastructure, infostructure and services, results in new preoccupations bursting into the telecoms regulators' world - issues that fall outside the sole objective of promoting a competitive environment. Both trends raise new questions for public authorities, which may require innovative regulatory approaches.

3.1   New Market Structure and Transverse Regulation

If taking the example of France, fifteen years after the liberalization of the sector of electronic communications, the market is now structured around five main operators, which all propose multiple-services offers, and even content. Some of these actors can sometimes play simultaneously the roles of equipment suppliers, network operators, providers of services and content editors. They become horizontally integrated operators - see for instance the acquisition of the totality of SFR by Vivendi (a company featuring pay television, music, video games) finalized in June 2011.

Convergence worldwide leads to partnerships and acquisitions, involving actors that were not originally present in the electronic communication market, according to a great variety of configurations. For example, suppliers of connected TV equipment with editors of contents (in Europe: Philips with YouTube, TomTom, eBay, Meteo-Group, etc. In France: Samsung with TF1 and with Orange). Another illustration is the activity of mobile devices suppliers, which give access to content that they validate themselves (e.g. Apple's App Store is firmly interwoven with Apple's terminals such as the iPhone and the iPad, similarly as Google Play services with Android based handsets). One can observe increasingly complex architectures of companies (or groups of companies), associating network operators, CAPs and equipment suppliers – an obvious example being Google, which acquired Motorola Mobility in August 2011, tested Google Voice in September 2011 in Europe, became a virtual operator in Spain in 2011, etc.)

For regulators, these complex structures raise questions, on the one hand, regarding the boundaries of their scope of competences, and, on the other hand, regarding the relevance of their traditional modus operandi for regulating markets.

Regarding the first aspect, the creation of these horizontally integrated operators, and the deepening relations between the different sectors (e.g. the links between terminals and software platforms) trigger specific challenges for public authorities. First, they must look after maintaining effective competition inside each activity (equipment supplier, network operator, service provider, content editor). This can be achieved by instance through guaranteeing certain conditions in case of merging of different actors[10]. A second type of question -specifically for EC regulators- is to know which actors, or parts of actors, can be considered "operators of electronic communications", which is the only category directly subject to their powers. An

---

[10] For example in France, the Competition Authority had imposed specific conditions when authorizing the acquisition of TPS by Canal +, which lead to the creation of a dominant actor on the market of distribution of pay TV. These conditions aimed at allowing the remaining distributors (principally broadband providers) to access to contents attractive enough to build competitive ay TV offers. The same Authority recently observed that these conditions has not been fulfilled, and consequently imposed penalties on Canal + (property of Vivendi) (decision n° 11-D-12 of 20 September 2011).

increasing diversity of organizations invest in networks and/or propose services that fall into the ECNS category – typical examples are Skype or Google. More specifically, some actors may deploy strategies to be recognized in one (or several) categories, for instance to be able to require access or interconnection agreements with an established operator. It can be noted here that, according to the new regulatory framework, such access could be obtained by stakeholders that are not necessarily operators (typically CAPs), and such relations may be subject to dispute settlements, with the NRA being competent to solve some of these disputes. In general, regulators will consider that their rules apply to the relevant activity of a concerned stakeholder, whatever its other businesses. However, in practice, such "isolation" of an activity, for technical or accounting purposes, is not always easy to simulate.

Furthermore, beyond the difficulty in identifying the activities that fit within the ECNS definition, there may be a need in the future to better address those that seem to fall outside this scope. Today's uncertainties in this regards are underlined in the Ecory's study mentioned above (see footnote 12), which considers that there may be some gaps in the regulatory package: "(…) the current regulatory framework is typically designed to manage the contractual relation between access seekers and access providers and the contractual relation between operators and end-users. Is the regulatory framework endowed to manage the upstream contractual relations between over-the-top service providers and operators as well? In other words, is the framework ready to deal with the transition towards an internal market in which operators can exert market power in the contractual relation with content and over-the-top service providers?" Without necessarily envisaging a profound rewriting of the framework, a clarification of regulatory responsibilities seems unavoidable in the coming years. One of the possibilities, although not the only one, would be to explicitly extend the competences of telecoms regulators.

The second aspect leads to examine whether the current methodology that determines the need for regulation, and the obligations applied, is well adapted to this new environment.

The European regulatory framework is currently based on a cleavage of markets according to the different types of substitutable services (fixed telephony, mobile messaging, broadband access...) and the two main categories of relations (wholesale, retail). This segmentation is used for the market analyses, which are at the core of European regulation: in each pre-identified market, one or several operators are declared dominant (which means that they can exert a significant influence on the market, i.e. they enjoy "significant market power" - SMP), and consequently remedies are decided to guarantee effective competition on that market.

To understand this methodology, one must remember than, in Europe, sectorial regulation only should happen when competition law, which is recognized as the optimal reference by the ECNS directives, is deemed insufficient. Such situation is to be demonstrated via the fulfillment of three criteria: existence of strong and lasting barriers to entry, no perspective of sustainable competition in the time horizon considered, impossibility to solve issues through ex-post regulation. The underlying logic is that, in the longer run, as barriers progressively disappear or weaken, sectorial regulation should cease and give way to competition law alone. However, in an ever evolving sector such as telecommunications, where innovative networks and services are constantly emerging, barriers to entry are created regularly, causing new competition issues. This is reflected in the considerable evolution undergone by the list of relevant markets (those eligible to regulation) in the course of regulatory reviews.

More generally, convergence creates the need to think anew this regulation based on pre-identified markets, to move towards a transverse regulation. As an illustration, an operator that would not be deemed dominant on the fixed, mobile and broadband market considered separately, could nevertheless exert a significant influence on the whole market thanks to multiple play offers. This could happen for instance by increasing the switching costs between sub-elements of the bundles[11]. It could also stem from creating or reinforcing the "club effect" at household level: all the inhabitants of a home may be incited to migrate towards the same operator for all their communications needs[12]. An additional possibility is the cross usage of customers database, that can represent an undue advantage - particularly for an incumbent operator, if he uses the databases inherited from its previous position of public monopoly, in order to conquer customers on other markets[13].

3.2   New Preoccupations Challenging Regulators

The considerations above concern primarily asymmetric regulation, which played a central role in the first era of liberalization of the market (as described above). Since convergence structures the market according to a more symmetric shape (groups of large entities, diversified and integrated), a more symmetric regulation is needed. This covers, on one side, competition issues: the regulator must not limit its supervision to the incumbent operator, but must be vigilant regarding the practices of all actors in the oligopoly. On the other side, this symmetric regulation pursues wider objectives, such as maintaining a sufficient quality of service and preventing abuses towards consumers (e.g. inappropriate subscription clauses, barriers to switching, etc.) An example will be given below with the net neutrality topic, where the regulator aims at promoting end users' access to contents and applications of his choice.

The questions triggered by the evolving market structure particularly stem from the overwhelming importance of the infostructure, where happen most of interactions between new entrants and operators already present in the market place (in particular the incumbent). It is quite understandable, indeed, that these operators warily consider the interference with their network of other stakeholders, in particular if these players are external to the telecommunications world. Nicolas Curien, in the interview mentioned above (cf. footnote 9) narrates a similar form of mistrust already met much earlier in the French telecommunications history: "(...) at the end of the seventies, I remember that executives from the general Directorate of telecommunications fiercely opposed a perspective, which was already indicated by the evolution of the northern-

---

[11] This case was envisaged in ARCEP public consultation on its market analysis of mobile call termination for Free, Lyca, and Omea, which ended on the 10 October 2011.

[12] This situation was envisaged in the opinion n° 10-A-13 of 14 June 2010 by the French competition Authority.

[13] This case was also envisaged in the opinion n° 10-A-13 of the 14 June 2010 by the French competition Authority.

American market: the possibility for external agents, "foreign agents" somehow, to penetrate and manage the intelligence of the network. The counter-arguments that were put forward at that time were vague and not very convincing: they underlined the extreme complexity of a network system, the impossibility of an effective coordination by the market, the absolute necessity that a unique company controls the totality of the system, otherwise this could cause a catastrophic drop in quality of service. History rapidly proved wrong this centralist and over-planning vision, inherited from the management of the classical telephony network, which was not sustainable anymore in the digital era, marked by autonomy of action, decentralized initiative and flexibility."[14]

Nowadays, similar questions around the interaction at infostructure level are raised in the scope of Internet services. They encompass matters such as security, resilience and protection of private data. The network is continuously attacked or hijacked, which threatens its integrity and sustainability. The ways to address such threats are subject to intense public debates, concerning the degree of control that operators will exert, on their sole responsibility, on traffic conveyed on the networks. Such perspective raises concerns for end users and civil parties, because they fear that communication usages may be spied on, or that important sets of personal data may be stored in vulnerable places in the operator's network. On the other hand, delegating for instance such management to external parties raises relevant questions for operators, particularly in terms of efficiency. Clearly, years to come will see the need to balance these often-conflicting constraints of network integrity and security, users' privacy, as well as the challenges they pose on interoperability of services. The objective of interoperability, although it is put forward by the regulatory framework[15] and has proven central in the explosive development of the Internet ecosystem, is not always an obvious choice to go after. In some cases, full interoperability, despite its potential positive externalities, may deter certain forms of innovation, particularly when high initial investments are concerned. In such cases indeed, business protections such as exclusivities or restricted usage can make sense. In fact, economic theory does not allow determining, on a general basis and for all situations, whether an open and interoperable system will provide more value than a closer environment.

Another range of concern relates to the control of contents, which circulation is deemed illegal by relevant jurisdictions. Although the EU regulatory framework has recognized the limited liability of operators and hosting providers as regards the contents exchanged or made available through their services, they may be required to apply restrictions upon legal order. Such processes are for example established in laws regarding the protection towards child abuse, online games, the infringement of copyright, etc. Such legal orders generally fall outside ECNS regulators' competences, although some of them have been entrusted with responsibilities in this field. This is the case for instance in the United Kingdom, where the regulator OFCOM is involved in the process of implementing the legislative provisions adopted regarding copyright infringement.

---

[14] English translation of N. Curien's quotation by the author of this article.

[15] Article 8.3.b of the Framework Directive: « *National regulatory authorities contribute to the development of the internal market, in particular (...) by encouraging (...) interoperability of pan European services and end-to-end connectivity* ».

3.3   Innovative Regulatory Approaches

The description above of the new market structure has evidenced the need, for competition-focused asymmetric regulation, to address a variety of complex situations, in particular oligopolistic market structure and trans-market issues. Two provisions of the European regulatory framework may prove particularly helpful in this respect. The first one is the possibility (provided for in article 14(2) of the Framework directive) to declare several operators "jointly dominant" on a market, hence providing a tool for regulators in certain oligopolistic situations. However, this provision has arguably proved quite uncertain to apply in practice[16].

The second one deals with leverage of market power: the new framework explicitly provides for NRAs to impose conditions in circumstances where an actor can exert leverage of dominance, via article 14(3) of the Framework directive[17]. Traditional examples of such markets could be couples of retail markets (e.g. retail Leased Lines) and wholesale markets (in the same example: wholesale end-to-end call packages offered to resellers). There might indeed be very strong links between the retail markets and the corresponding upstream markets on which the provider is dominant – for instance, in the case where innovative, complex, solutions are offered on the retail market, without the alternative operators being able to easily replicate them, in the absence of adequate technical specifications on the wholesale market. Effectiveness of competition in such markets could thus be dependent on preventing the dominant provider from distorting the market by leveraging its dominance from the upstream market (such regulation may be very limited, e.g. in the form of a price publication remedy). In the context of convergence, such approach may be increasingly interesting for markets that display a "horizontal close link". Although when analyzed in isolation a dependent or adjacent market might appear to be effectively competitive, in practice the effectiveness and sustainability of that competition may depend on the regulation in place to control dominance in the adjacent market. It is a similar kind of reasoning that the one applied by the Commission in the famous Microsoft case (enjoying dominance in operating systems and thereby imposing its browsing system), or currently under examination in the Google case (enjoying dominance in search engines and thereby potentially imposing abusive conditions on the online advertising market).

Leverage effect and joint dominance are two regulatory approaches that allow accommodating and extending the definition of market power. However, the most difficult upcoming challenges for regulation may not be about market power (as subtle as

---

[16] See on this matter: *"Joint Dominance and Tacit Collusion: Some Implications for Competition and Regulatory Policy"*, Patrick Massey and Moore McDowell, in European Competition Journal, Number 2, August 2010. The article takes as its starting point the Irish telecom regulator, ComReg's, finding of joint dominance in the mobile phone market in Ireland. The case raises wider questions about the whole concept of joint dominance as it has evolved under EU competition law and economic analysis.

[17] This article states that: *"Where an undertaking has significant market power on a specific market, it may also be deemed to have significant market power in a closely related market, where the links between the two markets are such as to allow the market power held in one market to be leveraged into the other market, thereby strengthening the market power of the undertaking."*

this may be defined), but rather about promoting some key principles along all the segments of the digital chain. The evolution from monopolistic to oligopolistic structures, and the parallel growing importance of symmetric regulation, was already underlined above. But a perhaps even more drastic move can be foreseen in the future, if ECNS markets massively undergo a transformation from "portfolio" commercial models to "platform" models. The latter has shown both successes (e.g. IBM, Microsoft) and failures (e.g. WAP) in the past, and currently rides high with the impressive reach of Apple, Google, or even Facebook, constellations. In such "coopetitive" environment, it will be hard to define a clear-cut dominance on a firmly delineated market – but there are still concrete threats of undue discrimination, restrictions of users' ability to choose, anticompetitive behavior, etc. particularly from firms capable of controlling (at least partly) the access of end users to Internet services.

Convergence thus requires that regulators adapt their methodologies, and prioritize the prevention of new types of risks against a competitive, innovative and qualitative ECNS environment. Such evolution in regulation techniques is well illustrated by an important topic in today's regulatory agenda: the net neutrality debate.

3.4 An Example: The Net Neutrality Debate

The set of issues related to net neutrality reflects, to a certain extent, the impact of the new business context on the ECNS regulatory arena. This last part will attempt to show how some questions can be addressed by the existing (old and recent) principles of regulation – applied through a combination of available tools and modern regulatory approach.

3.4.1   Scope of the Debate

According to Tim Wu, the "father" of this terminology, net neutrality can be defined as a « network design principle » whereby « (…) a maximally useful public information network aspires to treat all content, sites, and platforms equally. This allows the network to carry every form of information and support every kind of application. »

Tim Wu's definition appears to be looking at networks as a whole. Among them, however, special attention is paid by public authorities to Internet and the services it conveys, since they have acquired a considerable significance over the recent years, in both our economy and our society. Analyzing them with regards to this net neutrality principle seems particularly relevant, because the swift development of the Internet "ecosystem" can precisely be attributed to its open and non-discriminatory nature - a neutrality that allows anyone to offer content or services, whether commercial or not, to all Internet users, to test innovations, business models, to communicate ideas, swap and share without having to obtain prior agreements or permission, and with no economic, regulatory or social "thresholds effect". This explains why many policy makers believe that it is in everyone's interest that these essential characteristics continue to exist, as much for technical-economic reasons as for reasons of social responsibility.

The current debate is thus centered on the Internet platform, but at the same time it involves various dimensions, either economical, or associated to human freedoms, and often with the question of contents lawfulness. It corresponds also on a broader thinking about the rules and rights applicable to all – in particular for the "transport" function (principally endorsed by ISPs) and the "transported services" (undertaken by CAPs and internet users). All these stakeholders have a role in the degree of openness and efficiency of the "Internet ecosystem", and their diversity of relations may, or may not, favor easy access to certain contents, long term innovation, resilience of the infrastructure, etc.

Some of the questions raised by the issue of Internet neutrality may actually fall outside the realm of the rules and regulations that usually apply to electronic communications networks. Here lies one aspect of the net neutrality issue complexity: the borders of the applicable regulatory scheme are often unclear. Furthermore, players cannot always be easily classified. For instance, several big CAPs (e.g. Microsoft or Google) also operate big scale (private) networks – this may include proprietary MPLS architecture, applying traffic management and peering contracts with ISPs. Some of them therefore appear to be in the position to prioritize certain contents and applications. Is this within the scope of net neutrality?

Electronic communications networks operators, in the classical understanding, nevertheless occupy a central place in the "Internet chain" and among the players that populate it. Indeed, the entities that operate these networks have a special responsibility because of their function of routing traffic between users. They are consequently the first ones affected by the demand for neutrality, which explains why, in its most recent works, Tim Wu has developed more precise recommendations regarding the specificity of their role. He advises that it remains separate from the provision of contents and applications that they transport: "those who develop information, those who control the network infrastructure on which it travels, and those who control the tools or venues of access must be kept apart from one another."

In any case, and whoever the category of players concerned, the net neutrality debate feeds into more general trends, related to the development of the digital economy. Among these, one must first mention the growing interference of economics and law in a previously tacit and technical universe (which partly explains the "hot" debates on ACTA, on Hadopi law in France, etc.). A second important aspect is the growth of exchanges, and of the values exchanged, on the Internet – this being partly diverted away from the physical economy to the Internet. Such trends lead to questions around the growth of bandwidth needs and how to support the associated costs, in parallel with debates on how to apply pre-Internet legislation and find the right balance between human freedoms (e.g. property rights vs. freedom of expression). An additional dimension relates to the weight and impact of new stakeholders in the digital economy, and the search for a sustainable balance between all actors of the value chain.

In this context, public authorities must conciliate the challenges of, one the one hand, preserving a digital public space that supports innovation and freedom of expression and, on the other hand, ensure the proper financing of networks, and protect copyright and intellectual property. While pursuing those targets at their own level, ECNS regulators must bear in mind the specific importance of Internet for the economy and the society, which has been recognized by the European Commission[18], the Council of Europe, and in France by the Constitutional Council[19].

---

[18] « *The Commission attaches high importance to preserving the open and neutral character of the*

With regards to operators having a role in the market access to Internet, symmetric regulation thus tries to preserve or promote a principle of "neutrality", which can be understood in the following way: avoiding that an operator favors contents produced by its close partner, and throttles deliberately the contents of rival solutions on its network. Operators may, in some cases, invoke justifications linked to the protection of the network, notably when facing traffic spikes provoked by the explosion of video video traffic; in many of these cases, the appropriate response consists in further investing on the Internet infrastructure and the associated services, rather than blocking certain types of traffic!

3.4.2   Regulatory Approach

Taking into account the background presented above, NRAs are expected to include net neutrality within their regulatory objectives. This primarily invites them to pursue their efforts to develop competition in the markets, since this is the first guarantee of net neutrality. Indeed, the availability of a diversity of offers enables the users to choose the access to contents that is best adapted to their needs. As we have seen previously in this chapter, competition has been ensured in Europe thanks to a strong asymmetrical regulation of broadband. Its efficiency however depends on the ability of users to "choose with their feet". This ability should be further enhanced, particularly via increased transparency and lower switching costs – the revised regulatory framework includes new powerful provisions in this respect.

But regulators shall also adapt to the complex trends in the markets, such as the growing asymmetry of data traffic (with more and more traffic, in particular video, flowing from Internet giants to "eyeballs" end users), or the appearance of exclusive or privileged agreements – which are much more difficult to grasp than classical vertical integration. In this changing environment, NRAs must keep focus on promoting the access to content, particularly through monitoring the quality of service of Internet access offers. In this respect, the 2009 telecom package gives the regulators the power to impose minimum quality requirements (article 22.3 of the Universal Service Directive), which is a key safeguard in the event of excessive degradation of the access to Internet. This could happen for instance if operators decided to invest essentially in their own, closed environment services, rather than on sufficient capacity for the open internet platform.

As discussed earlier, there are new, complex and constantly evolving relations between ECNS and the other parts of the Internet ecosystem – which invites regulators to develop a prudent approach. This can be illustrated by the three-step approach of ARCEP in France. This consisted first in identifying the objectives that shall be conciliated in its market – a process that leveraged on a wide consultation of all stakeholders in 2010 (auditions, conference, public consultation) and enabled to emphasize the following stakes: the liberty of choice for the user; a sustainable functioning of networks; innovation everywhere (both at the core and at the edge of networks). Sub-

---

Internet, taking full account of the will of the co-legislators now to enshrine net neutrality as a policy objective and regulatory principle to be promoted by national regulatory authorities » - Commission declaration on net neutrality (2009/C 308/02), 18 December 2009.

[19] See: decision n° 2009-580 DC, on 10 June 2009, where Internet is recognized as a fundamental mean to exercise one's freedom of expression.

sequently, the Authority published some "soft law" guidance[20], including a global vision of good practices and of methodologies to evaluate the market situation. The document puts forward large range principles, which could constitute a basis for case-by-case appreciation later on. It also presents tools that would be used to monitor the relevant markets. The third step is currently on-going: implementing those recom-mendations in practice, primarily through co-regulation, but being ready for more prescriptive measures if deemed necessary.

Upon a demand from the French Parliament, ARCEP has recently published an update and follow-up on the national situation regarding net neutrality, together with further clarifications about the principles put forward in 2010. A public consultation was held in June 2012, raising substantial comments, in particular regarding the anal-ysis of traffic management practices in the light of ARCEP's main criteria (relevance, proportionality, efficiency, non-discrimination between parties and transparency). Consultations were held also at European level, on similar aspects, notably initiated by BEREC, which published elements of assessment of traffic management practices (or differentiation practices). The last part of this article will however focus on anoth-er burning aspect of the discussions, which relates to the interaction between ECNS operators and other players – particularly CAPs and handset manufacturers, and how this materializes at various levels of the ecosystem: interconnection agreements, diffe-rentiated treatment of applications, end users' conditions...

3.4.3   Latest Developments

Internet is now at the heart of billions of humans' lives, both in developed and devel-oping countries. It is an incontrovertible tool for communicating and working, for leisure and information. It plays a crucial role for citizens' empowerment and free-dom, as the 2011 spring Arab revolutions (launched on Facebook and Twitter) have demonstrated. Its social importance is becoming considerable, which can be illu-strated for instance with a recent study in France[21], showing that 74% of persons own-ing a home Internet access connect everyday, whereas 41% of users say they can't do without Internet for more than a few days. This worldwide, spectacular success can be explained in a number of ways, but a major one lies in how players and networks have spontaneously maximized their interconnection capabilities, without any restrictive legal framework.

Interconnection

A recent article published in ARCEP's newsletter describes how economic theory applies to this significant development: "(...) externalities of adoption are particularly positive in a telecommunications network. In other words, very user connected to the network values it all the more than the number of other connected users –both pro-ducers and consumers- raises, to the extent that available capacities do not affect ne-gatively its own comfort of use. Internet players have perfectly understood this eco-nomical principle and have spontaneously applied it in practice (...) through a pyra-midal architecture inherited from the pre-commercial times of the Internet, where a

---

[20] « *ARCEP proposals on Internet and network neutrality* », published on 30 September 2010, available in English at www.arcep.fr

[21] Conducted in 2011 by CREDOC.

few "tier 1" transit operators passed the traffic between ISPs at the edge of the networks (...). This transit created a cost, and often sub-optimal performance (...), thus FAI attempted to directly exchange traffic between them"[22]. This (simplified) story illustrates the development of secondary peering, and the constitution of peering points (named IX for Internet eXchange), which enabled significant efficiency gains, despite punctual tensions, usually rapidly solved without the intervention of public authorities.

The continuous development of Internet raises the importance of some questions, first about handling the risks of attack without affecting individual freedoms, second about the security and resilience of exchanges when interconnection relations are getting more and more complex. Thirdly, parties debate about sharing the costs of the development and maintenance of the infrastructure, at a moment when operators are forced to re-dimension their networks permanently to face the increased number of users, the lengthening of time spent on-line and the success of bandwidth-hungry services (such as streaming). Network operators are consequently exploring various means to have CAPs (who benefit from the traffic volume growth) contribute more to these costs: they may introduce paid peering, or offer to prioritize some types of traffic (against remuneration) on their local networks, or propose enhanced interconnection conditions (for instance via telco CDN services). In front of these options, regulatory authorities will need to be vigilant regarding potential anticompetitive effects, which would impact the online services markets, and more generally the long-term dynamic effect of certain models on innovation.

Nevertheless, such anticompetitive effects could also be a consequence from other players' behaviors. In this respect, we mentioned above the growing weight of some major players on the CAP side. It is therefore both types of parties, who could need to be defended in the event of a dispute. In this context, what are the current, and perhaps desirable in the future, competences given to regulators by the ECNS framework on these matters?

Competence of regulators over CAPs/ISPs interaction

BEREC recent report on "Differentiation practices and related competition issues in the scope of Net Neutrality" has started looking into this kind of issues, in particular on the great variety of interaction and behavior of this "upstream" part of the Internet ecosystem. European regulators indicate that the current text of the telecom directives does provide some legal background to regulators in order to intervene, at least partially, on relations between OTT and network operators for telecommunications issues. In this regard, references to the framework are two-folded:

- On the one hand, regulators are entrusted with objectives to promote the access to content, and a suitable competitive environment to achieve this (see in particular articles 8.2b and 8.4g of the Framework Directive). Such provisions do not constitute specific regulatory powers in themselves, and

---

[22] Translation, courtesy of the author, of « *Peering et net neutralité : pérenniser la croissance et le dynamisme de l'internet* » in *Les cahiers de l'ARCEP*, n°8, June 2012.

should be read in conjunction with other objectives when applying the existing powers and tools of the directives;

- On the other hand, certain competences of regulators have been enlarged or further specified in order to better take into account these aspects – e.g. transparency on traffic management (article 20/21 Universal Service Directive), ability to impose minimum quality requirements in case of degradation of certain traffic (art 22.3 Universal Service Directive). One modified provision of the revised framework is of particular interest here: article 20 of the Framework directive, on dispute settlement.

Regarding the first aspect, it is useful to consider the wider background of the revised telecom framework: although these provisions covering transmission do not cover the content of services delivered over electronic communication networks, the European legislator recognizes that content and carrier are inherently linked to each other. This is reflected for instance in recital 5 of the Better Regulation Directive: "The separation between the regulation of transmission and the regulation of content does not prejudice the taking into account of the links existing between them, in particular in order to guarantee media pluralism, cultural diversity and consumer protection." This reference helps reading the policy objectives in the Framework Directive, which provide guidance for how the provisions of the ECNS framework should be understood. These goals, drawn from article 8 on the goals of regulation, could be summarized likewise: to achieve the overarching objective of guaranteeing access to content for the interest of the citizens of the European Union; to ensure that electronic communications networks run smoothly, in other words to guarantee a satisfactory quality of service (including matters of integrity, security and interoperability); to enable the long-term development if the networks and services thanks to innovation and the development of the most efficient technical and business models.

BEREC "guidelines on quality of service and net neutrality" further discuss how to consider these provisions: "(...) access to content is an objective, which is interlinked with relevant parts of the electronic communications regulatory framework. As content is being made available through networks, (...) without prejudice to the eventual outcome of a careful and balanced consideration of interests, BEREC does recognise the idea that, according to article 8(2)(b) FD, NRAs shall ensure that there is no distortion or restriction of competition in the electronic communications sector (...). The ability to regulate content is also contingent on it being accessible, which links with the article 8(4)(g) FD objective of "promoting the ability of end-users to access and distribute information or run applications and services of their choice". The objectives pursued by content regulation are of a general interest nature, such as: "freedom of expression, media pluralism, impartiality, cultural and linguistic diversity, social inclusion, consumer protection and the protection of minors".[23] (...) These policy objectives therefore play a role in how NRAs approach their discretionary powers [...]"

---

[23] Framework Directive, recital (6).

Regarding the second aspect, it is particularly interesting to consider the enlarge-ment of the scope of article 20[24], Framework Directive, which should be read in con-junction with modified article 2, access directive (where the definition of "access" was updated in order to explicitly take into account the impact of ECNS on the access to content, and therefore on OTT activities[25]). How should this enlargement be un-derstood?

On the parties of the dispute, clearly the revised framework opens up the possibili-ty for NRAs to handle disputes between network operators and undertakings, which do not fall into this category. OTT/CAPs players could therefore be parties to a dis-pute resolution in the scope of this article. On the subject of the dispute, conversely, no particular element in the revised text allows inferring that the matters, which can be addressed through such provision, are modified with the telecom package. ECNS regulators (except when they have extra responsibilities in their national environment) do not have competence, for instance, in evaluating aspects related to the content itself: e.g. rules governing its distribution, exclusivities, property rights, etc. Their competence is limited to the transmission aspects of a situation, i.e. the conditions in which this content is transported.

The revised framework thus gives some interesting new tools to ECNS regulators. But are these sufficient? Outstanding issues may lie in particular in the technical and economic conditions associated with telecom devices.

The specific role of terminals manufacturers

Relatively to the core question of the net neutrality debate, i.e. the ability of end users to access the content of their choice without undue restriction, it seems relevant to also question the potential anchor role of the device used to access the Internet, and its conditions of use. This device can either function on fixed networks (e.g. set-top box-es and connected TVs) and/or on mobile networks (e.g. smartphone). Indeed, while this paper already mentioned the importance of the changing relations between ISPs and other players, operators and terminal manufacturers share, to a certain extent, the same crucial specificity in the ecosystem, which is that they both control an access "gate" to the Internet, that an end-user can not easily circle (in particular because such

---

[24] Article 20 of the FWD previously provided for an *ex post* tool of dispute resolution between network operators. The revised version of this article reads as follows: *"In the event of a dispute arising in connection with existing obligations under this Directive or the specific directives between undertakings providing electronic communications networks or services in a Member State, or between such undertakings and other undertakings in the Member State benefiting from obligations of access and/or interconnection arising under this direc-tive or the specific directives, the national regulatory authority concerned shall, at the re-quest of either party, and without prejudice to the provisions of paragraph 2, issue a binding decision to resolve the dispute in the shortest possible time frame and in any case within four months, except in exceptional circumstances.*

[25] [access] *"means the making available of facilities and/or services to another undertaking, under defined condition, on either an exclusive or non-exclusive basis, for the purpose of providing electronic communications services, including when they are used for the delivery of information society services or broadcast content services."*

devices are expensive to change). End users may become all the more "captive" that, with terminals becoming more sophisticated and smart, they concentrate a growing amount of information from their owner, with high personal and economic value. This information is frequently complex to extract from the device and transfer it to a new one, if the user so desires.

In this context, and with the development of vertically integrated platform, terminal manufacturers increasingly have the capacity to influence or restrict the usage of the consumers: what service they can download in their device, which application they can run, etc. On these aspects, ISPs may have little or no control at all, whereas the risk of anticompetitive practices grows with the closeness of manufacturers' proprietary environment. Such vertical offerings nevertheless present some concrete interest for users (simple and safe platform), and thus may justify such industrial policy – an approach mostly carried out by American actors today.

The difficulties identified here are susceptible to considerably restrict users' ability, both to access the content or applications of their choice, and to change provider of ECNS. The emerging nature of such issues, the diversity of situations concerned and the numerous types of players involved, may require that public authorities, and perhaps regulators, propose specific measures to tackle the "manufacturers" topic.

4   Conclusion

It is often heard, as regards big network-based industries (such as energy, telecommunications and transports), that everything was simple before the eighties. State monopolies were to face the huge infrastructure investments that, supposedly, the private sector could not bear. Progressively, however, the interest of allowing the entry of private competitors on the market became a more seductive idea, and was followed by the concept of sectorial regulation. Indeed, liberalization seemed to require, in addition to competition authorities, the presence of regulation institutions. They were to set a legal framework enabling market entry, and thereafter supervise, based on common competition law and subject to relevant jurisdictions, of economic players' behavior. Furthermore, as mentioned at the beginning of this article, other objectives such as universal service, networks security or industrial policy, were embedded very early into the regulator's remit. According to Marie-Anne Frison Roche, professor of law at Sciences Po, the definition of this role "was first informal. Then it crystalized (…)" – in France was first born the authority of financial markets, then the regulator of telecoms.

In the subsequent years, the major role of ex ante regulators has thus been to enable the transition from a (mostly) monopolistic configuration to a (mostly) competitive environment. This appears to be a long term mission, which final goal (the setting of an effective competitive situation) is not reached yet. In the meantime, regulating the economics sector by sector becomes more and more complex. This article particularly examined the thinner frontiers between electronic communications markets, especially in the context of development of the Internet, and all the more that growing needs appear for regulating at a more global scale, since "markets have internationalized", as Marie-Anne Frison Roche explains. She also notes the interdependence of some regulated markets, for instance between energy and finance... the latter having significantly evolved due to the usage of Internet.

This changing environment raises serious challenges for regulators, and some of them have been discussed in this article: which players can be the subject to electronic communications sectorial rules? What is the scope of ECNS regulation within the Internet ecosystem? What are its means of action, when actors interact in supranational markets? These questions will need to be faced by tomorrow's regulation, which asymmetric component will probably have considerably diminished, to the profit of ex post law, whereas its symmetric role may gain importance. Policy makers are indeed particularly keen on the establishment, monitoring and enforcement of such symmetric rules for the ECNS sector, since these markets support the major transformations of our times: the digital revolution. In this context, it is crucial to avoid market bottlenecks, which could be lethal to the digital development dynamics.

Some of the key principles, which should guide ex ante regulation in the future, have already been designed and applied in the past (e.g. transparency, non-discrimination and, to a certain extent, interoperability). In fact, the evolution of regulation needed to adapt to the new context may rather concern the right methodology to implement these principles. For instance, some believe that regulators should adopt a less prescriptive, more incentivizing, attitude – like "hostesses in a cocktail, who facilitate the meeting and collaboration of players", as describes Nicolas Curien, previous member of ARCEP. To understand this view, one should first refer to the original aim of regulation: "maintaining a complex system in a sustainable state of dynamic equilibrium, according to the definition given to the term "regulation" by the physician Ampère". Yet, a fundamental issue for institutional regulators is that, whereas they must implement an external control to the system, players in the markets naturally adapt their strategies and exert a reciprocal influence on regulation.

Such de facto interaction must be fully taken into account by regulators, who should not conceive their action as a purely independent organization of the market, nor as mere punctual problem solving. The participation of stakeholders in finding common solutions should be facilitated at all stages. This approach seems all the more necessary that there appears to be an intimate relationship between the balance found in the ECNS framework, and innovation in the digital era. In this scope, if regulation is to be at the service of the digital revolution, it must not interfere in excess with its fertile unpredictability – the development of Internet splendidly advocates this, by demonstrating "a strong link between fundamental unpredictability and an amazing innovation capacity" as Elie Noam and Nicolas Curien have underlined.

It will undoubtedly be difficult for tomorrow's regulators to restrict their natural tendency to fix long-term sustainable rules and to eradicate uncertainties. This challenge is reinforced by the fact that some policy objectives will remain stringent: ensuring that networks function properly and safely, protecting the most fragile populations by maintaining appropriate "safety nets", some of them designed for users with specific social needs, while some of them aim at protecting the rights of all users – which lives depend more and more on ECNS services. Regulation will therefore need to find the right balance between these vivid preoccupations and a soft approach, openly involving all parties and giving enough leeway for innovators to create the future.

References

1. Laffont, J.-J., Tirole, J.: Competition in Telecommunications. MIT Press, Cambridge (2001)
2. Curien, N., Maxwell, W.: La neutralité d'Internet, La Découverte (2011)
3. The telecom package first includes directive 2009/140/CE of European Parliament and Council (Better regulation) amending directives 2002/21/CE (Framework), 2002/19/CE (Access) and 2002/20/CE (Authorization). The second part is made of directive 2009/136/CE (Citizen's Rights), modifying directives 2002/22/CE (Universal service) and 2002/58/CE (Privacy) as well as regulation (CE) n°2006/2004 on cooperation between national authorities in charge of consumer protection. Lastly, a new regulation (CE) N° 1211/2009 creates the new regulators' body BEREC. These texts were published in EUOJ (December 18, 2009)
4. Ecorys: Steps towards a truly Internal Market for e-communications delivered - In the run-up to 2020 (November 14, 2011)
5. Wu, T. (Columbia University, Law School): Network Neutrality, Broadband Discrimination. Journal of Telecommunications and High Technology Law 2 (2003)
6. Internet governance principles, Council of Europe Conference in Strasbourg, April 18-19 (2011)
7. Through the Law of 22 March 2011, French Parliament has asked ARCEP to provide an update on the status of net neutrality. ARCEP submitted on 20 September 2012 its report to Parliament and the Government on this issue. French and English information can be found here: http://www.arcep.fr/index.php?id=8652
8. BEREC has published a significant amount of findings and guidance on net neutrality. Most recently, it has adopted two Reports (on differentiated practices and related competition issues, and on IP interconnection), as well as Guidelines on Quality of Service, at the BEREC Plenary on 6 December 2012, after a public consultation during the previous summer (report on the consultation also available). All this material, together with useful overview and summary documents (which provide a concise description of three years of BEREC's activities in the field of net neutrality) can be found here: http://berec.europa.eu/eng/news_consultations/whats_new/1281-berec-has-adopted-two-summaries-and-the-updated-reports-on-net-neutrality
9. The quotations from Marie-Anne Frison Roche (translation courtesy of the author of this article) are from her interview with Benjamin Cruard in Sectorial regulators: hostesses in a cocktail (November 10, 2011)

Virtualizing Devices

André Paul and Stephan Steglich

Fraunhofer Institute for Open Communication Systems,
Kaiserin-Augusta-Allee 31, 10589 Berlin, Germany
{andre.paul,stephan.steglich}@fokus.fraunhofer.de

Abstract. Device categories are converging, operating systems proliferating and physical devices are becoming more and more interconnected. However, to develop an application for different devices is extremely difficult and complex whereby Web technologies are a good candidate to solve this problem. To support application developers multiple approaches currently exist that providing solutions for platform independent application development based on Web technologies. In this chapter an overview about current Web application related activities is given and the webinos Web runtime is introduced. Webinos goes another step further by also exposing features of remote devices and services as well as allowing developing distributed Web applications.

Keywords: Web, Future Internet, Widgets, Web Applications, Cross Domain Development, Cross Device Development.

1 Introduction

The last years have shown the increasing importance and usage of connected devices. Especially with the introduction of Web 2.0 technologies and the ability for users to contribute to their favorite Web sites the range of available Web based applications was significantly increased. One of the main advantages of such Web applications is that they can be accessed from various types of devices. It does not matter whether a Microsoft Windows or Linux based PC is used or even if mobile devices such as smart phones or tablets are used to access a Web page. The success of this is heavily based on the standardization of the underlying technologies like HTTP, HTML, CSS or JavaScript. But as of today Web technologies do not allow access to device specific functionalities in a common way and across various types of devices.

This chapter discusses activities that aiming to push the Web even further in order to reduce the need for native and operating system dependent applications to a minimum. A comprehensive comparison of related technologies and projects is given and the webinos project is introduced as midterm approach that introduces personal zones in order to share device features even across devices. Before going into the main sections a rough summary of non-Web technology based approaches and the past day of fragmentation is given.

E. Bertin et al. (Eds.): Telecommunication Services Evolution, LNCS 7768, pp. 182–202, 2013.
© Springer-Verlag Berlin Heidelberg 2013

Interoperability – The Early Days

In computer science interoperability and platform fragmentation is not a new problem. With the upcoming availability of a number of different home computer and gaming consoles the fragmentation problem reached the consumer marked.

For example the popular game 'Karateka' (1984) was available for, Apple II (6502 CPU), Armstart CPC (Z80A CPU), Atari 800 (6502b CPU), Commodore 64 (6510 CPU), IBM PC (8088 CPU), ZX Spectrum (Z80 CPU), Atari 7800 (6502c CPU), Atari ST (68000 16bit CPU), Nintendo Game Boy (LR35902 CPU). In total nine different underlying CPUs, graphics hardware, OSs, sound chips etc. For all platforms, almost everything was written again from scratch. With this being said interoperability problems and the demand for cross platform development is not new for today and already started several years back.

2   Background

Let's take a look into different approaches that promising to solve, or at least to ease, the platform fragmentation problem. Well platform fragmentation means that there are significant differences between different devices that hindering interoperability between them. Thus, standardizing the platform could be an approach to follow. This was already done back in the early 1980s by a number of companies that wanted to create a platform that can compete with the dominating platforms from Atari and Commodore.

The MSX home computer architecture defined fixed hardware and operating system specifications. With this all programs that were written for the MSX platform are able to run on all MSX based machines. MSX compatible computer were for example offered by Sony, Sharp, and Canon but the approach did not really worked in a competitive market. Because of long standardization process innovation was stifled and the platform was quickly outperformed by other products.

The MSX example shows that hoping to standardise hardware in a still emerging technology is not easy and success is by far not guaranteed. Standards for interfaces are, however, a good idea.

In this section a brief introduction to cross platform development tools and a deeper look into Web technology based tools is given. The section closes with an overview about standardization efforts that aiming to establish the Web as the application platform of the future.

2.1   Cross Platform Development

The demand for interoperability quickly created several approaches to abstract hardware from software which allowed easier application development and code reuse on different platforms. For example libraries originally were used to get easy access to system specific functionalities. Today a huge number of libraries for different devices are available that can be used for more or less each task that must be executed multiple times. Table 1 summarizes the most common classic abstraction technics.

Table 1. Cross platform development approaches.

Technique	Advantage
Cross-Compilers	No more machine language
Linked libraries	Re-use system specific binaries
BIOS	Abstraction from hardware I/O
Graphic libraries	Abstraction from graphic cards
Dynamic linked libraries	Libs do not need to be distributed with binaries

Later interpreted languages made a big step forward but early attempts, for example with Pascal p-Code (used mostly by USCD Pascal), did fail due to lack of processing speed. By 1995 home computers were powerful enough to run virtual machines with sufficient performance for many applications. Most prominent example is Java which promised "Write once, run everywhere". But in reality not that many desktop applications are available and it is mainly used on the server side with Servlet and Java Enterprise extensions. Java was followed shortly by JavaScript, Jscript and the related standardization ECMAscript. These and other scripting languages didn't even require compilation to byte code.

Later in this chapter JavaScript is used as one of the key technologies for Web based cross platform development. Before showing how it is used a short overview over classic cross platform development approaches is given.

Cross Platform Application Development Approaches

As of today a number of different application development environments are available. For example Wikipedia list 60 different approaches just for mobile development. The techniques used can be categorized into three classes which will be briefly introduced.

1. Fat Binaries
2. Runtime Environments
3. Cross Compilation

Fat Binaries are computer programs, which run natively on multiple architectures. Theses software packages include machine code for multiple instruction set architectures (ISA) at once. Because of this the resulting distributable compiled software is larger than a common one. Popular examples for this are the FatELF file format for Linux distributions or the so-called universal binaries from Apple that were used several times while switching from on hardware platform to another one (e.g., from the 68k to PowerPC or from PowerPC to Intel x86).

The group of runtime environment based approaches uses a middleware that translates code from a generic development language to a target machine. The complexity of dealing with different hardware is moved to the middleware and the developer does not need to take care about it. Depending on the actual approach an intermediate language is used and source code must be compiled (e.g., most prominent example Java) or code is directly interpreted during runtime (e.g., JavaScript).

Finally the class of cross compilation approaches creates native binaries for a target machine based on one input source code. This can either be done directly or through an intermediate step that produces platform specific source code, for example as with ParticleCode. This mostly involves heavy usage of compiler directives and switches for platform specific code that will be used by the compiler based on the requested target machine.

Web-Based Cross Platform Application Development Approaches

With the increasing distribution of the Internet and constant improvement of related technologies (network transmission rates, Web technologies), the World Wide Web (WWW) has developed to a dominant service platform in recent years. The original Web was designed for standard desktop computers (powerful, sufficient resources) and standard Internet connections (high speed, stable). With the convergence of devices in different domains, Web technologies are promising candidates to be also used in other environments. Especially mobile devices (e.g., (smart) phones in mobile telecommunication networks), consumer electronics devices (e.g., TV sets, set-top boxes and gaming consoles) as well as in-car entertainment system devices should be mentioned here.

Currently, there is no proven technology for delivering a single feature rich application to many device types and different device domains. This absence is a barrier to convergence, a cost to industry, an inconvenience to the consumer and can lead to an uncompetitive technical landscape.

Against this backdrop the Web and Web 2.0 technologies are showing themselves to be a strong candidate solution; the web designed for ubiquitous information sharing is proving itself to be a powerful applications platform. Strong evidence exist that PC, mobile and media industries are moving towards the web as an application platform solution.

Making Web applications the choice for platform independent application development needs two general building blocks. First one is the Web application runtime itself which is needed to interpret and execute Web technology based applications (HTML, CSS, JavaScript,...). The second block is related to the level of functional coverage that the runtime can provide to applications. To compete with native applications it is essential to provide as much as possible features that are commonly only available to native applications. Web based approaches can be classified into three categories:

- Native binary packaging
- Operating System Level integration
- Installable Web runtimes

Native Binary are standalone native applications that including a runtime for Web applications. Both parts are packaged together as common platform application such as an iOS or Android applications. The included Web runtime just needs to provide access to the features needed by the bundled Web application. Since each Web application that is deployed using this approach is bundled with its own Web runtime in total more storage space is needed. Example implementations of this approach are Appcelerator Titanium [2] and PhoneGap [3].

OS Level brings direct and integrated support for Web applications. The OS can handle application packages directly without additional need for Web runtime installations or for applications to come bundled with a specific Web runtime. Examples for this are HP's WebOS [20], Mozillas Boot2Gecko [21] and Google's ChromeOS [22].

Installable Web runtime approaches extending native operating systems to support the execution of Web application packages. A separate Runtime for executing applications must be installed on the device prior using the Web applications packages that are supported by the runtime. Examples for this are the Nokia WRT [1], Opera Widget Runtime [23] or the FOKUS Media Web Runtime [24].

Overall the best possible option is a deep integration of Web runtimes into operating systems. Each application only needs access to the features it really uses and declares and only one runtime component is needed. But most prominent advantage is that applications do not differ from other (native) 1st class application citizens of the OS. The user would not know whether he is using a native or a Web application. Following the Nokia WRT, phoneGap and Titanium are presented as representative technologies that are already widely used.

PhoneGap is an open source Web application runtime project developed by Nitobi. While PhoneGap also addresses the platform fragmentation issues it is not a Widget runtime like WRT. Thus, PhoneGap does not provide the possibility to download and execute Widgets as Widget runtimes would do. PhoneGap provides a Web runtime that can be packaged together with a Web application which are afterwards compiled to a native application. PhoneGap is available for iOS, Android, Blackberry, WebOS, Windows Mobile, and Symbian. As PhoneGap also exposes device functionalities to Web applications via JavaScript the concrete set of available features depends on the platform to be used. Due to PhoneGap's technological approach the compatibility with each of the platform specific application deployment schemes is given. In October 2011 Adobe acquired Nitobi Software and it was announced that phoneGab will be contributed the Apache Foundation where it is currently in an Apache Incubation state as Apache Cordova [25] after it was called "Project Callback" for a while.

Titanium from Appcelerator has an equal approach as PhoneGap. It is a cross-platform mobile application environment which allows developers to write mobile applications with familiar Web technologies and then deploy them as native applications. Consequently Titanium also exposes multiple device features via JavaScript to Web applications. Beside of just providing access to device features Titanium also exposes access to native UI libraries like buttons, alerts, menus, and navigation bars (which differs between the targeted platforms). Thus, with Titanium it is possible to create Web applications with a look and feel that comes close to the look and feel of native applications.

So why Developing Web Apps: There is lots of momentum today. For example Adobe included support for PhoneGap in its DreamWeaver CS 5.5 HTML editor and acquired Nitobi Software. After originally Palm's WebOS Mozilla also started a new purely Web based OS project.

Developing based on Web technologies allows massive reuse of existing skills. Web skills are easier to find and less costly than native app development skills. They are easy to use and have big user communities to ask and lots of documentation.

Using new frameworks hooking into the underlying OS is possible through technologies know to web developers which allows to create an app for multiple platforms at the same time including rapid prototyping with using just a Web Browsers. Even if some adaptations for certain devices are needed code and design assets can be reused.

Risks in Developing Web Apps: Web apps as standalone HTML5 apps running within an invisible browser window. They do run the risk of feeling more like web sites and less like mobile apps respectively like native apps of the specific platform unless implemented with sufficient care and attention.

A lack of interface "flow" and usability still exists. Input and output latency may be higher than with native apps. Low latency makes using smartphones fun but without attention HTML based apps run the risk of feeling jerky. User interface could easily feel inappropriate for the specific target platform. Poor performance is possible, particularly where functionality that makes lots of calls to the OS is used and there are still some potential compatibility issues with different CSS, JS, and DOM implementations.

Finally, depending on the platform and toolset used, there is some lack of access to every by the underlying platform provided native functionality.

Native vs. Web: There is no absolute this or that answer. It depends on the specific needs of a specific application idea. But to summarize, with native development you get what you want (if the OS permits it) but commonly with more costs. By design you create application interfaces that the user expects from the device with better performance. And you get access to all features the OS provides.

Using Web based cross platform tools you create applications more cost effective for cross platform purposes and you are faster to market. Web apps are easier to repurpose like white-labeling and doing device adaptations for specific devices without re-doing everything again. Finally development relies on less-costly less-specialist skills for implementation. Table 2 shows the results of a future application development study that was done by infoQ [13].

Table 2. Mobile Development Platforms

Technology	%
A mixture of native and web technologies	44.8
Exclusively native technologies (Object-C, Java)	39
Exclusively web technologies (with phoneGap or similar)	27.4
Appcelerator or similar cross platform development tools	19.7

2.2 Related Standardizations

There are a lot of those standards: de-facto standards, industry standards, national committees, international committees and others. The situation is better with web standards than with many others. Let's showcase the 'most influential' standards from the various domains first.

As PhoneGap, Titanium, Boot2Gecko and all the other approaches all exposing device features via JavaScript the concrete implementations are not compatible. Today multiple different organizations are working on the standardization of JavaScript device APIs. The main target is to harmonize the exposed APIs in order to reduce fragmentation on the API layer.

A first attempt in the mobile domain was made by the former Open Mobile Terminal Platform (OMTP) with its BONDI project in 2008 [4]. BONDI aimed at the development of a standardized open source Web and Widget based application environment designed to run on any platform. BONDI was not intended to be a commercial product but it was a first joint step of different major mobile operators to create related industry standards in the area of Web applications and Widgets. During the BONDI life cycle already 15 JavaScript APIs and a policy based security mechanism were developed. BONDI was discontinued in early 2010 whereas the produced specifications were contributed to the newly created Wholesale Applications Community (WAC) [5].

Together with the Joint Innovation Lab (JIL) WAC continued the work that was started with BONDI. Recently, WAC released already Version 2.1 of their Web applications industry standards. In addition to JavaScript APIs and Security mechanisms WAC defines a wholesale infrastructure that allows applications easily to be distributed to multiple application stores across participating operators. Commonly a developer has to submit its applications to each application store separately. The advantage of the WAC infrastructure is that there is no need for separate submissions. WAC provides one entry point to submit applications and in turn the developer receives a single aggregated payment for all application sales at all participating stores.

In 2010 the W3C Device APIs and Policy Working Group [6] was which aims to create W3C recommendations in the field of device APIs with an equal scope as BONDI. Within the next years this will result into harmonized APIs which will reduce the appearance of fragmentation on the JavaScript device API layer. Beside this some of the HTML5 Working Group specifications defining device APIs, e.g., the File API that allows file I/O operations.

In addition, the W3C Web Application Working Group [7] is working on several Widget standards [8] including packaging, signing, configuring, and updating Widgets. W3C Widgets are client side Web applications that are authored using Web standards such as HTML5, JS, and CSS. Its content is zipped to make it portable and includes an additional XML configuration file that contains multiple meta-data and runtime parameters. In addition the W3C Device APIs Working Group [6] is working on the standardization of JavaScript device APIs.

The previous initiatives are mainly targeting the mobile and the general Web domain. Apart from these also the TV and automotive domains are looking into standardizing Web based components for their application eco-systems. The OIPF Forum defines a Declarative Application Environment (DAE) [26] for TV sets which is based on CE-HTML. DAE adds APIs such as channel switching, PVR, TV metadata access.

The GENIVI alliance [9] targets to define a full platform (OS, middleware and APIs) for the automotive in-vehicle infotainment (IVI) industry. GENIVI APIs covering car information, navigation, driving safety, maintenance and more.

As we can see beside of W3C there are lots of standardization efforts in the industry and there will be even more standardization needed when it comes to cross domain application environments where not only applications can make use of local APIs but also can make use of device capabilities that are available on remote devices.

3   A Cross Domain Cross Device Application Execution Environment

Using state of the art projects and technologies enables the creation of a number of innovative feature rich Web applications. Given the fact that Web runtimes allowing the development of cross platform applications and related device APIs allowing using device specific features from within Web applications the next question is why not combining all the device and platform specific Web runtimes in a common way in order to share the exposure of device features across device and platform boarders. The open source project webinos [10] addresses this idea by defining APIs, protocols, and security mechanisms for distributed usage in the PC, mobile, TV and automotive domains. But before going into the details of webinos a closer look into the target scope using scenarios is given. The following user story is used to give an impression about what kind of scenarios could be realized with future internet Web runtimes.

3.1   Example Use Case

Alice is sitting in front of her Internet enabled where she goes to a social community site in order to create a new account. As usual, there is some profile information like nick name, age, etc. that must be provided to complete the registration procedure.

Due to common remote control restrictions, such as the absence of easy to use text input facilities, this is not an easy and comfortable task. Alice could use each connected device that provides text input capabilities (e.g., PC with keyboard, smart phone, Bluetooth or WiFi connected keyboards) to insert text for an application running on a TV set. Providing user interaction input sources to other input processing devices means also that there is no need for yet another keyboard for yet another screen; each keyboard could be used for each screen. Or, even better, only one keyboard is needed to control all the devices.

The web application needs some information from Alice and therefore the application presents alternative input methods. Alice decides to use her smart phone and in addition she selects to use it also in the future without asking.

To complete the registration Alice wants to attach a picture of her to the profile. Because her TV is not equipped with a camera she wants to use her mobile phone's camera capabilities. The web site provides a list of usable cameras and Alice selects her smart phone again. She also decides to use her smart phone any time in the future if a camera is requested by the application. After the picture was taken it is shown within the web site and attached to her profile.

3.2   Distributed Resource Access

For the moment the issues addressed by the story can be summarized under the term "virtual device". This means each hardware or software based service that is running on any supported device could be used by any of the other devices. For an application itself it does not matter where a service is actually executed. It just can query for a desired service type and the "virtual device" framework does the rest.

For example using a mobile phone's camera to take a picture and directly present it on the TV screen without any direct user interaction for the transfer of the data and without the need for applications to be adapted to the specific devices.

To realize this, a platform independent application runtime that allows the execution of applications no matter on which platform the application is currently running is needed. In addition an approach that allows using distributed device features or services on demand is in order to not mandate predefined usage of certain devices for certain tasks, no matter if the feature or service is located on the a local or remote device. Defining such an approach would also cover the aspect that even uncommon components of certain devices can be used in an integrated way from an application running on another device. Fig. 1 shows a distributed App running on certain devices in order to provide a better service to the user.

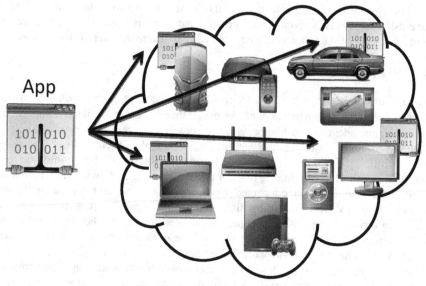

Fig. 1. Distributed Application

One approach to achieve remote access to resources could be to just allow applications to move some pieces of code between devices. These small code pieces then could do local API access and do kind of application to application communication between the main application and the small exported "child application".

On the one hand each API can just directly be used without specifying comprehensive RPC mechanisms because every device API access is done locally. In addition some remote deployment, device discovery and communication APIs are needed and must be defined also on protocol level.

But anyway, this approach has some drawbacks. First, sending code has always some risks. It's basically unknown what some piece of code is doing. Second one is that in the described case each device that wants to take part in the "virtual device" environment needs to support the execution of applications. That's not appropriate for some cases like sensor and actuator access or just for each device that as limited processing power but provides access to services. Thus, webinos uses a comprehensive RPC mechanism for remote service access but also allows for distributing applications across multiple devices.

3.3   Multi User

The just introduced scope is only talking about distributed access of device resources for Web applications in general so far. But we need to define boarders here. For example, not each device in the world should be automatically allowed to access each other device's services no matter where the device is or how the owner of the device is. Since webinos provides access to sensitive data such as the user location, calendar data or contact list information this would raise huge privacy and security issues. In our natural surroundings typically devices belong either to users or organizations. This being said in the first instance it makes sense to group the visibility of devices to users. In webinos the concept of grouping devices based on its owner is called Personal Zone (PZ) which is detailed following.

3.4   Architecture and Building Blocks

The overall architecture of webinos is based on putting the user in the center. Each user can create a Personal Zone that manages all the user's devices that should take part in the webinos environment. Prerequisite for a device to take part in a Personal Zone is basically that it must be connected somehow. Means the device must be accessible to other devices using any network barrier. Today not only the home computer is connected to a network. Also mobile phones, TV sets, home entertainment systems, gaming consoles and even cars or actuators like ligh switches or door openers are connected. Fig. 2 visualizes what type of devices could take part in such a Personal Zone. As shown, basically each device type can contribute to the PZ with exposing device capabilities as services to other devices. With this a PZ acts as an overlay network that abstracts from the underlying physical network that is needed to connect to certain devices.

While the Personal Zone is just a concept the Personal Zone Hub (PZH) and the Personal Zone Proxy (PZP) are the responsible architectural components in webinos that are used to establish Personal Zones. Using a PZP and PZH together ensures that device features can be shared across device, network and even user boarders in a secure manner. Let's take a closer look into what each of the components actually is.

Fig. 2. Personal Device Cloud

In webinos each device is represented by a PZP which is a piece of software running on the device. The primary tasks of a PZP are:

1. providing a web application runtime for executing webinos applications
2. providing access to device capabilities via JavaScript APIs to applications
3. acting as policy enforcement point
4. discovering devices such as Bluetooth, UpnP, NFC, ZigBee or other locally enabled devices

The PZH is responsible for managing and maintaining the Personal Zone of a user and should be an always available entity. Thus, it should run on a server available via a public IP address or name and with this a PZH can be identified by a URL. The primary tasks of a PZH are:

1. device management
2. user management
3. distributed device and service discovery
4. policy management and enforcement and enabling access to the personal zone

Following the key components of a personal zone hub and personal zone proxies are detailed to highlight the key features a distributed Web based application runtime needs to support.

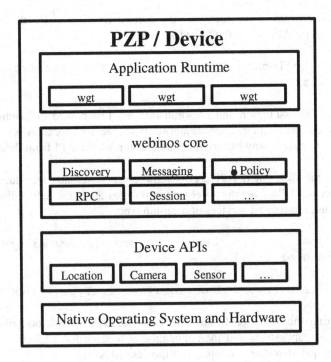

Fig. 3. Personal Zone Proxy

Web Runtime

The main task of a full PZP is to provide an application runtime environment for Web based applications. This is very comparable to what other Web application based solutions offer. Webinos basically extends the W3C Widget [8] specifications to fit the needs of a fully distributed environment and provides an application runtime that allows installing, executing and maintaining webinos applications. Webinos application in this case just means that it is an application that follows W3C Widget specifications but uses at least one of the APIs provided by webinos.

To also integrate devices that are not capable of providing a web application runtime, for example due to lack of processing power or lack of user interaction capabilities, it is also possible to have PZPs without them. This basically allows small devices to also directly take part in a personal zone and expose its features with respect to all security and privacy features.

Discovery and Device Capabilities

Device capability access is also comparable to other Web runtimes that provide more than just common Web APIs to applications. Through the PZP several supported device features are exposed to Web applications and can directly be used by the developer. For example for accessing the current position of the device using the W3C geolocation API would look like following:

```
navigator.geolocation.getCurrentPosition(successFunction,
errorFunction);
```

In this case successFuntion and errorFunction are two passed in functions that are invoked by the geolocation implementation if the devices location was determined respectively in case of any occurred errors that hinder the API from determining the location.

To meet the distributed API access requirements webinos introduces a second option to access APIs. Therefore webinos introduces a central service discovery API that can be used to request services of a certain type.

```
serviceType   =   {   api   :   'http://www.w3.org/ns/api-
perms/geolocation' }
```

```
Webinos.discovery.findServices(serviceType, findCallBack)
```

For requesting the W3C geolocation API serviceType would look like following where the key 'api' states that the application is looking for a specific API and the value is a unique identifier that represents the desired API.

For each API found the success callback will be called and passes in a service object that represents the API. The service object provides some Meta information about the service such as the id, a narrative name, a narrative description and an icon that can be shown to the user. In addition, and most importantly, the service object finally allows to actually binding to the service. Binding makes the service usable by the application, which means that, for example, any resources needed for service execution can be acquired by the service implementation. After the service was successfully bound it can be used via the same APIs that are known from the original direct accessible API as in the previous example.

```
findCallBack = function (service){
      service.bind({onBind:bindCallBack});
};
```

```
bindCallBack = function () {
      service.getCurrentPosition(successFunction,
      errorFunction);
}
```

The two step separation between discovery and binding was made because of two considerations. Potential needed resource requisition and security and privacy restrictions.

Having in mind that webinos service discovery allows finding several services of the same type that are hosted by multiple different devices shows that a number of service objects can be provided to the application. In most cases only one of them will be used at the same time. Requesting service resources already during the discovery phase would unnecessarily increase costs like CPU time or memory usage. Even for some services, for example a camera, it's only allowed to be attached to one service user at the same time. For these services a service discovery with direct binding would block the usage of the service for other interested applications even if it turns out that the services will not be used.

Security and privacy considerations are related to the differentiation between the allowance of being able to see the availability of services and being allowed to actually use a service.

After introducing how service discovery can be used by the application developer it's time to show how the distributed service discovery is working behind the pure JavaScript API.

As noted, one of the tasks of PZPs is to provide access to local device capabilities via JavaScript APIs to Web applications. Another part of this is to also expose these APIs to other devices via RPC mechanisms. With the in webinos applied service discovery and RPC mechanism it makes no difference for application developers to use a local capability or a remote one. For example it's just the same code if the geolocation API provided by the local device or if a geolocation API provided by another device, such as a car, is used.

To allow the service discovery API to also find remotely available services each PZP needs to provide a list of its accessible services to the PZH. The PZH then holds a master list of services about which services are available on which device and therewith in the personal zone. The master list can then be queried by PZPs in order to search for services. This allows PZPs to easily find and bind to services without directly contacting each available device.

As mentioned webinos uses RPC mechanisms for using remotely available services. This RPC mechanism is purely based on JSON-RPC. Thus, each JavaScript API call is mapped to appropriate RPC messages which are send through the communication channels. To support this webinos comes with a comprehensive RPC API that on the first hand was used by the webinos development team to create the mappings between RPC and JavaScript and to transport the RPC messages. Since we have these APIs available in the core of webinos it can also be used by application developers so that it is relative easy to make web applications itself available through JavaScript APIs using webinos service discovery.

Incorporate Non-webinos Devices

As previously introduces PZPs and PZH together forming the webinos personal zone overlay network which allows addressing services provided by devices without actually addressing them using their physical addresses. So far only such IP enabled devices were considered where it is possible to install and execute a webinos PZP. There are several cases where this is not possible at all – so called non-webinos enabled devices. For example small sensor or actuator devices which just can provide some data or respectively allow setting some values in order to trigger certain functionalities. Another example is any kind of complementary devices such as Bluetooth headphones, GPS devices or human interface devices. Also several USB devices or any other device that can be accessed to a certain barrier can be considered here.

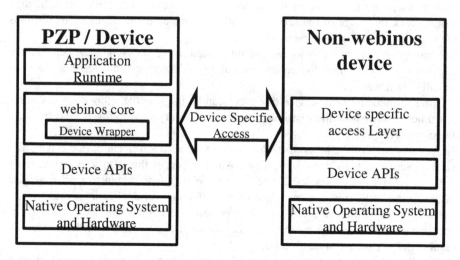

Fig. 4. Inclusion of non-webinos enabled devices

All these devices providing valuable services to the end user and so it is worth to also make them accessible through the personal zone. To provide such functionality a special PZP version is needed where the device API implementations are not restricted to use local device capabilities only. Means the PZP has some API implementations which are wrapping webinos RPC API calls into device specific remote calls. The same is true for the responses. Device specific responses are wrapped into webinos specific API objects which are then send back through the RPC channel to the original service requestor.

Therewith the complexity of accessing services using USB, Bluetooth, NFC or other barriers is completely hidden in the API implementations of a PZP.

User and Device Management

With the user management of a PZH a user is able to connect its personal zone with personal zones of other users. This allows sharing services even across multiple users. Since the PZH is addressable using a URL this can be used to make two different personal zones known to each other. The URL can be shared between users like telephone numbers or email addresses are shared. If a user got the address of another person he can log-in to his PZH and attach the other PZH to his zone.

The device management component of a PZH is responsible for setting up the personal zone through maintaining webinos enabled devices. The most important thing here is to add devices to a personal zone.

Security and Policy Enforcement

In webinos security is mainly addressed at two fronts. The first is that multiple devices can share services that can be used by each other. This is a big security issue because it should not be allowed that each device simply can connect to other devices and use their services. The second front is on the application level. Applications may harm the user by accessing sensible or privacy related data or APIs. For example an application may generate costs by using SMS or telephony APIs or may ignore the user's privacy concerns, which is not acceptable. A comprehensive access control system is therefore essential.

Communication between devices in a personal zone and across different personal zones is mutual authenticated. To achieve this PZHs are acting as certificate authorities that issuing certificates for each newly added PZP. When a user set-ups his PZH a PZH certificate is created that holds the PZH identity. When a new device is added to the PZH a binding between the PZH and the PZP that is running on the device is made. Therefore the PZH interface shows a bar-code that can be scanned by the PZP. Alternatively the token that is represented by the bar-code can be entered manually to the PZP interface.

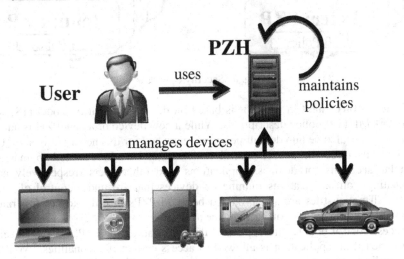

Fig. 5. Personal Zone Hub

After the user has set-up the PZP with providing its PZH address the PZP contacts the PZH and provides the token. After successful checking the token the PZH creates a new certificate for the new device/PZP and sends both, the PZP and PZH certificates to the PZP. From now on each communication between the PZP and the PZH is based on encrypted standard transport level security (TLS) sessions and the certificates are stored in a secure storage. The PZP trusts the PZH because it got the PZHs certificate during binding. The PZH trusts the PZP certificate because the PZH has created the certificate. The PZH also synchronizes all certificates of other registered devices to the PZP and thus, because the same PZH issued the certificates, trusted PZP to PZP communication is also possible.

Adding a PZH, basically to add a friend, to a personal zone is comparable. The user enters the address of the other PZH to his PZH interface. Then the other PZH is contacted and asked for binding. The owner of the queried PZH has to accept the binding. After that the PZH certificates are exchanged so the afterwards communication between both PZHs can be authenticated.

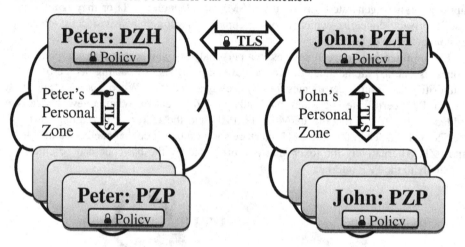

Fig. 6. Security Overview

Policy enforcement in webinos is based on the WAC security model [18] which uses XACML [19] policy descriptions. While a new device or a new PZH is added to a user's personal zone hub default policies are created for this new relationship. Using the PZH interface the access control policies can be administrated to make fine granular decisions for devices, applications, and other users (respectively access originating from applications running on devices that are under control of another PZH). All policy files are synchronized between PZPs in order to not frustrate the user with defining policies on each device again.

Access control policies are applied at the PZH and on the PZP. On PZP level it is determined if an application is allowed to access certain functionalities. To achieve this, applications need to state their intentions about which APIs they need to have access to. At application installation these intentions are shown to the user for acknowledgment (this for example is comparable to who the policy framework in android is working) where the user can select between two options for each intention. Allow every time and ask when an API is accessed. If the second option is used each time the related API is accessed the user is asked for permission. During runtime of an application again multiple options are possible. Allow every time, allow one time, disallow and allow during this time execution of the application.

On the PZH side requests coming from other PZHs/users are evaluated and based on this the service request is either forwarded to the actual device where the service should be invoked or the request is already rejected at the PZH. Fig. 6 summarizes the security features of webinos.

3.5   Webinos APIs

This section will give an overview about the APIs available through webinos runtimes. Overall webinos defines 27 API available to webinos application developers [14]. Therefrom 15 APIs are either completely new developments or are based on existing specifications from W3C or WAC but with modifications or extensions. Table 3 lists these APIs wherefrom following the TV, Vehicle, and Event APIs are highlighted.

Table 3. webinos: list of new and extended APIs

API	Description
Authentication API	Authentication API for providing applications with information about whether the current user has authenticated, and requesting re-authentication at runtime.
Context /Analytics API	API that provides statistical information about application and API usage.
Events API	API that provides local and remote application to application communication.
AppLauncher API	API that allows activation of webinos applications.
Messaging API	Providing access to SMS, MMS, and Email functionalities.
NFC API	API that allows data exchange with NFC enabled devices.
Payment API	API that provides generic shopping basket functionality to provide in-app payment.
Sensor API	Generic Sensor API that provides access to data from sensors.
Discovery API	The Webinos Discovery API provide web applications with an API to discover services.
TV API	API for accassing basic TV set functionalities.
User Profile API	Access to information of the user while extending the Contact API
Vehicle API	Provides access to specific vehicle data.
Widget API	Extended W3C Widget specification.

The TV API enables application developers to take control over TV devices. In the first version of the API different TV sources of a TV can be listed. TV sources, for example, can be just the DVB-S or DVB-C receiver of a TV or set-top-box or even the AV or HDMI input devices. On TV sources it is possible to list the available channels which then can be set to be displayed on the TV.

Another option of the TV API is to get access to the channel stream that is currently selected. This stream can then be used as input source for the HTML5 video tag which enables Web application to render TV channels directly within the application context.

The Vehicle API is based on W3C's DOM Level 3 Events model [16] and defines several events for getting information about the vehicle. This includes features such as the trip computer (if any), gears, the park distance sensors, or the climate control. In addition the API allows to push POIs to build in navigation systems in order to request guidance.

Location, speed and orientation data are not part of the vehicle API because for these dedicated APIs are available in webinos. Implementations of webinos for vehicles may map these APIs to vehicle specific hardware.

The Event API provides mechanisms for application to application communication even across devices without relying on external message transport services. Specifically it provides two approaches. A publish subscribe method for just firing events which will be received by interested applications, i.e., by applications that have subscribed to the event. And a common peer to peer massaging approach that allows to send messages to one or more specific recipients.

In addition to the already mentioned APIs webinos refers to 12 more APIs that are available to application developers within webinos runtimes. These APIs were not changed or adapted by webinos at all except of the possibility to request access to these APIs through the webinos service discovery API.

Table 4. webinos: list of referenced APIs

API	Description
W3C calendar API	Access to a user calendaring service.
W3C contacts API	Access to a user unified address book.
WAC device status and vocabulary API	Access to device status information like CPU or battery info. The vocabulary defines the information available in the device status API.
WAC device interaction API	Access functions that allow to interact with the end user (like vibration).
W3C device orientation event API	Defines several DOM event types that provide information about the physical orientation and motion of a device.
W3C File, File Writer and Directories and System APIs	Programmatically access to file objects including access to their data including APIs for writing to files and navigating the file system hierarchies.
W3C Gallery API	Access to the media items stored in the device gallery.
W3C Geolocation API	Access to geographical location information of the device.
W3C Media Capture API	Access to audio, image and video capture capabilities.

3.6   Platform Implementations

Webinos was implemented so far for Windows, Android, Linux and Linux based vehicle and TV platforms PZPs as well as PZHs are implemented using node.js [15], a JavaScript based application server. This allows re-using mainly code of the webinos core components, such as messaging, discovery, RPC, the policy enforcement, and the JavaScript API to native API wrappers on the different target platforms. Therefore node.js was ported for the Android platform.

Implementations are available as open source code at github [17] under the Apache License, Version 2.0. So everybody can fork the code and use it for free or contribute to the webinos master code base by creating pull-requests.

The webinos platform and demo applications were already demonstrated and presented on different conferences and exhibitions. Most notable here is Mobile World Congress 2012 in Barcelona, Spain, and the DroidCon 2012 in Berlin, Germany.

4   Applications

So far multiple demo applications were implemented to highlight both the local Widget part with device API access on different platforms and the distributed application part. The demos are covering applications like a distributed poker game where the TV is used as public screen and smart phones are used for the private cards.

Another demo highlights the distributed usage of the File APIs and the TV API in by providing a distributed media sharing applications. A number of applications focuses on using locally available features like an communication app with address-book and massaging (SMS, MMS, eMail) integration, a picture that directly publishes taken pictures to Flickr, or an event app that shows upcoming events related to the device's location with calendar, messaging, and contact list integration.

5   Conclusions

The chapter described a middleware concept especially for the use in distributed environments and different domains. Webinos introduces the personal zone concept and implements it using the personal zone hub and personal zone proxy components.

With the webinos runtime implementations for the different domains and the respective demo applications the webinos project is showcasing the huge possibilities that the future Web can enable when applying technologies as described during this chapter. Especially that the "Web" is not anymore just for Web sites. It reaches all devices and platforms in terms of comprehensive application execution environments.

Compared to others Web applications are relative simple to develop which can turn out as benefit when looking into developing applications for several platforms at once. Also multiple standardization efforts are closing more and more the gap between native and Web applications.

Acknowledgements. The webinos project described in this chapter has received financial support from the European Community frame work program FP7-ICT-2009-5 – Objective 1.2 under grant agreement number 257103. As webinos is a cooperative project with over 20 partners several peoples where involved in carrying out the webinos architecture, security framework as well as the APIs. Their valuable contributions to the project are hereby acknowledged in all.

References

1. Nokia Web Runtime, http://www.developer.nokia.com/Community/Wiki/Category:Symbian_Web_Runtime
2. Appcelerator Titanium, http://www.appcelerator.com/
3. Nitobi PhoneGap Project, http://www.phonegap.com/
4. Open Mobile Terminal Platform, BONDI Project, http://bondi.omtp.org/default.aspx
5. Wholesale Applications Community, http://www.wacapps.net/
6. World Wide Web Consortium (W3C), Device APIs Working Group (DAP), http://www.w3.org/2009/dap/
7. World Wide Web Consortium (W3C), Web Applications Working Group (WEBAPPS), http://www.w3.org/2008/webapps/
8. World Wide Web Consortium (W3C), Widget Standards Family, http://www.w3.org/2008/webapps/wiki/WidgetSpecs
9. GENIVI, http://www.genivi.org/
10. webinos, http://www.webinos.org
11. FatELF: Universal Binaries for Linux, http://icculus.org/fatelf/
12. Particle Code, http://www.particlecode.com/
13. InfoQ, A Survey on Mobile Development, http://www.infoq.com/news/2011/05/A-Survey-on-Mobile-Development
14. webinos API specifications, http://dev.webinos.org/deliverables/wp3/Deliverable32/API_specifications.html
15. Joyent Inc. Node.JS, http://nodejs.org/
16. World Wide Web Consortium (W3C), DOM Level 3 Events Specification, http://www.w3.org/TR/DOM-Level-3-Events/
17. webinos, open source code repository, https://github.com/webinos/Webinos-Platform
18. Wholesale Applications Community, Core Specification – Security and Privacy, http://specs.wacapps.net/core/index.html#security-and-privacy
19. OASIS, eXtensible Access Control Markup Language (XACML), http://www.oasis-open.org/committees/tc_home.php?wg_abbrev=xacml
20. WebOS, Hewlett Packard, http://www.hpwebos.com/us/products/software/webos2/
21. Boot2Gecko, Mozilla Foundation, https://wiki.mozilla.org/B2G
22. Chrome OS Google, http://www.cHROMIUM.org/chromium-os
23. Opera Widgets SDK, http://dev.opera.com/articles/view/opera-widgets-sdk/
24. Fraunhofer FOKUS, Media Web Runtime, http://www.fokus.fraunhofer.de/en/fame/projects/current_projects/mwr/index.html
25. Apache Cordova, http://incubator.apache.org/cordova/
26. OIPF, Decalarative Application Environment Specification, http://www.oipf.tv/docs/Release1/OIPF-T1-R1-Specification-Volume-5-Declarative-Application-Environment-V1_0-2009-01-06.pdf (accessed April 30 2012)

Virtualizing Platforms

Roberto Minerva[1,2], Corrado Moiso[1], Antonio Manzalini[1,2], and Noel Crespi[2]

[1] Telecom Italia, Future Centre, Via Reiss Romoli 274, 10148 Torino, Italy
[2] Institut Mines-Telecom, Telecom SudParis, 9 Rue Charles Fourier
91011 Évry Cedex, France
{roberto.minerva,corrado.moiso,
antonio.manzalini}@telecomitalia.it

Abstract. The technological and market scenarios of cloud computing is dominated by web companies. They are offering cloud services in a walled garden fashion creating a wide segmentation in the market. Telcos will successfully compete in this market if they bring disruption at the technological and at the market level. This means to introduce new technical capabilities as well as new business models that exceed the value proposition of the "pay per use" and are catalysts of new ecosystems. The chapter describes how Telcos can meet this challenge.

Keywords: Cloud Computing, Grid Computing, Autonomic Networking, Internet of things, Map Reduce, Hadoop.

1 Introduction

The term Cloud Computing is nowadays a common jargon for users and providers. It refers to a computing environment that provides computational services typically in a client server fashion. Services can range from on demand infrastructural capabilities like storage or computing capabilities to applications and services like Customer Relationship Management applications.

"The National Institute of Standards and Technology (NIST) defines cloud computing as a "*pay-per-use model for enabling available, convenient and on-demand network access to a shared pool of configurable computing resources (e.g., networks, servers, storage, applications and services) that can be rapidly provisioned and released with minimal management effort or service provider interaction*" [1].

Fig. 1 <<Editorial Note: in the current version some of the figures are "copied" by other papers; in the final version these will be modified or appropriate references will be added>> depicts a typical configuration of a Cloud Computing infrastructure.

In this representation, user systems can access to "clouds of resources/services/applications" by means of the Internet. Each cloud can provide capabilities on demand (users buy resources, platforms and services just for the time they need them). Relationships between the different clouds can vary according to business relationships among the providers of the infrastructures.

E. Bertin et al. (Eds.): Telecommunication Services Evolution, LNCS 7768, pp. 203–226, 2013.
© Springer-Verlag Berlin Heidelberg 2013

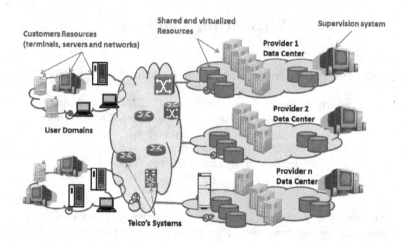

Fig. 1. A typical cloud computing configuration. Customers' resources and systems (lecft) are connected to the Telco's infrastructures (center) and to Cloud Providers' systems. The entire infrastructure is decoupled and resources interact at a low level. Interoperability between different Data Centers is usually based on proprietary interfaces and mechanisms.

According to NIST [1], a Cloud Computing system is characterized by a set of essential characteristics, such as:

- On-demand self-service, i.e., the capability offered to a user to directly manage all the needed infrastructure.

- Broad network access, i.e., the ability to access to Cloud Services by means of common (Internet based) mechanisms independently from the underlying networks (fixed, mobile) and compatibly with the most common devices (PC, Mobile phones, tablet and the like).

- Resource pooling, i.e., the Providers can dynamically integrate needed resources in order to satisfy customers' needs. Examples of resources are storage, processing, memory, and network bandwidth.

- Rapid elasticity, i.e., the capability to flexibly allocate the needed resources according to availability and customer's demand.

- Measured service, i.e., the Providers should make available to customers a precise accounting of resources allocated and used.

The features and capabilities of a Cloud system can be summarized into a well renowned model that foresees three majors Service Models:

- Software as a Service (SaaS), i.e., services and applications are delivered to users by means of a web browsers and /or specific client applications.

- Platform as a Service (PaaS), i.e., all the typical functionalities of a software platform (e.g., libraries, tools, services) are provided to the users by means of a browser or a client application.

- Infrastructure as a Service (IaaS), i.e., basic capabilities, like processing, storage, and connectivity, are provided to the user that can configure them (e.g., through a web browser of client applications) in order to deploy and execute his/her own services and applications.

From an ecosystem point of view, the NIST definition implies a very simple business model: the pay per use one. It could be implemented by obvious Web Companies (like Google and Amazon), by relevant IT Companies and by Telecom Operators (Telcos).

From a deployment perspective, the NIST definition includes four options:

- Private cloud. A full infrastructure (comprising management capabilities) is offered to a single organization.
- Community cloud. The infrastructure is offered and provisioned for exclusive use by a specific community of consumers.
- Public cloud. The cloud infrastructure is offered and provisioned for open use by the general public. This refers mainly to SMEs and residential (but not only) customers.
- Hybrid cloud. The cloud infrastructure is an integration of different cloud infrastructures that remain separated, but are capable of interoperating by means appropriated technology and business goals.

Fig. 2 is derived from the taxonomy as defined by NIST.

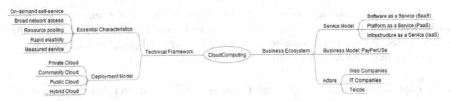

Fig. 2. The NIST taxonomy for cloud computing enriched with a Technical Framework (left) that comprises essential characteristics and deployment models and a Business ecosystem (right) comprising Service Models, Business Model (pay per use) and Ecosystem Actors.

This chapter will try to provide a wider view at the technological and business level of this cloud computing definition aiming at correctly positioning the Telcos proposition in the market and in the technological scenario.

2   A Market Driven Evolution of Cloud Computing

The recent evolution of cloud computing (actually cloud computing is a derivative of old and well-known ideas related to utility computing [2]) has been heavily influenced and led from the innovation of web service platforms as provided by big companies like Google, Amazon and others. These companies have been instrumental in the technological transformation of Application Servers in very complex (and highly distributed) data centers. They had to put in place high capable and available data centers able to provide services (e.g., search or selling of goods) to a large audience and with a highly variance in demand. Their infrastructure was dimensioned in such ways to be able to provide an answer to each worldwide customer in less than a second. Their infrastructures count for many hundreds of thousands of general purpose computing machines [3].

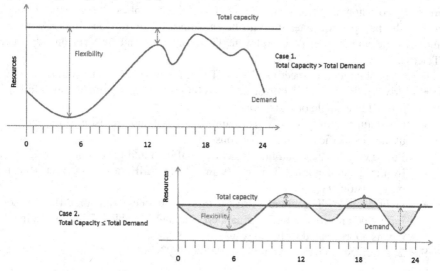

Fig. 3. Flexibility in capacity allocation in Data Centers. Flexibility coincides with spare capacity (*top left*). It can be allocated on demand to requesting customers. When all the capacity is used (*bottom right*), some processing can be postponed (e.g., batch execution) and resumed when resources are deallocated by higher priority tasks.

The opportunistic approach of these giants is based on the fact that they deployed an enormous capacity that seldom is totally used for providing in-house services. There is a lot of spare capacity that they can reuse or can offer to clients. An example is gmail, the e-mail service offered by Google. In order to index and organize information, the Californian companies had developed over the years a gigantic infrastructure that is capable of storing a large part of the known web. They have spare capacity and they can use it flexibly in order to provide to user large repositories for collecting mails. The variance between the deployed capabilities and the real usage of them is the key for providing cloud computing services. Fig. 3 depicts two typical situations, the first one in which the total capacity is always greater than the demand for resources (in this case the business goal is to sell the spare capacity, i.e., shown as flexibility in Case 1); the second one depicts a situation in which sometimes all the resources are over-allocated, a sort of negative flexibility that can hamper the working of the system (in this case a better allocation strategy is to be implemented, e.g., able to optimize SLAs and to reduce penalties [28]).

In a quest for flexibility in resource allocation, virtualization techniques are playing an important role. Virtualization "means to create a virtual version of a device or resource, such as a server, storage device, network or even an operating system where the framework divides the resource into one or more execution environments.." [4, 5]. Virtualization can be applied at different levels, e.g., hardware, operating system and application/service. Fig. 4 represents different perspectives on virtualization.

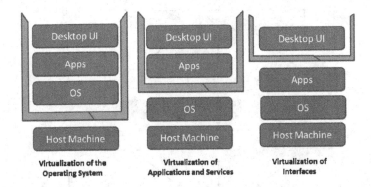

Fig. 4. Examples of virtualization at different layers. Virtualization of the Operating system (*left*), i.e., several OSes and related applications can be virtualized on the same host; virtualization of applications (*center*), i.e., application can be virtualized in such a way to run on the specific OS; virtualization of the interfaces (*right*), i.e. a system can offer different virtualized interfaces (e.g., the Linux desktops).

3   Some Technology Trends in Cloud Computing

The technological panorama of Cloud Computing is vast, in this section a few aspects of its evolution will be taken into consideration. They are relevant for understanding how the current market propositions are put forwards by major actors and their implications from a service ecosystem point of view.

Emphasis on Data Management
The current offering of services and applications in cloud computing is derived largely by the capability of some companies in dealing with huge data sets. Two of the major actors in this field, namely Google and Amazon, are were instrumental to new ways for dealing with large datasets and the use of advanced techniques. Google has been using the MapReduce approach [6] in order to implement n indexing mechanism able to perform on a large infrastructure of general purpose machines. The MapReduce method applies a sort of conquer and divide approach to data processing. Large set of data are reduced to chunks and chunks are dealt with in parallel by several processes. Intermediate results are sorted out and combined by other processes in an order sequence (as depicted in Fig. 5).

The Google approach was inspirational and this has led to the well know approach of the Hadoop Open Source platform [7]. MapReduce and Hadoop mechanisms are often offered as a service in cloud computing platforms (e.g., see Amazon Elastic MapReduce Service).

Another example of data processing innovation is the Amazon platform. It is intended to support the variety of services that Amazon is supporting (see Fig. 6).

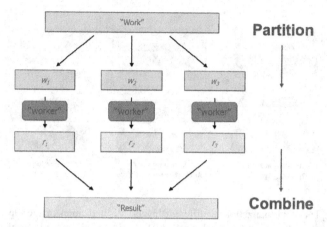

Fig. 5. A MapReduce example. A global task is partitioned between different workers, each worker performs a limited sub-task. Sub tasks results are collected and combined in order to get a final result

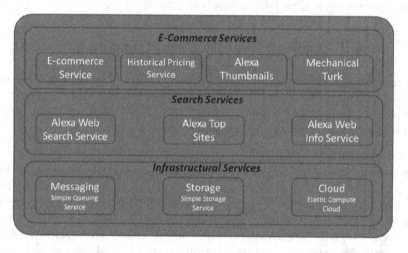

Fig. 6. The Amazon Cloud Infrastructure. The upper layer deals with e-commerce related services, the middle layer comprises search services, while the bottom layer provides basic cloud services like message queuing, storage and processing.

Particularly interesting in the realm of data manipulation is the Amazon solution for the Simple Storage Service (S3). Dynamo [8] is a highly available, proprietary distributed storage system. Its goal is to provide databases services in a highly distributed environment. In order to reach the goal it is based on a key-value approach and it uses distributed hash tables (DHTs) for pointing to data. Functions similar to Dynamo are offered through SimpleDB web service by Amazon which also offers elastic basic storage services through S3. Dynamo is one example of a consistent trend in database evolution named noSQL, it is not following a traditional relational database management system approach, instead it tries to support the high distribution and partition of huge datasets by means of a distributed, fault-tolerant architecture. Other example of this trend are the Facebook's internal platform Cassandra and the already cited MapReduce and Hadoop systems. Actually the design choices for Dynamo are: scalability in order to add new systems to the network minimizing their impact; symmetry, i.e., each node has no special roles, in fact all features are in all nodes; decentralization, the Dynamo design do not foresee any Master node(s); Highly Availability, data are replicated in the network nodes and they must be always available; speed, the system should provide access to distributed data in a very quickly and consistently with user requirements. These design guidelines have left out the consistency of data (or better adopted a "weak consistency" model), in fact the Dynamo system (according to Brewer's CAP theorem [9, 10]) privileges availability and partition of data over consistency. In other terms, data will be distributed and always available even if replicas of data could be in different (and inconsistent) states. Another interesting feature is that data are always writable because conflicts are dealt with during "reads".

Another relevant example of availability and timeliness in providing information is given by the functions implemented by the Twitter architecture, which, in the near future, could become interesting services offered by some provider according to the cloud-based model. In this case the problem is not only indexing information in order to allow a fast retrieval to users, but also to tag the information and made it available in the shorter time possible to user that are monitoring specific hashtags. In fact the Twitter engine is based on a PubSub model [11] and each single event to publish is indexed and delivered to interested users. A glimpse of the Twitter architecture that puts together a message queue engine (Kestrel), a Hadoop base Content Store with a noSQL metadata store à la Cassandra [12] is given in [13]. Also in this service, consistency is a minor requirement compared to quasi real/time availability.

Generally speaking, an approach that favors availability instead of consistency can deal with huge data and can provide very fast response time by disregarding the needs of consistency of all the data replicas. However, in certain cases, the consistency requirement could be a major need (e.g., in financial and transactional related applications). A network able to support high standard of high availability and sure parameters related to delay could be needed in case consistency should be pursued by relaxing requirements on high availability and real-time responses.

Virtualization

Virtualization is widely used in cloud computing solutions. Actually the progress of the virtualization techniques is not penalizing to much from the performance point of view. The concept of Hypervisor and related technologies have matured so much that now different options are possible and each of them is not penalizing too much the overall performance of the hosting machines. Typical configurations are depicted in Fig. 7.

Virtualization has been applied mainly to processing and storage changing the face of utility computing and taking progressively advantage of multicore systems [30].

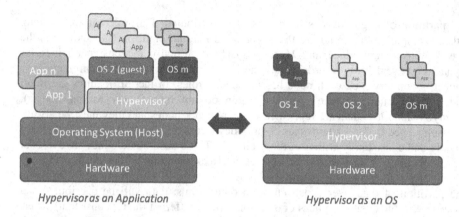

Hypervisor as an Application   *Hypervisor as an OS*

Fig. 7. Examples of Hypervisor applicability: Hypervisor as an Application running on top of a Host Operating system (*left*) and Hypervisor as an Operating System able to support different Operating Systems and Applications (*right*)

OpenNebula is an interesting open source solution which provides a uniform and homogeneous view of virtual resources, abstracting away from different virtualization technologies by means of drivers (new drivers can be created to add support to new virtualization technologies). It uses a scheduler, which can be easily tailored or changed, to take VM placement decisions (e.g. to balance the workload or to consolidate servers).

Focalization on Perimeterized Solutions

Cloud computing comes also with a number of drawbacks, for example clouds are designed to interact within an homogeneous environment. Usually providers prefer to impose a close and proprietary environment instead of looking for interoperability with other systems. This is due to the possibility left to user to cope with interoperability within the customer domain (e.g., interoperability between resources in Cloud Domain 1 and in Cloud Domain N has to be sorted out within the Customer Domain). Fig. 8 depicts one of such situations.

Actually the interoperability is a major difference between cloud and grid computing [14, 15], the latter is more complicated in terms of interfaces and mechanisms but it can support interworking of heterogeneous systems. The concept behind grid computing is the possibility to put together heterogeneous resources provided by multiple providers in order to integrate them into a virtual organization. Resources are negotiated for and are chosen according to specific needs of the applications. Resources can be seen as a collection of them or even as single elements. In addition, grid computing is trying to standardize a set of programming interfaces in order to allow the development of customized applications and services fulfilling particular needs and requiring specific arrangements of resources. Obviously this architectural characteristic comes with a price: programming at collective or single resource level implies more complexity and a clear knowledge of how to compose and organize resources.

On the other side, in cloud computing, interoperability at customer level can be alleviated by means of virtualization, in fact if all the involved domains are providing virtualized resources of the same type, the customer applications can have an homogenous view on available resources independently from the specific cloud. In any case, the creation of walled gardens is a market strategy of Cloud providers in order to segment and perimeterize the Cloud offering.

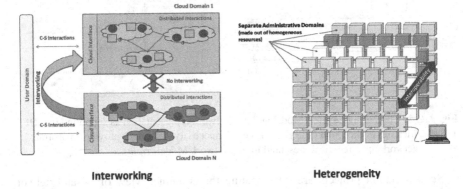

Interworking   **Heterogeneity**

Fig. 8. Cloud Computing: current Interoperability (*left*) and Heterogeneity (*right*) between different technological and administrative domains approaches leave to customer applications the goal to sorted out the integration

Lack of solutions considering network issues

Another major issue of cloud computing is the lack of any references to the underlying networks. The assumption is that connectivity is granted and it will be provided according to a best effort arrangement. It is also assumed that the capacity of the supporting networks is sufficient for services and application to deliver the expected behavior. Actually this could be an big issue as pointed out in [16]. The assumption that the network per sè will always be available providing the expected services is wrong and dangerous and it could lead to disruptive effects on services. Many cloud computing solutions are designed in such a way to cope with dynamic behavior of networks and they try to trade off the unreliable behavior of the network by increasing processing and storage capabilities at the edges (in the user domain and in the cloud). As an example of this trend, the Amazon Silk browser dynamically splits computation between the servers and the end device (in this case a tablet) in order to optimize the resources and the processing load between components. This is done to mediate the adverse cases of a malfunctioning network status. Actually some programming languages like Ambient Talk [17] have been designed in order to cope with network fallacies. It is based on the possibility of communication processes to keep working while hiding to the programmers the need to check the network connectivity status.

A major difference between cloud and grid computing is the view on resources with special reference to the network. While current commercial solutions for cloud computing are mainly focusing on processing and storage (giving simple representation and access to virtualized images of these types of entities), grid computing is representing resources at different layers and by means of well-defined interfaces. Fig. 9 represents a high level architecture for grid computing.

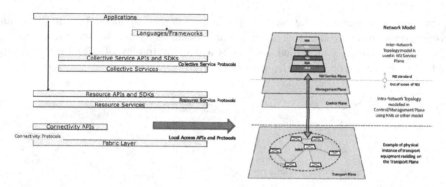

Fig. 9. Grid Computing Layered Model and the Network representation as supported in GDF 173 specification of the Open Grid Forum. The Connectivity APIs (*left*) provide an abstract view on network resources as represented in the Network Model (*right*).

Some research projects are investigating the combined view of IT and network virtual resources. For instance, IRMOS project has introduced the concept of Virtual Service Network (VSN), which consists in an aggregation of VMs, virtual links and virtual storage nodes. The VSN description, an ontology-based graph model (OWL), specifies hardware and QoS requirements for each of the virtual resources integrating the network. In the IRMOS platform, a VSN is created for each application as part of an automatic SLA negotiation process. During such process, an ISONI provider (i.e. provider of virtual resources) able to fulfil the hardware and QoS requirements of the application is dynamically discovered and selected (all virtual resources will be provided by the same provider). Resources are then reserved and integrated into the VSN where the application will run. At run-time, the initially signed SLA can be renegotiated, but only the amount of resources assigned to the VSN can be modified (not the type of resources, and not their provider). SLA renegotiation, and the subsequent VSN modification, can be triggered because the application end-user changed the QoS requirements of the application, because the initially amount of reserved resources was not enough to satisfy the signed SLA, or as a response to some scalability rules specified for the application.

Applications at the upper layer have different interfaces that can be used to control and manage resources (or group of resources termed as collective) at different layers and with different granularity. In this way an application can negotiate and allocate a collective resource (an aggregate of functionalities provided by a group of resources that can be controlled and manages as a single entity), or it can access to resources and to connectivity for linking them together. In the specification [18.] of the Open Grid Forum, a model for a network of network is given in order to present to applications and services an interface for requesting and controlling the composition of connectivity among different networks. A simpler specification [19] is provided within the framework of OGF by the Open Cloud Computing Interface, OCCI, initiative. It provides an object model for describing how resources can be connected by means of links and network interfaces. The goal is to allow applications and Cloud Infrastructures to cope with the complexity of supporting networks and to orchestrate the needed resources on a dynamic basis.

Another relevant initiative for the integration of network virtualization in cloud infrastructure is related to OpenFlow [20] and to the definition of a Network Operating System [21] and its applicability to data centers [22]. OpenFlow is the parent of new initiatives related to the so called software defined networking. The goal is to allow the opening up interfaces within network resources in order to allow virtualization and programmability in a similar way as cloud and grid computing are offering with processing and storage entities.

Soft Defined Networking (SDN) is about virtualizing network equipment and decoupling them from network management and control; not only this, a key facet of SDN is introducing API for programming network services. In principle, this could mean morphing routers into commodity (low cost) programmable boxes controlled and programmed (through API) by an outside source. This research avenues may have a deep impact on Cloud Computing. For example, in [23], it is mentioned how two-thirds of the cost of WAN bandwidth is the cost of the high-end routers, whereas only one-third is the fiber cost. So, simpler network nodes (e.g. routers) built from commodity components (as SDN is planning to have) deployed in WAN, may provide costs dropping more quickly than they have had historically, enabling new paradigms of interactions Cloud – Network.

In this direction, OpenStack is an open source cloud project and community with broad commercial and developer support. OpenStack is currently developing two interrelated technologies: OpenStack Compute and OpenStack Object Storage. OpenStack Compute is the internal fabric of the cloud creating and managing large groups of virtual private servers and OpenStack Object Storage is software for creating redundant, scalable object storage using clusters of commodity servers to store terabytes or even petabytes of data. Interestingly, OpenStack has a network connectivity project named Quantum (project page). Quantum looks to provide "network connectivity as a service" between interface devices managed by other OpenStack services. Quantum itself does not talk to nodes directly: it is an application-level abstraction of networking. It requires additional software (in the form of a plug-in) and it can talk to SDN via an API.

4   Cloud Computing from a Telco Perspective

As seen the cloud computing technological and market scenarios are largely dominated by Web and Information Technology companies. The technological pace is determined by needs and solutions stemming from the web companies that were able to create walled gardens with proprietary technologies. Each major web player is also able to directly and autonomously develop and master its own specific solutions. From this perspective the technical gap between the Web and the Telecom industries is striking and probably insurmountable. In addition, major web companies have a significant footprint in the provision of services to residential users and their services are deperimeterized (i.e., they can be accessed independently from an owned network).

Competition under these circumstances is hard especially if Telcos are continuously playing the role of "intelligent buyers" and do deliver services on platforms developed by IT companies.

In order to improve this situation, Telcos should change the rules of the game at the technological and at the business level.

In the following sections a divergent perspective on Cloud Computing for Telcos is presented and discussed. It is based on the assumptions that market and customer differentiation is a premium, that there is not only a "pay per use" business model behind cloud computing, that residential and business market segments have different needs and expectations. From a technical perspective the integration of connectivity within private and federated cloud is a key element for bringing cloud solution to enterprises, that network programmability is a means to support enterprise requirements and a pass thru for delivering better distributed services that can support consistency of data when customers' needs require such a feature.

Approaching the Cloud Computing in a different way means also to have a another view on the taxonomy of Fig. 2. In fact new dimensions and aspects of the Cloud Computing proposition could be introduced. Fig. 10 illustrates a few new viewpoints that an Operator must consider in entering in the cloud competition.

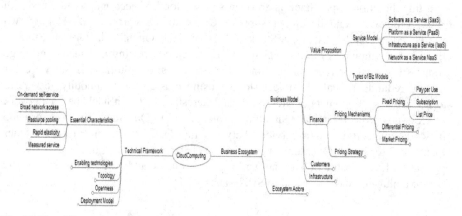

Fig. 10. New Viewpoints on the Cloud Taxonomy. Business aspects are extended to encompass pricing, customers and Business Infrastructure aspects (*right*). While Technical Framework is extended encompassing also Enabling technologies, Topologies, Openness and Deployment Models (*left*).

From a business perspective some new considerations for the cloud market are related to the value proposition to associate to the Service Models, some consideration related to pricing mechanisms and even more important to pricing strategies. A better definition of target customers could help in tailoring solutions that fit the expectations of the users. The business infrastructure is the company attitude to pursue a cloud related offering. And finally the Actors of the ecosystems are those stakeholders that have relationship with the Telco and can help or contribute or have to be involved in order to make a viable business.

On the technical side, new dimensions are related to the enabling technologies to be used for a viable implementation of a cloud infrastructure able to support the business objectives. Topology deals with the organization and the kind of infrastructure to be controlled. Openness point to a major feature of the platform: the ability of the proposed platform to be extensible and flexible in such a way to extend and improve the functionalities and services provided over the time. The deployment model extend a bit the one proposed by NIST and tries to figure out some viable and meaningful deployment from the Telco perspective.

4.1   On the Cloud Business Ecosystem

Two aspects of the Business Ecosystem will be briefly sketched in this section: the business models and opportunities reasonably pursuable by a Telco and the composition of a supporting Business Ecosystem. They strongly characterize the possibilities and the approaches that a Telco can attempt.

The Ecosystems Actors
The ecosystem of a cloud offering (from a Telco perspective) is quite articulated and complex because Telcos do need to have a direct link with customers and because the construction of the Telco Cloud requires a lot of links with other stakeholders. In addition Telcos are not relying on a "make", but on a "buy" approach and then the construction phase is made also of relationships and integration with other entities. They have to seek cooperation of a large number of other stakeholders in order to put in place a cloud offering. Fig. 11 (bottom links) depicts a possible set of stakeholders for a cloud platform.

Central to the approach is a clear and valuable link with the users. It is mandatory to be able to have a different approach to customers compared to the one established by web companies: in this case there is the need to have a direct communication with customers in order to support them, to integrate their systems and to fulfill their requirements by means of a day by day cooperation. Clients in this case are also Enterprises that seek a greater integration of their private platforms into a cloud. Communities (in a large sense) are also important in order to grasp requirements and in order to promote the solution and the functionalities to a large audience. Communities are also important for extending and tuning the offered capabilities (a sort of Beta test). From a development point of view, the internal IT and Network organizations have to cooperate in order to design and agree the best specification for a cloud platform, they should also cooperate in order to define a target list of services and the condition for integrating the platform and its systems into the Telcos processes and workflow. Other actors involved in the definition, design and implementation of the platform are technologies vendors, developers and integrators. Here the goal is to avoid as much as possible a lock in situation in which the Telco is forced to follow the design and product evolution decisions of a specific vendors. In such a competitive market (in which the Telco is not the primary choice for many customers) flexibility and readiness to modify and extend the capabilities ids of paramount importance. Advisors and consultancies agents should cooperate in this phases in order to advice on trends and best practices of the industry. From a more commercial point of view, Resellers and even other Telcos can be useful to enlarge the potential market of the cloud platform in order to exceed the rigid boundaries determined by the need to deploy networks in specific geographic areas. Government and Regulation have a role in regulating the possibilities and the limits of Telcos in this market. Governments can also be seen as potential customers for usage of cloud solutions in many situations.

Telcos have to nurture new ecosystems in the field of cloud computing allowing a more open model for application development and for the integration within customers systems. Interoperability between different systems and environments and new interfaces are important in order to catalyze new developments that are portable over different cloud computing platforms. The expected contribution from enterprises and developers is the be part of a federated environment that is open and can exploit and leverage the contribution of each stakeholder.

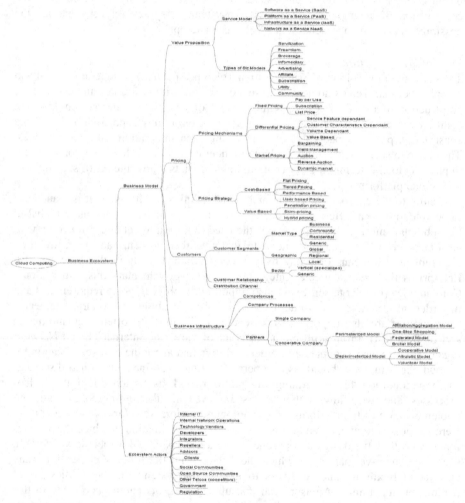

Fig. 11. Additions to the taxonomy of cloud computing from a Business ecosystem point of view and from the Telco perspective

The Business Model
The Business Model definition should encompass at least the following aspects:

A value proposition, i.e., a clear definition of the value chain and the perceived benefits for customers and the other stakeholders. This is a combination of the service model (XaaS) and the types of Business Model applied to the service model. As described in [23], there are several business models for cloud computing and the Internet. For a complete list refer to [24]. The Telco proposition should be aligned to the real possibilities that an Operator can have in the market. Some types of business model are out of scope (such as Manufacturer, or others) while the Broker one seems to fit well in the tradition and skills of Telcos. Another viable option is the possibility to help customers to better enter in the realm of servitization by means of a cloud solution, i.e., the Telco, the customer and the users can establish a B2B2C relationship in which the cloud platform enables the customer to move from the selling of products into the selling of product-related services. The capillary presence of Telcos in the territory and the support of customer care department can make this even more appealing and possible.

Pricing is another important aspect of the construction of a sustainable business model. Different pricing schemas can be applied to Cloud services. They can have a fixed price structure in which the user pays for resources usage, or a subscription fee. However, cloud computing can be charged also according to the perceived value of the customer. Fig. 12 illustrates the value that customers give to the different service models.

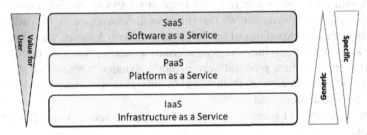

Fig. 12. The value of Cloud layers and functions s perceived by the user. The more the service is specific and tailored to customers' requirements, the more it is valuable (*left triangle*), the more the functionality is basic and related to the Infrastructure, the less it is perceived as specific and then valuable (*right triangles*).

A hybrid pricing model could be offered to customers: basic and generic functionalities of the Infrastructure and platform could have a fixed price or a differential one (depending on quantities and volumes), while specific and tailor services could be feature dependent. Other interesting options for are related to the possibility to dynamically make the price by means of auctions or bargaining with customers for resources and features made available. Google is using a complex auction mechanism in bidding for personalized advertisement. Other pricing strategies should be carefully analyzed in order to align the pricing schemas to the cost structure of the cloud solution that the Telco is building.

Another relevant issue is determining the target customers. As said, web companies have a supremacy in the SME, no-profit initiatives and residential market, but sometimes they lack the same grip on businesses. One possible step for the Telco is to address mainly the business market by leveraging its local customer management and channel distribution capabilities. In addition, Telcos could differentiate services and feature of the cloud platform in terms of vertical markets, i.e., the cloud offering could be instrumental for many business for better cover and exploit specific markets (such as Public Administration, e-health, smart cities and the like). Another major point is the possibility to focus on a national market or to have an international footprint. In this latter case, the Telco should create a network of relationships and allies in those market in which a direct presence is not possible. In addition, the Telco could take the opportunity to leverage different deployment models in order to create a global cloud solution. As a rule of thumb, a Telco should adopt and promote the federation of cloud solutions in order to create a global coverage of the market, at the same time, it should act locally by promoting hybrid solution in local markets. The combination of a Federated and a hybrid approach allows to provide to customer a large portfolio of standardized and generic services. These services could be locally tailored to the needs of the specific market or even customers. This flexibility and elasticity should be supported at the technical infrastructure level by high degree of programmability and composition of services.

Eventually, a Telco should take care of its Business Infrastructure, i.e., the combination of skill/competences, processes and company attitude in doing business. Processes and IT skills are quite important for a successful deployment of cloud infrastructures, however they should also be supported by the right capability of doing business in a cooperative way (e.g., by involving partners or with a doing yourself approach). Another dimension of the Business Infrastructure is the willingness to pursue an open or a closed model for the cloud platform. A closed way of operating in the market naturally excludes deperimeterized coverage because the company is reluctant to operate in a practical way within a dynamic scenario of short term or opportunistic relationships and alliances. In this case a perimeterized model (and market) is more appropriated.

The previous Fig. 11 summarizes some of the aspects related to the Business model dimension.

4.2   On the Cloud Technical Framework

The NIST technical framework under which cloud solutions can be designed and implemented is extended in this section. The reasons for this broadening lay in the need to better leverage from a Telco perspective the network assets and to promote them to the general attention. This leverage is not pursued with a traditional perspective (the network has value and it provides Quality of service related features), instead the networking capabilities are framed within a highly distributed environment compatible with the end to end principle of the Internet.

One of the beliefs is that networking aspects will be more considered in the future of cloud computing and will not be treated as minor issues in the provision of cloud solutions. If Nielsen's Law holds true (i.e., a high-end user's connection speed grows by 50% per year [25]) then the users will be limited by the network capabilities [26]. This means that the growth in bandwidth will lag behind the grow in processing power. From a cloud computing perspective, this Law could have interesting consequences: the commoditization effect on processing will be faster than on bandwidth (i.e., 18 months for doubling the processor power vs. 21 months to double the available bandwidth); bandwidth could maintain a premium value over computing. If this Law holds valid than a sort of paradox could emerge: Cloud Computing Providers started by providing a value added service, but they will end up providing a commodity service, while Telcos are starting by providing a commodity service and will end up offering a value added connectivity service needed to the whole cloud ecosystem. Scarcity of bandwidth could be an important factor for the optimization of network resources.

The enabling technologies of cloud computing cover a broad spectrum. They range from virtualization up to data management. Virtualization has been applied so far mainly to processing and storage. New emerging technologies are bringing virtualization benefits also to other kind of resources: networking resources have been briefly covered discussing the advancements of projects like OpenFlow, smart objects and sensors will be virtualized as well leading to a decoupling of local proprietary sensor solutions from the virtual representation in the cloud of virtual and smart objects. The combination of virtualized communication, processing and storage capabilities coupled with smart objects within the cloud will make possible new kind of applications related to Internet of Things and Ambient Intelligence. Any real object could be in the near future virtually represented by means of a clone in the cloud. The relationship between a real and a virtualized object creates a sort of continuum that allows to interact, manipulate and govern real objects that can be augmented in terms of features and intelligence. The number of distributed smart objects will increase over time and it will soon become difficult to control and manage them by means of human intervention, These objects will progressively expose intelligent behavior and the ability to self-organize in complex situations becoming autonomics. Autonomics capabilities and ubiquitous communication will make these object pervasive. Pervasiveness will determine the possibility to be involved and actually support and control large parts of production life cycles, or processes in the home or in the enterprises. Their strong relation with cloud computing will bring an increase in the perceived value of cloud based application and services. Objects will need to communicate each other in order to adapt to the execution context and to the desiderata of end users. The topology of cloud infrastructures will change because pervasiveness, heterogeneity of intelligent entities and objects governed by cloud services, dynamicity and elasticity of service environments will require the ability to integrate different resources into autonomic and intelligent systems. They will be arranged in a distributed fashion, but for certain specific applications there will be the need to centralize resources and architectures. In addition, (virtualized) resources are to be programmed and controlled, extensibility and programmability of resources will be a common requirement. In environments operating closely with the final customers there will be an increasing need for trust also in the software development. Open source implementations could find a further boost because they are controlled and extended by large communities of programmers that continuously check for bugs and malicious developments. Deployment models will greatly vary from closed environment (e.g., private clouds) to federated solutions or even "clouds of clouds" (i.e., interclouds) in which capabilities and resources of heterogeneous and different infrastructures will be negotiated and then integrated in a seamless platform. This evolution will emphasize the need for interoperability between different clouds, the value of connectivity for creating dynamic link between resources and consequently will require trusted and regulated stakeholders. Telcos will have a chance to play a relevant role in this context by leveraging assets such as connectivity, identity management and a regulated behavior that is respectful of users privacy.

Cloud computing will also extend its essential capabilities by offering choices between consistency and availability of data. Programmers and developers of services will be able to choose between different solutions for guaranteeing transactions and consistency to financial services or high availability and real-time speed data stream management. Terminals will be more and more integrated in the cloud, initially as simple clients but progressively they will become active nodes in the provisioning of services.

Fig. 13 is providing a view on the technical framework of the upcoming cloud computing.

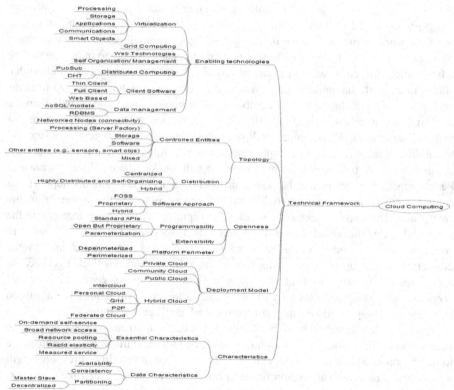

Fig. 13. A taxonomy of technical aspects of cloud computing from a Telco perspective

5   Examples of Telco Services in a Cloud Context

Telcos have to use the Cloud approach for providing services mainly to enterprises and business customers. This choice is dictated by the following reasons: business customers are more interested in creating a long lasting relationship with the provider, this link can also leverage customer relationship management systems; the existing billing relationship for connectivity services can be exploited in order to promote a sort of one stop shop approach for many services; the Telco can leverage the local footprint and to provide integration capabilities at a global level, for certain enterprises this can capabilities can make a difference.

The Telco's approach to the cloud has to promote and leverage the interoperability and integration of different complex IT systems into a federated infrastructure with a rich service portfolio. However this large infrastructure should be flexible enough to accommodate for private systems. Enterprises should be able to decide which processing, storage, communication and sensing capabilities to keep in-house and which ones to externalize.

In the following section, examples of Cloud services (in general according the PaaS or SaaS model) based on these foundations are given. A Business to Business to Customer approach is usually pursued in order to leverage the assumed capabilities of a Telco's cloud platform.

Intermediary in the Internet with Things
The Internet of Things is an environment in which some intermediary functionality can have value. In [27], the assumption is made that Telcos could play the role of intermediary between small (wireless) sensor network providers and final customers. The Operator could even promote the wide adoption of (wireless) sensor network by subsidizing the small sensor providers. The goal is to collect a set of meaningful data that can be exploited by determining macro trends within a community or a specific location.

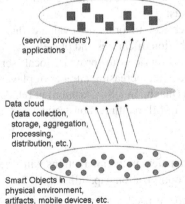

Fig. 14. The Intermediary service in an Internet of Things Context. The data cloud (*middle*) can offer intermediary functions and interfaces between (wireless) sensor networks (*bottom*) and application providers and developers (*top*).

In particular the Cloud platform could be extended for offering functions aiming at a «Data Cloud»:

- To collect data from sensors networks geographically dispersed nd to integrate them with other data sets (e.g., from the Public Administration in an open data fashion, from users' devices, and automotive embedded devices);
- to store large data sets to be dynamically updated and to analyze (data mining) and aggregate data into information;
- to provide message based engine and to derive information from complex events management;
- to distribute to Service providers' applications relevant and updated data with the request aggregation level and according to the agreed dispatching mechanism (e.g., pub-sub, continuous query, big tables,…).

This service could be characterized by:

- frequent interaction with aggregation systems of distributed sensor networks;
- elasticity in processing and storage allocation depending on data and processing to be dealt with;
- interaction with centralized and traditional applications
- Data cloud capabilities offered as SaaS and SaaS.

Fig. 14 describes the service.

Massively Multiplayer Online Games (MMOG)

MMOG Providers at a global level could request cloud computing services aiming at:

- Optimizing the processing and storage load balancing;
- Optimizing the network features in order to provide a better service to their clients, e.g., optimization of latencies for the users, dynamic increase in bandwidth allocation (e.g., to download large files), etc.

The Cloud Computing Provider, in addition, could provide specific functions for the MMOG Provider such as:

- Load prediction service, in order to evaluate the servers load based on a prediction of distribution of entities and players;
- Resource allocation service: to provide local servers and rebalance the processing load due to an increasing number of players.

The service should aim (maybe in a Silk fashion) at rebalancing the processing and storage load in order to fulfill realtime constraints and real time capabilities as negotiated with the users.

Features of this service are:

- support of QoS parameters in the interactions with user terminals;
- load balancing and optimization capabilities.

Similar features could also be used to better support multimedia service provision within a specialized cloud.

They could be packaged in a specific PaaS offering for MMOG or generic Multimedia Providers.

Virtual Terminals

Physical devices could be virtualized in the cloud and augmented with additional features or capabilities (e.g., more processing power or more storage). The physical device could use its virtual image for the execution of background processing; for the migration (teleporting) of tasks that do require too many physical device resources [30]; migration of tasks that requires more resources than those available in the physical device or that have nonfunctional requirements (e.g., performance, security, reliability, parallel execution) that the physical terminal cannot satisfy; delegation of tasks to be executed when the physical device is not connected to a network; extension of storage for storing all the events forwarded or generated by the terminal. Feasible scenarios are related to the usage of this service in the context of network PC provided to an Enterprise for supporting Teleworking capabilities.

The major features of the service are:

- elasticity in allocation of processing and storage capabilities as a consequence of the dynamic needs of running applications

- migration of the virtual terminal based on the actual location of the corresponding physical mobile device.

Also in this case the Virtual Terminal capabilities can be packaged as PaaS and/or SaaS offering.

6   An Agenda for Telco Oriented Cloud Platforms

As seen, web companies have an edge from the technological and the market perspective over the complex, Telcos. In order to recover the gap there is the need of a coordinated and standardize set of actions aiming at the definition of an open, programmable and federated cloud platform.

Following the offering of the web companies using proprietary platforms (maybe acquired by IT companies) does not solve the problem, Also IT companies are lacking behind and to many proprietary solution do even more segment the cloud computing market. Operators should take action in order to move towards a grid based approach. This means to embrace the heterogeneity of the platform components and the ability to mix and match resources pertaining to different administrative and technological domain. The task is more complex that aiming at the construction of a single and proprietary solution, but the risk is to be kept at the margins of an ever increasing market.

In addition, virtualization capabilities are emerging also in the realm of sensors and smart objects as well as in the networking itself. This will configure a situation in which the dynamic combination and programmability of processing, storage, sensing and communication resources will move intelligence, services, applications and infrastructures towards the edge of the network and within the customers' domain. The Telcos can offer to this edge environments programmable and on demand connectivity as well as the ability to support mechanism for self-management of complex edge networks s well as complement the locally missing resources with virtualized ones. This is a daunting objective and it should be approached with a step to step strategy. The starting point is interesting from a technical and marketing point of view: the integration of Enterprise IT systems within a federated cloud approach. From a marketing perspective this means to create a sort of hybrid cloud in which the enterprise IT systems maintain their importance but can cooperate with remote systems and access to specialized applications in order to improve and enrich their functions. Such an hybrid cloud platform could become a sort of cooperative environment in which different enterprises can implement or integrate companies' processes, functions, applications, services and market places for conducting business.

The cooperative cloud is then instrumental to create an ecosystem in which different enterprises contribute in terms of resources and final customers can access a large set of specialized services.

In order to make such a platform a reality, Telcos should be instrumental to the definition of open architectures within important standard bodies. The more time elapses without this standardization effort the more the cloud computing business is in the hands of web companies proposing walled gardens.

Some core specifications already exist and they are in the field of Open Grid Forum and Web Services. Telcos should somehow endorse them and to promote a further level of standardization and visibility. The concept to "virtual Organization" behind the grid computing fits well with the possible business proposition that Telcos should pursue and strive for. In addition support to network virtualization (e.g., OpenFlow) should be guaranteed. Software defined networks are the next step towards a change in the connectivity and communication proposition of Operators. The possibility to create virtualized views on network capabilities and to offer them in an integrated manner with Virtual Private Networks or even better with Virtual Organizations will provide a viable business framework for the Operators. A large ecosystem of application developers, process system integrators and IT companies could exploit the capabilities offered by such a different cloud platform.

References

1. Mell, P., Grance, T.: The NIST Definition of Cloud Computing (Draft) Recommendations of the National Institute of Standards and Technology. Nist Special Publication 145, 7 (2011)
2. Ross, J.W., Westerman, G.: Preparing for utility computing: The role of IT architecture and relationship management. IBM Systems Journal 43(1), 5–19 (2004)
3. Minerva, R., Demaria, T.: There a Broker in the Net ...its name is Google. In: ICIN Conference Bordeaux France (2007)
4. Definition of virtualization,
   http://www.webopedia.com/TERM/V/virtualization.html
5. Barham, P., Dragovic, B., Fraser, K., Hand, S., Harris, T., Ho, A., Neugebauer, R., Pratt, I., Warfield, A.: Xen and the art of virtualization. In: Proceedings of the Nineteenth ACM Symposium on Operating Systems Principles (SOSP 2003), pp. 164–177. ACM, New York (2003), http://doi.acm.org/10.1145/945445.945462, doi:10.1145/945445.945462

6. Dean, J., Ghemawat, S.: MapReduce: simplified data processing on large clusters. Commun. ACM 51(1), 107–113 (2008), http://doi.acm.org/10.1145/1327452.1327492, doi:10.1145/1327452.1327492
7. White, T.: Hadoop: The Definitive Guide, 1st edn. O'Reilly Media (June 2009)
8. DeCandia, G., Hastorun, D., Jampani, M., Kakulapati, G., Lakshman, A., Pilchin, A., Sivasubramanian, S., Vosshall, P., Vogels, W.: Dynamo: amazon's highly available key-value store. In: Proceedings of Twenty-first ACM SIGOPS Symposium on Operating Systems Principles (SOSP 2007), pp. 205–220. ACM, New York (2007), http://doi.acm.org/10.1145/1294261.1294281, doi:10.1145/1294261.1294281
9. Brewer, E.: Towards Robust Distributed Systems. In: Proceedings of the Annual ACM Symposium on Principles of Distributed Computing, vol. 19, pp. 7–10 (2000)
10. Brewer, E.: A certain freedom: thoughts on the CAP theorem. In: Proceedings of the 29th ACM SIGACT-SIGOPS Symposium on Principles of Distributed Computing (PODC 2010), pp. 335–335. ACM, New York (2010), http://doi.acm.org/10.1145/1835698.1835701, doi:10.1145/1835698.1835701
11. Baldoni, R., Contenti, M., Virgillito, A.: The evolution of publish/subscribe communication systems. In: Schiper, A., Shvartsman, A.A., Weatherspoon, H., Zhao, B.Y. (eds.) Future Directions in DC 2002. LNCS, vol. 2584, pp. 137–141. Springer, Heidelberg (2003)
12. Lakshman, A., Malik, P.: Cassandra: a decentralized structured storage system. SIGOPS Oper. Syst. Rev. 44(2), 35–40 (2010), http://doi.acm.org/10.1145/1773912.1773922, doi:10.1145/1773912.1773922
13. Information about Twitter architecture, http://engineering.twitter.com/2011/11/spiderduck-twitters-real-time-url.html
14. Foster, I., Kesselman, C.: The Grid: Blueprint for a New Computing Infrastructure. Morgan Kaufmann, San Francisco (1999)
15. Foster, I., Kesselman, C., Nick, J., Tuecke, S.: The Physiology of the Grid: an Open Grid Services Architecture for Distributed Systems Integration. Technical report. Global Grid Forum (2002)
16. Rotem-Gal-Oz, A.: Fallacies of Distributed Computing Explained (The more things change the more they stay the same) (2006), http://www.rgoarchitects.com/Files/fallacies.pdf
17. Dedecker, J., Van Cutsem, T., Mostinckx, S., D'Hondt, T., De Meuter, W.: Ambient-oriented Programming in AmbientTalk. In: Thomas, D. (ed.) ECOOP 2006. LNCS, vol. 4067, pp. 230–254. Springer, Heidelberg (2006)
18. Roberts, G., Kudoh, T., Monga, I., Sobieski, J., Vollbrecht, J.: Network Services Framework v1.0, Specification of the Open Grid Forum GFD.173 (December 2010), http://www.ogf.org/documents/GFD.173.pdf
19. Metsch, T., Edmonds, A.: Open Cloud Computing Interface – Infrastructure, Specification of the Open Grid Forum GFD.184 (June 2011), http://ogf.org/documents/GFD.184.pdf
20. McKeown, N., Anderson, T., Balakrishnan, H., Parulkar, G., Peterson, L., Rexford, J., Shenker, S., Turner, J.: OpenFlow: enabling innovation in campus networks. SIGCOMM Comput. Commun. Rev. 38(2), 69–74 (2008), http://doi.acm.org/10.1145/1355734.1355746, doi:10.1145/1355734.1355746
21. Gude, N., Koponen, T., Pettit, J., Pfaff, B., Casado, M., McKeown, N., Shenker, S.: NOX: towards an operating system for networks. SIGCOMM Comput. Commun. Rev. 38(3), 105–110 (2008), http://doi.acm.org/10.1145/1384609.1384625, doi:10.1145/1384609.1384625

22. Tavakoli, A., Casado, M., Koponen, T., Shenker, S.: Applying NOX to the Datacenter. In: Proc. HotNets (October 2009)
23. Armbrust, M., Fox, A., Griffith, R., Joseph, A., Katz, R., Konwinski, A., Lee, G., Patterson, D., Rabkin, A., Stoica, I., Zaharia, M.: Above the clouds: A Berkeley view of cloud computing. Technical Report UCB/EECS-2009-28, University of California at Berkeley (February 2009)
24. Rappa, M.: The utility business model and the future of computing services. IBM Systems Journal 43(1), 32–42 (2004)
25. Rappa, M.: Business Models on the Web. Managing the Digital Enterprise (May 2003), http://digitalenterprise.org
26. Nielsen's Law, http://www.useit.com/alertbox/980405.html
27. Nielsen's contributions, http://en.wikipedia.org/wiki/Nielsen%27s_law#Contributions
28. Bohli, J.M., Sorge, C., Westhoff, D.: Initial observations on economics, pricing, and penetration of the internet of things market. SIGCOMM Comput. Commun. Rev. 39(2), 50–55 (2009), http://doi.acm.org/10.1145/1517480.1517491, doi:10.1145/1517480.1517491
29. Fito, J., et al.: SLA-driven Elastic Cloud Hosting Provider. In: Proc. 18th Euromicro Conference on Parallel, Distributed and Network-based Processing, pp. 111–118 (2010)
30. Sotomayor, B., Montero, R.S., Llorente, I.M.: Virtual infrastructure management in private and hybrid clouds. IEEE Internet Computing 13, 14–22 (2009)
31. Byung-Gon Chun, B.-G., Maniatis, P.: Augmented smartphone applications through clone cloud execution. In: Proceedings of the 12th Conference on Hot Topics in Operating Systems, HotOS 2009 (2009)

Virtualizing Network

Roberto Minerva[1,2], Antonio Manzalini[1,2], Corrado Moiso[1], and Noel Crespi[2]

[1] Telecom Italia, Future Centre, Via Reiss Romoli 274, 10148 Torino, Italy
[2] Institut Mines-Telecom, Telecom SudParis, 9 Rue Charles Fourier
91011 Évry Cedex, France
{roberto.minerva,antonio.manzalini,
corrado.moiso}@telecomitalia.it

Abstract. The challenge for the Telco is to find a viable technological and market perspective for escaping from the consolidation of current business. The paper argues that the virtualization and the creation of a platform for supporting a Virtual Continuum between real objects and their clones in the cloud can be a means to radically transform the present service paradigm. In order to achieve this goal the Telcos have to design, implement and deploy a new platform for future networks that enables the role of Service Enabler. The platform has to displace the consolidate client server paradigm addressing enabling distributed processing technologies like: software defined networking, overlay, and autonomic networking.

Keywords: Network of Networks; Virtualization; Overlay Networks; Self-Organization; Virtual Terminals; Virtual Environments, Virtual Continuum; Internet of/with Things.

1 Guessing the Future of Networks, Technologies and Markets

Technological evolution is difficult to predict but what is even more difficult to foresee is the market acceptance of possible technologies. However, the technological evolution of future networks seems to have taken some identifiable trajectories that, if accepted and pushed by the market, will lead to changes in the current communication environment.

Actually, technology trends for developing future networks are progressing at an impressive rate: processing is continuing to follow the Moore's curve and it is doubling in capability roughly every 18 months; storage capacity on a given chip is doubling every 12 months driving increases in connectivity demand for accessing to the network; optical bandwidth is doubling every 9 months – by increasing the capacity of a single wave length and by putting multiple wavelengths of light on a single fiber. Also technology adoption is constantly accelerating: for example the cell phone took less than 10 years to reach 25% of the US population, while the fixed telephone took over 30 years.

This technological evolution, from the standpoint of the Operators, will exacerbate even more the current consolidation of the market. In this section a few possible pictures of the future are sketched in order to figure out a possible global scenario in

E. Bertin et al. (Eds.): Telecommunication Services Evolution, LNCS 7768, pp. 227–256, 2013.

which Operators will operate in a ten years timeframe. A set of assumptions, that roughly can resemble to scenarios, are put forward and used to delineate possible situations in which the Operators could be acting in the future.

One major consequence of these technology trends is that networks will become more and more pervasive and dynamic, capable of interconnecting larger and larger numbers of nodes, IT resources, machines, smart things (e.g. consumer electronics devices) embedding communication capabilities. In the future, anything will be a network node. Actually, with the development of Internet of-with Things [1] in a few years there will be many billions of electronic devices connected with each other and to the Internet.

The paper argues that the virtualization and the creation of a platform for supporting a Virtual Continuum between real objects and their clones in the cloud can be a means to radically transform the present service paradigm. In order to achieve this goal the Telcos have to design, implement and deploy a new platform for future networks that enables the role of Service Enabler.

Far from being precise, scientific [2] or necessarily true, the primary use of this analysis is to identify and understand trends and circumstances that can have an impact on telecom approaches to market and technologies.

This evolution will have a deep impact from a socio-economic viewpoint, influencing economy development as a whole, public institutions, social relations, diffusion of information, privacy of citizens, etc. Moreover, it raises technical challenges and important socio-economic issues for stakeholders to consider: from simplifying such emerging complexity when managing future networks to identifying new business opportunities and models.

Connectivity picture. In the considered period, the trends towards higher (both fixed and wireless) bandwidth availability will substantially increase. From the point of view of fixed networks, fiber will reach a large part of homes and enterprises in many advanced countries, in addition new optical technologies [3] will provide to homes essentially unlimited bandwidth[1] with a very low cost per bit. In certain locations, the fiber deployments will not necessarily be led by Operators. Local administrations or governments agencies could have an important role in these infrastructure deployments. There could also be the case that the deployment is driven directly from user communities [5]. Availability of fixed bandwidth will also have an impact on mobile networks. Fibers deployments will foster and help in providing backhaul connectivity for next generation mobile networks, that, on the other side, will be able to provide to mobile users enough connectivity for executing complex multimedia services. LTE and its evolutions (e.g., LTE+) will be capable to deliver up to 100 Mbit/s in the downlink and 50 Mbit/s in the uplink if a 20 MHz is used (in a shared fashion). Sometimes mobile connectivity could be competing with fixed one also and so cannibalizing part of the fixed market (e.g., advanced ADSL like offering could be outplaced by mobile offering). Moreover, short range connectivity (e.g., 802.11ac) will also increase consistently offering to user a lot of bandwidth with very low costs. Terminals will also be able to act as routers and will dynamically create

---

[1] Bandwidth consumption will be largely determined by video and multimedia services. With new technologies [4], the bandwidth available in the home will be sufficient to cover all the human needs and senses.

islands of connectivity that devices of the same user (or related people) could exploit for accessing to applications and functions.

This situation will likely have two major consequences: high bandwidth connectivity will be available everywhere (and often at a very low price); and the market will move towards flat rates also for mobile.

Personal Connectivity picture. One first hypothesis (derived also from the general connectivity picture, is that each user will be Always Best Connected (ABC). This ABC connectivity will be substantially different from what Operators were expecting, actually it will be provided in a transparent way (user always connected at the lower prices and best bandwidth), but the change of connectivity means and networks will be terminal and user based instead that network determined. This will be also supported by a strong integration (at the terminal level) between mobile and fixed networks (i.e., terminals will be able to adapt and to physically connect to different networks). Users will dynamically connect to smaller, more efficient and cheaper cell. Cognitive Radio [6] (terminals will adapt to the available frequencies and exploit free channels aiming at the optimization of communication) will exacerbate the situation from the Operators point of view, it will provide dynamic capabilities to highly evolved terminals that will exploit it in order to optimize the communication from the user point of view. The concept of ABC will likely have an impact also on the static relationships between customers and network providers leading to the possibility to rapidly change of Providers and even further to dynamic business models for connectivity. For example, the customer could dynamically negotiate with Network Provider for connectivity for a specific area and for a limited period of time, or to negotiate connectivity for a group of users or a community. The situation could be termed as a Telecommunication Supermarket [7], in which customers are not obliged to have a long lasting relationship with a provider, but they can dynamically choose for the best offering of the day.

(Personal) Data Picture
Importance of personal data [8] will be eventually recognized by final customers and consequently many current approaches to exploitation and profiling of customers will be hampered or made obsolete in favor or new methods that embrace the principle that personal data are owned by users. This will increase the level of privacy and control that users will exert on their data sets. A first consequence will be the seamless access to personal data (that thanks to the wide spreading of cloud based solutions will be more and more stored in the network). This will allow (under the direct control of the users and regulated by user defined contracts) the capability to dynamically create, aggregate and update personal data. The single user will be able to collect all its personal data, including any single transaction with other users or with services/applications or digital environments. User will have a sort of life-log including all the meaningful actions and information they produced or used. This will lead to a sort of transaction based world in which each single interaction between users and digital environments will be represented and sent to the user that will be able to store it in order to create a representation in the network of its behavior. This will imply the creation of new data types and sets strongly related (and deeply) representing the user, their preferences, and their behavior and interactions. These

data sets will be used by "private" applications[2] that will help users to analyze their behavior and to improve their personal capabilities. Many interactions will take place in digital environments and consequently there will be a strong integration between real and virtual related data, making them indistinguishable and an integral part of the user characterization. Under the control of users, services related to social relationships will be transformed and will allow a better (and more meaningful) profiling of users. Services will became even more personal and intimate. Social sciences will be an important element in the definition of services and applications. Having such a deep representation and understanding of a user will also impact on the way Identity will be managed. Identity Management will make use of biometric techniques allowing a very strong association between the user, its associated devices and the surrounding environment. The user, however, could still assume different roles and identities according to its needs and wishes and also the digital environment in which he is operating (e.g., in a banking transaction, identity will be treated in much different way that in the access to a social network). Pseudonyms will be allowed and different levels of anonymity will be granted in a networked environment. The role of the SIMs will likely diminishing in favor of other (software based) mechanisms that will be able to relate the user to the specific environment and its played role and identity.

The Terminals Picture

Terminals will have a fundamental role under many perspectives. From a technical perspective, there will be an abundance of storage in mobile terminals (1TB in the terminal, toward infinite in the network). This will change the way services will be conceived and provided. For example, the equivalent of a current SD card could store all the movies produced during many years, so the video on demand service could access to the movie locally, while the authorization will be carried out by means of a network. The high processing capabilities in the terminals will allow to locally control the context. Context-awareness will mainly reside in terminals while the network will just support the availability of stored information. In addition, the capability to interoperate and adapt to the specific context will be, as said, embedded in terminals and for many situation it will be downloadable Over The Air (OTA). So terminals will highly adaptable to different situations, different environments and different technologies. Actually, the software embedded in the terminal will make more and more the device a personal service platform than a product. They will be personalized according to specific user needs and interests.

Pervasive Communication Picture. The flexibility of terminals, the availability of cheap connectivity will make possible the ubiquitous connectivity, i.e., users and machines will be constantly able to connect. This will push towards the rise of broad classes of communicating objects (smart object, beacons, smart materials, sensors, actuators, micro-machinery, etc). This will increase the number of personal data produced and to be managed by users. Ubiquity of connectivity will have the effect to stimulate the explosion of Augmented Reality and Internet of Things (IoT)

---

[2] i.e., applications that operate on and interpret personal data, but do not export these data outside of the user environment and control.

applications. With the development of the IoT, any object will be empowered with intelligence and with the capabilities to interconnect with any other object, machine and people anywhere, anytime. Several applications are envisioned today: from health to domotics, from energy management to security to types of digital enterprises. Whilst the IoT foresees billion of things potentially communicating with one another, the Internet with Things (IwT) foresees a growing number (in the hundreds of millions initially, to become hundreds of billion) of objects that will become accessible to human beings through the Internet. The IwT shares several technologies and architectures with the IoT although the "communications interface" should be adapted to meet human needs and the form factor of the object matters since the object is "visible" and its physical characteristics are a selling point, as important as its functionality. In the IoT the functionalities exposed are the ones designed by the producer of the "T"; in the IwT a significant number of functionalities will be mashed up by third parties.

Actually a sort of virtual continuum will be created between physical objects and their virtualization into the digital world. Actions in the digital world will have impacts and could modify the behavior of physical objects and progressively also their material Smart objects will respond to stimuli from the digital environments and will adapt in order to ease the usage and the experiences of people.

The pictures depicted so far have broad implications from a market point of view, some of them are briefly presented:

- Connectivity will be a commodity, in a world in which connectivity is always available and provided by different competing providers the users will always able to choose a convenient offering or proposition. The pure connectivity provider will compete with decreasing (and low) margins.
- Terminals are flexible and personal service platforms. Services will still be provided in a client server fashion (and for this reason data centers will be larger and larger), however their capability will be extremely useful to personalize the user experience and for balancing the functionalities that can have to be executed in the "cloud" with those that can be performed locally. In addition the availability of local environments able to provide storage, processing, networking and sensing capabilities will further modify the equation that all the intelligence has to be provided in the servers.
- Service personalization and adaptation will be pursued and provided in order to enable the user to have better and richer social relationships. Services will try to capture the essence of the specific people and help in providing and creating favorable environment for social interchange.

From a business perspective there will be many different business models based on supporting ecosystems. In certain cases, the ecosystem will see services as a means and not a goal, i.e., services will be provided for free because the ecosystem will find its revenue from other mechanisms than the selling of service features. Advertising will be still a major business model of such a type, but other business models will consolidate [9] or emerge. On the other side, programming and mashup technologies will be such that users will be more and more active in service provision/creation. On the other side, many industries that now focus on "products" will try to move the focus on services associated to that product. The "servitization" trend [10, 11] is of paramount importance for Operators that could help by means of network enablers and platforms in this transformation.

2   Lean vs. Smart, the Operators Dilemma

The global picture depicted in the previous section could be taken into consideration as a general context into which framing the future line of actions of typical Operators. A first point to observe is that complexity of the networks will drastically increase, above all at the edge (where almost "everthing" will become a node, e.g. Users' devices, machines, sensors, actuators, etc). Currently the public networks are organized hierarchically with different segments of the network specializing for collecting and optimizing the flows at different aggregation points. Evolution of these networks is already moving towards an architectural simplification, through "flattering" of layers and reduction of segments; on the other hand, the edges of the infrastructure will see an increase of dynamicity and complexity (implying this several interworking issues). In other words, public networks' architectural evolutions going towards simplification (especially through the deployment of "long" optical access) while edge networking is morphing to master complexity and to face the challenges of an environment composed by a sheer number of interacting devices capable to connect to different core networks.

One can easily imagine a scenario in the near future where virtual links are dynamically created and destroyed by applications and services to produce a very dense, interconnected environment of processing and storage resources, sensors, actuators, machines, etc. The edge will be the business arena of multiple Players (e.g. Network and Service Providers, Over-The –Top (OTT), Enterprises, etc.) interacting with each other as in a natural ecosystem, providing all sorts of services and data.

An interesting situation will likely occur: different networks will adapt each other in order to better fits the users requirements. This yields to the concept of a network of networks, i.e., a highly dynamic complex systems made out of many heterogeneous networks, systems and intelligent endpoints that cooperate and compete in order to achieve their goals pursing the satisfaction of customers' requirements. Many customers can use this network of networks aiming at satisfying their specific communication (but also computing, storage and sensing) needs sometimes. Available resources (pertaining to different administrative domain) will try to optimize their behavior by adapting to customer requirements, but also pursuing a common "network or resource goal".

If not mastered, such an increasing complexity will result in:

- Costly infrastructure difficult to install, manage and integrate;
- Lack of optimization of usage of resources;
- Lack of knowledge of the "network" as a whole and how it is globally and locally behaving in supporting customers' requests.

Eventually, the edge of network infrastructures will be a sort of no man's land (demilitarized zone) in which different sub-networks, nodes and devices will try opportunistically to get and (potentially) share connectivity, processing, storage and other functions. It is in this area that probably there is the major need for a cooperative optimization of resources. This can be achieved by means of self-organization leading to the concept of 0-Touch networks, i.e., networks that do not necessarily assume the human intervention for working, providing services, configuring and generally speaking support a number of management functionalities.

This evolution will require that the intelligence controlling network resources and their services will be implemented through sets of controllers (interacting with each other and properly orchestrated), embedding certain levels of automaticity (to ease human operation and mitigate mistakes) and decoupled from data forwarding and processing [12], [13].

Software Defined Networking (SDN) can be seen as a step in the direction of this network transformation. In SDN architecture, control and data planes are decoupled, and so network infrastructure is abstracted from business applications. This is expected to bring about greater programmability and the flexibility to build multiple networks (on the same physical infrastructure) offering multiple network services. Network services, for example, will include routing, multicast, security, access control, bandwidth management, traffic engineering, quality of service, processor and storage optimization, energy usage, and all forms of policy management, custom tailored to meet business objectives.

If an Operator aims at being a bit carrier or better a Lean Operator, it will avoid to provide functionalities, systems or resources coping with the edge complexity problem. The major goal of such an Operator will be the one of just providing the better connectivity towards the edge and to optimize by delayering the network and by using at the larger extend optical connectivity. The focus of a Lean Operator will be on Transport (prevalently at Level 1 and 2). This implies that such a Lean Operator will provide just a few basic transport services (maybe supporting virtual private networks and possibly some degrees of negotiable Quality of Service, QoS). The needed control platform will be designed in order to optimize (i.e., minimizing) the usage of transport resources and to provide a set of basic improved functionalities. The main goal is to reduce underutilization of resources and to increase the network capability (i.e., the bandwidth provided to the edge). An example of a simple infrastructure that could be of interest to a Lean Operator is represented in Fig. 1.

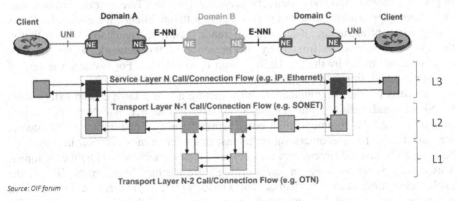

Fig. 1. A Lean Operator will try to keep all the traffic at level L1/L2 because operating at this level is less cost intensive that at L3 (mainly at the IP level). In this way the Lean Operator could optimize the transport at lower level and occasionally to deal with more consuming and possibly slower operation at higher layers.

"De-perimeterization" of Services

The current service offering of Operators are strongly tied to the network, Services are thought of, deployed, offered, and maintained in a strong synergy with a network. An operator very seldom will propose a service without a connectivity offering. Still services are thought as extending the value of the underlying network infrastructure. In addition, services are designed in order to replicate over and over the usual scheme of the network intelligence (i.e. services reside in the network and the edge terminals and servers are exploiting connectivity to provide and support their features). Apparently this approach has been rejected in favor of a client – server paradigm, but in reality the "interpretation" of this model is still related to the leverage of network functions.

On the contrary, the Internet has since a long time decoupled the (inter)network layer from the services. The Internet Protocol, i.e., the slim waist of the IP hourglass), is highly standardized and effectively implemented all over. In addition, http and html standardization has allowed the creation of a well-defined and easy to use environments for implementing services in a client – server fashion. The clear result of this separation is the possibility to transport bits and packet all over the world in a very effective way, and the possibility to access to services independently from the location and the networks used to forwards packets. This "de-perimeterization" of service allows the possibility for each small Web company in the world to effectively competing with major actors of the web. As a byproduct of this independency from the network, a web service can be reached from anywhere, and hence the "long tail" of web services is global. Vice versa, the strong tie between networks and service offering still carried out by Operators is confining Operators services to a smaller footprint essentially determined by the presence of the Operator's network. Even the biggest (mobile) Operator footprint is smaller than the potential footprint of a small web company. This has also an effect on the marginal costs of a global infrastructure and "software client" development. Operators can address well defined markets and their investment have to keep into account the deployment of a network, while web companies have a global reach and investments on networks are limited to those needed for connecting different data centers. Other costs are similar: the cost for put in place or extend the service delivery platforms (i.e., the Telco service layer versus Data Centre approach), the costs for developing software clients, the costs related to a management infrastructure. The main difference then is the reachable market that in the case of operators is limited by the presence of the network, while for Web companies is limited by the availability of an open Internet. For instance the case of Skype is illuminating. The Skype architecture is represented in Fig. 2.

The costs for the communication infrastructure are to a large extend externalized by Skype (and possibly put on the shoulders of Internet and Network Service Providers), i.e., the communication costs between any two end nodes in the Internet are paid for by the customers subscriptions, costs for communication interworking between an IP and a different network (skypein or skypeout) are paid by the customer. This allows Skype to have an interworking infrastructure between the IP and the public telecommunication networks. The service delivery platform comprises client nodes, supernodes and the Authentication infrastructure. Direct costs are essentially paid for the authentication and billing infrastructure, client nodes costs are those related to the development of the software client (there are no cost for skype in the usage of CPU and storage and connectivity of the client/customer), supernodes are often allocated for free or at a low price. The real infrastructural costs are related to the authentication and billing infrastructure (as well as the data center for downloading the skype client). It should be noted that the more skype clients are downloaded than the less their marginal costs are. The peer to peer network scalability has a positive effect on the costs of the client. This is a clear example of how virtualization of a network (the peer to peer network of skype) offers advantages in terms of scalability, global footprint and marginal costs.

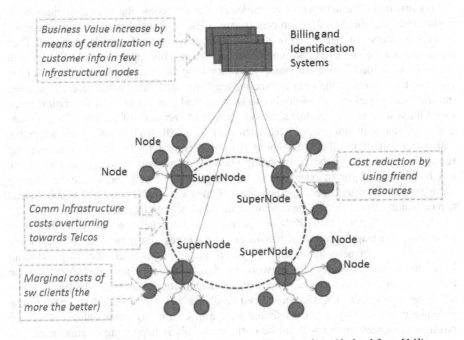

Fig. 2. Skype Architecture and some cost related considerations (derived from [14])

These considerations lead to a further requirement from the Operator's perspective: to support and seek for the "de-perimeterization" of services. Another related issue is the service delivery paradigm, Operators are lagging behind the web companies in infrastructures (e.g., cloud computing) and technologies (big data, real time web) and the technological gap is enlarging. Another issue should be considered here, many web companies are "technological" companies, i.e., they develop directly the technologies they need. Many web companies are in the forefront of technological innovation (e.g., twitter, google, amazon), while Operator, at the service layer, are at the most, best buyers.

Another consequence of the "de-perimeterization" of services is that web companies can use standardized technologies at the service layer, but still they can create walled garden and proprietary solutions. They do so by using http and xml derived means, while they create their own and proprietary environments and APIs. Operators instead are still seeking general consensus and interoperability between different networks and related service environments. Examples are RCS [15] or WAC [16]. Another consequence is that web companies can focus on how users interact with their services, while Operators need first to reach interoperability and then differentiation and personalization. The results are unmistakable: new interfaces and new modality of using services are a clear domain of web and it companies.

FON is an interesting example of how users can share resources and create a large scale communication community. FON is based on the possibility to create separate networks supported by the same WiFi access point. This dual network mechanism allows the access to the Internet by means of a FON based network. Another interesting example along the same line but even more socially oriented is Guifi [17]. They aim at the construction of a network of networks able to overcome the current limitations in connectivity and the digital gap in certain areas. They put together wireless connectivity as well as fibers in order to create a network infrastructure collectively managed. They are an officially recognized telecom operator in Spain. This approach could fit very well with the one named "home with tails" [5] which proposes the idea that single customers could be the owners of the fiber connecting the "last mile". This could create a different infrastructure based on the possibility to share optical connectivity within communities. Other interesting initiatives related to the concept of "network of networks" are Village Telco [18] and some military projects such as [19] or [20]. All these approaches together with other initiatives like Mantychore [21] are heading to the fact that networking resources can be put together and forming a network of network. This composite network can be virtualized (or in other words be "de-perimeterized") and it can be offering services to the connected people. Such a paradigm is a powerful one and it is able to lead to a radical transformation of the communication business and service delivery.

The de-perimeterization of Services leads also to the need to have means to recompose the fragmentation of the different resources and networks. Such a means could be a sort of network operating system whose major goals are: to provide an harmonized view on underlying network capabilities and to offer a framework for the execution of services (e.g., security, management, reusable functions). The relationship between real and virtualized resources has to be well designed because virtualized and overlay networks should have a link with the real resources otherwise physical resources' usage will not be optimized. This is happening in current peer to peer networks. So the relationship between real and virtual resources should be maintained and exploited in order to build a link between the network and the service layers. Approaches similar to ALTO [22] could be considered.

If a Lean Operator will try to keep all the traffic at level L1/L2 because operating at this level is less cost intensive that at L3 (mainly at the IP level), a Smart Operator will then be strongly involved in the definition, design, deployment and operation of such a network wide operating system. Its goal is the optimization of the available resources and the creation of a Virtual Continuum between real objects and their clones in the cloud can be a means to radically transform the present service paradigm. In order to achieve this goal the Telcos have to design, implement and deploy a new platform for future networks that enables the role of Service Enabler.

3   Choose a Strategy, Network Will Follow

In Future Networks, the role and the business goals of Operators will be extremely important in order to determine the network architecture. Three major business driven roles are sketched in Fig. 3 and briefly described here:

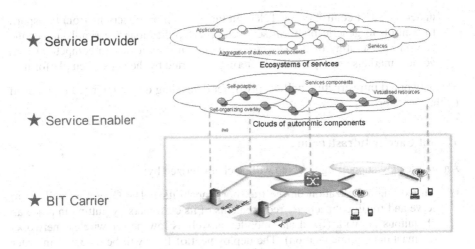

★ Service Provider

★ Service Enabler

★ BIT Carrier

Fig. 3. Possible Roles for a Telco in Future Network Scenarios (e.g., Next Generation Networks)

- Bit carrier, in this role the Operator will focus on the most efficient and performing transport of bits. It will try to deliver and forwarding bits in the quickest and most economical way trying to move big chunks of data to the closest or more appropriate sink.
- Service enabler, it will focus on positioning its infrastructure as an enabler for the creation and development of data and information related services. It will put together controllers [23], functions and components that abstract the underlying network infrastructure, but do provide value to the final users as well as to Service providers and application developers. This architecture comprises reusable components that are able to self-organize themselves into reliable overlays that support the communication, processing, storage and sensing capabilities of the users. The Operator is not involved in the direct development of applications for the customers, it is instead enriching the platform services by developing platform components that can be re-used by service developers and service providers for creating new applications. These components are designed in such a way to optimize the usage of networked solutions. The Operators playing the Service Enabler role will be concerned with traffic optimization at several levels (L1/L2/L3) as well as the execution of functions at higher level (at the application layer of the ISO/OSI stack). At this level, openness, well defined platform services and components, and a wide set of established APIs are of the paramount importance because they are instrumental for application development and hence for attracting and nurturing a wide ecosystem of developers and service providers.
- Service Provider, it will organize its infrastructure in such a way to be able to rapidly manage the entire service and application lifecycle. The network and the Network operating system are the infrastructure/platform on top of which the operator will build and provide and deliver directly to customers (residential or business ones) its services and applications. Potentially this platform could be a walled garden to be used exclusively by the Operator or a set of other actors

under the strict control of the Telco. In this case all the functions from transport, to control, to generic platform services up to applications are rigidly under the control and scrutiny of the Operator that acts in such a way to compete also in vertical markets with specialized offering supported by the networked platform.

The networked infrastructure will deeply differ depending on the intended role played by the Operator.

The Bit Carrier Infrastructure

An architecture supporting this role will be characterized by:

- An extreme focalization on the transport capabilities. The Operators will try to serve and fulfill connectivity requirements of its customers by putting in place an ubiquitous network (fixed and mobile, as well as low power wireless networks for machine communication). The deployment of fiber will be essential in order to create synergies between the fixed and mobile communications. Data will transit in the network in an optimized fashion, i.e., they will use minimal resources, they will be transported preferably by optical technologies (and at lower layer), usage of functions at L3 and up will be minimized and the major goal of such a bit pipe will be to deliver the chunks of data faster and in the shorter time possible to the data center where bits will be processed and transformed into data an information (generally outside of the domain of the Carrier). The network will be optimize for getting rid of bits as quickly as possible.

- A basic control infrastructure. Since revenue will be generated by bit transport, the control functionalities will focus on the best management of the infrastructure by to minimize the usage of valuable resources as well as the time for packet processing and delivery. The goal of the Operator will be to have the leanest infrastructure able to support the foreseen traffic. Network optimization will be of the greatest importance.

- A few basic service. The platform will still be able to provide a few services. They will be strictly related to the transport. Apart from billing and accounting of the network resources, the infrastructure could provide QoS related capabilities in order to allow service providers to adapt the allocated network infrastructure to the varying traffic conditions, some private virtual network functionalities in order to accommodate the need of companies for creating their own network infrastructure and to connect it to customers and employees. Mobility will still be a major service and probably the major revenue stream for the Carrier. It will be optimized and integrated with different access capabilities (from LTE and LTE+ to Wi-Fi and its evolutions to other techniques). Some interfaces and services will be offered in order to support the needs and requests of Virtual (Mobile) Operators that will create inter-regional or sovra-national virtual networks combining capabilities and capacity offered by carriers. Probably this type of carrier will also be proposing to customer the possibility to dynamically bid for connectivity when resources are under a certain threshold.

Fig. 4 represents a possible infrastructure for such a type of Operator.

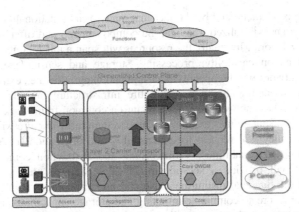

Fig. 4. A Possible Network Architecture supporting the Role of Bit Carrier

The Service Enabler Network

The network infrastructure needed to play the role of Service Enabler has to be radically different from the one of the Carrier. Three major differences must be emphasized: a) the communication focus moves from the lower layers (L1/L2) to upper layer L3 and UP (i.e., the network has to deal with IP and application player protocols), b) the network is not only based on communication resources, it has to integrate and offer processing, storage and sensing/actuating capabilities; 3) the focus moves from bits to data and information, the network has to provide means to gather, process and delivery to customers real time information. The networked infrastructure for playing the Service enabler role is represented in Fig. 5.

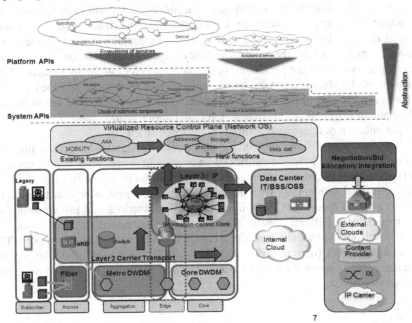

Fig. 5. A possible Network Architecture supporting the Role of Service Enabler

This platform is characterized by the fact that many of its functionalities and services can be abstracted and virtualized, they can be componentized and offered by means of API to the external world. Internally the resources will span a much larger intent that the simple communication capability: processing, storage and sensing/actuating will be integrated. The network will be open to extension and integration, i.e., external resources could be asked for and included in the entire infrastructure in order to allow the integration of customers network and systems into a common framework. For instance, banks and other financial entities that have a large system infrastructure will not move to the cloud, instead they will request for extensibility and integration (under their direct control) of networked capabilities. Virtualization and abstraction come to help. The Service Enabler will provide a set of virtualized capabilities that will extend the infrastructure of the financial institution. Also end user capabilities could be integrated and used in order to create complex computing and storage capabilities. For example a Nanodatacenter [24] could be dynamically built by integrating end user terminals into a virtualized data center. User could be remunerated for allowing the usage of their resources for a certain period of time. The integration relation is based on contract that can have a limited in time validity.

The platform should be able to accommodate also for smart objects, this pushes for introducing different communication paradigms that differ from the prevailing one (i.e., the client – server). The Service Enabler network should be able to provide a Complex Event Processing (CEP) engine capable of dispatching in real time events and commands to a multitude of smart objects as well as to derive usable information by analyzing event patterns. This real time event engine will be a sort of twitter of things where each smart thing will be able to send (and receive) events about its perception about the status of an environment, resources or system. Transactions, i.e., a set of events that describe the occurrence of a functionality, will became more and more important. Users will want to be informed of the final status of actions performed on their behalf from financial systems, or security related applications. Users will want to trace all the actions that they, or their terminals, or smart objects temporarily associated to the person are performing on behalf of the individual. These transaction will be able to represent the digital experience of users, and they need to be collected and passed to the users in real-time. A pubsub engine [25] seems to be a technical possibility to allow this transaction based digital world.

A representation of the twitter of things is provided in Fig. 6.

All these functions will be provided by means of componentized functions that will be instantiated as programmable entities of an overlay network. They will be resilient and self-organizing in order to allow the developers to focus on the functionalities of the service instead than coping with the complexity of the system organization. Each entity will provide specialized APIs in order to offer functions and programmability to the applications. Different levels of APIs will be requested in order to exploit different levels of abstraction that the Service Enabler network can support. The differentiation of API (represented in Fig. 5 as a ladder) are useful for allowing the service designer to choose the level of granularity and control on networked resources that the service needs.

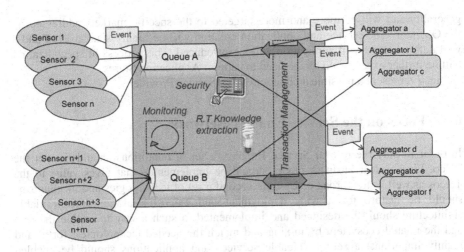

Fig. 6. A PubSub engine will be instrumental to support the passage from the Client – Server Internet to a Transactional Internet

The Service Provider Infrastructure

The Operator playing the role of Service Provider will opt for a different infrastructure. Its value is in the creation of applications, so all the platform will be customized at several levels (from the resource level to the upper layers) in such a way to take advantage by special feature and capabilities. The platform will lose

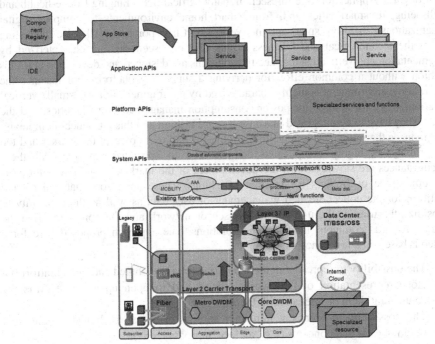

Fig. 7. A possible Network Architecture supporting the Role of Service Provider

generality and will be more and more targeted to the specific markets addressed by the Operator. The service and application creation will be highly standardized and a well defined registry of application will be introduced. This process of specialization will be further exacerbated by the need to support Application Stores.

Fig. 7 represent a possible architecture for a Service Provider.

4   Focus on the Service Enabler Network

In order to play the role of Service Enabler, a set of conditions should be met the Telco. First a clear business model should be implemented that gives value to the Telcos as well as to a broad ecosystem; second a set of technologies and mechanisms should be mature for a wide deployment and extensive usage; third a viable architecture should be designed and implemented in such a way to enable the role and the related ecosystem by mixing and match the needed technologies; forth (and mainly important) a set of valuable services and applications should be enabled and made possible by the architecture. The lack of one of the conditions, or a bad "execution" of one of them, can hinder the success of the entire approach. In the following these fourth conditions are further discussed and analyzed.

A New Business Model for the Telcos

There are many expectations about the forthcoming Internet of Things. It should provide an environment in which objects can collaborate and help humans in many aspects of their day life. Applications are foreseen in many vertical fields ranging from e-health and well-being, to smart cities and, from smart home environments to complex digital organizations [26]; from smart automotive to smart transportation. All these interesting (form the technological and business points of view) scenarios are characterized by fragmentation and verticalization, i.e., the solutions are designed and developed in a silos fashion without a common effort for deriving a supporting platform. For instance the smart home environment is highly characterized by the fragmentation of "small" vertical solutions (e.g., for alarms, for power consumption management, for domotics, and the like). They have to be integrated in a case by case fashion and this introduces complexity and reduces the reuse of solutions. In addition, the end users percept the market and the opportunity as highly complicated and devoted to specialized people. All these circumstances are slowing down the development of the market. A possible solution is the emergence of Brokers for Internet of Things. These are actors that can offer a platform for the collections and management of user data as well as the capability to subsidize the user or the use of wireless sensor network and the ability to drive the market towards common standards and solutions. The approach proposed here for a Telco is based on a few concepts:

- The possibility to represent in the cloud (i.e., in a distributed and open platform) a clone representation of real world objects and to open up a set of APIs for controlling them or interact with them;
- The possibility to represent non only sensors or actuators, but also other real world objects and concepts (e.g., a place, a product, etc.);

- The possibility to transform a product and an object into a service by means of its virtualization and representation in the cloud.

This is a relevant step forward from the internet of Things to the Internet with Things in which possibly all the objects and many "concepts" can be virtualized, represented and "programmed" in the Internet by means of open interfaces. Fig. 8 depicts the Internet with Things and a few of its characteristics.

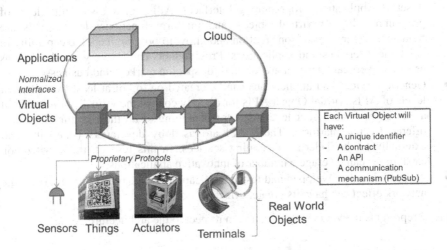

Fig. 8. Towards the Internet with Things

This approach will leverage the concept of *servitization*, i.e., the capability to leverage a product and make it a services. For example, a dishwasher can be just lent to the user and it will pay for each washing cycle, or the service provider can suggest what cleaning products to buy, and many other similar patterns.

Sometimes the servitization works better with the so called Network Effect, i.e., the increase of value of a product or service depending on the number of people that use it. Internet with Things works well either with or without the network effect. For small services that needs very specific applications, the virtualization can produce good effects in terms of sharing of the underlying infrastructure and means for programming it, For more general services, the Internet with Things can leverage the social effects of virtualized objects and creating large communities that share services, virtual objects and especially data generated by them. For instance, wireless sensor networks for the home environment could collect various data about the usage of resources, these data can be neutralized and be shared within a community in order to determine virtuous behavior in the usage of valuable resources such as energy, gas and the like. People sharing these data could engage in a sort of competition aiming at reducing their carbon footprint.

The value proposition of the Telco in this approach is differentiated: it relies on an extended communication capabilities:

- The connection between a real object and a virtualized one is based on Always Best Connected communications, i.e., the communication infrastructure (the object itself and the network of networks) will strive to provide a reliable link offering the maximum capability possible depending on the context of use of the resource.

- The platform provides a set of functions and means for exerting the expected behavior of the virtual object, e.g., processing, storage and communication capabilities (e.g., PubSub engine, data store). In addition it provides means and functions for controlling, managing and monitoring the virtual objects (e.g., the object repository for brokering of objects and resources).

- A set of Application Programming Interfaces, APIs, for allowing high level of programmability of virtual objects and platform functions/objects. APIs are fundamental for service construction and allow to programmers the capability to create new services and applications. Programmers can create general solutions as well as vertical ones that are tailored for specific markets and businesses.

- Generic services and applications can be created on top of at least two different levels of APIs: virtual Object APIs for directly control the virtualized instance of a real object, and higher level APIs for benefiting of all the rich functionalities offered by the platform. These API are used by developers (Internally and externally to the Telco) for creating services. In this respect, the servitization capabilities can leverage a number of innovative applications.

- A set of already developed and tested applications by a large ecosystem (here the network effect can have its greater effect).

Fig. 9 represents the value proposition with respect to the architecture.

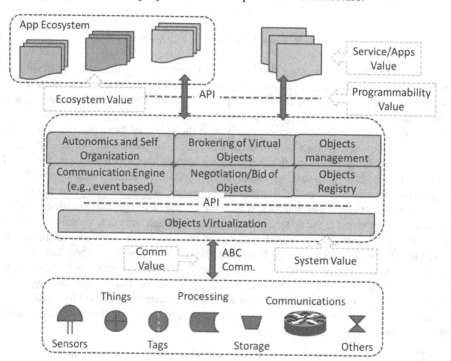

Fig. 9. Some valuable features of a Service Enabler Platform

It is worth to consider the difference of this approach respect to the traditional attitude of Telcos. In a traditional business proposition, the Telco was trying to create a full offering by acting a number of different roles in the value chain of a service (from infrastructure, to platform up to service provider). This was done by leveraging the network and its capabilities. In this approach, the Telco will focus mainly on the role of Platform Providers and will act in order to collect and integrate different infrastructures (processing, storage and communications) as well as to allow different service development capabilities. For certain services, the approach still allows the Telco to play the full set of roles (i.e., the service provider) or to focus on the communication infrastructure (connectivity provider). This flexibility will guarantee the possibility to choose the best role depending on the service proposition.

A representation of the new ecosystem is given in Fig. 10.

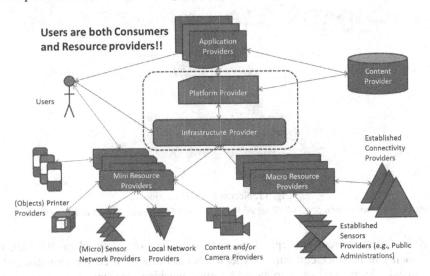

Fig. 10. The Ecosystem envisaged for the Service Enabler Platform

One of the major differences is the role of the user: it is not only a customer, it can be a provider of resources and be a partner of the Telco. The platform in fact is built also by putting together and integrating resources pertaining to different administrative domains (and end users will have a key role in this). One requirement of the platform is to be able to easily and dynamically integrate resources, systems and networks of other actors in such a way to cooperate in the creation of a synergic network of networks.

Virtualization for the Service Enabler Platform

Service Enablers' networks will therefore rely more and more on highly-developed software, which will accelerate the pace of innovation as it has done in the computing and storage domains.

Virtualization [27] technology, introduced by IBM in 1973, became very popular with systems like the hypervisor Xen and VMware. These systems have been widely used to enhance isolation, mobility, dynamic reconfiguration and fault tolerance of IT systems. The concept of virtualization has been migrated to networks.

Of course, network virtualization already exists in virtual private networks (VPN) which generally use the multi-protocol label switching (MPLS) technology, operating on the link level layer. Another form of virtualization is to segment the physical local area networks into virtual local area networks (VLAN). An overlay network is yet another form of network virtualization which is typically implemented in the application layer (Fig. 11), though various implementations at lower layers of the network stack do exist.

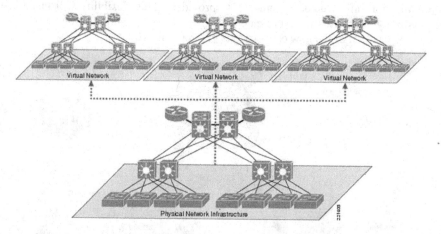

Fig. 11. Network Virtualization
(Source: http://www.cisco.com/en/US/docs/solutions/Enterprise/Network_Virtualization/PathIsol.html)

Nevertheless current concept of network virtualization is based on the idea of introducing in network equipment hypervisors (as formerly used for virtualizing IT resources). An hypervisor, also called a virtual machine manager, is a program that allows multiple operating systems to share a single hardware host. Each operating system appears to have the host's processor, memory, and other resources all to itself. However, the hypervisor is actually controlling the host processor and resources, allocating what is needed to each operating system in turn and making sure that the guest operating systems (called virtual machines) cannot disrupt each other.

For example, the principle of a virtual router is that one physical router is divided into several virtual routers residing inside virtual machines.

Network virtualization is a powerful technique as it provides flexibility, promotes diversity, promises security and increased manageability: by allowing multiple heterogeneous network architectures to cohabit on a shared physical substrate, network virtualization is a diversifying attribute of the future networks. Network virtualization allows achieving multiple advantages: for example, the crash, or the misuse, of a virtual resource is confined in a virtual network (e.g., by applying fault recovery policies enforced by self-healing capabilities) and it has no impact on other virtual networks; it is possible to put in place, in each virtual network, specific logics and policies (e.g. to optimize the usage of allocated resources according to SLA).

This evolution will require new management approaches capable of operating, in an integrated way, both real and virtual network resources. A way to implement this operational intelligence is based on decoupling data processing-forwarding from sets of controllers (interacting with each other and properly orchestrated), embedding certain levels of automaticity (to ease human operation and mitigate mistakes).

Software Defined Networking (SDN) [28] which can be seen as a step in the direction of this network transformation. In particular, in SDN architecture, network control and data planes are decoupled, so that network infrastructure is abstracted from business applications (see Fig. 12). This is expected to bring programmability and flexibility to build multiple networks (on the same physical infrastructure) offering multiple network services. Network services, for example, will include routing, multicast, security, access control, bandwidth management, traffic engineering, quality of service, processor and storage optimization, energy usage, and all forms of policy management, custom tailored to meet business objectives.

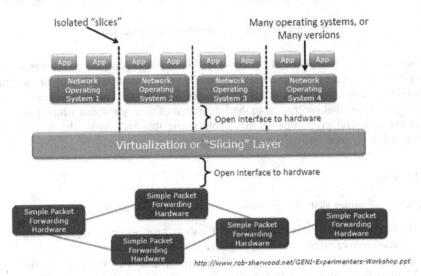

Fig. 12. Decoupling network control and data planes to abstract network infrastructure from business applications [28]

This network transformation should also pay attention to open-source initiatives aiming at providing "network connectivity as a service". For example OpenStack is an open source cloud project developing two technologies: OpenStack Compute and OpenStack Object Storage. OpenStack Compute is the internal fabric of the cloud creating and managing large groups of virtual private servers. OpenStack Object Storage is software for creating redundant, scalable object storage using clusters of commodity servers to store terabytes or even petabytes of data. Interestingly, Quantum is project of OpenStack looking to provide "network connectivity as a service" between interface devices managed by other OpenStack services. In other words, Quantum is an application-level abstraction of networking: it requires additional software (in the form of a plug-in) and it can talk to SDN via an API. Fig. 13 represents a possible integration between the two solutions.

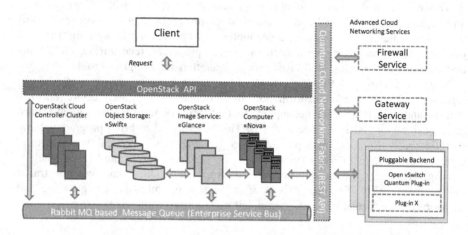

Fig. 13. Integration of OpenStack and Quantum

Eventually future network of networks will look like a complex environment (e.g. ecosystem) of resources and associated controllers in a continuous and dynamic game of cooperation and competition. As known, complex systems exhibit properties (e.g. self-organization) that emerge from the interaction of their parts and which cannot be predicted from the properties of the single parts: this will make the architectural design and the Operations particularly challenging.

Architecture

The Service Enabler Platform (a network of networks) will strongly depend on:

- the virtualization of resources (communication, processing, storage, sensing);
- the cooperative orchestration of single or subsystems' resources;
- the introduction of self-organization capabilities in order to achieve an autonomic, cognitive [12] behavior of applications and resources (the highly dynamic and unpredictable behavior of a network of networks requires the real-time adaptation to different contexts);he introduction of different (from client server) paradigms for the cooperation of distributed (virtual) objects.

Overlay networking is a real distributed processing paradigm and it fits properly in this dynamic environment. The combination of these technologies will lead to a programmable networked environment such as the one represented in Fig. 14.

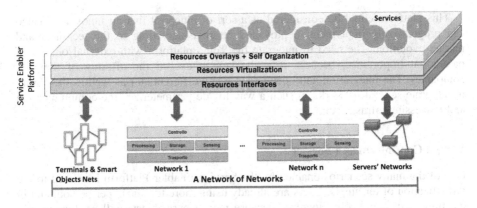

Fig. 14. A Service Enabling Environment and its basic principles and layering

The Service Enabler platform is a sort of Network Operating System, that, through the representation and virtualization of networked resources spanning across many subsystems and different administrative domains, will allow applications to negotiate for "virtualized" and autonomic resources, to allocate them, to control and program their functionalities according to the specific needs and requirements. The upper layer is made out of overlay network that comprises basic resources. These basic resources can be extended or can be integrated with new specialized ones in order to allow for the provision and offering of many services. It is important to stress out the role of end-users terminals and networks. They provide to the entire network a set of capabilities and the possibility to the entire network to rapidly grow (similarly to peer to peer networks in which end users contribute to the resources of the system that can scale up).

A broader view of the architecture is given in Fig. 15.

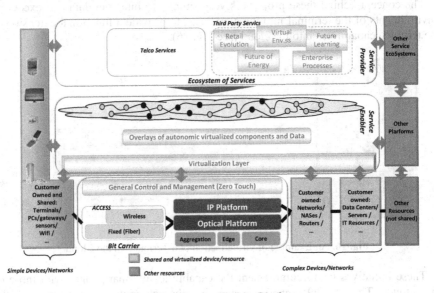

Fig. 15. A Service Enabler Platform

This platform could be considered as a sort of blueprint that an innovative Telco can progressively implement, deploy and improve according to the technical and market evolution. The need to integrate the Telco platform with external ones is of paramount importance, because it is the key to exceed the offering of the web companies. The integration and openness is a key differentiator as well as the ability to integrate several networks in such a way to "de-perimeterize" the communication and processing infrastructure.

Virtual Continuum as a Service

One of the many scenarios enabled by the Service Enabler Platform is related to the virtualization of terminals. Users are already using more terminals per person, and in the future this trend could increase because more smart objects will be dynamically associated to the single user. The virtualization capabilities promised by the Service Enable Platform promise to nurture an very valuable service portfolio related to terminal virtualization.

The Virtual Terminal

The concept of virtualization of mobile phones is getting more interest worldwide. There are already some initiatives related to the definition of Virtual Terminals and Virtual Environments. For instance the Clone Cloud project within Intel Research Center in Berkeley aims at "clone the entire set of data and applications from the smart-phone onto the cloud and selectively execute some operations on the clones, reintegrating the results back into the smart-phone". Also NTT is working on a Virtual Terminal with the idea of offloading many time consuming processing tasks from the terminal into the network.

The concept behind these projects is very simple: to integrate data and execution environments of the terminal into the cloud, i.e., to provide a functional extension of the terminal capabilities into the cloud (see Fig. 16).

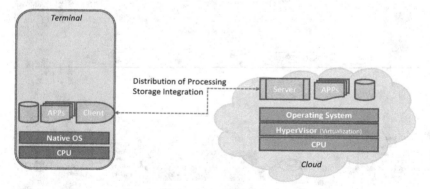

Fig. 16. An Example of virtualization of a Terminal in the Cloud

These initiatives try to complement the capabilities of smartphones with those of the cloud. The typical functions can be the computation off-load or the synchronization of data between different clones (e.g., like silk of amazon [28]). These are important functions that in the short – medium term can have market relevance. They can increase the capabilities of simple terminals (e.g., those of plain vanilla 2G terminals) or to extend the battery life of power demanding terminals. The service could offer a continuous presence of the customer in the network (e.g., in the social networks) and the ability to aggregate around the Virtual Terminals the many specific terminals used by the single customer.

Operators have a clear idea of the real social network of the customers. Actually the entire set of call and message related information does clearly define the social network of customers. Many services can be created exploiting this knowledge of the customer (exceeding those enabled by the address book: e.g., the Skydeck service was building the social network of the customer by storing all the messages sent and received as well as the records of all the calls).

Some Examples
Moving the SIMs into the Virtual Terminal. A user could map one or more physical terminals onto a (subscribed) virtual terminal in order to synchronize them or to extend their capabilities. The user decides how to deal with communications and processing services, however the different terminals can create a sort of mesh network and can partition information and computational tasks among them. See Fig. 17.

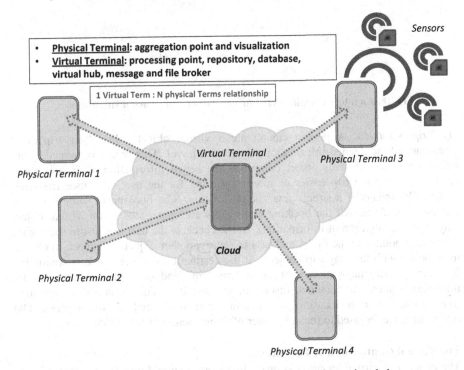

Fig. 17. A 1-to-n mapping between n real terminals and one virtual clone

Another situation is depicted in Fig. 18: a user has many virtual terminal subscriptions and it associate the unique physical terminal to all it virtual images in order to integrate all the services into a single end-point.

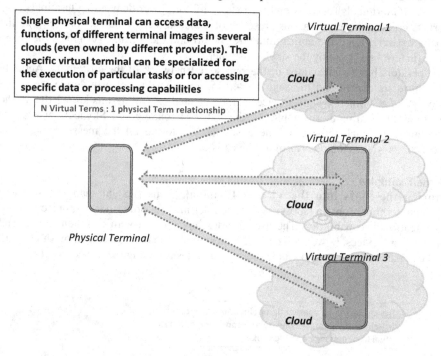

Fig. 18. An n-to-1 mapping between a physical terminal and n virtual clones

My Trip Scenario. A person can create a virtual object called "my trip" that represents all the needed information related to a travel. This object is created in the virtual environment. This object comprises the set of information, data, and alerts needed to make the trip easier or more rewarding for the user. The user first visit virtually by means of a street view, the destination. S/he bookmarks some points of interest with alerts. All the booking and tickets are aggregated to the virtual object "my trip" (aggregation of information). At the check-in the user has just to share with the clerk a pointer to the ticket and gets in return another object (the check-in object) to associate with the "my trip" object. At the destination the user can start wandering and can ask the navigation support to "my trip" and can get also some useful information about monuments, restaurant and the like. This instance of "my trip" (plus some addition location information) can be stored in the system. Old information can be used to recall the user of things done or seen in that place.

The Virtual Continuum: A Definition

The concept of virtual terminal is just a first step: it should be gradually extended to encompass and integrate other physical objects. Virtualization in the network of physical objects aims at the creation of a "virtual continuum" between the real and virtual environments. There will be a constant entanglement between real objects and their representations in the network. Events, actions, data on a physical object will be represented in the virtual world and vice versa.

The Virtual Continuum will enable the exploitation of the Service Enabler Platform. It will be enriched and personalized with a huge set of applications and services that largely exceeds the portfolio of communication related services supported by current and future communication platforms. The opportunities related to virtual environments and the related platform can be also a means to change or shape new markets like Augmented Reality, Internet with Things, Ambient Intelligence / Context Awareness, Social Media, Entertainment, Micro and Distributed production and the like.

There is the need to design and develop a set of APIs and functionalities that virtualize the Terminal (an open and licensable physical and logical architecture of the terminal). The agreement between many Telcos could be important to ensure a significant market for application developers.

The virtualization of terminals and objects straightforwardly leads to the aggregation/integration of clusters of objects and consequently to the ability to virtualize entire real environments. An environment can be a living room or a house, but also a store or a shopping center, a business or a hospital, a whole global telecommunications network or a distributed data center. The concept of virtual environment is important because it allows a Telco to build global offers independently from the direct control of resources (more often owned by others) or networks. This feature should be well understood and analyzed because it is the key to the "de-perimeterization" of services and the ability to create a "network of networks" (e.g., integrating the specific Telco owned network with those of other Telcos or enterprises networks) or "overlay networks" that span over other networks. Overlaying capabilities will be a means to provide a global coverage of services and virtual environments (a sort of roaming feature) and to introduce the concept of resource brokering.

A virtual environment is a software feature that allows customers to use features tailored to their specific needs. The allocation and adaptation is mediated/optimized considering the customer's needs and the possible allocation and exploitation of existing local physical resources. In addition, the functionality of virtual environment allows third parties to develop services that may be provided regardless of the actual availability of specific local resources by means of an intelligent use of remote and virtualized resources. A Virtual Environment will gather different resources pertaining to different domains and will integrate them in a dynamic infrastructure. Virtual environments will be designed and operated like complex systems capable of self-organizing. Fig. 19 represents the problem domain addressed by the Virtual Environment and Virtual Continuum concepts.

The concept of virtual environment can support future enterprises' needs by seamlessly integrating different technologies like cloud computing, virtualization and composition of networks, sensors and actuators. A business operates in its own environment, made out of its resources (physical, logistical, intellectual, contract).

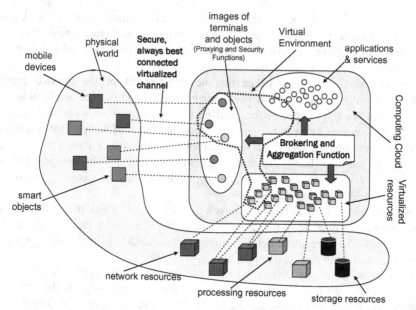

Fig. 19. A Virtual Environment as supported by the Service Enabler Platform

In the coming years, the businesses will tend to transform their organizational structure moving from rigid and hierarchical structures (e.g., organizational or functional units) to open environments in which resources and processes are not directly controlled and they can even reside outside the enterprise perimeter. New flexible organizational models need to be supported by the ICT infrastructure. They will be characterized by a loose coupling of dynamically associated heterogeneous resources pertaining to different domains; their integration and aggregation will be so dynamic that human intervention for configuring the environment is not possible. Virtualization and autonomic networking will be used in order to support the self-organization of the environment according to self-CHOP features.

5   Conclusions

In the future context draft by the Service Enabler Platform proposition, a Telco can leverage its traditional assets like: management skills of complex systems, the offer of multi-channel communications, identity management of users, integration with (and within) various business sectors and institutions and its global value within the national and international relationship system, and disrupt the market (currently dominated by the service offering of the web companies) making new compelling service offering within an open environment. The proposition and the related architecture leverage the role and the resources of users, giving them a central role in the entire approach.

Moreover, adopting this approach does not implies to disregard existing business models, instead it means to build a new compelling offering that shifts the focus from physical point to point connectivity to a higher meaning of "connectivity": customers' needs are to be supported by the creation of secure and flexible communication environments made out of virtualized resources that dynamically adapt to the context of usage in order to meet customers' needs at the best. In a sense, for businesses it is a move from simple integrated communication offering to the next step of communications: the integration of cloud computing, storage, communications and sensing/actuators; while for the mass market it is the move from the "access gateway" or the set-top-box to the next level of communications made out of the integration of content, data, information, social relationships (i.e., a move towards an information centric networking).

Why Enter This New Course

Part of the value will be in the deep knowledge of the customers and its data. This knowledge can be monetized in terms of security services (e.g., to protect privacy and data ownership) or in term of profiling seen as a service to the user), controlled by the user (the profiled data will be used according to the allowed and agreed mechanisms negotiated with the users).

The virtualization allows the Telco to leverage its assets (connectivity and management) for entering into new businesses that have the potential to transform the current processes and business models: from virtual reality to the Internet with Things.

The real interest for moving in this direction is twofold: on one side the possibility of a repositioning and re-appropriation / sharing of the value that terminals and smart objects will continue to build, and on the other side the possibility to reposition the Telco infrastructure as a global platform and an enabler of services. Taken together, these aspects can slow down and possibly reverse the fall in revenues and importance of the traditional business of Telcos.

References

1. OECD, Machine-to-Machine Communications: Connecting Billions of Devices. OECD Digital Economy Papers, No. 192. OECD Publishing (2012), http://dx.doi.org/10.1787/5k9gsh2gp043-en
2. Hsia, P., Samuel, J., Gao, J., Kung, D., Toyoshima, Y., Chen, C.: Formal Approach to Scenario Analysis. IEEE Softw. 11, 33–41 (1994)
3. Prat, J. (ed.): Next-Generation FTTH Passive Optical Networks: Research Towards Unlimited Bandwidth Access (2008) ISBN: 978-1-4020-8469-0
4. Saracco, R.: An Exciting Future, presentation available in Comsoc Distinguished Lecture, http://www.comsoc.org/about/memberprograms/distinguished-lecturers/on-line
5. Wu, T., Slater, D.: Homes with Tails (November 24, 2008), Available at SSRN: http://ssrn.com/abstract=1306745 or http://dx.doi.org/10.2139/ssrn.1306745
6. Akyildiz, I., Lee, W.Y., Vuran, M., Mohanty, S.: NeXt generation/dynamic spectrum access/cognitive radio wireless networks: A survey. Computer Network 50(13), 2127–2159 (2006), http://dx.doi.org/10.1016/j.comnet.2006.05.001
7. Minerva, R., Crespi, N.: Unleashing the Disruptive Potential of User-Controlled Identity Management, in Telecom World (ITU WT), 2011 Technical Symposium at ITU (October 2011)

256   R. Minerva et al.

8. Personal Data: The Emergence of a New Asset Class edited by: World Economic Forum
9. Rappa, M.: Business Models on the Web. Managing the Digital Enterprise (May 2003), http://digitalenterprise.org
10. Bikfalvi, A., Lay, G., Maloca, S., Waser, B.R.: Servitization and networking: large-scale survey findings on product-related services. Service Business, 1–22 (June 2, 2012), doi:10.1007/s11628-012-0145-y
11. Information about servitization available in, http://www.servitizer.com/servitization-defined.html
12. Manzalini, A., Deussen, P.H., Nechifor, S., et al.: Self-optimized Cognitive Network of Networks. Oxford Journals, The Computer Journal 54(2), 189–196 (2010)
13. Manzalini, A.: Mitigating Systemic Risks in Future Networks. Submitted to The International Workshop on Computer-Aided Modeling Analysis and Design of Communication Links and Networks (2012)
14. Baset, S., Schulzrinne, H.: An Analysis of the Skype Peer-to-Peer Internet Telephony Protocol. IEEE Infocom (April 2006)
15. Information about Rich Communication Services available in http://www.gsma.com/rcs/
16. Information about Wholesale Applications Community available in http://oneapi.gsma.com/developer-article-oneapi-and-the-wholesale-applications-community-wac/
17. Information about Guifi available in http://en.wikipedia.org/wiki/Guifi.net
18. Information about Village Telco available in http://villagetelco.org/about/
19. Information about DirecNet available in http://opengroup.org/direcnet/
20. Information about LandWar available in http://www.army.mil/aps/06/maindocument/Text_addendum_B.html#part20
21. Information about Manthycore available in http://www.mantychore.eu/
22. Gurbani, V., Hilt, V., Rimac, I., Tomsu, M., Marocco, E.: A Survey Of Research On The Application-Layer Traffic Optimization Problem And The Need For Layer Cooperation. IEEE Communication Magazine 47(8), 107–112 (2009)
23. Chiang, M., Low, S.H., Calderbank, A.R., Doyle, J.C.: Layering As Optimization Decomposition: A Mathematical Theory of Network Architectures. Proceedings of the IEEE 95(1), 255–312 (2007), doi:10.1109/JPROC.2006.887322
24. Information about Nanodatacenters available in http://www.nanodatacenters.eu/
25. Baldoni, R., Contenti, M., Virgillito, A.: The evolution of publish/Subscribe communication systems. In: Schiper, A., Shvartsman, A.A., Weatherspoon, H., Zhao, B.Y. (eds.) Future Directions in DC 2012. LNCS, vol. 2584, pp. 137–141. Springer, Heidelberg (2003)
26. Information about iCore availbale in http://www.iot-icore.eu/
27. Definition of virtualization available in http://www.webopedia.com/TERM/V/virtualization.html
28. McKeown, N.: Software Defined Networking. Infocom (April 2009)

Internet of Things

Gyu Myoung Lee[1], Noel Crespi[1], Jun Kyun Choi[2], and Matthieu Boussard[3]

[1] Institut Mines-Telecom, Telecom SudParis, 9 rue Charles Fourier 91011 Evry, France
{gm.lee,noel.crespi}@it-sudparis.eu
[2] Korea Advanced Institute of Science and Technology,
291 Daehak-ro, Yuseong-gu, Daejeon 305-701, Korea (Republic of)
jkchoi59@kaist.edu
[3] Alcatel-Lucent Bell Labs France
mathieu.boussard@alcatel-lucent.com

Abstract. This chapter addresses the Internet of Things (IoT); from the concept and fundamental characteristics to the advantages of machine-to-machine communications, as well as the key requirements for the IoT. Examples of the IoT are illustrated, including their core technologies. Architectural models for the IoT are presented to identify related functionalities. This chapter also introduces recent efforts towards standardization of the various technical aspects.

Keywords: M2M, IoT, WoT.

1 Introduction

The Internet of Things (IoT) is one of the hottest and one of the most divisive topics in Information and Communication Technology (ICT) today. There are many different views on the IoT, from those who judge it an ambitious concept to others who purport a kind of infrastructure. As the authors of [1] point out, this variety of viewpoints (and resulting definitions) stems from the locution itself, mixing the notion of 'Internet' – which itself can cover many different realities, from networking aspects up to a collection of socially-meaningful data and services - and the notion of 'things' – which is even more subject to interpretation, although in the IoT context it usually refers to network-able things, i.e., connected physical objects or virtual things that have a cyber-existence (a piece of content, a service, the representation of a physical object). The result is that a first splitting of viewpoints emerges, based on whether the considered actor has an Internet-oriented (i.e., focused on the communication infrastructure and mechanisms, typically resulting in the Machine-to-Machine (M2M) field) or an Object-oriented view (i.e., focused on the possibilities offered by having real-world objects reflected in the network or augmented with Information Technology (IT) services as is the case with Radio Frequency Identification (RFID) or smart objects). Another major resulting dimension, which pertains more to computer science, is the notion of complex distributed systems. As more and more heterogeneous objects get connected to an Internet of Things, novel means to manage, describe, discover, and use these connected resources and the data

E. Bertin et al. (Eds.): Telecommunication Services Evolution, LNCS 7768, pp. 257–282, 2013.

they produce become necessary. A number of initiatives borrowing from the fields of autonomous or intelligent systems and semantic technologies, etc. go in this direction. Fig. 1 gives an idea of the variety of topics brought by these three viewpoints that make up the Internet of Things landscape. It is also important to note that this diversity of actors and viewpoints results in an equally important diversity of application fields (examples are given in Section 3.2). With so many diverging opinions, there have been many attempts to define the IoT so that it can move forward with a common understanding in a global perspective.

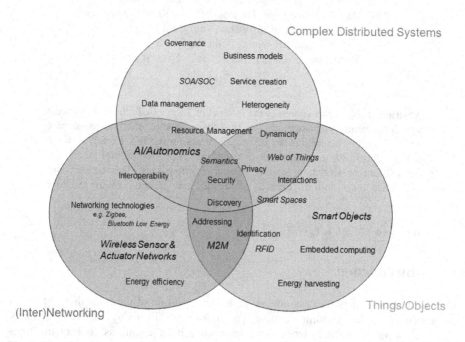

Fig. 1. The three viewpoints of the Internet of Things and their associated concepts and topics (Freely adapted from [1])

After considering the existing definitions put forth by different organizations, the ITU-T has defined the IoT as follows: "The IoT can be perceived in a broad perspective as a vision with technological and societal implications. The IoT can be viewed as a global infrastructure for the information society, enabling advanced services by interconnecting (physical and virtual) things based on both existing and evolving interoperable ICTs. Through the exploitation of identification, data capture, processing and communication capabilities, the IoT makes full use of things to offer services to all kinds of applications, whilst maintaining the required privacy" [2].

As a result of the IoT vision, many different kinds of devices connect to the network and take part in the exchange of communication. End points of this communication may be humans, or objects such as devices/machines. As a result, two distinct modes of communications are commonly described for the IoT [3, 4, 5, 6]:

- Human-to-Object (Thing) Communication: humans communicate with a device in order to get specific information (e.g., IPTV content, file transfer) including remote access to objects by humans.
- Object-to-Object (Thing-to-Thing) Communication: an object delivers information (e.g., sensor-related information) to another object with or without the involvement of humans. As objects include physical devices and products as well as logical contents and resources, M2M communication is a subset of object-to-object communication.

In the IoT, things are objects of the physical world (*physical things*) or of the information world (*virtual things*), which are capable of being identified and integrated into information and communication networks. All of these things have their associated information, which can be static and dynamic [2].

- Physical things exist in the physical world and are capable of being sensed and/or actuated upon and/or connected. Examples of physical things include sensors of surrounding environments, industrial robots, goods, and electrical equipment.
- Virtual things exist in the information world and are capable of being stored, processed and accessed. Examples of virtual things include multimedia contents, application software and service representations of physical things (e.g. avatars or Virtual Objects [7]).

Objects that contain sensors can interconnect with one another and can be monitored by distant servers or people. Many everyday objects already incorporate embedded microcontrollers and will increasingly include (often wireless) networking interfaces. Typical microcontrollers incorporate a microcomputer, storage, software, and interfaces for sensors and actuators that can reside onboard everyday objects. With the addition of a network interface, people and machines can monitor and control such objects from a distance, via the Internet. Software that resides in servers and/or in Internet-connected objects can initiate a sequence of events, with or without human intervention. The combination of embedded microcontrollers, sensors, actuators, network interfaces, and the greater Internet makes it possible for the Internet to evolve from a network of interconnected computers to a network of interconnected objects. Accordingly, the things in the IoT influence each other depending on their functional capabilities (e.g., computational processing power, network connectivity, available power, etc.) as well as on their context and situations (e.g., time, space) and will be actively involved in different processes [8]. Based on these concepts, the fundamental characteristics of the IoT are identified as follows [2]:

- Interconnectivity: Any type of thing will have the potential to be interconnected with the communication infrastructure.
- Things-related services: The IoT is capable of providing thing-related services within the constraints of things, such as privacy protection and semantic consistency between physical things and their associated virtual things. In order to provide thing-related services within the constraints of things, the technologies in both the physical world and the world of information and communications will change.

- Heterogeneity: IoT devices are heterogeneous, ranging from tiny sensors and actuators to mobile devices and large computers, and based on different hardware platforms and networks. They can interact with other devices or service platforms through various networks.
- Dynamic changes: The state of devices changes dynamically, e.g., sleeping and waking, connected/disconnected, etc. as does their context, including location and speed. Moreover, the number of devices can change dynamically.
- Enormous scale: By 2020, there will be 50 billion things that will need to be managed and to communicate with each other [9, 10]. Even more critical will be the management of the data generated and its interpretation for application purposes. This aspect relates to the semantics of data, as well as its efficient handling.

The following section introduces technology trends for beyond M2M – visions and requirements for the IoT. The state of the art and examples of the IoT are then introduced. Next, architectural models for the IoT are presented. The relevant activities for standardization are summarized in the last section.

2   Beyond M2M

2.1   Towards an Internet/Web of Things and People Post-M2M

M2M is about enabling the flow of data between machines and machines, and ultimately machines and people. M2M communications involve the automated transfer of information and commands between two machines with no human intervention at either end of the system [11]. There are many different choices to make, such as how each machine is connected, what type of communication is carried out, and how the data is used. However, there are four basic stages that are common to virtually every M2M application [12]:

- Collection of data from a machine;
- Transmission of selected data through a communication network;
- Assessment of the data via integration; and
- Response to the available information depending on the circumstances.

While M2M is a specific capability that enables machines to connect and then to interact over a network, the IoT is so much more than M2M, and its potential has only just begun to be explored. The IoT it is about interacting with the objects around us, even static non-intelligent objects, and augmenting such interactions with context provided by geo-location, time and other information. In this context, M2M is a subset of the IoT [13]. Through the evolution of smart objects, a smart object becomes aware of its characteristics, context, and situation (Fig. 2). These smart objects communicate with each other and with various types of mobile media and devices based on standard communication protocols. Recently, we have seen the substantial increase in the production of smart objects in everyday life thanks to the advances in embedded IT. Consumers are quickly learning how to access them, mainly through communication technologies such as Near Field Communication (NFC), accessible through smart phone applications.

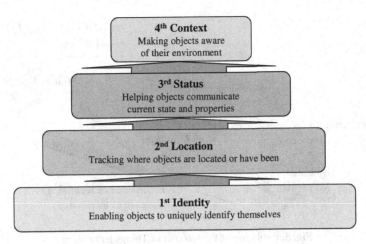

Fig. 2. The evolution of smart objects (source: [14])

Regardless of the number of low-power network protocols developed recently to facilitate these connections, embedded devices are still located in isolated islands at the application layer: developing applications using them is a challenging task that requires expert knowledge of each ecosystem. As a consequence, integrating smart objects into applications to support a smart connected world remains a difficult task. Meanwhile, the Internet with Web on top shows how open standards can be used to build millions of flexible systems over heterogeneous hardware and software platforms and still preserve efficiency and scalability. Websites no longer offer only pages, but Application Programming Interfaces (APIs) that can be used by other Web resources to create new, ad-hoc and composite applications running in the computing cloud and accessible by desktops or mobile computers. The Web of Things (WoT) [7, 15] is a way of realizing the IoT wherein everyday devices and objects are connected by fully integrating them to the Web. Web standards are used to access the capability of the devices, which makes it possible for users to interact with the devices using Web interfaces. The WoT can provide capabilities such as device reusability, portability across several heterogeneous networks, and accessibility based on the Web and with Web standards [16, 17].

Thanks to the loose-coupling, simplicity and scalability of RESTful architectures, and the wide availability of Hypertext Transfer Protocol (HTTP) libraries and clients, RESTful architectures are becoming one of the most ubiquitous and lightweight integration platforms. Using Web standards to interact with smart things thus appears to be increasingly adequate. Although HTTP introduces a communication overhead and increases the average latency, it is sufficient for many pervasive scenarios where such longer delays do not affect user experience [18, 19].

Recently, a new approach for a human interaction model for the IoT, the so-called 'Social WoT' [20, 21], has been introduced as an interaction paradigm for connecting people to the IoT. While the IoT has focused mainly on establishing connectivity in a variety of challenging and constrained networking environments, the social WoT enables interactions among people to be translated into representations in the real physical world in a way that provides some of the same ambient awareness that the social network services provide online. Therefore, it allows people to connect, use, share and compose physical and virtual things in order to create personalized and pervasive applications.

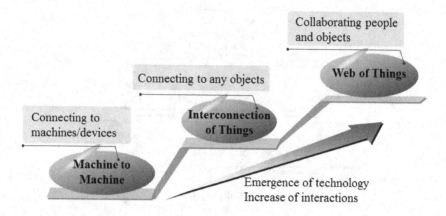

Fig. 3. Evolution of the Internet of Things technology

Fig. 3 shows the technical evolution from M2M to WoT. When we consider various devices, including tiny sensors for M2M, providing connectivity is the fundamental challenge for the communication technology. From the interconnecting of things, to link to any object in the real world will be as critical as the extension of end points. In addition, Web-enabled objects (i.e., WoT) will support the easy creation of applications and sharing of data from objects and people.

A recent white paper [22] points out that a 'pluridisciplinary' approach to develop the requisite new technologies, concepts, and models is needed. This would include Integrated Circuit development, energy management, communications systems and principles, embedded systems, and packaging data acquisition and processing. Among the key challenges for the IoT, the following three points should demand the most attention:

- Integration of smart, autonomous interconnected objects such as sensors, actuators and processors working under severely constrained energy and physical environments;
- Coping with the potentially billions of objects [9] that can be interconnected over secure, flexible networks providing secure and ubiquitous service provisioning; and
- Accomplishing the fusion of the data obtained by sensors, the network and service management, distributed data treatment, and ambient intelligence.

2.2   Vision and Impact

The vision of the IoT suggests that there would be a "world-wide network of interconnected objects uniquely addressable, based on standard communication" [23]. Everything from individuals, groups, communities, objects, products, data, services, and processes will potentially be connected by the IoT. Connectivity will become, in the IoT, a kind of commodity. In addition, there will be the need to create the best situation-aware development environment for stimulating the creation of services and appropriate intelligent middleware to understand and interpret the information, to ensure protection from fraud and malicious attack and to guarantee privacy [9].

With this vision, and making use of intelligence in the supporting network infrastructure, things will be able to autonomously manage their transportation, implement fully automated processes, and thereby optimize logistics. They may be able to harvest the energy they need. They will automatically configure themselves when exposed to a new environment; exhibit an 'intelligent/cognitive' behavior when faced with other things, and deal seamlessly with unforeseen circumstances. Ultimately, they could even manage their own disassembly and recycling at the end of their lifecycle, helping to preserve the environment and freeing humans from exposure to dangerous components.

The IoT infrastructure allows combinations of smart objects, sensor network technologies, and human beings, using different but interoperable communication protocols, capable of realizing a dynamic multimodal/heterogeneous network that can be deployed in inaccessible or remote locations and in cases of emergencies or hazardous situations. In this infrastructure, different entities or things discover and explore each other and learn to take advantage of each other's data by pooling resources, dramatically enhancing the scope and reliability of the resulting services.

The IoT can benefit from the latest developments and functionalities through the provision of new, intuitive user-centered and individually configurable, self-adapting smart products and services for the benefit of businesses and society [24].

Fig. 4 summarizes the vision and impact of the IoT. One of the ultimate objectives of the IoT is to meet the challenge of seamless communications between any things (e.g., humans and objects). The IoT will have to encompass the following:

- Ubiquitous connectivity allowing for whenever, whoever, wherever, and whatever types of communications;
- A pervasive reality for effective interfaces to provide connectable real world environments; and
- Ambient intelligence allowing for innovative communications and providing increased value creation.

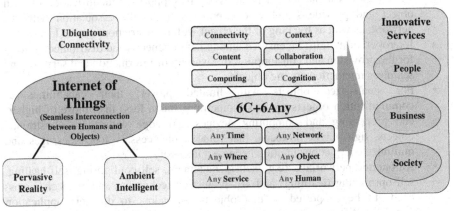

Fig. 4. The Internet of Things: vision and impact

From communications for transmitting information, evolution will effectively integrate connectivity and content with computing, context, collaboration and cognition. Therefore, the IoT will be a global network of interconnected objects, enabling the identification and discovery of objects as well as semantic data processing via 6Cs+6Anys [5, 25]. Here, the 6Cs include:

- Connectivity: connection for mobile and constrained objects;
- Content: massive data produced from objects;
- Computing: cloud computing and content storage service;
- Context: context aware design to improve performance;
- Collaboration: cooperative communications, inter-objects and service sharing;
- Cognition: mining the knowledge from massive data and providing autonomous system adjustment for improvements.

6Anys stands for Any time, Any where, Any service, Any network, Any object and Any human.

From the vision, the IoT is beginning to transform how we do business, the run the public sector and the daily life of people. The IoT will thus enable innovative services for people, business and society involving the use of technologies such as Bio Technologies (BT), Nano Technologies (NT) and Content Technologies (CT), thereby allowing the provision of services that go beyond traditional telecommunication and IT services. These innovative services, including interdisciplinary services, will require extensions in terms of networking and service capabilities as well as the availability of all sorts of objects [5, 26].

2.3   Requirements

The following is a list of high-level requirements that have specific relevance for the IoT [2, 3, 27]:

- Each object will need to be connected to the network and be able to consider heterogeneous identifiers. It is necessary to support the identification of each object and provide seamless communication via the association with the network, as well as tracking of the object with no restrictions on the location.
- Interoperability must be ensured among heterogeneous and distributed systems for the provision and consumption of a variety of information and services and seamless interaction among objects.
- For small-sized objects with limited power, their capabilities as communication objects are less (sometimes much less) than those of higher-end processing and computing devices. To cope with these constrained objects, lightweight protocols that remove unnecessary loads/messages and minimize energy consumption become a necessity.
- Autonomic networking (e.g., self-management, self-configuring, self-healing, self-optimizing (learning) and self-protecting techniques and/or mechanisms) needs to be supported so that objects can adapt to different application domains, different communication environments and a wide variety of devices. To support self-configuration, context information plays a critical role in supporting context-aware networking for changing communication

environments, and in supporting a semantic as the virtual representation of physical objects.

- For autonomic service provisioning, the services need to be able to be provided by the automatic capture, communication and processing of the data of things based on the rules configured by operators or customized by subscribers. Autonomic services may depend on the techniques of automatic data fusion and data mining.
- Objects can move from one place to another and may become attached to another network with a different technology. Object mobility management is required to provide seamless communication among mobile objects for location-based communications and services. This may be constrained by laws and regulations, and should comply with security requirements.
- Network size is increasing as more and more objects are connected to the network. Scalable solutions are required in order to cope with the increase of traffic and routing table sizes and the shortage of IP addresses.
- To support end-to-end connectivity, each object will need to be addressable and should therefore have a unique address. Adequate address space is a prerequisite to allow the huge number of objects expected in the IoT to be connected to the network. Alternatively, each object would be required to provide their direct connectivity via a host or gateway with a unique IP address.
- The required Quality of Service (QoS) and Quality of Experience (QoE) levels must be respected. Reliable services require on-time handling along with a verifiable level of accuracy.
- Security and privacy concerns must be managed appropriately, as the IoT connects many sophisticated objects, which may cause untold damage –even life-threatening damage – if their security is breached. The IoT needs to support privacy protection during data transmission, aggregation, storage, mining and processing.
- Self-management must be supported to ensure normal network operations. IoT applications usually work automatically without human participation, but their overall operation process should be manageable by the relevant parties.
- Middleware architectures for the IoT often follow the Service Oriented Architecture (SOA) approach. The adoption of the SOA principles is required for the decomposing of complex and monolithic systems into applications consisting of an ecosystem of simpler, well-defined components [1].

3   The State of the Art and Examples

3.1   Key Technologies for the IoT

Progress in the following technologies will contribute to the development of the IoT as its enabling building blocks [4]:

- M2M interfaces and electronic communication protocols to set the rules of engagement for two or more nodes on a network.

- Embedded computing with the computer chips (e.g., microcontrollers) that are designed to be embedded into objects other than computers.
- Wireless communication, which has the potential to play an important role in the IoT, including short-range and long-range channels as well as bidirectional and unidirectional channels.
- RFID technology, which can identify multiple objects concurrently. Some RFID tag-reader architectures support security features such as requiring a human operator to input a challenge code before decoding an ID. RFID can have varying sizes (from a few cm to hundreds of meters), power requirements, operating frequencies, amounts of rewriteable and nonvolatile storage, and software intelligence.
- Energy harvesting technologies to capture small but usable amounts of electrical energy from the environment. Current energy-harvesting research and development concentrates on advantageous temperature variations, ambient sound and vibration, and ambient radio frequency.
- Sensors that can detect changing attributes in the environment and report them to a system, along with sensor networks to exploit the benefits of sensing at more than one location. Actuators detect an incoming signal and respond by changing something in the environment.
- Location technology to assist people and machines in locating objects and to determine their physical whereabouts. For example, fixed or orbiting transmitters have known locations. They can broadcast timing signals, and receiving devices triangulate by calculating the amount of delay from each transmitter.
- Software comprises a broad domain of development. Development of the IoT will rely on many dimensions of software capabilities, including distributed execution, self-describing data structures, and much more.

3.2   IoT Examples

From the key characteristics of the IoT, new opportunities can be created to meet business requirements: creating new services based on real-time physical world data, gaining insights into complex processes and relationships, handling incidents, addressing environmental degradation (e.g., pollution, disaster, global warming, etc.), monitoring human activities (e.g., health, movements, etc.), improving infrastructure integrity (e.g., energy, transport, etc.), and addressing energy efficiency issues (e.g., smart energy metering in buildings, vehicles' fuel efficiency, etc.) [8].

The IoT is disruptive and will omnipresent. Accordingly, the IoT will significantly impact all fields of our lives in the future. As shown in Fig. 5, the major application fields for the IoT are the creation of smart environments/spaces and self-aware things (e.g., smart transport, cities, buildings, energy, living spaces, etc.) that will be activated to realize logistic, agriculture, food, energy, mobility, digital society and e-health applications [28, 29]. In the IoT, applications can be created through the integration and combination of technologies such as BT, NT and CT. Therefore, it is necessary to combine BT, NT, CT as well as IT in support of network, platform, content and objects for the IoT.

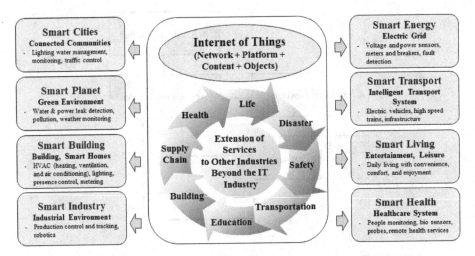

Fig. 5. Internet of Things examples (illustration inspired from [5, 28])

Communication networks have been supporting the evolution of information processing and service capabilities within IT industries. However, the capabilities of networks benefiting from ubiquitous networking will soon be impacting other industries such as medical technology, education, finance, transportation/ distribution, etc., resulting in new requirements for specific services to be incorporated into the IT field [3].

4   Architecture Model

4.1   IoT Ecosystems

The IoT sets the stage for a business ecosystem composed of a variety of business roles and players. Each business player could play at least one business role, but additional roles are possible. Some of the identified IoT business roles are shown in Fig. 6 [2]. The identified business roles and their relationships do not represent all the possible relevant roles and relationships that can be found across IoT business deployments.

- The **device provider** is responsible for devices, providing raw data and/or content to the network provider and the application provider according to the service logic.
- The **network provider** plays a central role in the IoT ecosystem. In particular, the network provider performs the following main functions:
  - Access and integration of resources provided by other providers;
  - Support and control of the IoT capabilities' infrastructure; and
  - Offering the IoT capabilities, including network capabilities and resource exposure to other providers.

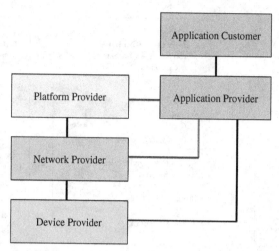

Fig. 6. An Internet of Things ecosystem (illustration from ITU-T Y.2060 [2])

- The **platform provider** provides integration capabilities and open interfaces. A platform serves as a foundation or base for realizing a particular functionality. Different platforms can provide different capabilities to application providers. Platform capabilities include typical integration capabilities, as well as data storage, data processing, device management etc. Support for different types of IoT applications is also possible.
- The **application provider** utilizes capabilities or resources supplied by the network provider, device provider and platform provider to deliver IoT applications to application customers.
- The **application customer** is a user of IoT application(s) provided by the application provider.

The rest of this section provides details of the architectural aspects in each layer related to the IoT ecosystem. First we present the IoT reference model and functional groups (Section 4.2), and then describe enablers and an implementation model to support the IoT (Section 4.3).

4.2   IoT Reference Model and Functional Groups

Fig. 7 shows the IoT reference model and its functional groups, which began as a reference model from ITU-T [1]. The relevant functional groups developed by the IoT-A project [30] are shown in the figure to make the key functionalities of each layer clearer.

The IoT reference model is composed of four layers (application, service support/application support, network, and device layers) as well as management and security capabilities associated with the four layers [2]. From a functional viewpoint, seven functional groups (IoT Applications, Process Execution & Service Orchestration, Virtual Entity & Information, IoT Service & Resources, Device Connectivity & Communication, Management, and Security) were identified to meet the requirements in the IoT-A [30]. The following items explain the information shown in Fig. 7 in more detail:

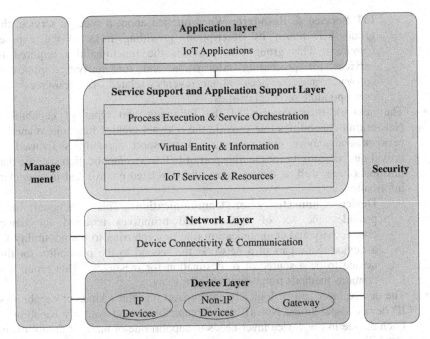

Fig. 7. Internet of Things reference model and functional groups (illustration compiled from ITU-T Y.2060 [2] and IoT-A [30])

- The application layer contains IoT applications.
    - **IoT Applications:** This group describes the functionalities provided by applications that are built on top of an implementation of the IoT architecture.
- The service support and application support layer consists of the following two capabilities: 1) Generic support capabilities, which are common capabilities that can be used by different IoT applications, such as data processing and data storage; and 2) Specific support capabilities to cater to the requirements of diverse applications. These may consist of various detailed capability groupings assembled to provide different support functions to different IoT applications.
    - **Process Execution & Service Orchestration:** This functionality group organizes and exposes IoT resources so that they become available to external entities and services. Through this set of functionalities, and the APIs that expose them, IoT services become available to external entities and can be composed by them.
    - **Virtual Entity & Information:** This group maintains and organizes information related to physical entities, enabling the search for services that expose resources associated with physical entities. It also enables the search for services based on the physical entity they are associated with. When queried about a particular physical entity, this functionality group will return the addresses of the services related to that particular physical entity.

- **IoT Service & Resource:** When queried about a specific service, this group will return its description, providing links to the exposed resources. This group also provides the functionalities required by services for processing information and for notifying application software and services about events related to resources and corresponding physical entities.

- The network layer consists of the following two types of capabilities: Networking capabilities that provide the relevant control functions related to network and device connectivity; and transport capabilities focused on providing connectivity for the transport of IoT service/application specific data information, as well as the transport of IoT-related control and management information.

  - **Device Connectivity & Communication:** This functional block provides the set of methods and primitives required for device connectivity and communication (the first referring to the possibility for a device to be part of a network, the second to the possibility for that device to be a source of or destination for messages). This group also contains methods for content-based routing.

- The device layer can be logically categorized into three kinds of capabilities: IP device capabilities, Non-IP device capabilities and gateway capabilities. Each device in the device layer needs to support one or more of the following capabilities:

  - Direct communication with the network layer for IP devices: devices that can gather and upload information directly (i.e., without using gateway capabilities) to the network layer and directly receive information (e.g., commands) from the network layer;

  - Indirect communication with the network layer for non-IP devices: devices that can gather and upload information to the network layer indirectly, i.e., through gateway capabilities; and

  - Gateway capabilities: gateway capabilities include but are not limited to:
    - ✓ Support for multiple interfaces: Support for devices in the direct layer to be connected to the network layer via various types of wired or wireless technologies, such as controller area network bus, ZigBee, Bluetooth, Wi-Fi, etc. Within the network layer, the gateway capabilities can communicate through various technologies, such as Public Switched Telephone Network (PSTN), Second Generation/Third Generation (2G/3G), Long Term Evolution (LTE), Ethernet, and Digital Subscriber Line (DSL).; and
    - ✓ Protocol conversion: There are two situations where IoT gateway capabilities are needed. One is when communications at the device layer use different device-layer protocols, e.g., ZigBee technology protocols and Bluetooth technology protocols. The other situation is when inter-layer communications use different protocols, e.g., ZigBee technology protocol at the device layer and a 3G technology protocol at the network layer.

- **Management:** To manage computational resources efficiently, management should be administered by a group of functionalities.

- Device management, such as remote device activation and de-activation, diagnostics, firmware and/or software updating, sensor node working status management;
- Sensor network topology management; and
- Traffic and congestion management, such as the detection of network overflow conditions and the implementation of resource reservation for time-critical and/or life-critical data flows.

- **Security:** Security functions must be applied consistently by the different groups of functionalities. Specifically, access-control policies should be applied consistently to prevent unauthorized applications from obtaining access to sensitive resources.
  - At the application layer, these include authorization, authentication, application data confidentiality and integrity protection, privacy protection, security audit and anti-virus programs and policies;
  - At the network layer, security needs motivate the use of authorization, authentication, use data and signaling data confidentiality programs, signaling integrity protection policies, etc.; and
  - At the device layer, secure procedures include authentication, authorization, device integrity validation, access control, data confidentiality and integrity protection programs.

In the next section, more specific enabling functionalities are shown to identify key capabilities from a generic reference model and standard functional groups.

4.3   Generic Enablers and Implementation Model to Support the IoT

The relevant Generic Enablers (GEs) for IoT service enablement were specified by FI-WARE [31], making it possible for objects to become citizens of the Internet – available, searchable, accessible, and usable – so that future Internet services can create value from real-world interaction, enabled by the ubiquity of heterogeneous and resource-constrained devices.

Management functionalities are provided for the devices and IoT domain-specific support is provided for the applications. As shown in Fig. 8, there are four groups of GEs for the IoT service enablement to be adopted and integrated:

- **IoT Communications** provide common and generic access to every kind of thing, regardless of any technological constraint on communications, typically having to integrate several protocols and manage the discontinuity of connectivity for nomadic devices. The GEs for IoT communications allow application providers to gain homogeneous access to dedicated things and devices and to be able to manage QoS in communication with those devices.
- **IoT Resource Management** proposes unified service and operational support management functions, enabling the different IoT applications and end users to discover, utilize and activate small or large groups of IoT resources and manage their properties. In doing so, the IoT service enablement focuses on global identification and information model schemes for IoT resources, providing a resolution infrastructure to link them with relevant things and developing a common remote management tool for configuring, operating and maintaining IoT resources on a large scale and with minimum human intervention.

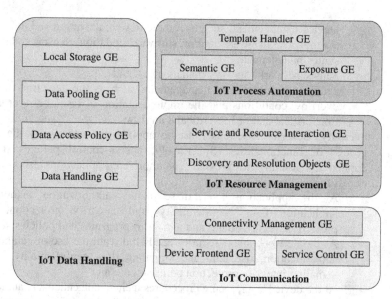

Fig. 8. Internet of Things generic enablers (GEs) (illustration from FI-WARE [31])

- **IoT Data Handling** is essential for application and data service providers to collect large amounts of IoT-related data, produced by a huge number of IoT resources almost in real-time. The GEs for IoT data handling are supported by security- and privacy-regulated policies in their collecting and forwarding of data to application/services.
- **IoT Process Automation** provides application/service providers with generic automation capabilities, enabling them to use subscription and rules templates that ease the programming of automatic processes involving IoT resources. They allow high-level conditions to be set up, which may in turn trigger new actions in a self-propagating process.

As shown in Fig. 9, from the telecom operators' perspective, they have a network infrastructure and service platform for providing telecom services using IP Multimedia Subsystem (IMS) and (mobile) Internet services thorough telecom enablers and Internet/Web enablers, which includes related capabilities for location, presence, calls, messaging, multimedia and so on. A service delivery platform for converged services and IoT enablers can support various IoT applications and services as well as 3rd party services through an open service platform, as shown in Fig. 8. A unified service delivery platform is needed to integrate resources from different networks and support multiple applications. That unified platform thus allows telecom operators to have a major role in the overall ecosystem through service creation, service execution and service delivery management. A telecom operator also needs to support access networks with various wired/wireless interfaces via gateways, according to the local environment.

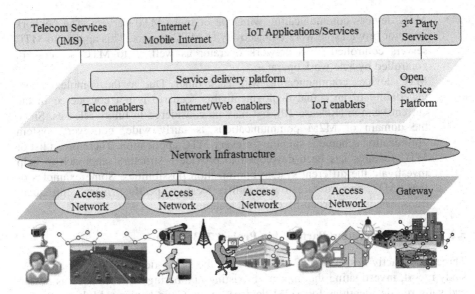

Fig. 9. An implementation model for the Internet of Things

This section presented an architectural model based on results from standards and related projects. The IoT functional model promotes a common understanding of the IoT. In particular, the analysis of an IoT reference model and its functional groups provides a favorable positioning of key capabilities. The IoT GEs make a large number of things and associated resources to become available, searchable, accessible and usable for the enabling IoT services. Finally, this section has provided an implementation model for the IoT in the telecom operator perspective.

5   Standardization for the IoT

The growth of the IoT industry has led to the need for interoperability between IoT solutions. Towards this direction, all major standardization bodies have established working groups dedicated to IoT technology. Most Standards Developing Organizations (SDOs) have only recently been formed and the overall specifications are therefore still under development. Few specifications have been published; these mainly address the overall system requirements and architecture and do not delve into the specifics of detailed solutions. The recent activities of SDOs related to the IoT are presented here to identify the gaps and to focus the search for new items for future standardization [32, 33].

5.1   Third-Generation Partnership Project (3GPP)

There is a significant amount of on-going standards work focused on M2M communications. The initial M2M standardization effort in 3GPP was started by the Service and System Aspect Working Group 1 (SA1 WG), which defined the service requirements for Machine Type Communications (MTCs). During the study of MTCs in 3GPP, the SA1 WG identified two scenarios:

- MTC devices communicating with one or more MTC servers. The network operator provides network connectivity to MTC servers. This applies to MTC servers controlled by a network operator as well as to MTC servers not controlled by a network operator.
- MTC devices communicating with each other. Due to the complexity and uncertainty of an actual deployment, this scenario is not considered in the current version (Release 10), but may be considered in future releases. Since the domain of M2M communications is fairly wide, not every system optimization scheme is suitable for every MTC application. Therefore, a list of MTC features has been developed to provide a structural approach to help investigate the different system optimization possibilities. Some examples of these MTC features are low mobility, location-specific triggers, infrequent transmission, and group-based MTC features.

5.2   Third-Generation Partnership Project 2 (3GPP2)

Three major activities in 3GPP2 are related to the M2M field: developing an M2M study report, investigating the impact of existing numbering schemes used as device and subscription identities for M2M devices over a Code Division Multiple Access (CDMA) network, and working on network enhancements to accommodate future M2M devices.

The study also reports that architectural enhancements, such as various M2M communication models, need to be considered for efficient network operation. Moreover, the architecture might need a communication adaptation protocol and a new terminal class for M2M devices so that the network can distinguish M2M devices from traditional wireless devices. Potential M2M-related enhancements to the 3GPP2 radio network are also identified.

Another M2M activity at the 3GPP2 Steering Committee (SC) level is to investigate the impact on the current addressing and numbering schemes due to the presence of a large number of M2M devices in the cdma2000 network.

5.3   European Telecommunications Standards Institute (ETSI)

The ETSI has published the first release of its M2M service standards, providing a standardized platform to manage the complexity of multiple M2M services and technologies.

M2M communication services are already showing strong revenue growth with the number of deployments steadily increasing. Large-scale managed M2M services will become a feature of this industry, but today the technology landscape is fragmented, which discourages investment.

Leading industry players participating in ETSI's Technical Committee (TC) for M2M communications (i.e., TC M2M) have now developed a set of standards which provides a complete horizontal service layer for M2M communications. The ETSI TC M2M standardization work mainly focuses on the service middleware layer, not the underlying access and network transmission technologies. M2M services will be implemented on top of three entities: the M2M service platform, M2M gateways, and M2M terminals. To support a wide range of M2M applications, the ETSI TC M2M is defining a set of standardized service capabilities (in all layers) that provide functions that are shared by the different M2M applications. These service capabilities can use core network functionalities through a set of exposed interfaces and can interface to one or more core networks. This set of service capabilities can be implemented in an M2M platform located in the network domain, in an M2M device (terminal), or in an M2M gateway [34].

The ETSI M2M Release 1 standards enable the integration of different M2M technology choices into one managed platform. ETSI M2M Release 1 is built upon proven and mature standards from the ETSI and other bodies such as the IETF, 3GPP, the Open Mobile Alliance (OMA) and the Broadband Forum. The business benefits are clear: reduced complexity of M2M deployments, reduced deployment time for new M2M services, and ultimately reduced costs for operation and investment, etc. The ETSI M2M standards specify architectural components including M2M devices, gateways with associated interfaces, applications and access technologies, as well as the M2M Service Capabilities Layer. They also offer security, traffic scheduling, device discovery and lifecycle management features. The ETSI M2M Release 1 standards are published as a set of three specifications available for download from the ETSI website [35]:

- Requirements in ETSI TS 102 689;
- Functional architecture in ETSI TS 102 690; and
- Interface descriptions in ETSI TS 102 921.

The publication of the ETSI M2M Release 1 standards marks a new milestone for the M2M industry. They unlock the potential for wide-scale deployment of M2M services and technologies, and encourage investment in new applications, which one day will bring about a true IoT.

5.4   International Telecommunication Union (ITU)

ITU-T, Internet of Things Global Standards Initiative (IoT-GSI)

The IoT-GSI [36] promotes a unified approach in ITU-T for the development of technical standards (Recommendations) enabling the IoT on a global scale. The ITU-T Recommendations were developed under the IoT-GSI by the various ITU-T Questions groups, in collaboration with other SDOs, and will enable worldwide service providers to offer the wide range of services expected by this technology. IoT-GSI also aims to act as an umbrella for IoT standards' development worldwide.

The IoT-GSI aims to accomplish the following objectives through meetings and related activities involving groupings of rapporteur groups working on the IoT:

- Develop a definition of the 'IoT';
- Provide a common working platform by collocating meetings of IoT-related rapporteur groups; and
- Develop the detailed standards necessary for IoT deployment, taking into account the work accomplished in other SDOs.

So far, the following IoT related recommendations have been developed in the ITU-T:

- Y.2060, "Overview of the Internet of Things";
- Y.2061, "Requirements for support of machine-oriented communication applications in the NGN environment";
- Y.2062, "Framework of object-to-object communication for ubiquitous networking in Next Generation Network";
- Y.2063, "Framework of the Web of Things"; and
- Y.2069, "Terms and definitions for the Internet of Things".

ITU-T, Focus Group on Machine-to-Machine Service Layer (FG M2M)

The ITU's new Focus Group on the M2M (i.e. FG M2M) [37] was established in April 2012.

Considering the wide range of M2M's possible applications – enabling services across vertical markets including healthcare, logistics, transport, utilities and countless others – while these predictions may hold true, they certainly cannot be realized without the interoperability enabled by global ICT standards. A common M2M service layer, agreed to at the international level by stakeholders in the M2M and relevant vertical markets, will provide a cost-efficient platform that could easily be deployed across hardware and software platforms, in a multi-vendor environment, and across industry sectors.

The FG M2M has been identifying a minimum set of requirements common to vertical markets, and thereby creating the knowledge base needed to begin the development of open, international ITU standards. In analyzing the requirements of vertical markets, the group is initially focusing on the healthcare market by investigating APIs and protocols supporting e-health applications and services.

ITU-R

ITU-R's "Wide Area Sensor Networks" essentially deals with M2M communications. ITU-R Working Party 5A is focused on "Mobile wireless access systems providing telecommunications for a large number of ubiquitous sensors and/or actuators scattered over wide areas as well as machine communications in the land mobile service", under Study Group 5 Question ITU-R 250-1/5.

5.5   Open Mobile Alliance (OMA)

The scope of the OMA [38] is to develop mobile service enabler specifications to support the creation of interoperable end-to-end mobile services. Towards this direction, the OMA promotes service enabler architectures and open enabler interfaces that are independent of the underlying wireless networks and platforms. OMA's data service enablers are intended to work across multiple devices, service providers, operators, networks, and geographies.

As there are several OMA standards that map into the ETSI M2M framework, a link has been established between the two standardization bodies in order to provide associations between ETSI M2M Service Capabilities and OMA Supporting Enablers [39]. Specifically, the expertise of OMA in abstract, protocol-independent API creation, as well as the creation of API protocol bindings (i.e., REST, SOAP) and especially the expertise of OMA in RESTful APIs is expected to complement the standardization activities of ETSI in the field of M2M communications. Additionally, OMA has identified areas where further standardization will enhance support for generic M2M implementations, i.e.:

- Device management;
- Network APIs addressing M2M service capabilities;
- Location services for mobile M2M applications; and
- The messaging of sleeping M2M devices.

The overall aim of the collaboration between ETSI and OMA is twofold. On the one hand, it must be ensured that the APIs defined by OMA to describe service capabilities map into the ETSI M2M framework. On the other hand, there must be a mapping of OMA service enablers to the ETSI M2M framework.

5.6   Internet Engineering Task Force (IETF)

IETF Working Groups (WGs) [40] are created to address specific problems or to produce one or more specific documents aimed at speeding up the standardization process. The duration of these groups depends solely on the achievement of their objectives, and they manage almost all of the work through mailing lists. Each WG has a charter, which specifies the scope of the work to be carried out and lists how the objectives will be achieved. Currently, there are three active working groups dealing with protocols for the IoT, covering routing, IP-based addressing and application domains:

- 6LowPAN(IPv6 over Low power WPAN): An international open standard for IP enablement of the smallest devices, such as sensors and controllers, by enabling IEEE 802.15.4 and IP together;
- ROLL(Routing Over Low power and Lossy networks): Routing over low power and lossy networks via ZigBee and Bluetooth; and
- CORE (Constrained RESTful Environments): A framework for resource-oriented applications designed to run on constrained IP networks.

In addition, a WG for implementation guidance in lightweight TCP/IP protocol suites for constrained devices has been set up:

- LWIG (Light-Weight Implementation Guidance): This WG focuses on helping the implementers of the smallest devices. The goal is to be able to build minimal yet interoperable IP-capable devices for the most constrained environments.

5.7   Open Geospatial Consortium (OGC)

OGC members work to specify interoperability interfaces and metadata encodings that enable real time integration of heterogeneous sensor Webs into the information infrastructure. Developers will use these specifications in creating applications, platforms, and products involving Web-connected devices such as flood gauges, air pollution monitors, stress gauges on bridges, mobile heart monitors, Webcams, and robots, as well as space and airborne earth-imaging devices. OGC members have developed and tested the following candidate specifications [41, 42]:

- Observations & Measurements (O&M): Standard models and XML schema for encoding observations and measurements from a sensor, both archived and in real time;
- Sensor Model Language (SensorML): Standard models and XML schema for describing sensor systems and processes associated with sensor observations in order to provide information required for the discovery of sensors, location of sensor observations, processing of low-level sensor observations, and listing of taskable properties, as well as supporting on-demand processing of sensor observations;
- Transducer Model Language (TransducerML or TML): A conceptual model and XML schema for describing transducers and supporting real-time streaming of data to and from sensor systems;
- Sensor Observations Service (SOS): A standard Web service interface for requesting, filtering, and retrieving observations and sensor system information as the intermediary between a client and an observation repository or a near real-time sensor channel;
- Sensor Planning Service (SPS): A standard Web service interface for requesting user-driven acquisitions and observations as the intermediary between a client and a sensor collection management environment;
- Sensor Alert Service (SAS): A standard Web service interface for publishing and subscribing to alerts from sensors; and
- Web Notification Services (WNS): A standard Web service interface for asynchronous delivery of messages or alerts from SAS and SPS Web services and other elements of service workflows.

As the OGC has identified the need for standardized interfaces for sensors in the WoT, the OGC has created a new Standards Working Group (SWG) on the sensor Web interface for the IoT. The sensor Web interface for the IoT SWG aims to develop such a standard based on existing WoT portals with consideration of the existing OGC Sensor Web Enablement (SWE) standards. This group will develop a candidate standard for access to sensor observations including location information well-suited to IoT and WoT deployment environments.

5.8   Other Activities

OneM2M

Considering the increasing momentum for a standard system-level M2M architecture, seven of the world's leading ICT SDOs (i.e., ARIB and TTC of Japan, ATIS and TIA of the USA, CCSA, ETSI, and TTA of Korea) have launched a new global organization, called OneM2M, to ensure the most efficient development of M2M communications systems [43]. The new organization will develop specifications to ensure the global functionality of M2M, allowing a range of industries to effectively take advantage of the benefits of this emerging technology.

This section has introduced related activities from SDOs on the IoT and M2M. For M2M, 3GPP/3GPP2 and ETSI have produced relevant standards and continued the work for considering many application areas. Dedicated groups on the IoT have also been established to enhance capabilities in a wide range of scope from the M2M concept. Standardization activities in specific areas are aligning in the umbrella of the IoT for a more synergic approach. A new approach for a global standard among SDOs is emerging and will become more and more important in terms of interoperability.

6   Conclusion

This chapter has introduced the concept and fundamental characteristics of the IoT and investigated the key technologies and requirements for the evolution from M2M to an IoT/WoT, considering the vision and technology trends. Major application fields of the IoT have also served to reveal the significant potential impact to other industries using ICT. Based on relevant activities to develop architectures from the ITU-T and related research projects, this chapter has shown some of the architectural models to identify related functionalities. Many standards on the IoT are developing concurrently in related SDOs, and these standardization efforts are becoming increasingly important due to the necessity of global standards for interoperability among various solutions. To realize the IoT, leading technologies are expected to become highly integrated, such as autonomic networking, data mining and decision-making, security and privacy protection, as well as cloud computing, with technologies for advanced sensing and actuation varying according to specific use cases.

7   Acronyms

3GPP	3rd Generation Partnership Project
6LoWPAN	IPv6 over Low power Wireless Personal Area Network
API	Application Program Interface
ARIB	Association of Radio Industries and Businesses
ATIS	Alliance for Telecommunication Industry Solutions
BT	Bio Technology
CCSA	China Communications Standards Association
CDMA	Code Division Multiple Access
CORE	Constrained RESTful Environment
CT	Content Technology
DSL	Digital Subscriber Line
ETSI	European Telecommunications Standards Institute
FG M2M	Focus Group on Machine-to-Machine service layer
GE	Generic Enabler
HTTP	Hypertext Transfer Protocol
ICT	Information and Communication Technology
IETF	Internet Engineering Task Force
IMS	IP Multimedia Subsystem
IoT-A	Internet of Things – Architecture
IoT-GSI	Internet of Things Global Standards Initiative
IoT	Internet of Things
IT	Information Technology
ITU	International Telecommunication Union
ITU-R	International Telecommunication Union- Radiocommunication Sector

ITU-T	International Telecommunication Union- Telecommunication Standardization Sector
LTE	Long Term Evolution
LWIP	Lightweight IP Protocol Stacks for the Internet of Things
M2M	Machine-to-Machine
MTC	Machine Type Communication
NFC	Near Field Communication
NT	Nano Technology
O&M	Observations & Measurements
OGC	Open Geospatial Consortium
OMA	Open Mobile Alliance
PSTN	Public Switched Telephone Network
QoE	Quality of Experience
QoS	Quality of Service
RFID	Radio Frequency Identification
ROLL	Routing Over Low power and Lossy networks
SAS	Sensor Alert Service
SC	Steering Committee
SDO	Standards Developing Organizations
SensorML	Sensor Model Language
SOA	Service-Oriented Architecture
SOS	Sensor Observations Service
SPS	Sensor Planning Service
SWE	Sensor Web Enablement
SWG	Standards Working Group
TC	Technical Committee
TIA	Telecommunications Industry Association
TML	Transducer Model Language
TTA	Telecommunications Technology Association
TTC	Telecommunication Technology Committee
WG	Working Group
WNS	Web Notification Services
WoT	Web of Things
WWW	World Wide Web

References

1. Atzori, L., Iera, A., Morabito, G.: The Internet of Things: A survey. Computer Networks 54(15), 2787–2805 (2010)
2. Overview of Internet of Things, ITU-T Y.2060 (June 2012)
3. Framework of object-to-object communication for ubiquitous networking in Next Generation Network. ITU-T Y.2062 (March 2012)
4. Disruptive Technologies Global Trends 2025. Appendix F: The Internet of Things (Background), SRI Consulting Business Intelligence (2010)
5. Overview of ubiquitous networking and of its support in NGN, ITU-T Y.2002 (October 2009)
6. Lee, G.M., Crespi, N.: Shaping Future Service Environments with the Cloud and Internet of Things: Networking Challenges and Service Evolution. In: Margaria, T., Steffen, B. (eds.) ISoLA 2010, Part I. LNCS, vol. 6415, pp. 399–410. Springer, Heidelberg (2010)

7. Boussard, M., Christophe, B., Le Berre, O., Toubiana, V.: Providing user support in Web-of-Things enabled smart spaces. In: Proceedings of the 2nd International Workshop on Web of Things, vol. (11) (June 2011)
8. Guillemin, P., Friess, P., et al.: Internet of Things - Strategic Research Roadmap. The Cluster of European Research Projects on the Internet of Things (CERP-IoT) Strategic Research Agenda (SRA) (September 2009)
9. Evans, D.: The Internet of Things – How the Next Evolution of the Internet is Changing Everything. White Paper, Cisco (April 2011)
10. More than 50 billion connected devices. Ericsson White Paper (February 2011)
11. Brown, A., Moroney, J.: A Brave New World in Mobile Machine-to-Machine (M2M) Communications. Strategy Analytics. Forecast and Outlook Snapshot (July 2008)
12. What is M2M communications, http://www.m2mcomm.com/about/what-is-m2m/index.html (viewed October 1, 2012)
13. M2M vs. Internet of Things (August 2010), http://weblog.cenriqueortiz.com/internetofthings/2010/08/02/m2m-vs-internet-of-things/ (viewed October 1, 2012)
14. Accenture, Sensor telemetry (2005), http://www.accenture.com/SiteCollectionDocuments/PDF/sensortelemetry.pdf (viewed October 1, 2012)
15. Guinard, D., Trifa, V., Mattern, F., Wilde, E.: From the Internet of Things to the Web of Things: resource oriented architecture and best practices. In: Architecting the Internet of Things, pp. 97–129. Springer (2011)
16. Framework of Web of Things. Work in Progress. ITU-T Y.2063 (July 2012)
17. Pfisterer, D., Romer, K., Bimschas, D., Kleine, O., Mietz, R., Truong, C., Hasemann, H., Kroller, A., Pagel, M., Hauswirth, M., Karnstedt, M., Leggieri, M., Passant, A., Richardson, R.: SPITFIRE: Toward a semantic Web of Things. IEEE Communications Magazine 49(11), 40–48 (2011)
18. Tridium Web of Things. White paper (September 2009)
19. Shelby, Z.: Embedded Web services. IEEE Wireless Communications 17(6), 52–57 (2010)
20. The social Web of Things – a social network for your devices (February 2011), http://www.ericsson.com/thinkingahead/idea/110217_social_network_for_you_1968920151_c (viewed October 1, 2012)
21. Pintus, A., Carboni, D., Piras, A.: Paraimpu: a Platform for a Social Web of Things. In: The International World Wide Web (WWW) Conference, Demos Track, pp.401-404 (April 2012)
22. Les Instituts Carnot, Smart Networked Objects and Internet of Things, which takes an ever broader view of the practice and potential of IoT. White paper, v1.1 (January 2011)
23. INFSO D.4 Networked Enterprise & RFID INFSO G.2 Micro & Nanosystems, in co-operation with the Working Group RFID of the ETP EPOSS, Internet of Things in 2020, Roadmap for the Future, Version 1.1 (May 27, 2008)
24. Uckelmann, D., Harrison, M., Michahelles, F.: An architectural approach towards the future Internet of things. In: Architecting the Internet of Things, pp. 1–24. Springer (2011)
25. InterDigital, Standardized M2M Software Development Platform. White Paper (2011)
26. Fundacion de la Innovacion Bankinter, The Internet of Things – in a connected world of smart objects (2011), http://www.fundacionbankinter.org/system/documents/8189/original/XV_FTF_Interneto_of_things.pdf (viewed October 1, 2012)

27. Zorzi, M., Gluhak, A., Lange, S., Bassi, A.: From today's Intranet of Things to a future Internet of Things: A wireless-and mobility-related view. IEEE Wireless Communications 17(6), 44–51 (2010)
28. Internet of Things. Pan European Research and Innovation Vision, European Research Cluster on the Internet of Things (October 2011), http://www.internet-of-things-research.eu/pdf/IERC_IoT-Pan%20European%20Research%20and%20Innovation%20Vision_2011_web.pdf (viewed October 1, 2012)
29. Gubbi, J., Buyya, R., Marusic, S., Palaniswami, M.: Internet of Things (IoT): A vision, architectural elements, and future directions. The Computing Research Repository, CoRR (July 2012)
30. Internet of Things – Architecture (IoT-A), Project Deliverable D1.2 – Initial Architectural Reference Model for IoT, http://www.iot-a.eu/public/public-documents (viewed October 1, 2012)
31. FI-WARE, Internet of Things (IoT) Services Enablement, http://forge.fiware.eu/plugins/mediawiki/wiki/fiware/index.php/Internet_of_Things_%28IoT%29_Services_Enablement (viewed October 1, 2012)
32. Yang, D.-L., Liu, F., Liang, Y.-D.: A survey of the Internet of Things, pp. 358–366. Atlantis Press (2010)
33. Krishnan, V., Sanyal, B.: M2M technology: challenges and opportunities. White paper, Tech Mahindra (2010)
34. Chang, K., Soong, A., Tseng, M., Xiang, Z.: Global wireless machine-to-machine standardization. IEEE Internet Computing 15(2), 64–69 (2011)
35. ETSI website, http://www.etsi.org/WebSite/homepage.aspx
36. ITU-T IoT-GSI website, http://www.itu.int/en/ITU-T/gsi/iot/Pages/default.aspx
37. ITU-T FG-M2M website, http://www.itu.int/en/ITU-T/focusgroups/m2m/Pages/default.aspx
38. OMA website, http://www.openmobilealliance.org/
39. Internet-of-Things Architecture (IoT-A), Project Deliverable D3.1 - Initial M2M API Analysis, http://www.iot-a.eu/public/public-documents (viewed October 1, 2012)
40. IETF WGs website, http://datatracker.ietf.org/wg/
41. Fairgrieve, S.: Sensor Web standards and the Internet of Things. In: Proceedings of the 2nd International Conference on Computing for Geospatial Research & Applications, vol. (73) (May 2011)
42. OGC, Sensor Web Enablement DWG, http://www.opengeospatial.org/projects/groups/sensorwebdwg
43. OneM2M website, http://www.onem2m.org

Internet of Services

Javier Soriano[1], Christoph Heitz[2,3], Hans-Peter Hutter[2,3], Rafael Fernández[1],
Juan J. Hierro[4], Juergen Vogel[5], Andy Edmonds[2], and Thomas Michael Bohnert[2]

[1] School of Computer Science, Universidad Politécnica de Madrid, Madrid, Spain
{jsoriano,rfernandez}@fi.upm.es
[2] Zurich University of Applied Sciences, Winterthur, Switzerland
{heit,hans-peter.hutter,edmo,thomas.bohnert}@zhaw.ch
[3] Swiss Institute of Service Science, Switzerland
www.service-science.ch
[4] Telefónica I+D, Madrid, Spain
jhierro@tid.es
[5] Bern University of Applied Sciences, Falkenplatz 24, Bern, Switzerland
juergen.vogel@bfh.ch

Abstract. As the relentless march towards an Internet of Services (IoS)
continues, it is of utmost importance for the telecoms industry to understand
what the IoS is and upon what foundations and methodologies the IoS is based
and built on. Further, how the telecom industry can leverage IoS research and
push IoS capabilities on and beyond through innovation and how those services
within the IoS should be designed and implemented need to be understood. Not
only are these questions answered but also so as not to remain stationary in the
world of IoS, the telecoms industry must comprehend the upcoming challenges
and opportunities that the IoS will present. Within this chapter there are two
perspectives taken on the more specific aspects of engineering services for the
IoS. The first takes a first principles approach whereas the second takes one
from the basis of an innovative methodology. This chapter will provide
information and insights that seek to answer the former questions, starting with
a discussion on what exactly a service is, moving through the innovation,
design and implementation of IoS and its services, and finally arriving at a
demonstrator of IoS that points towards its own future.

Keywords: Internet of Services, Service Science, Service Engineering,
Web-based Service Industries, Global Service Delivery Framework, Service
Mash-up, Service Composition, Service Orchestration, Service Pricing, FI-
WARE.

1 Introduction

Services are omnipresent; in the Telco, IT, and software industry and much beyond.
In fact, in particular applying to the western hemisphere, modern economies have
long embarked, not necessarily explicitly and willful, on a service strategy that drives
transforms inherent structures away from classic product-orientation towards service-
orientation. In other words they morph into so-called service-economies.

E. Bertin et al. (Eds.): Telecommunication Services Evolution, LNCS 7768, pp. 283–325, 2013.

This transformation is meanwhile well known and considered vital for the survival of economies in high-income societies, like Switzerland, Germany, or the USA. Prime and fundamental causes are a.) products easily turn into commodities with very low profit margins, b.) high labor and thus production costs, c.) fierce competition from emerging powerhouses in Asia but also South America for instance, d.) and eventually societal and economic changes that force people and enterprises to focus on core expertise and needs which requires to consume complementary expertise , knowledge, workforce, etc. as services provided service providers of all sorts.

This transformation is ongoing, unstoppable, and present in all our daily lives since years. But most notably, all this became immensely amplified with the advent of the Internet, which facilitates offering and consumption of services of all sorts. To order books over the Web, manage personal or corporate financials, keeping in touch with friends and family, even personal partnering facilitated by partner brokers meanwhile became absolutely natural, just like going in the grocery store next corner.

All this renders on matter fact particularly stunning, namely that the discipline of "Service Engineering" is still little understood at best. While the production of goods is backed up by a massive body of knowledge, just think of the production efficiency, effectiveness, and ultimately quality of car production, there very few if at all commonly agreed upon and implemented engineering principles for the design, implementation, and provisioning of services.

One fundamental problem that contributes to this artifact, artifact since we believe that this state is ultimately ephemeral, is the inherent intangible nature of services. While goods provide solid intuition by means of physical existence and structure, services are virtual and relate to experience confined to the very moment of consumption. These features make the establishment of a commonly agreed definition difficult. Something utmost visible in the Internet, where classic Telco incumbents face new, Web-based market entrance that challenge the old Telco-world-order.

This chapter is aimed to complement this book with a different perspective on services, namely the so-called Internet of Services. This concept emerged in the European cooperative research framework (FP7) and provides a theoretical and practical framework for the delivery of services by means of Internet infrastructure, platforms, applications and services. It intentionally complements the other chapters of this book, which tend to represent the classic Telco perspective on services and business. It also represents business and strategy of powerful yet very recent Internet phenomena, which is companies like Google, Amazon, Facebook, Tencent, and the likes. All these together present themselves as fierce and successful challengers of the previous Telco-oriented world order.

2   Services: A Conceptual Consideration

2.1   What Are Services?

The concept of the Internet of Services refers explicitly to the term "services" which is a somewhat ambiguous notion. Depending on the context, service may have very different meanings. On a technical level, a service may just be a functional piece of software available over Internet with a defined interface. However, the real power that is unleashed in the emerging of the Internet of Services can be better understood if a broader concept of services is used.

Traditionally, service has been defined as something that creates "intangible products" and is characterized by a simultaneous consumption [1]. This is motivated by a traditional manufacturing view that tries to explain the difference between classical products (such as cars, for example) and services (such as a consulting service). In many contexts this distinction makes sense, but describing services as special products is not very suitable for describing the intrinsic nature of services. In the research literature of the last years, several new service definitions have been proposed. In our context, a simple but still very useful definition is the one of Vargo and Lusch: "Service is the application of competences for the benefit of another." [2].

This is clearly the case for a classical IT services where the "application of competences" corresponds to the execution of a functional software code that has been written and provided by another party than the one that is using it. However, the definition is much more comprehensive and encompasses many other forms of service delivery that might or might not have IT services as an intrinsic part.

2.2 The Nature of Services, Service Dominant Logic, and Service Science

Vargo and Lusch have derived a completely new business logic around their service concept which has become known as Service Dominant Logic (SDL) [3]. SDL is described by 10 foundational premises (FPs), which express a specific view on economic activities in general, interpreting every economy activity as a manifestation of a service. Service is considered the fundamental basis of exchange (FP1, [3]), and goods are viewed simply as distribution mechanism for service provision (FP3, [3]).

While it may be argued that it is not necessary to re-define economy for understanding services, Vargo and Lusch have developed a clear conceptual framework for services during their research. They start from the basic notion of value creation, and with the realization that the classical and widely used value-in-exchange concept is not suited for services. The value-in-exchange concept states that value is created by production of a good, and the value is identical to the price for which the product can be sold on the market. In contract to this value definition, Vargo and Lusch base their concept on the value-in-use concept, which is the second popular value concept that can be traced back to Aristotle. The value-in-use concept states that value is created during the usage of a product or a service, and that the user determines the quality and the quantity of the value. This concept is much more suited to understand value creation in services, but can be applied to classical manufacturing as well.

According to SDL, the process of value creation in services can be described by three steps. The first step is the value proposition of the provider: A provider suggests using its service. This is typically done by a functional promise (e.g. "You will be able to reach others with your mobile phone.") and a compensation scheme (e.g. "Monthly flat rate of $50"). The second step is the acceptance of this offer by the user, which may or may not include a formal contract or a payment. The third and final step is the actual use of the service – only then value for the user is created.

SDL seems to establish itself as the theoretical foundation of the emerging field of service science, a new scientific approach to understand service [5,6,7]. The basic object of research in service science is the so-called service system, which is defined as an arrangement of resources (including people, technology, information, etc.) connected to other systems by value propositions [5]. A service system's function is to make use of its own resources and the resources of others to improve its circumstance and that of others. Service systems can be individuals, groups, organizations, firms, and governments.

2.3   Implications for Telco Services

While it is beyond the scope of this contribution to discuss the concepts of SDL and service science in depth, we may derive some important implications of the service concepts that have been developed so far in these recent efforts to understand services.

A first insight is that the fundamental and constitutive property of a service is neither its technical implementation nor its functionality but rather its value proposition: What is the benefit the user is supposed to enjoy if he uses the service? Especially when coming from a technical background, one is tempted to describe a service by its implementation and the functional abilities of this given implementation. While this may be a technically consistent and even exhaustive description of a service, it misses the central point, which is the type and process of value creation by the user. Eventually, the success or failure of a service depends on how the users perceive their individual value creation – of course this depends on the technical functionality, but many other user-related factors play a relevant role. This explains why so many technically excellent solutions fail.

The second insight that might be derived from the recent service science research is that a service is a mutual and intrinsically relationship-based issue. A service happens in the relationship of a provider and a client (often mediated by technology). Usage of the service creates value for the client, but in order to be sustainable it must also create value for the provider. Typically, the value creation for the provider contains a financial element (payment for the service) but often there are additional non-financial value elements. As an example, a consulting firm does not only receive a financial benefit from performing a project with a client, but also develops its own competence by working with the client, gets a better market standing by an additional reference customer, and so on.

So, not only the value creation for the user of a service is a relevant issue, but also the value creation for the provider. A service can only be sustainably successful if it creates both value for the user (otherwise it will fail on the market) and value for the provider (otherwise there is no way of sustaining the service over a longer time period). When developing a new service, both dimensions have to be taken into account, and it is an important part of the design of a service to specify these value generation processes.

For a third insight, we might ask ourselves what the real drivers for the future development of the internet of services are, and which factors push the evolution. From a service science perspective, the fundamental and underlying basic driver is not the technology but rather the possibility of making new value propositions and creating new service systems that could not be realized up to now. Technology is key, though, because only the availability of new technology (in particular internet and mobile technology) makes the creation of these new services possible. However, the role of technology is the role of an enabler, not the role of a driver.

So, a successful development of a future internet of services will only partly depend on the technological solutions, but much more on innovation in the field of new value propositions by using these technological solutions. Successful innovation will have to put the value proposition and value creation process into the center, and carefully design these value-related aspects, and then build the appropriate technological solutions for realizing the concept.

3   Service Innovation and Design

There are various definitions of the terms "Service Innovation" [1,8], "Service Design" [9], and "New Service Development" [1,10] with quite some overlap. We will adhere in the following discussion to the definitions found in [8]: *Service Innovation* is the process of devising a new or improved service concept that satisfies the customer's unmet needs. *Service design* refers to all activities involved in implementing this concept and bringing it to market. The *New Service Development* process comprises the whole process starting with Service Innovation to the final launch of the new service. Instead of providing an overview of the research literature about service innovation the following sections try to summarize the process needed for successful service innovation and design [8,11].

3.1   Service Innovation

The customer is the central part of every service since the value of a service, in contrast to the value of a product, is only created when it is *used* by the customer, and it is the customer who defines the value of a service for him and assesses the success of the service based on its outcomes. Therefore, successful service innovation comes from understanding, how the customers define value.

Service innovation must therefore be customer-centered from its very beginning, i.e. it must start with the jobs the customer has or wants to do, his goals, his tasks, and his needs. There are different categories of service innovation, that normally are distinguished [8,1]:

- New Service Innovation
  refers to a major innovation where a new service addresses new customer jobs in a new or existing market. These new jobs the customer wants to do nowadays often result from innovations in ICT. Facebook, e.g., is a new service innovation for people to socially interact with each other in a virtual place.
- Core Service Innovation
  is a new or fundamentally improved service for a core job (major goal or task) an existing customer wants to do, e.g. an app store is a core service innovation to purchase and install new applications on a mobile device.
- Service Delivery Innovation
  is an innovation how the customer can consume the value/benefit of a service. Examples of such innovations are 24/7-, drive-in, mobile or one-click access to existing services.

- Supplementary Service Innovation

  means innovations in services accompanying a product to help get the most value out of it. These services may help the customer to select, compare, purchase, install, learn, move, store, maintain, upgrade, or dispose a product. These services often contain important value propositions from the customers' viewpoint.
- Service Improvements

  are rather augmentations, changes in features or styles of existing services that a company currently offers. Service improvements help service providers to distinguish their services from similar propositions of its competitors or to react to changes in the needs of the current customers of the service.

The first step in any service innovation is to define the customer group(s) to target and the innovation focus, i.e. which of the above innovation categories to address. Then the scope of the investigation has to be defined, i.e., which core job(s) and goals of the target customers should be taken into consideration.

3.2 Uncover Customer Needs

The 2nd and very important step in service innovation is to uncover the needs of the target customers in trying to get the selected job(s) done [8]. It is important to note here that it is not the idea to bluntly ask customers what they want or which features or ideas of an existing or intended service they like. The task is to find out what the customer actually wants to achieve by using a specific service and also why he wants to achieve that goal.

There are several techniques known from the User-Centered Design discipline to uncover these user needs that are also applicable to services [9], e.g. interviews (contextual, field), focus groups, direct observation, shadowing, diaries, task analysis, surveys. Some additional techniques specific for services are found in [11], e.g., service safaris, customer journey maps, customer journey canvas and expectation maps.

The result of all these activities should be a list of job statements, i.e. a goal to be accomplished or a problem to be solved or avoided. To be useful a job statement should reflect the goal a customer is trying to accomplish not just the task to be performed to reach that goal. This kind of job statements are an efficient mean of analyzing the customers problem to be solved and play a similar role that user stories play in agile software development. A job description should be relevant for the whole customer group not only one individual. It should be stable over time, specific and precise enough so that it triggers an unambiguous course of actions. E.g. from the mobile area could be: "Communicate with a remote person when on the move", "Find all persons I know within an area of 1km".

Once the job statements are identified, the outcomes, i.e. the functional goals, the customer desires for a successful execution of the job have to be specified. This is very important for two reasons. Firstly, the outcomes are the metrics the customer will use to define the success of a service hired for that job. Secondly, the outcomes are valuable sources for improvements of a service. A job outcome must be specific in what the customer actually wants to control, it should be unambiguous and it should be truly a measure. A job outcome normally starts with a verb, often minimize, maximize or increase/decrease, followed by a unit of measure, e.g. time, likelihood, number, amount, frequency. An example outcome statement could be "Minimize the time it takes to find an empty parking lot in a car parking". Some jobs may have only five outcomes to consider but others may have up to 100 outcomes. The uncovered and carefully worded job statements and outcomes should be discussed with the customer in order to make sure that they really reflect what the customer is trying to do and what the desired outcomes are.

3.3   Prioritize Customer Needs

In the next step of service innovation the needs, i.e. the job and outcome statements, have to be prioritized since the best opportunities for a new service or a service improvement are the most important needs that are not well satisfied by today's services [8]. To that end, a representative sample of the targeted customers are asked to rate the uncovered needs according to the two criteria importance and satisfaction, e.g., on a 5-point Likert-scale. Ulwick [12] proposes a simple opportunity algorithm to be used

$$Opportunity = impor\tan ce + max(impor\tan ce - satisfaction, 0)$$

The *importance* and *satisfaction* are calculated from the percentage of customers that rate the importance/satisfaction in the top two options, i.e. important/satisfied or very important/very satisfied. These percentage figures are then divided by 10 for convenience. E.g. if an outcome of a job was rated important or very important by 80% of the customers, and only 30% of them rated the current outcomes at least as satisfactory, then the opportunity figure would give 8.0 + max(8.0-5.0,0) = 13.0 which is a great opportunity for a new service, as any value > 10 is considered as a promising opportunity. This opportunity figure may be calculated for different subgroups of customers or even for different contexts in which a customer's job is to be done, e.g. answering an e-mail while in the office, at home, or while commuting.

All jobs and outcomes that have been uncovered and prioritized, e.g. according to the above opportunity measure, form the basement for the development of a service strategy, discussed in Section 3.5.

3.4   Discovering Innovation Opportunities

This section elaborates on the ways how service innovation opportunities can be discovered for the different innovation categories by systematically identifying customer jobs and outcomes [8].

For a New Service Innovation a good starting point to find opportunities are the jobs for which the existing services of a company are already hired. The aim of customer interviews is then to find out what customers are trying to accomplish when using this service, what are their goals or objectives, what problems does this service help them to prevent or resolve, and in what context (where, when, with whom). Another important question that should be asked to customers in an interview is what an ideal service would help them to accomplish. Other questions should focus on the jobs a customer is trying or would like to get done before, after and during the company's current service. E.g. ([8], p. 31), a mobile service provider might ask his customers what other tasks they are trying to do related to the call itself. The answers will probably be, among others, scribbling notes and checking their calendar, which themselves are solutions for a couple of jobs to get done. A follow-up question in this direction might reveal that the customers are taking notes during a call for capturing important points like name and callback number of a call, share key points of a call with others, make changes to their calendars, or create a to-do list based on the call. All these jobs could be the basis for new or improved services of the mobile service provider.

In order to uncover more jobs of a specific customer group is to try to abstract given jobs of the customers to more general types of jobs the customers want to do, e.g. the given job "Update customers with latest product news" may be generalized to "jobs related to maintain customer relationship" or even "jobs related to run a small business". The next step is to find out what are the customers trying to accomplish in this job area, what are their goals and objectives, i.e. what are they trying to do, to determine or decide, to prevent or resolve and so on. It is also a good idea to consider the *actions* relevant for that job type, i.e. to try to identify or even anticipate the verbs in the job statements for that specific job area. With these verbs questions for new jobs can easily be formulated, e.g. "What else are you doing to maintain the relationship with a customer?"

A special class of jobs, for which services might be hired, is experience jobs of customers. Customers may want to experience e.g. nature, entertainment, competition, physical or mental challenge, or a specific time period. They hire specific services that provide this experience, like theater, adventure, or nature trips and many more. Even if a customer job is mainly functional the customer may choose a service that also accomplishes his experience-oriented jobs. E.g., eating in a restaurant fulfills the functional job of getting a meal without having to cook, but customers may well choose a specific restaurant in order to also experience the atmosphere of a foreign culture. In order to uncover experience jobs the same kind of questions can be asked as for functional jobs with only the verbs being changed to experience related verbs e.g. experience, discover, appreciate, learn, inspire, escape, become, achieve, support, share, remember, or forget. It may also be useful to identify categories of possible experiences for the target customer group, e.g. "discovering who you are", "growing as a person", "understand the world" and "build relationships".

The 3rd kind of jobs to be discovered are emotional jobs which can be further separated into jobs dealing with what a person wants to feel or avoid feeling, and jobs dealing with how a person wants to be perceived or avoid being perceived, e.g. smart, good parent, or unprofessional, resp. Customers will define the value of these services by how well their emotional need is satisfied. Functional jobs may also have an emotional component like "overcoming depression" or "relieving stress", but here, the customer will still define the value of a service on how well the functional goal is accomplished. Emotional jobs are easily identified by the verbs "feel", "avoid feeling", "be perceived as", or "avoid being perceived as" in the job statement. Questions for revealing emotional jobs therefore also use these verbs, e.g. "How would the ideal service for this job make you feel, or how would you be perceived?"

Customer jobs normally remain quite stable over time. New customer jobs emerge mainly for three reasons: new technologies or solutions, advances in knowledge, changes in laws, policies, or regulations, and --- last but not least --- trends. It is therefore important for New Service Innovation to systematically track and analyze the technological developments but also the trends and policies relevant to the company in order to timely reveal emerging jobs and customer needs related to these developments.

Once all relevant jobs and outcomes for the targeted customer group have been identified and prioritized as described in the previous section, the job(s) with the highest opportunity ranking are selected to develop a new service concept.

For Core Service Innovations the starting point is an existing service and the question what core job is the customer trying to accomplish with it. Then, this core job is divided into steps the customer must take to successfully complete the job. A job step must be relevant to anyone doing the job and must specify what the customer is ultimately trying to accomplish (fundamental goals), not what he is doing in the current service. At each step the customer is looking for certain outcomes and will assess the service by these outcomes. Each of these steps may therefore be an opportunity for a Core Service Innovation. Bettencourt [8] proposes a universal job map comprising the following nine universal steps that are found in nearly any core job: Define (what the job requires), Locate (the inputs required), Prepare (job execution), Confirm (readiness or priorities), Execute, Monitor (results and environment), Resolve (problems), Modify, and Conclude.

Further insights in Core Service Innovation opportunities are derived by uncovering and prioritizing the outcomes of the different steps of the core job. Essentially three types of outcomes are considered by the customers for each step, i.e. outcomes related to input (e.g. speed, mental effort), output (e.g. problems, quality, bottlenecks), and the process (optimized results). To reveal these outcomes, customers should be asked the following three groups of questions for each step: 1. What makes (this step) time-consuming or slow? What makes it cumbersome or inconvenient? 2. What makes (this step) problematic or challenging? What causes it to be inconsistent or to go off track? 3. What makes (this step) ineffective or the output of poor quality? What would the ideal result look like?

Discovering opportunities for Supplementary Service Innovation are especially interesting for manufacturers. There are essentially four approaches for supplementary service opportunities: 1. Core job for which customers use the product(s) 2. Consumption chain jobs related to owning and using the product(s), i.e. what job must the customers get done to receive the value from a product? 3. Improve how technical support is delivered. 4. Help executors of related jobs get their jobs done. There are three types of related job executors: Adjacent job executor (e.g. a nurse assisting a surgeon using an operation tool), job observers (i.e. managers), and job beneficiaries (e.g. patient in a surgeon job using a tool).

When the target is service delivery innovation the consumption chain for obtaining a specific service must first be analyzed and defined independently of the form of service delivery. Job statements for obtaining a service often have verbs like obtain, get, take, receive, or have. Example for such job statements are: "Take a class", "Receive Internet access", but also "Rent a car". Once the job of obtaining a service is defined, innovation opportunities can be identified in a similar way as with Core Job Innovation, i.e. the delivery job is divided into different steps and for each step the outcomes that customers use to judge success are collected. A universal job map for this kind of jobs and sample outcomes can be found in [8], p. 80ff.

There are also abundant opportunities for service delivery innovation from the provider perspective, i.e. innovations on how to deliver a consistent service with the desired quality in a profitable manner. The job of the employees, which are the internal customers, is "to provide a service to customers" and they hire internal systems, technology, and processes to do that job. Exceptional value can be created by systematically discovering and exploiting any opportunity to address struggles and inefficiencies for these internal customers. The first step to that end is again to define the job an employee is trying to get done, e.g. "resolve a claim", "teach a class", or "open an account". Then the steps involved in doing that job are defined, e.g. "define or assess customer needs", "prepare customers for their role", or "deliver service". Several of these job steps parallel or support the steps of the customer in obtaining the service, other steps normally occur behind the scene, e.g. "determine resource needs" or "coordinate with service partners". Combining the job map for obtaining service with the one for providing the service gives a complete view of what must happen for a successful service delivery. Although this looks like a service blueprint the important difference is that the combined job map shows what has to be done for a successful service delivery (requirement) whereas a service blueprint shows how a specific service is provided (solution). The job map provides a framework for uncovering the outcomes the service provider uses to define success at every step.

Important questions at each step are: What are the high-opportunity outcomes related to efficiency, consistency, cost, and results? What would the ideal scenario look like from the company's perspective and the one of the employees? What problems could occur that detract from the service delivered to the customer and how can these problems be prevented? What must the employees do and what the customer? What system, equipment, material, information, process, and facility requirements must be met to deliver the service the customer needs?

The outcomes of each of these steps should be prioritized internally by the company since each step provides opportunities to improve service delivery from the provider's perspective. This internal perspective for providing a service can also guide the subsequent (re)design of a current or new service to satisfy the unmet needs of the customers.

3.5   Service Design

After customer needs have been uncovered and prioritized, a service strategy can be developed. This service strategy should be unique and deliver value to customers as well as the company. A critical part of the service strategy is the service concept. The service concept comprises two important aspects:

1.   What should the service provide to the customer to satisfy their needs and
2.   How the service is provided.

The first aspect of Service Design starts with the customers' job and outcome opportunities and their priorities. In order to describe these needs of the targeted customer group in a compact and engaging way, design teams often introduce so-called personas

[11]. A persona is a fictional person profile that represents the jobs, outcomes and needs of a whole customer group. If the service has to satisfy different groups of customers with different needs, a persona is introduced for each group. The service concept should emphasize the differentiating features of the service and how the service does help customers accomplish the jobs they are trying to get done and how they achieve the desired outcomes. The second aspect of the service concept should describe the service delivery system and how it provides value to customers and the company.

The service design process normally starts with an idea generation phase where an interdisciplinary team of employees, managers, customers, IT specialists, other stakeholders and service designers try to co-create ideas for service innovations. There are various techniques for idea generation, see e.g. [9,11], like brainstorming, six thinking hats, or even open innovation. The idea generation process should be focused on the jobs and outcomes with the highest opportunities. For these the key problems should be identified to satisfy these jobs and outcomes. The key problem may be an objective problem, a problem of context or just one of customer perception. If the problem is not only a matter of perception a cause-and-effect diagram can help to classify potential reasons for poor satisfaction of the customer needs. In the idea generation session a diverse set of new service ideas to satisfy these opportunities should be taken into account. Helpful questions in this process are: How have those in other industries dealt with similar customer or service delivery struggles? What are some examples of solutions or workarounds that customers have created to satisfy the high-opportunity jobs or outcomes? What is a far-fetched idea for a perfect completion of the job or achievement of the outcomes?

The next step is to create a first high-level concept out of the most promising service innovation ideas keeping the following questions in mind: Does the service concept deliver meaningful value to the targeted customer segment(s)? Does the service concept make appropriate trade-offs between benefits and costs and considering the different stakeholders (customers, company, providers, partners, etc.). Are the concept features and design elements internally consistent and is there synergy among them? Can the company develop and deliver on the service concept as designed and what capabilities and resources will be required. Are the costs of developing the service justified by the created value?

After agreement about the high-level service concept among the stakeholders has been reached additional details to the concept are added, normally in iterative design cycles. The detailed concept should not only describe what it will take to deliver the new or improved service but also what must happen at each step to ensure success in getting the customers' job done. The details on how the new or improved service should be delivered are classically visualized with a service blueprint [13, 11]. A service blueprint visualizes a service by showing the different steps of service delivery, the points of customer contacts (touchpoints), the roles of customer and providers, and the visible elements of the service (tangibles). In addition the user experience of a given or intended service can be analyzed, shown or discussed with e.g. design scenarios or story boards [11]. In addition, customer journey maps [11] can be used to provide a high-level overview of the factors that influence the user experience with a service. The customer journey map not only shows the sequence of touchpoints of the service the customer goes through, but also the user experience at each touchpoint and the other influencing factors on the user experience that happen before, after, or in parallel to the service, e.g. social networks, friends or family, which normally are beyond a service provider's control. One goal of this is to identify weak touchpoints as opportunities for innovation, the other to provide a consistent user experience through all touchpoints.

The evaluation of different service design concepts can be done with a range of methods [9, 11], e.g. with evaluation workshop, participatory evaluation, desktop walkthrough, service prototypes, or even service staging, where scenarios or service prototypes are acted out.

The service design and evaluation activity are iterated several times until the stakeholders agree on all details of the service concept. In the subsequent development phase the service concept is implemented in full scale.

4   Implementation of the Internet of Services

It is well-known that the major revolution behind Web 2.0 is not on the use of particular technologies, but rather on realizing that, on the Web, value largely resides on the data about and the communication between people, and that this value is subject to the well-known *network effect* [16]. However, Web Services never reached on the Web the critical mass that would justify the additional efforts and investment. In reality, they have hardly been adopted beyond the boundaries of enterprises [15]. This has ended with, *paraphrasing* [17], *the fall of Web Services and the rise of Internet Services,* the latter being significantly different from the former at the technology level as well as from the perspective of the nature of the service provided which will have a clear business focus rather than a predominantly functional nature.

The building of the Future Internet of Services will largely be driven by a number of innovations that will undoubtedly face a number of research challenges, but will also be at the origin of many business opportunities. From the technological perspective, the development of Internet-scale infrastructures to support and deliver services in the new, so called, *service economy* raises a number of challenges. From a business perspective, it also obliges us to re-think how value is created through services. In the reminder of this chapter we first analyze the state of the art and current research trends on a number of areas that we believe will have a crucial impact on the development of the Future Internet of Services, from a technological and a business perspective. We then introduce one of the most promising efforts towards the realization of the Internet of Services vision: The Future Internet Core Platform (FI-WARE[1]) and, specifically, its proposal for an Internet-scale Applications and Services Ecosystem and Delivery Framework. Finally, we comment a number of research initiatives and programmes that will help to set the road map for realizing the Future Internet of Services.

4.1   Global (Internet-Scale) Service Delivery Platforms

Opening SOA technologies to the Internet has important implications from both engineering and technological perspectives. Typically, these implications have been overlooked and, as a consequence, SOA remains mostly an enterprise-specific

---

[1] http://www.fi-ware.eu/

solution. Its adoption for supporting the creation of distributed systems on the Internet has largely fallen behind initial expectations.

Some recent initiatives have started to work towards an architecture and language stack for a service delivery platform to foster the Internet-scale adoption of service technologies. All of them together represent a step forward towards the realization of the Internet of Services vision.

4.1.1 Towards a Conceptual Architecture for the Internet of Services

Paving the way towards the Future Internet will require the integration and federation of service-based systems from various domains. The Internet of Services coexists in the Future Internet with a number of different trends like software as a service (SaaS), cloud computing, Internet of Things, and web 2.0/3.0, each of them requiring a different type of supporting architecture. Therefore, the Future Internet needs to be architected in a way that fosters the integration and federation of these differentiated service-based systems.

The NEXOF-RA[2] project represents an early effort to define a reference architecture for service-based systems that, accompanied by a set of guidelines, could serve as a construction kit to derive specific architectures for a particular project context. The experience gained during the project, saw that it was not feasible to develop a one-sized-fits-all, integrated reference architecture. Instead, the project chose a pattern-based approach based on the principle of separation of concerns [19], that allowed the consideration of the different, even contradicting demands of the various types of service-based systems that were identified as relevant at that moment, and that could be extensible to include new future trends. The objective of The NEXOF (NESSI Open Framework) Reference Architecture is to address the problem of specifying service-based software system architectures by partitioning the overall solution into several pieces of the design solution: patterns.

The central part of the reference architecture depicts a system of patterns that allows the integration of different families of systems addressing different types of service-based systems, e.g. a family for Enterprise SOA, or the Internet of Services.

Top-level patterns describe the characteristics of service framework families, including the Enterprise SOA (ESOA) top-level pattern, the Internet of Services top-level pattern and the Cloud Computing top-level pattern. The top-level patterns are refined by abstract design patterns that refer to abstract components and patterns. They can be defined and refined on several levels of abstraction until at least one specific component becomes part of the solution.

Nevertheless, specifying solely a map of patterns is not sufficient for the creation of reusable reference architectures for service-based systems. It has to be accompanied with several other elements that foster the instantiation. To this end, NEXOF-RA is composed of three elements: architectural Guidelines and Principles, the Reference Model and Glossary, and the Reference Specifications. The latter in turn is composed of three elements: the Pattern Ensemble, the Standards Catalogue and the Components Catalogue. Fig. 1 depicts the structure of NEXOF-RA.

---

[2] http://www.nexof-ra.eu

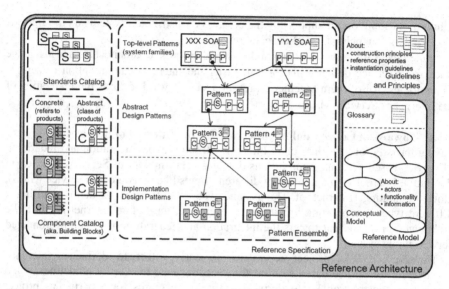

Fig. 1. Structure of NEXOF-RA Reference Architecture (taken from http://www.nexof-ra.eu)

The Internet of Services top-level pattern [20] provides an architectural design of a worldwide Internet-based platform to enable anyone to deliver, consume and *prosume*[3] services at global scale. It provides a very high level description of the overall functionality provided by such a global distributed platform, including SLA management, CR management, service management (service discovery, service delivery and consumption and UI management) and security management.

4.1.2 From Semantic Web Services to Linked Services

The SOA4All[4] approach to a Web-minded global service delivery platform proposes an architecture that extends SOA with essential principles upon which the Web builds: openness, decentralization, and communication driven by a 'persistent publish and read' paradigm rather than by messaging. Additionally, the project adopts semantic technologies as a means to lift services and their descriptions to a level of abstraction that deals with computer-understandable conceptualizations, so as to increase the level of automation that can be achieved while carrying out common tasks during the life cycles of services, such as their discovery, composition and invocation. Without automation it would not be feasible to scale service delivery platforms to the dimensions of the Internet. Automation is advocated by means of Semantic Web services. Services are annotated by means of Semantic Web languages, and the platform services operate on the semantic descriptions of services and processes, rather than the actual software implementation of the physical endpoints.

---

[3] *Prosumer* is a portmanteau formed by contracting either the word producer with the word consumer. The term *prosumer* is used in the context of the Web 2.0 to differentiate the traditional passive consumer with an active consumer role more involved in the process of creating value (i.e. the consumer becomes a producer).

[4] http://www.soa4all.eu/

One clear limitation to the proliferation of Web services on a web scale has been the limited expressivity and level of automation that can be achieved despite the considerable complexity of the technology stack. Semantic Web services have brought solutions able to reach a higher-level of automation throughout the life cycle of Web service-based applications by frameworks such as OWL-S[5], WSMO[6] and SAWSDL[7], but they have additionally increased the level of complexity both for humans and for automated processing.

Building on the success of the Linked Open Data Initiative, the SOA4All project has re-conceptualized Semantic Web services by developing an approach termed *Linked Services* [17]. Linked Services are services described and exposed as Linked Data, i.e. their inputs and outputs, their functionality, and their non-functional properties are described in terms of lightweight RDF-S vocabularies and exposed following Linked Data principles[8]. By virtue of these descriptions, and with appropriate infrastructure support, Linked Services can consume RDF from the Web of Data and thus represent a processing layer on top of the wealth of information currently available in the Web of Data, which remains unexploited. Moreover, Service descriptions, as produced by SOA4All tools, are transformed into Web resources and published as Linked Data. Therefore, they become addressable resources on which one can apply social networking solutions and technologies, which allows for further exploiting the relationship between users and services.

Nevertheless, SOA4All conceptual architecture does not respond to related issues such as service management or non-Web-based services such as mobile services or sensor networks that need to be integrated in order to fully enable the 'Everything as a Service' paradigm behind the Internet of Services.

4.1.3 Cloud-Based Services Architectures and Infrastructures

Traditionally, services are meant to provide access to application logic that may be distributed over an Intranet and/or the Internet, and typically the service provider also used to be responsible for hosting the service on one or more of his own machines. Cloud computing takes the service idea one step further by compartmentalizing the general computing resources of an application into services as well, i.e., by providing "everything" as a service (XaaS). Typically, cloud computing distinguishes among three different types of services [42]:

- Infrastructure as a Service (IaaS) denotes providing basic computing resources such as data storage, communication networks, and processing capabilities. IaaS providers such as Amazon AWS[9] usually run large data centers.
- Platform as a Service (PaaS) can be seen as an additional layer on top of IaaS that provides a preconfigured, virtualized runtime environment for (off-the-shelf or custom-made) applications, e.g., providing a web application server for web applications. Typically, PaaS providers such as Google with the App Engine[10] offer

---

[5] http://www.w3.org/Submission/OWL-S/
[6] http://www.w3.org/Submission/WSMO/
[7] http://www.w3.org/2002/ws/sawsdl/
[8] Tim Berners-Lee (2007) http://www.w3.org/DesignIssues/LinkedData.html
[9] http://aws.amazon.com/
[10] http://www.google.com/enterprise/cloud/appengine/

an entire ecosystem complete with libraries, development tools, and online communities to attract and support their customers.

- Software as a Service (SaaS) refers to an application that is executed within a cloud computing infrastructure. A SaaS offering can be accessed by its users, e.g., via a web client or a dedicated (thin) client (e.g., a mobile app) and requires usually very little IT infrastructure and setup from the SaaS consumer's perspective. For instance, SAP ByDesign[11] provides a fully-fledged on demand business application suite for enterprises serving up to several thousand users.

In service-based cloud computing, a SaaS application for an end consumer may therefore be a complex service network incorporating offerings from many different IaaS, PaaS, and SaaS providers who in many cases will not even be visible for the end consumer.

An important concept in cloud computing are *resource pooling* and *virtualization*, meaning that resources are shared flexibly and transparently among services so that the service provider can assign the same physical resource to several consumers at the same time in order to achieve maximum utilization of resources and flexibly migrate services between the available resources, on the one hand. On the other hand, virtualization means that the presence of a cloud environment is not perceived by the consumer other than that the consumed services scale up and down dynamically to meet changing resource demands. While virtualization usually refers to transparent resource sharing at the IaaS layer, *multi-tenancy* denotes the capability to transparently serve multiple independent consumers in parallel at the PaaS or SaaS layer by sharing (at least some) resources of a service, thus realizing efficiency gains. For instance, the same Java virtual machine at the PaaS layer may execute applications from different SaaS providers by shielding their address spaces from each other but sharing basic functionality like IO-management or garbage collection at the same time.

Many experts see the PaaS component as the key to a wide success of service-based cloud computing as its functionality may significantly lower the technical entrance barrier for the application providers. As with other technologies (e.g., mobile apps), the success of cloud computing eventually depends on the availability of (a high number of) attractive applications, and providing rich tools and reusable basic services to SaaS providers helps to create these applications because SaaS providers can then focus on their core competencies. However, commercial PaaS offerings currently available tend to be based on proprietary technologies so that switching providers becomes difficult for the consumer, leading to a so-called *vendor lock-in* [43]. This is a major obstacle for potential SaaS providers and consumers considering the relatively immature market at this stage.

To summarize, current technological and economic challenges in cloud computing include

- technologies to improve the resource efficiency of cloud components such as virtualization and multi-tenancy;
- achieving a high *elasticity* in cloud components via vertical and/or horizontal scaling in order to adapt to increased or lowered resource demands;

---

[11] http://www.sap.com/solutions/sme/businessbydesign/

- guaranteeing *security* of sensitive data and application logic that is hosted by third party providers;
- *economic* and *operational management* of XaaS offerings, including negotiations of business/SLA terms between service provider and consumer as well as handling contracts, payments, and revenue shares within established service networks;
- *interoperability* among XaaS offerings of different providers in order to allow seamless migration and prevent vendor lock-in.

In the EU FP7 project 4CaaSt[12], these challenges are being addressed (with the exception of security) [40]. The 4CaaSt platform is based on abstract service descriptions, so-called blueprints [44]. The blueprint of a service basically describes a service's requirements with respect to the cloud computing resources (i.e., consumed XaaS) it depends on, including runtime requirements (e.g., average and high-peak CPU consumption) and deployment recipes. For instance, a business application may require a web application server, which in turn relies on a Java virtual machine, which is connected to a database etc. Similar to the core principle of service-based computing that distinguishes between a service's interface and its implementation, this blueprint concept enables a high flexibility for the creation, deployment, and management of applications and services in the cloud. Blueprints enable any service at any layer to be combined or exchanged with other services as long as the requirements are fulfilled. Thus, the blueprint concept helps to prevent the vendor lock-in problem described above. Blueprints can also be translated automatically into a deployment plan for initializing and configuring all XaaS resources a particular service depends on. This minimizes the deployment and management effort for the service from both the consumer and provider perspective and therefore enables a greater flexibility and new business models in service value networks.

Once a SaaS application has been deployed on the PaaS, 4CaaSt automatically manages the dynamic scaling of these components. The elasticity mechanism is provided by two means:

1. The customer is able to define a set of elasticity rules that define how the application scales vertically and/or horizontally based on their preferences.
2. Furthermore, the platform may take automatic control of a multi-tier SaaS application by analyzing monitoring data and deciding which part of the application should be scaled and how.

From a business perspective, 4CaaSt provides a marketplace for trading of all types of XaaS in a unified way. Service providers may contract resources, platforms and even software (or deploy their own software) and sell services by themselves or through the 4CaaSt marketplace, while the customers may contract access to running services. Software developers may enable applications to be contracted and deployed on demand. Finally, service customers may contract a private instance of an application that has to be deployed. Service offerings are traded trades products based blueprints and associated prices (e.g., following licensing or pay per use models, see Section 2.2.2). 4CaaSt manages all the phases of a typical marketplace:

---

[12] http://4caast.morfeo-project.org/

- information on services, stakeholders, and service usage;
- negotiation and customization of service offerings;
- contracting and deployment of services;
- charging for actual service usage.

For this, the marketplace is tightly integrated with the PaaS layer so that information sources such as monitoring data from the service execution can be leveraged by the marketplace.

4.2   Business Frameworks for Global Service Ecosystems

With the rise of commoditized, on-demand services, the stage is set for the acceleration of and access to services on Internet scale that will have a profound effect on business and society. Internet is now conceived as a medium for offering and selling services. Service marketplaces, where service consumers and providers (and even *prosumers*) are brought together to trade services and so engage in business interaction, along with their associated business frameworks represent an enabling technology that need to be investigated so as to foster access, repurposing and trading of services in such large settings.

Specifically, innovative Internet-scale comprehensive approaches to service description and discovery, service pricing, revenue settlement and sharing, and SLA management are required to make them comparable and tradable in the global service ecosystem envisioned for the Future Internet. The next subsections tackle each of these areas that, together, define the required business framework for the Future Internet of Services, where Web-based IT-supported service ecosystems will form the base of service business value networks.

4.2.1   Leveraging Services on the Internet through Advanced Service
Description and Discovery

There exists a plethora of service description efforts [22], each having its own motivation and representation needs for capturing service information:

- Service-oriented Architectures (SOA) efforts aims at thinking about IT assets as service components and considers amongst its key components a service registry. The OASIS standards body introduced the concept of a platform-independent registry through its Universal Description, Discovery and Integration (UDDI[13]) specification. UDDI services shall be discovered from information such as address, contact, known identifiers, or industrial categorizations based on standard taxonomies. However, UDDI does hardly prescribe any schema for such information. From the perspective of service engineering, several standards bodies such as OMG, OASIS or The Open Group propose alternative modeling languages (OMG SoaML[14]) and reference models (OASIS SOA-RM[15], TOG SOA Ontology[16]) for Service-oriented architectures.

---

[13] http://uddi.org/pubs/uddi_v3.htm

[14] http://www.omg.org/spec/SoaML/

[15] http://docs.oasis-open.org/soa-rm/v1.0/soa-rm.html

[16] http://www3.opengroup.org/standards?tab=9

– Semantic Web Services efforts aim at automating the discovery, composition, and invocation of services in a SOA by ontology reasoners and planning algorithms. Many efforts have surfaced in literature, the most prominent of which are OWL-S and WSMO. With the many approaches around came the need to specify a reference model for semantic SOAs and, consequently, the OASIS standards body developed a Reference Ontology (RO-SOA[17]). In lightweight approaches to semantics, service annotations tend to be based on WSMO-Lite[18], a minimal extension to SA-WSDL[19] that empowers the creation of lightweight semantic service descriptions in RDF-S. MicroWSMO[20] is used to annotate services that are not described using WSDL, such as RESTful services or Web APIs. MicroWSMO is a microformat-based language that uses similar constructs from WSMO-Lite, but adapted to support the annotation of HTML-based descriptions, as they are usually available for this type of software façades.

– Software-as-a-Service efforts are rooted in the rise of on-demand applications that led to the notion of SaaS. The emphasis of *service* here implies that the consumer gets the designated functionality she requested together with hosting through a pay-per-use model. This difference triggered the Software-as-a-Service Description Language (SaaS-DL), which builds on WS-* to capture SaaS specificities in order to support model-driven engineering [24]. The strand of SaaS also contains a standard, namely, the W3C Service Modelling Language recommendation (SML[21]). One anticipated use for SML is to define a consistent way to express how computer networks, applications, servers, and other IT resources are described or modelled so businesses can more easily manage the services that are built on these resources.

– There are overarching efforts that draws attention mainly on capturing the purely economic aspects of services regardless of their nature, i.e. with little or no focus on IT services and in which attributes (e.g. resources, location, etc.) and properties (availability, price, payment, discounts, obligations, rights, penalties, trust, quality, etc.) are commonly specified in a non-machine readable way. Amongst these efforts it is worth pointing out those focused on describing service networks, i.e., the ecosystem and value chain relationships between services of economic value (e.g. the Service Network Notation, SNN) [26].

– Finally, service system and service science efforts [27, 28] take into account socio-economic aspects and a reference ontology for ontological foundations of service science which is founded on the basic principles of ontological analysis. This reference ontology forms the core part of the TEXO Service Ontology [25], which extends it by ontology modules for pricing, legal, innovation, or rating information.

4.2.2 Towards a Unified Service Description Language (USDL)

The individual efforts for describing services in a repository can be attributed to the following criteria: (i) whether the scope of the effort lies in capturing IT or business

---

[17] http://docs.oasis-open.org/semantic-ex/ro-soa/v1.0/
see-rosoa-v1.0.html
[18] http://www.wsmo.org/ns/wsmo-lite/
[19] http://www.w3.org/2002/ws/sawsdl/
[20] http://www.wsmo.org/TR/d38/v0.1/
[21] http://www.w3.org/TR/sml/

aspects of services or the whole service system. (ii) the purpose of the corresponding effort, e.g., enabling of normative data exchange, facilitation of software engineering, or acting as reference model. (iii) whether the effort is able to capture business network relationships between services. (iv) whether the effort is standardized. The Unified Service Description Language (USDL) [23] is the only effort that covers IT (i.e. technical, operational) and business aspects, serves both a reference and exchange purpose, considers business network related information and is about to be standardized[22].

USDL represents an interdisciplinary approach to a platform-neutral language for comprehensively describing nearly all kinds of services to make them comparable and tradable. It is provided by major investments through public co-funded projects, under the Internet of Services theme, where services from various domains including cloud computing, service marketplaces and business networks, have been investigated for access, repurposing and trading in large settings (e.g., FAST[23], RESERVOIR[24], MASTER[25], ServFace[26], SHAPE[27], SLA@SOI[28], SOA4All, 4CaaSt, and the Australian Smart Services CRC[29])

USDL is modularized to describe various aspects of services including those regarding participants, function, interaction, and capability to technical mapping, pricing, service level and legal aspects. An additional service module describes the general information about the service type, nature, titles, taxonomy and descriptions, and a foundational Module provides a coon set of concepts and properties, such as time, location, organization, etc. that are transverse to the remainder of the modules. Fig. 2 depicts these modules and their interrelationships.

Recently, the FI-WARE consortium has adopted USDL as an enabler of its core platform for wide leverage of services on the Internet. The kinds of services targeted for coverage through USDL include: purely human/professional (e.g. project management and consultancy), transactional (e.g. purchase order requisition), informational (e.g. spatial and demography look-ups), software component (e.g. software widgets for download), digital media (e.g. video & audio clips), platform (e.g. middleware services such as message store-forward) and infrastructure (e.g. CPU and storage services).

In the context of FI-WARE, USDL extensions for artefacts from other FI-WARE chapters are to be considered: Internet of Things (IoT) service enablement, security, privacy and trust, cloud hosting (XaaS monetization), or data/context management services.

---

[22] The standardization of USDL was discussed in the W3C USDL Incubator Group, which published the final report in September 2011. The common understanding and recommendation of the group members was to keep the alignment with Web standards and go for a W3C standardization process. So the discussion with the W3C has started to establish a new standardization group that could be in place in spring 2012.

[23] http://fast.morfeo-project.org/

[24] http://www.reservoir-fp7.eu/

[25] http://www.master-fp7.eu/

[26] http://141.76.40.158/Servface/

[27] http://www.shape-project.eu

[28] http://sla-at-soi.eu/

[29] http://www.smartservicescrc.com.au/

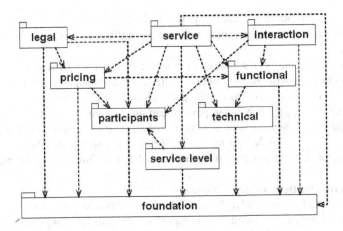

Fig. 2. USDL Modules and Relationships

4.2.3 Pricing

Depending on his business model, a service provider may choose one or more price models for each of his service offerings in order to meet different customer demands. Price models can be formally described in an appropriate data model such that they can be interpreted, e.g., for the automatic selection of the cheapest service offering or the calculation of payments to be made by the service consumer. The USDL service description model introduced above contains a comprehensive price model covering the most common cases and is leveraged by several projects including PremiumServices[30], 4CaaSt, and FI-WARE.

A USDL price model as used in 4CaaSt may contain several components [41], e.g., a monthly basic fee and a usage fee (per service call, per data volume handled, etc.). The overall payment required by the consumer then equals the sum of the payments generated by each of its components. A price model may also be restricted by a payment limit. If the payment is higher than the payment limit, only the amount equal to the payment limit is charged to the consumer. The semantic function of the payment limit is to allow the service provider to equip the price model with a cost control function. A price model component is a function that maps a number of consumed billing units to a payment and is applicable during a certain time frame. The billing unit is the unit per which the consumer is charged, e.g., the consumer can subscribe to a service and will then be charged per month. The function of the price model component depends on the concrete payment assessment metric such as

- subscription: the consumer pays for the timeframe during which the service can be used and the subscription fee applies independently from the quantitative consumption of the service within the subscribed time frame. Billing units are timeframes such as day, week, month, quarter, and year.
- pay per use event: the consumer pays for each event of interaction with the service. Billing units are events such as invocation, notification, transaction, and session.

---

[30] http://premiumservices.research-events.com/joomla/

- pay per use time: the consumer pays for the time of actual interaction with the service. Billing units are timeframes such as millisecond, second, hour, day, and week.
- pay per use quantity: the consumer pays for the quantity of resources consumed by interacting with the service. Billing units are quantity measures such as kilobyte, megabyte, gigabyte, data package, and CPU instruction.
- revenue share: the consumer pays a certain percentage of its own generated revenues, i.e., the consumer is a service provider itself who leverages a 3rd party service, e.g., a mobile app provider offering the app via the Apple App Store. The Billing unit in this case is revenue and the price function a percentage.

4.2.4 Revenue Settlement and Sharing

In the envisioned future Internet of Services composite services based on the aggregation of multiple (atomic or composite) services are expected to play an important role. Beyond the complexities of their management (design, provisioning, etc.), there is a complex issue to solve when dealing with the business aspects: both the composite and the atomic services must be accounted, rated and charged according to their business model, and each of the service providers must receive their corresponding payment. Therefore, there is an urgent need to standardize the way the revenues produced by a user's charges for the services consumed are split and distributed amongst the different services providers involved.

Nowadays, there are some examples in which revenue distribution is already needed. The best-known example is the Apple Application Store[31], which pays a percentage of the incomes from an application download to its developer. Another example is Telco API usage, with initiatives like Telefónica's BlueVia[32] or Orange's Partner[33], in which the application developers receive revenue share for the usage of those Telco APIs by the final users. There are also examples in the cloud computing services, like dbFlex[34] and Rollbase[35].

The service composition process ends up in a value network of services: an oriented tree in which the price model of each service and its share of participation in the overall services are represented. Depending on its business model, the business framework may play different roles in relation to the service providers. These realities will lead to different scenarios in which the revenues generated by the services must be settled between the service providers:

- If the business framework charges the user for the composite service, a settlement process must be executed in order to redistribute the incomes as in a clearing house.
- If the business framework charges for all the services in the value network, then besides the settlement function, there could be a revenue sharing process by which a service provider might decide to share a part of its incomes with the service provider that is generating the income.

---

[31] http://store.apple.com
[32] http://www.bluevia.com/
[33] http://www.orangepartner.com
[34] http://www.dbflex.net/
[35] http://www.rollbase.com/

In this context, a service must be understood in a broad sense, that is, not only as a remote decoupled execution of some functionality, but also considering other types of services: the business framework itself, content services, advertisement services, etc.

Revenue Settlement and Sharing Systems serve to the purpose to split the charged amounts and revenues among the different services providers involved in the delivery. Bearing in mind the open world assumption of the Future Internet of Services, these systems should offer at least the following functionality:

- Receive or interact with other external systems for loading business models regarding sharing and settlement.
- Define and store the different revenue sharing models to be applied taking into account Application and Services Ecosystems business models.
- Receive, store and load call data records or charging logs about the different sources of charges of the application and services ecosystem to the customers.
- Create aggregated information and data to be used to distribute the revenues.
- Store the information of developers or users to be paid.
- Daily revenue share execution and generation.
- Payment file generation and sending to the payment broker.

4.2.5 Service Monitoring and SLA Management

The management of Service Level Agreements (SLAs) will be an essential aspect of service delivery in the envisioned Internet of Services. In a competitive service marketplace, potential customers will not be looking for "a" service, but for "the best" service at the "best price". That is, the quality of services (QoS) – such as their performance, economic and security characteristics - are just as important as their functional properties. Providers who can offer hard QoS guarantees will have the competitive edge over those who promote services as mere 'functional units'. SLAs provide these hard guarantees: they are legally binding contracts, which specify not just that the provider will deliver some service, but that this service will also, say, be delivered on time, at a given price, and with money back if the pledge is broken. The cost of this increased quality assurance, however, is increased complexity. A comprehensive and systematic approach to SLA management is required to ensure this complexity is handled effectively, in a cohesive fashion, throughout the SLA life cycle.

Management of the SLA life cycle in the context of the Internet of Services is all about controlling its legal, systems and business impact in an integrated manner, in order to optimize business value on the whole ecosystem. Current standards and technologies offer at best only partial solutions: tackling either one aspect in isolation, or looking at the whole but with overly restrictive assumptions. What is missing is the big picture: the need for a comprehensive and highly integrated set of generic information & process models detailing SLA management over the entire SLA life cycle.

For the future Internet of Services, increasingly autonomic control of negotiation, service-delivery and monitoring is also expected. We also anticipate various management issues relating to the versioning of SLA templates (offers) and archiving of SLAs, monitored data, SLA state & negotiation histories, and any other information that may prove useful to the design of future service offers.

The Internet of Services needs an integrated SLA Model, i.e. a SLA content model, a SLA life-cycle model, and a SLA management model, that can serve as the foundation for the development of robust, Internet-scale SLA-aware applications and services. This SLA Model does not need to be designed from scratch, but will instead be consolidated from existing solutions. In particular work undertaken as part of the FP7 ICT Integrated Project SLA@SOI as well as other outstanding efforts such as WS-Agreement[36] regarding negotiation, WSLA[37] regarding content and monitoring, and SLAng[38] regarding monitoring, pave the way to the availability of an integrated SLA Model for the Future Internet of Services

4.3   An Second Perspective on Service Engineering

Service engineering is a new, structured approach to the analysis, design and implementation of service-based ecosystems in which organizations and IT provide value for others in the form of services. Service Engineering not only provides methodologies to handle the increased complexity of numerous business actors and their value exchanges, but also provides tools for constructing and deploying services that merge the IT and business perspectives.

4.3.1   Service Engineering Methodologies

Service Engineering requirements for the Future Internet of Services, along with the business framework-related requirements tackled in the previous sections were the basis for the TEXO project from the THESEUS[39] research program, which targets the development of an open platform for the development, distribution and provision of business services. One of the most outstanding outcomes from TEXO is undoubtedly the ISE methodology [21].

The ISE methodology provides the structured means for suppliers of services to describe and create new services for the Internet of Services, with a focus not only on a technical perspective, but also on a deep and prominent business perspective. The structuring is achieved by following the separation of concerns and model-driven design. A service in ISE is therefore divided into several individual models at different layers of abstraction, which are in turn integrated by using model representation formalisms (e.g. Meta Object Facility) and model transformation languages (e.g. QVT or the ATLAS Transformation Language) from the well-known model-driven approach to automatic model integration. Fig. 3 shows the different abstraction levels (perspectives) and dimensions (entities) of the ISE methodology, and the different artifacts assigned to each intersection of a perspective and a dimension.

Each of the abstraction levels of the ISE methodology can be regarded as a phase in the development process of services. Thus, the models and methods assigned to each of the layers support the development process from different view points (e.g., business, conceptual, logical, technical, and runtime).

---

[36] http://forge.gridforum.org/projects/graap-wg

[37] http://www.research.ibm.com/wsla/

[38] http://uclslang.sourceforge.net/index.php

[39] http://theseus-programm.de/en/index.php

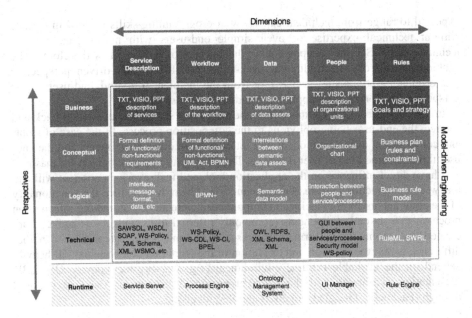

Fig. 3. Abstraction Levels and Dimensions of the TEXO ISE Methodology

4.4 Services Composition and Mashup

The recent social, economic, and technological developments lead to a new phenomenon often called *servification*, which is supposed to become the dominating principle in the economy of the future. Wikipedia, Amazon, YouTube, Apple's AppStore, Facebook and many others show the unprecedented success of Internet-based platforms in many areas including knowledge and content delivery, social networking, and services and apps marketplaces. Nevertheless, despite these success stories, few offers can really become killer applications alone, but many of them could have better chances in combination with others. Support of cross selling through composition would therefore become a highly desirable feature in the envisioned Internet of Services. However, most relevant applications and services ecosystems today do not incorporate these features or do not incorporate them at the right level, nor consider the right actors.

With the advent of the Web 2.0, phenomena like Wikipedia, Google Maps or YouTube have taught us how end consumers may become major drivers of innovation whenever suitable authoring tools, complemented by social tools that maximize their ability to exchange knowledge and gain recognition, are provided. However, while crowd-sourcing and social web technologies have experienced a relevant development in the area of information and multimedia content, they are still immature in the application and services space.

In the context of the future Internet of Services, applications and service ecosystems will need to strive to exploit the composable nature of the services technologies in order to support cross-selling and achieve the derived network scaling effects in multiple ways. The capabilities and skills of composite service creators are expected to range from technical experts with programming skills to domain experts without technical expertise or even simple end-users with no programming or technical skills. Service composition in the Internet of Services has therefore to be enabled either from the traditional back-end, IT-staff/providers-driven perspective (i.e. originating composite services), or from the incipient front-end, end-user-driven perspective (i.e. originating application and service mash-ups).

In the case of back-end composition, the composed service is yet another back-end service, the end-user being oblivious to the composition process. In the case of front-end composition, every component will interface both other components and the end-user through some kind of user interface. Thus the front-end composition (or mashup) will have direct influence on the application look and feel; every component will add a new user interaction feature. This of course will heavily influence the functionality of the components. While back-end components are created by atomizing information processing, front-end components (commonly referred to as widgets or gadgets) are created by atomizing information presentation and user interaction. Another difference is that the creation and execution of the front-end components will heavily depend on the available runtime environment (e.g. web-browser, device OS, 2/3D presentation platforms), and the different presentation channels they are exposed through (Facebook, Google Gadgets, Yahoo! Widgets).

4.4.1 Supporting Back-End, IT-Staff Driven Large-Scale Service Compositions

Composite services consist of a set of services along with the definition of the control and data flow among them. The actual exchange between elements in a composition can be understood as a workflow with specific actors (the services) and the flow of actions (e.g. a data dependency - one operation needs data produced by another operation) to be executed by them towards achieving the goals specified. Typically such a composition and the related workflow has to be created before the composite service can be executed and thereafter created compositions and workflows will be executed unchanged repeatedly in the same or in different contexts.

The explicit representation of the execution order of the composition steps in a workflow provides a clear and easy way to express chronological control dependencies. Typically, workflows can express sequential and parallel flows as well as use conditional statements. More advanced approaches can support multiple entry points, error and exceptions handling, and invocations of external services. Most often, workflows are defined implicitly (i.e. hard-coded) by implementations of applications written using typical imperative programming languages. To offer a more formal, programming language independent, declarative way of expressing the workflows several workflow definition languages were proposed and standardized. WS-BPEL[40] and BPMN 2.0[41] are technologies of choice for XML Web Services based workflows. Workflow scripts are then executed by an *orchestration engine* (e.g. a BPEL execution engine executes WS-BPEL workflows). The Topology and Orchestration Specification for Cloud Applications (TOSCA) [45], a recently initiated standardization effort from the OASIS Standards Body, aims at describing composite applications and their management in a modular and portable fashion so as to enable portability of cloud services.

---

[40] http://docs.oasis-open.org/wsbpel/2.0/OS/wsbpel-v2.0-OS.html
[41] http://www.omg.org/spec/BPMN/2.0/

Alternatively, workflows can be dynamically created or adapted during composition execution to address the on-demand nature of the Future Internet of Services. Suitable services are now identified and executed as needed on the current context, depending on external and internal events and results from previous service invocations, to provide tailored services on demand to users. Such workflows are valid only during execution time and under particular circumstances. They can be created through model-driven systems using inference procedures with a traceable line of reasoning based on application domain specific knowledge. One promising approach to model-driven dynamic composition is that based on composition templates or skeletons. The skeleton includes the main parts of the business logic of the composed service, but is not complete with regard to some implementation parts. Such points in a template are marked in a special way, so that these places can be found during execution. At run-time the composition engine is invoked at those places and it dynamically decides about what services (or further skeletons) to invoke or which data source to use based on constraints evaluated at that particular time. Essentially the composition engine is creating the workflow step-by-step during runtime, and different composition decisions can be taken depending on external events or on the return values of previously executed services. Ideally, composition engines focus on creating workflows on the fly, at runtime, and leave protocol implementation and service technology (e.g. WS, REST, SIP, RMI, CORBA, etc.) specificities to Composition Execution Agents (CEAs), which are responsible for enforcing composition decisions in a technology and protocol specific way.

Nevertheless, dynamicity is not the only concern when tackling the open world assumption of the Future Internet of Services: service orchestrations will also grow larger, more distributed and complex than ever, thus becoming a new source of concern. Their centralized approach to composition has scalability and single point of failure problems. The Future Internet of Services will therefore require additional support for *choreographies*, to compose services in a non-centralized, distributed manner, with no single point of failure. Choreographies are intrinsically more resilient than, although not as easily manageable as, orchestrations. As non-centralized distributed systems they have higher fault tolerance, adaptability, configurability, and freedom to grow.

Even though some choreography standards (e.g., WSCI[42] and WS-CDL[43]) have already been defined, to the best of our knowledge, none of them has been completely implemented, there are very few development tools available and there is still little research into the actual usage (deployment and enactment) of choreographies. Moreover, as the current ad hoc choreographies get larger and more intricate, they can easily become unmanageable.

The CHOReOS[44] project aims at assisting the engineering of software service compositions in the form of large-scale choreographies by implementing a middleware based on federated and distributed service bus, pervasive middleware and grid and cloud computing technologies. This will make possible the actual definition, deployment and enactment of large-scale choreographies, such as those that will be

---

[42] http://www.w3.org/TR/wsci/

[43] http://www.w3.org/TR/ws-cdl-10/

[44] http://www.choreos.eu/

needed for the Future Internet of Services [14,46], whilst sustaining adaptation and quality assurance.

4.4.2 Empowering End Users through Mashup Technologies

As previously mentioned, the Future Internet is expected to be composed of a mesh of interoperable services massively accessed, remixed and shared from all over the Web, with end users at the very heart of the vision. Moreover, the capabilities and skills of composite service creators are expected to range from technical experts with programming skills to domain experts without technical expertise to end-users with no programming or technical skills.

Nevertheless, this approach has not yet caught on since global user-service interaction and end-user driven service composition are still open issues. Successful building of composite services and applications still rely on heavyweight service orchestration technologies and programming frameworks that raise the bar far above end user skills. Thinking about professional developers as the only group capable of successfully build composite services and applications is however becoming a fallacy: the End-User Development paradigm [31] has started to gain momentum, and the Web 2.0 has shown us that the empowerment of end users is key to leverage network effects, also in the envisioned Internet of Services.

End-User Development

Software development is becoming a widespread, pervasive practice at an ever-increasing pace. People without programming skills, who are non-professional software developers, have also entered the scene and produce software solutions to support some "instant" goal (regarding their work or hobbies) in their own domains of expertise, for which they need computational support. According to statistics from the U.S. Bureau of Labor and Statistics, by this year (2012) in the United States there will be more than 55 million people using spreadsheets and databases at work, many writing formulas and queries to support their job, counteracts fewer than 3 million professional programmers [29].

This tendency has popularized the terms "end-user development" and "end-user programming", probably coined by Nardi [30] during her investigations into spreadsheet use in office workplaces. End-user development can be defined as "a set of activities or techniques that allow people, who are non-professional software developers, at some point to create or modify a software artifact" [31]. Most people polled in a survey conveyed by the EUD-NET Network of Excellence [32] respond that using EUD tools makes them more efficient in their tasks and makes their work itself more interesting. EUD represents for them a means for exploiting their domain expertise, thus creating more effective software to "instantly" support their activities, when traditional software development practices do not fit (implied 'time-to-market', lack of IT budget or required staff/resources, etc.).

Bearing this in mind, it is clear that we should leverage this tendency and put EUD (i.e. end users) at the very heart of application and service composition technologies for the Future Internet of Services.

One requisite to facilitate the use of EUD tools by end users is to choose the right abstractions for their problem domains. This means choosing the right concepts, choosing the right level of abstraction for such concepts, and supporting the design of custom data types, so that end-user developers can more easily process, validate and transform information between different formats. For example, a key to the success of the Google Maps API has been the relative ease with which end users can annotate geographical images with custom data types. Even so, the vision of end users developing their own solutions has not yet materialized.

This is a fundamental problem in many new domains of end-user development regarding the Internet of Services, such as mashup design tools and platforms (e.g. iGoogle, Yahoo! Dapper, OpenKapow, RoboMaker, Netvibes, PageFlakes, JackBe, M2O, AMICO, Marmite, EzWeb, WireCloud, QedWiki), and RSS feed processors (e.g., Yahoo! Pipes or Deri Pipes).

This will continue to be so unless we in both the industry and the research community set ourselves the ambitious challenge of devising end to end an end-user application development model for developing a new age of EUD tools.

In the SOA4All project, a first attempt towards EUD was made: a graphical editor allows users to define compositions (orchestrations) of semantic Web services (so-called lightweight processes) by means of a graphical notation [37]. This notation is basically a simplified subset of BPMN. The underlying process model is transformed automatically into an executable, BPEL-based process. In addition to semantic Web services (in WSMO-Lite format), SOA4All also supports human activities that are managed via an integrated task management system. For users not (yet) familiar with the basic concepts of graphical process modeling, a supported modeling mode was developed where a wizard explicitly guides users to perform a predefined series of modification steps [38]. The general SOA4All approach was evaluated in different use cases from the Telco, e-Commerce, and public administrations domains. For instance, Telco users combined communication services from British Telecom with services from Facebook to create a location-aware meeting application [39].

Application Mashups
Another major weakness of current approaches to user-service interaction, that impede the realization of the Internet of Services vision, lies in the abstraction of the underlying service front-end architecture rather than the infrastructure technologies themselves. A plausible approach is to offer end-to-end composition from user interface to service invocation, as well as an understandable abstraction of both building blocks and a visual composition technique that keep the composition process close to end-user skills. Such an approach has already been taken by the European FP7 FAST Project and, previously, by EzWeb[45] (a NESSI Flagship Project). In [36] the authors formalize this vision with regard to the next-generation front-end Web technology by presenting a novel reference architecture designed to empower non-technical end users to create and share their own self-service composite applications in the Future Internet of Services. In [34,35] the authors complete the picture by presenting and validating their proposed composition model and technique.

Telco Mashups
The convergence of Telecom, IT and content services is driving the emergence of new markets on an open Internet of Services. Mashups have been a major success in

---

[45] http://ezweb.morfeo-project.org/lng/en/

Web 2.0. The success of Web 2.0 services has encouraged Telcos to expose their services as Telco Mashups, in order to provide third parties with facilities to build their business. Moreover, the exposure of network infrastructure as services is facilitating the entry of new API-driven Telco agents that bring traditional Telco services (telephony, messaging, IP location, etc.) to the Web. Yet, the technologies underlying each of the different mashups types are heterogeneous, which makes integration challenging. Also, mashups do not offer a universal composition model either, since mashup development is not vendor independent. A mashup developed within a specific technology has to be re-coded in order to be deployed in another engine. OMELETTE[46] proposes an innovative process of service development based on a mashup-oriented approach, which will enable the development of multimodal services from the Telco domain in a seamless way.

4.4.3 Mediation

The heterogeneity amongst the different ways to represent data requested or provided by an application or a service, and to represent the communication pattern or the public process needed to request a functionality, are problems that arise as soon as a service has to be dynamically discovered and used at run-time as will be the case in the envisioned Internet of Services. For example, executing a composition in a different execution environment or implementing dynamic run-time changes might require a process mediation function.

There exist three types of mediation: data mediation, protocol mediation, and process mediation.

Data Mediation

Data mediation deals with data transformation between the different data models employed by the two ends of a communication. There are a number of mechanisms that can be utilized to perform data mediation:

- Using a library of built-in transformers in case of well-known formats.
- Using templates for more flexible data transformation capabilities.
- Using Domain Specific Languages (DSLs) or code components in order to fulfill more complex data transformation requirements.
- Using Lifting and Lowering (LILO) schemas and ontology mappings.

For highly dynamic cases, when services are discovered at runtime (a.k.a. late-binding of services), data mediation provides the glue between heterogeneous systems by providing semantic matching algorithms that can deal at runtime with discrepancies in exchanged data types from parameters and return values of services operations. These algorithms are based on semantic annotations/meta-data over service descriptions (SAWSDL, USDL), extracted from ontologies (RDF/S, OWL, WSMO, etc.).

Semantic annotations can be put on service descriptions and data-types. Additionally, service providers can issue pure semantic service descriptions using schemas such as OWL-S, WSMO and its light counterparts: WSMO Lite, MicroWSMO. Service consumers describe their needs in a similar fashion.

---

[46] http://www.ict-omelette.eu/

Protocol Mediation

Protocol mediation enables interaction between communicating parties where there is a shared conceptual model of the intent and purpose of the communication, but where the mechanics of communication interaction vary, i.e. the communicating parties are using different protocols to achieve the same or similar ends.

Process Mediation

Process mediation in open dynamic environments is based on the idea that, assuming that both the requester and provider adhere to some relatively fixed process models, and that those models are expressed declaratively, interoperability can be achieved by applying a process mediation component which resolves all incompatibilities, generates appropriate mappings between different processes and translates messages exchanged during runtime.

The process mediation component is primarily responsible for resolving service level and protocol level mismatches. However, more generally speaking, it has to address three problems: (1) identify possible information gaps and incompatibilities between the process models that impede the mediation, (2) find mappings between the two processes, and (3) provide suitable mechanisms for runtime mediation and translations.

Creating a mediator component is very challenging since this component must be able to identify and resolve various types of incompatibilities on the

1. data level, e.g., different representation of exchanged data elements,
2. service level, e.g., some information required by the provider is not provided by the requester, and
3. protocol level, e.g., different control flows.

Moreover, the mediation component has to be able to perform translations at runtime and also be able to respond to possible unexpected situations such as failures in communication.

A number of research and industrial initiatives are currently tackling the problem of data and service mediation. The SETHA2 software framework from THALES deals with dynamicity and heterogeneity concerns in the SOA context. A major part of SETHA2 is about providing libraries/facilities dedicated to dynamic data mediation. SOA4All Design Time Composer[47] provides some design time semi-assisted modeling features for data mediation and hybrid REST/WSDL based service compositions. Last but not least, PetalsESB[48] is an extensible ESB hosted by OW2 that supports all major industry standards (such as JBI, SCA, BPEL or WSDL). It has been successfully deployed in the SemEUsE[49] ANR project and is currently being deployed in the CHOReOS European/FP7 project.

4.4.4 Context-Aware Services

The information about the context in which service-based systems are executed effects the expected behavior and quality of the systems. There is a number of

---

[47] http://soa4all-dtc.sourceforge.net/

[48] http://petals.ow2.org/

[49] http://www.semeuse.org

research challenges to face when considering the context in which the service-based system is embedded [33]:

- Context modeling approaches to facilitate the description of the contextual information. This requires considering the different context facets ranging from the business context (e.g., stakeholders, regulations, business trends and business objects), to the user context (e.g. end-user preferences and settings, tasks and activities), or the lower level application operational context (e.g. protocols and networks, devices), amongst others.
- Context-driven service adaptation and monitoring. The broad, dynamic nature of the Internet of Services requires equipping service-based systems with the mechanisms necessary to quickly adapt to changes in the system's run-time. Context models are key to support the selection, realization and enactment of adaptation actions through service engineering and design. As input for extending the existing and for defining novel monitoring and adaptation approaches that are capable of explicitly considering and reasoning upon such information through service adaptation and monitoring techniques, context models need to be exploited, collected, refined, and integrated. This in turn requires identifying and codifying the relevant context information such that it can be monitored and exploited to trigger adaptations.
- Context issues in service discovery, selection and negotiation. Coping with the aforementioned broad, dynamic nature of the Internet of Services implies a growing need for automating the selection, negotiation and agreement of quality attributes (e.g. as stipulated by SLAs). This issue requires expliciting, gathering and considering user interaction and experience patterns developed for service engineering and design, as these may impact on the negotiation itself. Therefore, service discovery and registries constitute another relevant impact area of context. Specifically, feedback-based service discovery deals with finding the impact of human activities and social relationships among service users on the evaluation of the quality of experience in service consumption. Thus, bearing in mind that Internet of Services value is subject to the 'network effect', concepts which allow for gathering, storing, exchanging and evaluating quality of experience metrics (which are also relevant for service quality) are needed.

4.5 Realizing the Internet of Services Vision: The FI-WARE Applications and Services Ecosystem and Delivery Framework

FI-WARE[50] is supposed to play a key role as the main technological driver bringing together cloud computing, mobile networks, Web2.0, Apps, services, data sources, and things on a broadband Internet and enabling multi-channel consumption and mobile multi-device access. Its proposal for a novel Application and Services Ecosystem and Delivery Framework able to exploit the innovative value proposition of *servification* to its full potential from the technology as well as from the business perspective are envisioned as one of the main pillars of the Future Internet.

The Applications and Services Ecosystem and Delivery Framework in FI-WARE (FIWARE-Apps) builds from a set of generic enablers (i.e. reusable and commonly shared functional building blocks serving a multiplicity of usage areas across various

---

[50] http://www.fi-ware.eu

sectors) for creation, composition, sharing, discovery, delivery, monetization, and usage of applications and services on the Future Internet of Services. It aims to support the necessary life-cycle management of services and applications from both a technical and business perspective. The latter includes business aspects such as the management of the terms and conditions associated to the offering, accounting, billing, pricing, revenue sharing and SLAs, thus enabling the definition of a wide range of new business models in an agile and flexible way along with their association with the different applications and services available in the envisioned ecosystem. The capacity to monetize applications and services based on those business models, adapting the offering to users and their context and dealing with the fact that they may have been built through the composition of components developed and provided by different parties is a key objective for the FIWARE-Apps business framework infrastructure.

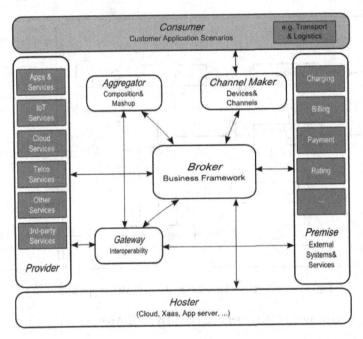

Fig. 4. FI-WARE Applications and Services Delivery Framework High-level Architecture

FIWARE-Apps considers the ability to uniformly access and handle services linked to processes, 'things' and contents, enabling them to be composed and mashed up in a natural way. The framework will bring the necessary range of composition and mashup tools that will empower users, from developers to domain experts to citizens without programming skills, to create and share, in a crowd-sourcing environment like the one envisioned for the Internet of Services, new added value applications and composite services adapted to their real needs, based on those offered from the available business frameworks. A set of multi-channel/multi-device adaptation enablers are also to be contributed to allow publication and delivery of the applications through different and configurable channels, including those social web networks which may be more popular at the moment, and their access from any sort of (mobile) device.

The high-level architecture[51] illustrated in Fig. 4 is structured according to the internal key business roles (aggregator, broker, gateway, and channel maker), the external key roles being considered (provider, hoster, premise, and consumer) and their relationships within the overall services delivery framework and existing IT landscapes.

4.5.1 Generic Enablers of the Business Framework

Fig. 5 illustrates the high-level architecture of the business framework infrastructure realizing the Broker, i.e. its core components, their interrelationships, and relationships to external parties and systems necessary to make the business framework infrastructure operational.

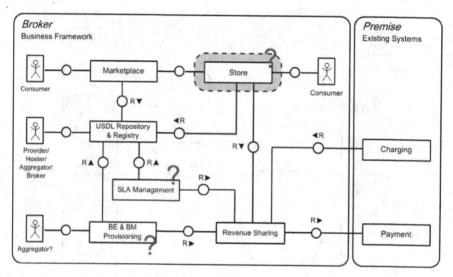

Fig. 5. High-level Architecture of the FIWARE-Apps Broker[52]

The set of Generic Enablers identified by FIWARE-Apps are:

- USDL Repository: The service repository is a place to store service descriptions and its use is required in order to prepare these descriptions to appear at a store, marketplace and other components of the business framework.
- USDL Registry: The service registry is a universal directory of information used for the maintenance, administration, deployment and retrieval of services in the service delivery framework environment.
- Marketplace: A store represents a specific (limited) service/app portfolio offered and fully controlled by a single service provider. The marketplace is a platform for many stores to place their offerings to a broader audience of potential consumers to search and compare services and find the store where to "buy" them.

---

[51] An early version of the FIWARE-Apps high-level architecture was released by the FIWARE Consortium on August 2011, as part of deliverable D2.2 (FI-WARE High-level Description).

- Business Elements and Models Provisioning System. The aim of the BE&BM provisioning is the monetization of services, applications, and their compositions/aggregations. The availability of a business model definition, i.e. a flexible way to define the manner in which services and applications can be sold and delivered to the final customers, is mandatory. While the USDL descriptions to be published in the service repository represent the public view of the business models offered to the customer, the business models define the way in which customers pay by applications and services and the way in which the incomes are to be split among the involved parties. Once, the business model is defined, it is necessary to provision these details in the rating/charging/billing systems.
- Revenue Settlement and Sharing System: In the future Internet of Services there is a need to manage in a common way how to distribute the revenues produced by a user's charges for the application and services consumed. When a consumer buys/contracts an application or service, she pays for its usage. This charge can be distributed and split among different actors involved (for instance store or marketplace owner earns money and mash-ups have to split the money). There will be a common pattern for service delivery in service-oriented environments. Independent of service type, composite services based on the aggregation of multiple atomic (from the viewpoint of composition) services are expected to play an important role in applications and services ecosystems. Beyond the complexities of the management of composite services (design, provisioning, etc.), there is a complex issue to solve when dealing with the business aspects. Both the composite and the atomic services must be accounted, rated and charged according to their business model, and each of the service providers must receive their corresponding payment. The Revenue Settlement and Sharing System serves to the purpose to split the charged amounts and revenues among the different services providers.
- SLA Management: The management of Service Level Agreements (SLAs) will be an essential aspect of service delivery in the Internet of Services. In a competitive service market place, potential customers will not be looking for "a" service, but for "the best" service at the "best price". That is, the quality of services (QoS) – such as their performance, economic and security characteristics - are just as important, in the marketplace, as their functional properties. Providers who can offer hard QoS guarantees will have the competitive edge over those who promote services as mere 'functional units'. SLAs provide these hard guarantees: they are legally binding contracts which specify not just that the provider will deliver some service, but that this service will also, say, be delivered on time, at a given price, and with money back if the pledge is broken. The cost of this increased quality assurance, however, is increased complexity. A comprehensive and systematic approach to SLA management is required to ensure this complexity is handled effectively, in a cohesive fashion, throughout the SLA life cycle.

4.5.2 Generic Enablers for Composition and Mashup

FI-WARE strives to exploit the composable nature of the application and services technologies in order to support cross selling and achieve the derived network scaling effects in multiple ways. It will enable composition either from the front-end perspective – mash-ups or the back-end perspective – composite services.

In FI-WARE, the mash-up and composition capabilities offered by the different types of supported components are expected to leverage their reusability as well as the creation of value-added applications and services not only by application and service providers but also by intermediaries and end users acting as *prosumers*. The supported framework will rely on a defined set of user, provider and intermediary roles defining the skills, capabilities and responsibilities of the actors and relationships among them. The value network spanned by the roles of the actors and relationships among them defines the creation and distribution of the value-added applications from the technical perspective. As the capabilities and skills of actors are expected to range from technical experts with programming skills to domain experts without technical expertise or even simple end-users with no programming or technical skills, all kinds of usability aspects, conceptual simplification, recommendation, autonomous provisioning (including composition, description and deployment), as well as procurement and user guidance will be taken into consideration.

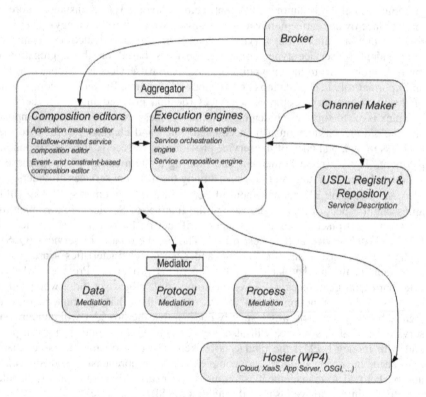

Fig. 6. High-level Architecture of the Aggregator and Mediator Generic Enablers

There are two main functional components that can be identified in service composition and application mashups: the aggregator and the mediator roles (Fig. 6). The aggregator allows the creation, exposition and execution of composed (or mashed up) services and applications. Whenever a composed service or application is used the need might arise to use a mediator for components to properly communicate and interact. The aggregator can be further split into a composition editing tool used for the creation of design time compositions (described by a specific composition language), an execution environment to expose and execute the composed services, and a repository for keeping the relevant information in the meanwhile.

Future convergent composition techniques require a smart integration of process know-how, heterogeneous data sources, management of things, communication services, context information, social elements and business aspects. Communication services are event, rather than process driven by nature. Thus, a composition paradigm for the Internet of Services needs to enable composition of business logic also driven by asynchronous events. The framework will support the run-time selection of Mashable Application Components (MACs) and the creation/modification of orchestration workflows based on composition logic defined at design-time, to adapt to the state of the communication and the environment at run-time. The integration of Things into the composition requires that the special characteristics of IoT services like lower granularity, locality of execution, quality of information aspects etc are taken into account. Moreover, the framework will allow the transparent usage of applications over many networks and protocols (HTTP/REST, Web Services, SIP/IMS) and corresponding execution platforms (both Web and native apps) via a multi-protocol/multi-device layer that adapts communication and presentation functionality.

4.5.3 Generic Enablers for Gateway

Acknowledging the necessity to deal with this heterogeneity, dynamic mediation solutions are required in FIWARE. Mediation will be the main functionality of FI-WARE Gateway Generic Enablers.

FI-WARE will offer three types of generic enablers for mediation: Data Mediation, Protocol Mediation, and Process Mediation. In all cases, the mediation component acts as a broker between service consumers and providers that provides some non-functional requirements like built-in monitoring and management capabilities, in order to be able to be automatically re-configured and to track mediation steps.

4.5.4 Generic Enablers for Multi-channel and Multi-device Access

The huge spread of mobile devices – smart phones, tablets, connected devices of all sorts- and the broad spectrum of social networking platforms have prompted the need for delivering Future Internet applications and services by means of multiple channels (such as social and content platforms, application marketplaces, and so on), while ensuring the best user experience at any time allowing their access from any kind of device (multi-device), adapting usability and presentation when necessary. It is also important to manage user's contextual information in order to support service composition adaptation corresponding to user's preferences and profile. The more detailed and relevant the information at hand and the smarter the ability to reach the end-user the greater are the chances to accelerate time to market, close a sale, or improve customer satisfaction.

In order to support the ideas behind this stage, Future Internet applications must be able to give up the control over their user interfaces to take advantage of an external multi-channel and multi-device access enabler. Applications must provide device-independent abstract user interfaces by means of a standardized user interface definition authoring language, in order to have it properly rendered according to the channel and device's properties and features, publicly available in a shared and standardized knowledge base. Moreover, giving up the control over the user interface also implies the adapter to be on charge of the interface workflow execution, which will be able to call back the application backend through service access points, and control the selection of rendered views.

Apart from solving rendering aspects, which is mandatory for enabling both multi-channel and multi-device access, multi-channel adaptation also requires dealing with the diversity of APIs and capabilities provided by the different channels. More specifically, each channel requires its own specific workflow, and thus there must be support for describing the application workflow in a generic enough abstract workflow language that can be concretized on demand to the target channel.

A workflow engine and a number of renderers, at least one per channel, leveraging the device's properties and the delivery context can tackle multi-device adaptation within a channel. Fig. 7 depicts the generic enablers for multi-channel and multi-device access and their interrelationships.

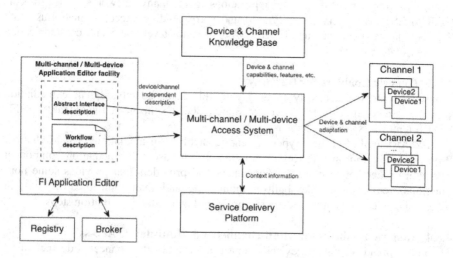

Fig. 7. Multi-channel / Multi-device Access System Generic Enablers

4.6   Key Research Initiatives and Programmes

At present, there are a number of research initiatives and programmes that, together, will help to set the road map for realizing the Future Internet of Services and, undoubtedly will influence future research directions:

- The Horizon 2020. EU investments in ICTs are due to increase by 46% under Horizon 2020 compared to the current EU research programmes (FP7)[52]. This EU investment will support the riskier ICT research and innovation that can deliver new business breakthroughs, often on the basis of emerging, key enabling technologies including micro- and nano-electronics, and photonics and, in

---

[52] http://ec.europa.eu/research/horizon2020/pdf/press/ fact_sheet_on_ict_in_horizon_2020.pdf

particular the development of infrastructures, technologies and services for the future Internet.

- The S-Cube Research Framework. S-CUBE[53] is the European Network of Excellence in Software Services and Systems, funded by the European Commission from March 2008 to February 2012. S-Cube set out to address cross-cutting research challenges faced when engineering, designing, adapting, operating and evolving the next generation of services and service-based systems for the Internet of Services. The research in S-Cube is guided by the S-Cube research framework [33], which clearly distinguishes between principles and methods for engineering and adapting service-based systems and the technology and mechanisms that are used to realize those systems. The benefit of adopting such an approach is that the S-Cube research framework provides a clear distinction between technology-focused approaches of the service technology layers and the cross-cutting principles, techniques and methods provided by the techniques and method planes that together exploit and integrate the capabilities of the technology layers. By synthesizing and integrating diversified knowledge across different research disciplines, S-Cube aims at delivering the novel principles, techniques and methods for the service-based systems of the future.
- Hola! Project. Being a dissemination instrument for Internet of Services projects, the HOLA![54] Project is aimed at developing (1) continuous, active collaboration amongst IoS projects, (2) horizontal knowledge management within the Internet of Services community, and (3) visibility of projects' results towards exploitation strategies.
- SEQUOIA Support Action. SEQUOIA[55] considers that one of the main building blocks of the Future Internet is the 'Internet of Services', together with the underlying networked infrastructures such as Software as a Service. It is therefore their priority to provide adequate support to ongoing and future research initiatives in order to improve their chances of success. Whereas the NESSI[56] platform has in principle addressed in a comprehensive way the essential aspects of technological interoperability and architectural harmonization for the Software as a Service (SaaS) domain, and is well-placed to do the same for the emerging Internet of Service (IoS), Internet of Things (IoT) and Internet of Content (IoC) areas of the Future Internet, many practical obstacles remain. The clearest challenge is how to transition from the collaborative context of EU projects to the competitive context of the marketplace. The SEQUOIA support action aims to measure the potential impact of already funded projects in the area of Software as a Service and Internet of Services by developing a sound socio-economic self-assessment methodology. SEQUOIA emphasizes the self-assessment, rather than the evaluation, of these and new research projects, i.e. aims to support them in maximizing their socio-economic impact and also support the transfer of results to SMEs through the adoption and application of the proposed methodology on their own.

---

[53] http://www.s-cube-network.eu/
[54] http://www.holaportal.eu/
[55] http://www.sequoiaproject.eu/
[56] http://www.nessi-europe.com/

5   Conclusions

The relentless march towards an Internet of Services will continue and it is of utmost importance for the telecoms industry to understand this. Through this chapter an understanding of what the Internet of Services are and upon what foundations and methodologies it is based and built on was given. Further, the means that the telecom industry can leverage IoS research and push IoS capabilities on and beyond through innovation was discussed. Importantly for the realisation of the IoS it was described how those services within the IoS should be designed and implemented. Through this chapter the upcoming challenges and opportunities have been discussed from the perspective of the telecoms industry to understand the potential of IoS for that industry. Such that that industry and others can vanquish challenges and seize opportunities within the IoS, two overarching methodologies were presented, culminating at the description of a particularly innovative one; the ISE methodology, a result of the THESEUS research programme.

Going forward the increasing adoption of IoS services will only be greater especially as more service providers leverage and take avail of cloud computing approaches. Cloud computing approaches and technologies are now very much a key stone to much of the cutting edge ICT research and innovation within Europe. From the context of the telecoms industry, the most interesting and innovative project is MobileCloud Networking[57]. MobileCloud Networking's aim is to bring all the concepts and advantages of not just cloud computing but IoS to the Telco world. MobileCloud Networking will research and implement the means to   move those concepts out from the data centre, across the core network and into the radio access network.

There are huge advantages to offer IoS services through cloud computing, however there still remains issues that need addressing today and into the future. Essential for further IoS uptake by businesses small and large is for key topics of service interoperability and dependability. Work from both the Cloud Computing Expert Working Group[58] and the Future Internet Architecture Working Group[59] all point to challenges related to standards, portability and interoperability. QoS, SLAs and service transparency are also noted in both. A clear indicator of the importance of addressing these issues is the focus of these topics in the European Cloud Partnership strategy[60]

---

[57] MobileCloud Networking Project.
http://www.cloudcomp.ch/research/foundation/projects/
mobilecloud-networking/
[58] "Advances in Clouds: Report from the Cloud Computing Expert Working Group".
http://cordis.europa.eu/fp7/ict/ssai/docs/
future-cc-2may-finalreport-experts.pdf
[59] "Design Principles for the Future Internet", Future Internet Architecture Working Group.
http://ec.europa.eu/information_society/activities/foi/docs/
fiarchdesignprinciples-v1.pdf
[60] "Unleashing the Potential of Cloud Computing in Europe".
http://ec.europa.eu/information_society/activities/
cloudcomputing/docs/com/com_cloud.pdf

These challenges are researched through some of the projects mentioned in Section 4.6 and further will be researched and continued on in the future. It is important to address the research challenges and it is exciting and encouraging to know that with the advent of Horizon 2020, the EU will support riskier ICT research and innovation that can deliver potentially more innovative solutions to these research challenges with impact demonstrated through new business breakthroughs.

Acknowledgements. This work is being partially supported by the EU co-funded IST projects FI-WARE: Future Internet Core Platform (GA FP7-285248) and 4CaaSt (GA FP7-258862). The authors thank the teams working on FI-WARE, especially those involved in its Application and Services Ecosystem and Delivery Framework Chapter from SAP AG, Atos Origin SAE, Deutsche Telekom AG, TID, Ericsson AB, Engineering Italia SPA, Telecom Italia SPA, UPM and Thales Communications SA, and 4CaaSt, especially from SAP AG, TID, and HSG.

References

1. Fitzsimmons, J.A., Fitzsimmons, M.J.: Service Management – Operations, Strategy, Information Technology, 7th edn. McGraw-Hill (2010)
2. Vargo, S.L., Lusch, R.L.: Evolving to a new dominant logic for marketing. Journal of Marketing 68, 1–17 (2004)
3. Vargo, S.L., Lusch, R.F.: Service-Dominant Logic: Continuing the Evolution. Journal of the Academy of Marketing Science 36, 1–10 (2008)
4. Vargo, S., Akaka, M.A.: Service-Dominant Logic as a Foundation for Service Science: Clarifications. Service Science 1(1), 32–41 (2009)
5. Spohrer, J., Maglio, P.P., Bailey, J., Gruhl, D.: Steps toward a science of service systems. Computer 40, 71–77 (2007)
6. Spohrer, J., Maglio, P.P.: The emergence of service science: Toward systematic service innovations to accelerate co-creation of value. Production and Operations Management 17(3), 1–9 (2008)
7. Vargo, S.L., Lusch, R.F., Akaka, M.A.: Advancing Service Science with Service-Dominant Logic: Clarifications and Conceptual Development. In: Handbook of Service Science. Service Science: Research and Innovations in the Service Economy (2010)
8. Bettencourt, L.A.: Service Innovation. How to Go from Customer Needs to Breakthrough Services, 1st edn. McGraw Hill (2010) ISBN 978-0-07-171300-9
9. Karwowski, W., Salvendy, G., Ahram, T.: Customer-Centered Design of Service Organizations. In: Salvendy, G., Karwowski, W. (eds.) Introduction to Service Engineering. John Wiley & Sons (2010)
10. Kim, K.-J., Meiren, T.: New Service Development Process. In: Salvendy, G., Karwowski, W. (eds.) Introduction to Service Engineering. John Wiley & Sons (2010)
11. Stickdorn, M., Schneider, J., et al.: This is Service Design Thinking. BIS Publishers, Amsterdam (2011) ISBN 978-90-6369-279-7
12. Ulwick, A.W.: Turn customer input into innovation. Harvard Business Rev. 80, 91–97 (2002)
13. Lynne Shostack, G.: Designing Services that Deliver. Harvard Business Review 62(1), 133–139 (1984)
14. Issarny, V., Georgantas, N., Hachem, S., Zarras, A., Vassiliadis, P., Autili, M., Gerosa, M.A., Hamida, A.B.: Service-Oriented Middleware for the Future Internet: State of the Art and Research Directions. Journal of Internet Services and Applications, JISA (2011)

15. Davies, J., Domingue, J., Pedrinaci, C., Fensel, D., Gonzalez-Cabero, R., Potter, M., Richardson, M., Stincic, S.: Towards the Open Service Web. BT Technology Journal 26 (2009)

16. Hendler, J., Golbeck, J.: Metcalfe's law, Web 2.0, and the Semantic Web. In: Web Semantics: Science, Services and Agents on the World Wide Web (2008)

17. Pedrinaci, C., Domingué, J.: Toward the Next Wave of Services: Linked Services for the Web of Data. Journal of Universal Computer Science (2010)

18. Pedrinaci, C., Domingue, J.: Web Services Are Dead. Long Live Internet Services. SOA4All White Paper (2010) http://www.soa4all.eu/pubs/SOA4All-WhitePaper-2010.pdf (retrieved April 26, 2012)

19. Stricker, V., Lauenroth, K., Corte, P., Gittler, F., De Panfilis, S., Pohl, K.: Creating a Reference Architecture for Service-Based Systems – A Pattern-Based Approach. In: Tselentis, et al. (eds.) Towards the Future Internet, pp. 149–160. IOS Press (2010)

20. Agassi, S., Bisson, P., Cantera, J.M., Jimenez-Peris, R., De Nigro, A., Desideri, D., Corte, P.: Internet of Services Pattern. NEXOF Reference Architecture (2010), http://www.nexof-ra.eu/sites/default/files/Internet%20of%20Service%200.6.pdf (retrieved April 26, 2012)

21. Cardoso, J., Voigt, K., Winkler, M.: Service Engineering for the Internet of Services. In: Filipe, J., Cordeiro, J. (eds.) Enterprise Information Systems. LNBIP, vol. 19, pp. 15–27. Springer, Heidelberg (2009)

22. Oberle, D.: Report on landscapes of existing service description efforts. W3C USDL XG Incubator Group (2010), http://www.w3.org/2005/Incubator/usdl/wiki/D1 (retrieved April 26, 2012)

23. Kadner, K., Oberle, D., et al.: Unified Service description Language XG Final Report. W3C USDL XG Incubator Group (2011), http://www.w3.org/2005/Incubator/usdl/XGR-usdl-20111027/ (retrieved April 26, 2012)

24. Sun, W., Zhang, K., Chen, S.-K., Zhang, X., Liang, H.: Software as a Service: An Integration Perspective. In: Krämer, B.J., Lin, K.-J., Narasimhan, P. (eds.) ICSOC 2007. LNCS, vol. 4749, pp. 558–569. Springer, Heidelberg (2007)

25. Oberle, D., Bhatti, N., Brockmans, S., Niemann, M., Janiesch, C.: Countering Service Information Challenges in the Internet of Services. Journal of Business & Information System Engineering (BISE) 1(5), 370–390 (2009)

26. Bitsaki, M., Danylevych, O., van den Heuvel, W.-J., Koutras, G., Leymann, F., Mancioppi, M., Nikolaou, C., Papazoglou, M.: An Architecture for Managing the Lifecycle of Business Goals for Partners in a Service Network. In: Mähönen, P., Pohl, K., Priol, T. (eds.) ServiceWave 2008. LNCS, vol. 5377, pp. 196–207. Springer, Heidelberg (2008)

27. Alter, S.: Service system fundamentals: Work system, value chain, and life cycle. IBM Systems Journal 47(1), 71–85 (2008)

28. Ferrario, R., Guarino, N.: Towards an Ontological Foundation for Services Science. In: Domingue, J., Fensel, D., Traverso, P. (eds.) FIS 2008. LNCS, vol. 5468, pp. 152–169. Springer, Heidelberg (2009)

29. Scaffidi, C., Shaw, M., Myers, B.A.: Estimating the numbers of end users and end user programmers. In: Proceedings of the IEEE Symposium on Visual Languages and Human-Centric Computing, pp. 207–214 (2005)

30. Nardi, B.A.: A Small Matter of Programming: Perspectives on End User Computing. The MIT Press (1993)

31. Lieberman, H., Paternò, F., Wulf, V. (eds.): End User Development — Empowering people to flexibly employ advanced information and communication technology. Kluwer Academic Publishers, Dordrecht (2006)

These challenges are researched through some of the projects mentioned in Section 4.6 and further will be researched and continued on in the future. It is important to address the research challenges and it is exciting and encouraging to know that with the advent of Horizon 2020, the EU will support riskier ICT research and innovation that can deliver potentially more innovative solutions to these research challenges with impact demonstrated through new business breakthroughs.

Acknowledgements. This work is being partially supported by the EU co-funded IST projects FI-WARE: Future Internet Core Platform (GA FP7-285248) and 4CaaSt (GA FP7-258862). The authors thank the teams working on FI-WARE, especially those involved in its Application and Services Ecosystem and Delivery Framework Chapter from SAP AG, Atos Origin SAE, Deutsche Telekom AG, TID, Ericsson AB, Engineering Italia SPA, Telecom Italia SPA, UPM and Thales Communications SA, and 4CaaSt, especially from SAP AG, TID, and HSG.

References

1. Fitzsimmons, J.A., Fitzsimmons, M.J.: Service Management – Operations, Strategy, Information Technology, 7th edn. McGraw-Hill (2010)
2. Vargo, S.L., Lusch, R.L.: Evolving to a new dominant logic for marketing. Journal of Marketing 68, 1–17 (2004)
3. Vargo, S.L., Lusch, R.F.: Service-Dominant Logic: Continuing the Evolution. Journal of the Academy of Marketing Science 36, 1–10 (2008)
4. Vargo, S., Akaka, M.A.: Service-Dominant Logic as a Foundation for Service Science: Clarifications. Service Science 1(1), 32–41 (2009)
5. Spohrer, J., Maglio, P.P., Bailey, J., Gruhl, D.: Steps toward a science of service systems. Computer 40, 71–77 (2007)
6. Spohrer, J., Maglio, P.P.: The emergence of service science: Toward systematic service innovations to accelerate co-creation of value. Production and Operations Management 17(3), 1–9 (2008)
7. Vargo, S.L., Lusch, R.F., Akaka, M.A.: Advancing Service Science with Service-Dominant Logic: Clarifications and Conceptual Development. In: Handbook of Service Science. Service Science: Research and Innovations in the Service Economy (2010)
8. Bettencourt, L.A.: Service Innovation. How to Go from Customer Needs to Breakthrough Services, 1st edn. McGraw Hill (2010) ISBN 978-0-07-171300-9
9. Karwowski, W., Salvendy, G., Ahram, T.: Customer-Centered Design of Service Organizations. In: Salvendy, G., Karwowski, W. (eds.) Introduction to Service Engineering. John Wiley & Sons (2010)
10. Kim, K.-J., Meiren, T.: New Service Development Process. In: Salvendy, G., Karwowski, W. (eds.) Introduction to Service Engineering. John Wiley & Sons (2010)
11. Stickdorn, M., Schneider, J., et al.: This is Service Design Thinking. BIS Publishers, Amsterdam (2011) ISBN 978-90-6369-279-7
12. Ulwick, A.W.: Turn customer input into innovation. Harvard Business Rev. 80, 91–97 (2002)
13. Lynne Shostack, G.: Designing Services that Deliver. Harvard Business Review 62(1), 133–139 (1984)
14. Issarny, V., Georgantas, N., Hachem, S., Zarras, A., Vassiliadis, P., Autili, M., Gerosa, M.A., Hamida, A.B.: Service-Oriented Middleware for the Future Internet: State of the Art and Research Directions. Journal of Internet Services and Applications, JISA (2011)

15. Davies, J., Domingue, J., Pedrinaci, C., Fensel, D., Gonzalez-Cabero, R., Potter, M., Richardson, M., Stincic, S.: Towards the Open Service Web. BT Technology Journal 26 (2009)
16. Hendler, J., Golbeck, J.: Metcalfe's law, Web 2.0, and the Semantic Web. In: Web Semantics: Science, Services and Agents on the World Wide Web (2008)
17. Pedrinaci, C., Domingué, J.: Toward the Next Wave of Services: Linked Services for the Web of Data. Journal of Universal Computer Science (2010)
18. Pedrinaci, C., Domingue, J.: Web Services Are Dead. Long Live Internet Services. SOA4All White Paper (2010) http://www.soa4all.eu/pubs/SOA4All-WhitePaper-2010.pdf (retrieved April 26, 2012)
19. Stricker, V., Lauenroth, K., Corte, P., Gittler, F., De Panfilis, S., Pohl, K.: Creating a Reference Architecture for Service-Based Systems – A Pattern-Based Approach. In: Tselentis, et al. (eds.) Towards the Future Internet, pp. 149–160. IOS Press (2010)
20. Agassi, S., Bisson, P., Cantera, J.M., Jimenez-Peris, R., De Nigro, A., Desideri, D., Corte, P.: Internet of Services Pattern. NEXOF Reference Architecture (2010), http://www.nexof-ra.eu/sites/default/files/ Internet%20of%20Service%200.6.pdf (retrieved April 26, 2012)
21. Cardoso, J., Voigt, K., Winkler, M.: Service Engineering for the Internet of Services. In: Filipe, J., Cordeiro, J. (eds.) Enterprise Information Systems. LNBIP, vol. 19, pp. 15–27. Springer, Heidelberg (2009)
22. Oberle, D.: Report on landscapes of existing service description efforts. W3C USDL XG Incubator Group (2010), http://www.w3.org/2005/Incubator/usdl/ wiki/D1 (retrieved April 26, 2012)
23. Kadner, K., Oberle, D., et al.: Unified Service description Language XG Final Report. W3C USDL XG Incubator Group (2011), http://www.w3.org/ 2005/Incubator/usdl/XGR-usdl-20111027/ (retrieved April 26, 2012)
24. Sun, W., Zhang, K., Chen, S.-K., Zhang, X., Liang, H.: Software as a Service: An Integration Perspective. In: Krämer, B.J., Lin, K.-J., Narasimhan, P. (eds.) ICSOC 2007. LNCS, vol. 4749, pp. 558–569. Springer, Heidelberg (2007)
25. Oberle, D., Bhatti, N., Brockmans, S., Niemann, M., Janiesch, C.: Countering Service Information Challenges in the Internet of Services. Journal of Business & Information System Engineering (BISE) 1(5), 370–390 (2009)
26. Bitsaki, M., Danylevych, O., van den Heuvel, W.-J., Koutras, G., Leymann, F., Mancioppi, M., Nikolaou, C., Papazoglou, M.: An Architecture for Managing the Lifecycle of Business Goals for Partners in a Service Network. In: Mähönen, P., Pohl, K., Priol, T. (eds.) ServiceWave 2008. LNCS, vol. 5377, pp. 196–207. Springer, Heidelberg (2008)
27. Alter, S.: Service system fundamentals: Work system, value chain, and life cycle. IBM Systems Journal 47(1), 71–85 (2008)
28. Ferrario, R., Guarino, N.: Towards an Ontological Foundation for Services Science. In: Domingue, J., Fensel, D., Traverso, P. (eds.) FIS 2008. LNCS, vol. 5468, pp. 152–169. Springer, Heidelberg (2009)
29. Scaffidi, C., Shaw, M., Myers, B.A.: Estimating the numbers of end users and end user programmers. In: Proceedings of the IEEE Symposium on Visual Languages and Human-Centric Computing, pp. 207–214 (2005)
30. Nardi, B.A.: A Small Matter of Programming: Perspectives on End User Computing. The MIT Press (1993)
31. Lieberman, H., Paternò, F., Wulf, V. (eds.): End User Development — Empowering people to flexibly employ advanced information and communication technology. Kluwer Academic Publishers, Dordrecht (2006)

32. Costabile, M.F., Lanzilotti, R., Piccinno, A. (eds.): Analysis of EUD Survey Questionnaire. EUD-NET: End-User Development Network of Excellence. Empowering people to flexibly employ advanced information and communication technology. Deliverable D4.2 (2003), `http://giove.isti.cnr.it/projects/EUD-NET/pdf/D4.2.pdf` (retrieved April 9, 2012)
33. Papazoglou, M., Pohl, K., Metzger, A., van den Heuvel, W.: The S-Cube Research Vision. In: Papazoglou, M., Pohl, K., Parkin, M., Metzger, A. (eds.) Service Research Challenges and Solutions. LNCS, vol. 6500, pp. 1–26. Springer, Heidelberg (2010)
34. Lizcano, D., Alonso, F., Soriano, J., López, G.: Supporting End-User Development through a New Composition Model: An Empirical Study. Journal of Universal Computer Science 18(2), 143–176 (2012)
35. Alonso, F., Lizcano, D., López, G., Soriano, J.: A New End-User Composition Model to Empower Knowledge Workers to Develop Rich Internet Applications. Journal of Web Engineering (JWE) 10(3), 197–233 (2011)
36. Alonso, F., Lizcano, D., Lopez, G., Soriano, J.: End-User Development Success Factors and their Application to Composite Web Development Environments. In: Proceedings of The Sixth International Conference on Systems, ICONS 2011 (2011)
37. Schnabel, F., Gorronogoitia, Y., Radzimski, M., Lecue, F., Mehandjiev, N., Ripa, G., Abels, S., Blood, S., Mos, A., Junghans, M., Agarwal, S., Vogel, J.: Empowering Business Users to Model and Execute Business Processes. BPM, Hoboken (2010)
38. Lombardi, J.-P., Vogel, J.: Wizard-based Process Modeling for Business Users. EUD4Services, Rome, Italy (2010)
39. Namoune, A., Mehandjiev, N., Owrak, A., Wajid, U., Stincic, S., Duke, A., Davies, J.: D8.7 Evaluation Prototype (2011), `http://soa4all.eu/`
40. García-Gómez, S., Lelli, F., Escriche-Vicente, M., Arozarena-Llopis, P., Taher, Y., Momm, C., Spriestersbach, A., Vogel, J., Jiménez-Gañán, M., Le Jeune, G., Dao, M., Carrie, S., Niemoller, J., Mazmanov, D., Biro, J., Giesmann, A., Junker, F.: 4CaaSt: Comprehensive management of Cloud services through a PaaS. In: Proc. of International Workshop on Clouds for Business and Business for Clouds (C4BB4C) in Conjunction with IEEE ISPA, Madrid, Spain (2012)
41. Junker, F., Vogel, J., Stanoevska, K.: Aggregating Price Models for Composite Services in Cloud Service Marketplaces. In: Proc. of International Workshop on Clouds for Business and Business for Clouds (C4BB4C) in Conjunction with IEEE ISPA, Madrid, Spain (2012)
42. Mell, P., Grance, T.: The NIST Definition of Cloud Computing, NIST Special Publication 800-145, Gaithersburg, MD, USA (2011)
43. Cusumano, M.: Cloud computing and SaaS as new computing platforms. Communications of the ACM 53(4), 27 (2010)
44. Papazoglou, M., van den Heuvel, W.-J.: Blueprinting the Cloud. IEEE Internet Computing 15(6), 74–79 (2011)
45. OASIS: Topology and Orchestration Specification for Cloud Applications (TOSCA), OASIS specification on (October 2011), `https://www.oasis-open.org/committees/tc_home.php?wg_abbrev=tosca` (retrieved October 4, 2012)
46. Issarny, V., Georgantas, N., Hachem, S., Zarras, A., Vassiliadis, P., Autili, M., Gerosa, M.A., Hamida, A.B.: Service-Oriented Middleware for the Future Internet: State of the Art and Research Directions. Journal of Internet Services and Application, JISA (2012)

Author Index